D0046566

HOW DOES YOUR GARDEN GROW

HOW DOES YOUR GARDEN GROW

ALBERT WILSON, M.A.
Botanist
Garden Consultant

STANFORD UNIVERSITY
1927 1934

Author of
"Distinctive Trees, Shrubs, and Vines in the Gardens of the San Francisco Peninsula"
"Gardeners All In California"
"These Were The Children"

HAPPY HOURS
P.O.Box 453
Menlo Park
Ca. 94026
U. S. A.

DEDICATED TO ALL
CRUSADERS FOR GOOD GARDENING

Library of Congress Catalog Card No. 73-79297

First edition, April 1949
Second edition, August 1955
Third edition, March 1966
Fourth edition, First printing, June 1973
Second printing, August 1982
Third printing, December 1984
Fourth printing, May 1987
Fifth Printing, February 1990
ISBN 0-933845-00-6

FOREWORD FOR THIS EDITION

The first professor of botany at Stanford University in 1891 was Dr. Douglas Houghton Campbell. He was one of Albert Wilson's teachers, just as he was one of mine. In the first book by Albert in 1938, Professor Campbell wrote: "In undertaking this survey of the Peninsula, Mr. Wilson has provided much valuable information which will be greatly appreciated by the the many gardeners and others who would like to know something about the many interesting plants that can be grown in this region".

The fourth edition of "How Does Your Garden Grow" gives testimony to the continuing progress of Albert Wilson's interest in the many garden plants, Old Timers and Newcomers, which will grow not only in the Peninsula but also in the rest of California and adjoining areas.

This huge territory, as large as several countries of Europe, with climatic zones from sub-tropical to alpine and desert, needs long and extensive experience to do justice in choosing the correct plants for a given condition. Further, good growth and longevity of these plant protegees need loving attention to satisfy the vicissitudes of the yearly seasons. These points are well brought out in this book, and both the novice-gardener as well as the Old Hand will find instructions in popular language. This book is designed to contribute to the ecology of our abode.

DR. L. A. WAITZINGER
Sometime Plant Breeder
Associate Professor at
Lingnan University,
Canton, China

Palo Alto, California
September 18, 1972

HOW DOES YOUR GARDEN GROW

The material of this book was gathered for broadcasts which started in 1945 on KNBC (then KPO). It is reproduced by permission of the National Broadcasting Company. But besides it owes much of its present form though none of its faults, to the expert help and kind encouragement and loyalty of the San Francisco staff of that company.

Though the material of this book has been broadcast from San Francisco, which has a special climate tempered by the Pacific fogs drawing in through the Golden Gate, it is no more limited to that climate than is the voice of the speaker. It is, in fact, built up of principles applying everywhere that plants can grow, including the foggy coast, the hot valleys, the foothills, the walled-in city gardens and the wider freer gardens out in the country.

ADDITIONAL ILLUSTRATIONS FOR THIS PRINTING BY
JOHN MILTON RAMM

PREFACE

Because of climatic conditions so different from those of the eastern United States, California gardeners need books especially written for them, and in these books there should be the variety of approach and treatment which the varying interests or experiences of their authors naturally provide.

Mr. Wilson's book, while valuable in itself, especially for the beginner, will supplement other books because his approach is on the operational side, his emphasis less on selection of plants or the finesse of arrangements than on the procedure or techniques necessary to the successful raising and later care of those things he has found to be the most widely desired or grown by the average gardener, whether these be annuals, perennials, roses, shrubs, fruit trees, or vegetables.

These papers, based on his deservedly popular radio talks, reflect them in their friendly and informal style, in their use of the interview, and in their very specific instructions and will have much the same appeal to the practical working gardener who wants to know just what to do in his California garden and when to do it.

SYDNEY B. MITCHELL

LETTER TO THE DEAR READER:

Now that you have bought this book I'm under no compulsion to recommend it, for I feel certain that to guard your purchase you'll read it through. So I can use this letter for other purposes and I propose to maneuver you into the mood which I have had in writing.

Last spring in Mill Valley I stopped at the curb one Sunday and asked my way. A little boy and his father were out there on all fours, and before the father could answer, the youngster shouted ecstatically, "Look, I'M helping weed the lawn."

The big idea is that gardening is a way of life. In fact it is one of the very best ways of life. It belongs to that wonderful clan of activities which enrich the home, draw its members closer together, make them hurry to the fascinating postponed tasks. There are of course several kinds of activities and of them gardening is only one. But it typifies them all.

I heartily believe that the new gardens springing up from raw soil with almost every new house and flourishing as never before with this majestic migration from crowded city to wide open country are rapidly strengthening the institution of the family.

ALBERT WILSON

Happy Hours
Menlo Park
California
Date: March, 1949

CONTENTS

CONTENTS

OPPORTUNE TASKS THROUGH THE YEAR

We must recognize here in California with our north to south coast line continuing almost 1000 miles, along with a climb from sea level to Sierra foothill, including many protected valleys, there is a difference in timing for the awakening of spring. Thus in San Diego and Southern California certain OPPORTUNE TASKS in gardens come sooner than they do for Central and Northern California. However, it is equally true as spring slides into summer the difference is little or even non-existent for these opportune tasks.

Chapter 1

ROSE . . . QUEEN OF THE GARDEN

(January: First Week, Second Week)

The rose is the flower beloved through the centuries. It's a flower of honest growth which thrives throughout the temperate zones where most of the world's people live. The blooms are of a refreshing shape and boundless beauty. With the rose, as with every other plant, the plan's the thing. Though we must never forget this, today we shall not discuss it, for our hands are full of rose culture. ***HISTORY***

Our roses are descended from the wild ones you find in the woods just as the Creator left them. The varieties have been made by hybridization, and by bud selection of good new qualities appearing in the plant by accident. They fall into distinct classes, according to their garden character, color tone, fragrance, disease resistance, repeated blooming, and strong necks not bent over. One, which we call the Golden Emblem, has shiny foliage, resists mildew, and has flowers with yellow-copper-toned petals and rich fragrance.

The repeated bloomer throws out flowers all summer long. It first appeared and instantly became famous in 1834, and with some degree of imagination was called the Hybrid Perpetual. We now use them as the white Frau Karl Druschki and red Star of Holland. The vigorous growing, strong stemmed, richly colored, intensely fragrant are called the Hybrid Teas — the kind you and I think of when we talk of roses; of these we use the Herbert Hoover, Texas Centennial, and Duchess of Penaranda. The kind that blooms 365 days per year, and some nights, in California is the Polyantha or Floribunda, now becoming so popular. The Baby Rose is a good example. The climbers are especially resistant to pests and bloom abundantly. The Belle of Portugal has one great blooming in spring; the Paul Scarlet is a steady bloomer, hundreds on the Stanford University fence, and it is the official rose of Santa Clara County. American Pillars are excluded from many gardens by mildew, but are exquisite in their place. Finally we have the Standard or Tree Rose, like the bush only budded upon long stems and trained high above the root.

WHEN TO PRUNE

January and February are good times to prune roses in California; move into the rose garden with sharp shears. Forget any little rose buds you might see for they belong to the past season, and the aim is to get the plants ready for the season to come. Prune to keep the plant growing and making new wood. Good flowers come only on the new wood.

The rose plant is really composed of two parts; the root system, and the branch system. Each has a definite function. The roots anchor and absorb moisture, while the branch system produces leaves and flowers. The roots can throw up strong new shoots if they do not have too many old ones hanging on. Therefore pruning really is a process of forcing. Strong shoots come also from the healthy older wood of good diameter, according to growth habit of the variety. But always prune out weak shoots even if they appear from leaders.

Your rose bush may be compared to your hand; from the ground comes the base support, the wrist; breaking from this is the scaffold, the palm; and from the scaffold come the canes, the fingers upon which are carried the blooms. The knuckles and joints of the fingers are where the buds develop.

RULES

We prune to form new canes. How is this done? What are the rules? First, cut out all the dead spindly wood. Second, take out the cross branches and center wood, for sunlight and air must get to the heart of the bush. Third, take out old canes, those showing cracking scaly wood. Old wood can produce only weak growth, can throw out only short stems, and it always harbors scale.

Leave the strongest canes, especially the new ground canes, those shooting up right out of the ground. These are always reddish and fresh looking because they are being given every encouragement by the roots themselves, which move into them the free-flowing sap. Should any doubt arise in your mind as to what to prune out, look upon your rose as your calendar. The tip of the cane will be the growth of last year. It began at a place where you can now see three or four horizontal lines; below these lines will be wood of the year before, that is the growth of 1947; this wood in turn developed from its horizontal lines which indicated the end of the growth of that year. The stem of the 1946 growth will look dark green, will feel hard, and may even show scars here and there where you picked a rose that spring. Cut back a certain amount of last year's growth. All the growth below the 1946 growth will be woody, will carry few thorns, and will show fissures which compare to the bark of the noble oak tree. This is old wood, and with too much of it your rose is not happy. On this woody bark and among the ravages of time flourishes the enemy scale. Its time has come; prune it all out and promote new growth from the roots.

WHERE & HOW

Having decided which canes must go, and which may remain, where and how should you cut? Along the stems of young green wood are the leaves; they are made up of several pairs of leaflets with one leaf ending the crown. Gently pull a leaf off the stem and you will find at the notch a little bud. Prune one half inch above this bud. They appear like the thorns up and down the stem, some facing inward toward the heart of the bush, others facing away from it. Select wherever possible the buds facing away from the center because you wish to open it up so the sun will reach in and kill the mildew. From these buds which gardeners call "eyes" new stems will develop upon which of course will appear flowers. The fewer eyes left after pruning the longer the stems, the more the blooms, and usually the better the quality of bloom.

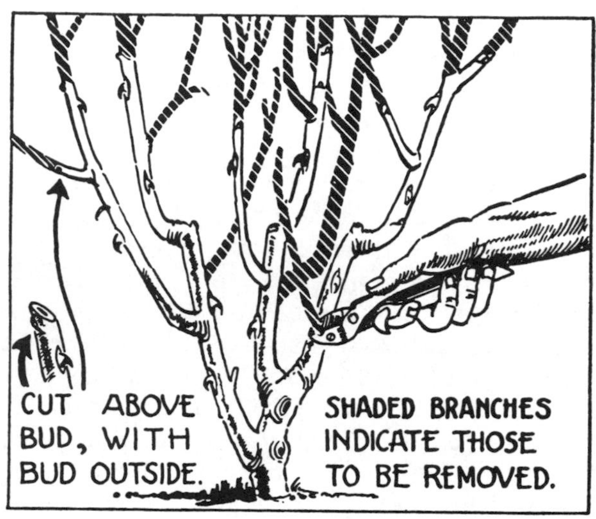
CUT ABOVE
BUD, WITH
BUD OUTSIDE.
SHADED BRANCHES
INDICATE THOSE
TO BE REMOVED.

Pruning determines both the quantity and size of flowers; there are three classes of pruning. First, severe pruning in which you thin out your rose leaving only three to five canes each of which will carry only two or three buds. Strong growing roses will thank you for this kind of pruning by sending out great new canes in spring each of which will carry blooms of the richest quality. Second, medium pruning which requires the same number of canes, but each may have from five to ten buds; here you will get a large crop of average flowers. And mild pruning in which you leave four to seven canes, each cut back to one half its height, leaving a large number of buds and from which develop a large crop of small blooms. Always make the cut on a slant as this causes moisture to move off the exposed surface keeping out disease and injury. When your job of pruning has been completed, all of the remaining canes should as nearly as possible be equidistant from each other, arranged around the plant, so that it presents a well-balanced appearance on all sides with an uncrowded center.

PRUNE *Floribunda*

We have been pruning the common rose of the garden so far. Now what about those having short canes ending in clusters — the Polyantha or Floribunda — how should they be pruned? These roses bloom practically every day in the year and all they require is complete removal of all dead wood, and the occasional cutting out of a few of the older canes. This may easily be done when the blooms are taken, and by their removal the roots are encouraged to send forth new growth. That is the way you prune your baby rose, the Cecil Brunner for instance.

PRUNE *Climbers*

And how do we prune the climber? Most require mild pruning, and the best time is right after the spring show. This enables the roots to throw up new canes which in turn carry the flowers next year. Long unwieldy canes must go, and now and then, though not every year, you take out down to the ground canes that are unproductive. Beyond this, climbers require little attention. It is undesirable to allow a climbing rose to become too rampant; that is, by the way, why Stanford University has that mile of glorious red roses every year; the superintendent instructs his crew to clear out excess wild growth and old spent wood, and to tie back only the most reliable new shoots. You will do well to follow suit with your own climbers, thin out old wood, keep the shiny stems' new growth, tie them back to the fence and wall, and enjoy their show of beautiful flowers. Look out for planting a naturally vigorous climber in a location where its growth must be restricted.

TREE ROSE

Standard or tree is the name given to the manner in which a rose bush is grown. The root and stem stock usually is of Japanese origin, one called I X L. This makes a trunk 36-40 inches tall for the Full Standard, 24 inches tall for the Patio Standard, and 9-10 inches tall for the Quarter Standard. At the top is budded any variety of rose that has proved adapted to the tree form. A good Standard rose has a dense umbrella-like head, can spread, and on which quality flowers develop, and includes kinds that drop old petals when finished. Good examples include Charlotte Armstrong, Mme. Henri Guillot, Golden Dawn, The Chief, and Christopher Stone, these among the Full Standards, budded at a height of 36-40 inches. Among the Patio Standards, budded at a height of 24 inches may be listed Helen Traubel, Picture, Fred Edmunds, and Golden Scepter. Among the Quarter Standards, budded only 9-10 inches and ideal for tubs, may be listed Chrysler Imperial, Eclipse, Peace and Lilibet.

The Standard rose is pruned exactly as the bush rose. Complete the job before the new leaves begin to appear; that is while the plant is still dormant. Cut out old wood, save new wood, and preserve the shape of the plant. Watch out in pruning the Standard that you do not cut below the bud, because then off goes the quality rose. Even more than with other roses make sure your shears are sharp. A dull blade crushes the stem. Seal over large cuts.

PESTS & DISEASE CONTROL

A word now on pests and diseases of the rose. At this time of year it is good to disinfect the soil so as to retard black-spot disease next spring and summer. Black-spot starts in the spring from spores on fallen leaves. It first turns the leaves in your plant sickly yellow, black spots develop, and the leaves drop off. The treatment is simple; a thorough spraying of the soil in and around the plant in the early winter and again in early spring before the leaves are out. Use ten tablespoons of Bordeaux to one gallon of water; or ten tablespoons of lime sulphur to one gallon of water. Be sure your equipment throws a forceful spray. This also controls rust, another enemy.

For the control of mildew, everywhere and always a plague to the rose, use sulphur; dust it on with a sulphur gun. Start in early April just before the leaves come out. And be conscientious. The idea is get sulphur on before mildew shows. Actidione PM sprayed on a mildew covered rose cleans off fungus, stops spread. If you want your roses available for picking at a moment's notice, spray rather than dust them. Use an oil emulsion spray. Be generous, apply regularly once a week. These materials leave a shiny coat on the foliage and neither bugs nor mildew have learned to unbutton that coat.

Of course, there are other than human admirers of the Rose Queen, and when warm weather comes they will appear in swarms. Among these are aphid, snout beetles, and leaf tier; these also will require conscientious treatment. Of course, there is the multipurpose spray. Use it. Follow directions on container.

The Opportune Task: Today, eat hot cakes and a rasher of bacon for breakfast. Then spring out to the rose garden and prune!

Let us add something about climbing roses. Did you ever come to paint your house and find the rose in the way? And be told by the painter to leave it to him? And when you got around again, found it and the trellis dumped on the ground; and what is worse, cut entirely off at the root? But next spring what happened? Vigorous new canes sprouted powerfully up the wall, and you saw blooms of quality that passed anything you had for ten years. The painter knew more than either you or he suspected. Of course we don't always have this painter to help us, and we won't always be so drastic.

We remember the calendar and the growth that go with 1948, 1947, and 1946. Get rid of cracking 3-year-old stalks first where the scale hangs out. This will make room for the new canes of 1949 to spray out from the roots. But of course if the plant has to get somewhere before you want it to bloom, as over a garage door, or pergola, leave the main stem regardless of age, and prune from there being sure to save two or three good buds.

Now for planting the rose. Out of the thousands of kinds select only a few, and several plants of each type. Remember to stick by those known to do well in your neighborhood. Your nurserymen will be glad to assist in the selection; you might ask him about the old shrub roses like the Scotch Rose with very spiny stems, the canary yellow Star of Persia, the Austrian Copper with its spectacular color tones of fiery scarlet on the upper surface of the petals and a copper yellow on the *PLANT* underside. Or ask him about the Rosa hugonis from North China named for another of our missionary friends, Father Hugo; and our famous Rosa rugosa, vigorous, adaptable and often used as a hedge. All of these roses are shrubs, they fill out, reach up three feet, grow independently, and require the simplest attention in pruning and care.

SOIL

What kind of soil? The best soil you can get is the best soil for roses. Whether it is clay or sandy is less important than the treatment you give it. One factor is adequate drainage; you do not want the roots to rot off, or to drown. Second, the soil should be thoroughly prepared at least to the depth of your spade, twice that for good measure. Roots that penetrate deep never worry about your vacation trips or about a close call from Old Sol. Third — always of interest to the amateur — is the acidity of the soil. Roses grow best when the soil is neutral or slightly acid. Lime or gypsum can be used to make soil less acid and sulphur to make it less alkaline.

HOW

Now for the mechanics of planting. First, plant your roses while they are still dormant. Dig the hole 12 inches deep, deeper if possible; loosen the soil in the bottom; if you have some, throw in bone meal, but cover it immediately with soil; use no manure in the bottom of the hole. You may top dress with manure, because that will serve as a mulch which later may be cultivated. At this time of year (winter months) roses come from the nursery bare-root. Some gardeners make up some soupy mud in a bucket and plunge the roots of the roses in this. Bare-roots have a way of drying out, and the cake of mud protects them. So that you can spread these roots freely in the soil, in the bottom of the hole, build a little mound of earth, and let the bare roots fall over this in all directions. Make certain that the hole is deep enough to permit the longest root to go down; never bend any root to accommodate it to the hole — that's as bad as bending toes in a shoe. Never crisscross the fine roots. Do not coil the root more than once around the hole. Throw in the soil up to the knob or bud scar. This knob should rest at ground level. Last, make the basin to hold the water and the compost top dress which you know is so helpful to the plants in the garden.

Sunshine, air and water are natural agents which make roses grow well. Nature gives them the first two freely here in California, but you and I must take care of the water. The rose like all other garden plants must never become distressed. Adequate water means constant beauty.

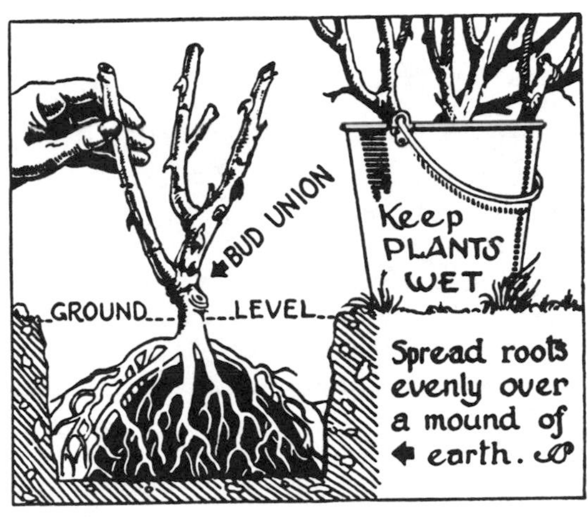

WHERE

Where shall we put the roses in the garden? The climbers of course belong on fences, pergolas, or along walls trained on trellises. The other roses must never be planted among shrubs, shoved up against a hedge, or choked in with vigorous perennials. They need light, air and space. They are not ordinary plants. They belong to themselves, they go best in a garden of their own. This is easy enough in a large garden, but there are ways of accomplishing it in the small garden, too. But certain combinations are good also. Lovely effects may be attained with the help of pansies, violas, forget-me-nots as ground covers under the roses, to enrich the design when the roses themselves are not at their best.

FLOWERS WITH ROSES

What of soil fertility? It must be maintained. If the rose bed has been well prepared to begin with, no further fertilizer will be needed during the first season of growth. But each year after adopt a definite program. Roses are vigorous feeders, and prosper only in soil rich in the essential elements — nitrogen, phosphorus, and potassium. At this time of year (winter months) supply generously organic fertilizers, that is, cow manure mixed with compost, and sheep manure. In spring and in early fall for the late flowers apply commercial fertilizer.

FEED

(January: Second Week)

Another Opportune Task in these dark days of winter ties itself up with the bright days of summer. January is the first month in the New Year; this is the second week of that month, and here is your task if you are an amateur and wish to succeed with growing tuberous begonias from seeds. Begin right now, and these are the steps you must follow:

HOW TO SEED TUBEROUS BEGONIA

1. Select an unbroken, clean flat; scrape out all old dirt; sterilize it with boiling water. You may also use a shallow clay pot called a pan.
2. Sift soil through a fine mesh, and sterilize it also. You may place soil in the oven and bake it, or you may pour over it a solution of clorox water: one tablespoonful to two quarts of water; you may pour this solution over your flat, too. It discourages algae and fungus enemies.
3. Let flats dry out in sun; and dry out soil.
4. In bottom of flat scatter in very coarse oak leaf mold; on top of this put down a layer of less coarse leaf mold; tamp down lightly so as to firm the bed. Then sift your soil over the leaf mold; the idea is to sift the soil very finely on top, smooth out but do not tamp. Notice that you use no peat.
5. Submerge flat in water till its contents become soaked.
6. Permit flat to drain.
7. Mix your very fine seed with very fine sand; scatter as evenly as possible over seed-bed.
8. Place glass over flat; place tar paper or several

sheets of newspaper over glass to keep out light. Put flat in a warm place.

9. Every morning lift the glass, you do this to get rid of the moisture drops; some gardeners turn the glass over each day, others wipe it off. But those big drops of water must not fall continuously onto the seed-bed. *CARE*
10. In daytime lift the glass, place under it a sliver of wood to create a crack so air will constantly circulate over the seed-bed; you do this to discourage fungus enemies.
11. For night-time close up this crack, let the glass rest snuggly on the flat.
12. Remove the paper just as soon as you discover the seeds have germinated. From then on be especially vigilant for damping-off fungus. (Seedlings attached by this enemy turn yellow, topple over and finally die). If you become suspicious of its presence then mix up a solution made with one tablespoonful of clorox to one gallon of water, and pour over seed-bed. Or you may use one of the commercial fungicides.
13. When the third leaf appears on your seedlings they are ready to be transplanted. Then your soil mixture should be made up of one part peat, one part coarse propagating sand, and two parts leaf mold. *SOIL MIX*

WATER
new plants
IMMEDIATELY
after
planting.

CHAPTER 2

(A) WINTER SPRAYS TO PROTECT SPRING AND SUMMER GARDENS

(January: Third Week)

Go into the garden armed to do battle, for we aim to protect our plants now so that they in turn may march out for us in spring dressed in their best. The success of their early pageant and their fruit offerings of summer depends almost entirely upon what you and I do in the garden during the next six weeks. The duty we must perform now is to spray upon these plants a coat for protection. But first, let us find out what sprays are needed now and on what trees or shrubs these sprays can be applied. You and I will discuss sprays and insects, once in the winter, and twice during the summer.* One difference between winter and summer spraying is that your trees have dropped their leaves and can stand a strong treatment from what we call dormant sprays. Those plants which keep their leaves can't take these sprays. I assume you know already about the fungus diseases which cause curly leaf on the peach tree, and shot hole of the almond; today we are not concerned with them. At the right time we will discuss the fungus diseases. Our program to fight them must wait till later, toward spring when conditions will favor us in our battle against them. But we are after the insects once more, especially the scale insects, the red spiders, aphids, and stray mealy bug. We are going after any adults we might find, and after all eggs that we suspect.

SCALE Let us begin with the job against scale. Suppose we walk out to that plum tree, to that cherry, or pear in the back yard. These trees have dropped their leaves and we can see the bare stems and branches.

*See December: first week; July; fourth week; August: fifth week.

If you can, bring a magnifying glass. Now look closely at that stem; what do you see? Is it a cluster of flat shells — brown or grey scale? Take your pen knife, scrape one off. If you find inside a hollow shell containing only a small amount of white, powdery dust, you have removed an empty shell from which hatched young, perhaps last August or September. But look further and you'll find here and there a flat brown scale that is alive. It is very small, being a young one, and has firmly attached itself for life. The newly hatched female moves out to a nice clean section of stem, and takes up housekeeping there. First she settles herself, then with a long beak she breaks the smooth bark, and works her way down. Then she pulls in her long legs and antennae, and anchors herself for life. She builds wax over her body; it mats and melts together and covers the body like armor. That is what you and I see now when we look closely for the fully grown adult. These females just stay put; there they reproduce, eat and cause the damage to the plant as I have described. The males develop wings, they can fly.

Recently, in San Jose, I was in the office of Mr. David Rayner, Agricultural Commissioner of Santa Clara County. I saw him scrape from a cherry twig a whole fingernail-full of brown scales, to show a man who had come in for help. Then further down on the twig, at the base of a flat flower bud, he showed us with a magnifying glass the individual scale. It was the size of a large pinhead. These scales are spending the winter in a half-grown condition, and by next May, June or July will be mature individuals. At that time they will lay eggs. And how many eggs would you guess a single female will produce? From a hundred to several thousand! Of course, conditions must be right for each egg to hatch, but just think of the mess you and I can have in our garden if we don't stop them.

Now let us move over to the orange tree. If you haven't an orange, look at your lemon or your holly tree. Move those outer branches and get inside. What do you find there? Many of you will find the same thing, scale all over the young stems and branches, and along the backs of the leaves. They will be flat, brownish; older ones will be black. Usually on the orange, lemon and on the oleander they are brownish, but on the holly and toyon, they are black. No matter the color, they are scale — the enemy we are after. Take a special look at your toyon. Do you find whole branches here and there that have died? Do you find branches where the smooth surface has given way to a rough one with deep creases and pock marks? Wouldn't you say that bark is decidedly injured and full of disease? Well, that is the work of a small scale insect.

KINDS Now there are many kinds of scale: the red, yellow, purple and black, the cottony cushion which threatens the orange industry, the San Jose type that came to us from China (it caused great damage to our fruit industry till a concerted and determined effort checked it, so that now it is found only in the garden of the amateur), the Italian olive-gray, the oyster-shell, the European, and the Chinese elm scale. There are scales that attack the pine trees, maples, apples, the boxwood, the ivy, virginia creeper vine, the rose, hawthorn, lilac, sycamore, pear and willow. Your garden and mine can be overwhelmed with scale insects if we haven't done something about it in the past. But today we are going to do something, because now we have a good chance to get the eggs. Later in the spring we'll tackle the job again. What we do now will help us next year and the years to come.

Let us continue our tour of inspection. This time, examine closely your apple tree. First of all, let us remind you of what you saw last summer. Remember those clusters of white wooly lumps that looked like cotton clinging up and down the stems and branches of your apple tree? Well, if you look hard now, in one or two places you might find them. On New Year's Day, I looked over my tree, and as I studied a scar on a branch where last year I had pruned, I found a few in the callus formed between the cracks on the thick

CHECK outer bark. These pruning scars are favorite places. And then, when I dug around the roots, I found lots of them, just waiting for spring, ready to climb up.

The individual wooly apple aphid is small, plump, and purplish red. Many live grouped together — the entire colony is completely bundled up with that white, cottony protective material which the insects exude from their bodies. May I remind you of one other thing? Did you find a lot of your apples dwarfed and all knobbed up, with bumps and lumps ruining the shape of the fruit? These apples were deformed and ruined by another aphid, the rosy or purple apple aphid. And the heart-rending feature about it is that this aphid does its miserable job early in the spring long before you are aware anything wrong is going on in your apple tree, and then in the summer you discover the damage. There is nothing, absolutely nothing you can do about it then. It is now, this afternoon, that you can get out and do something. That may sound authoritative, but if you will, get out and do it now! Then you'll have apples to cheat the doctor.

But still, before I tell you how to spray for these marauders, let me call upon your memory once again. Last summer, did you find your cherry tree with the tips of the branches all curled up and alive with black aphids and busy ants? The aphids were piled up on top of one another, and the ants were swarming around them. On the cherry, these black aphids have a very hard protective coat, and therefore we shall need to go after them with energy. And here again, it's what you do this winter that will help to keep that partnership of trouble out of your garden next spring and summer.

APHIDS & MOULD

And that plum tree, that hawthorn, cotoneaster, and pyracantha with leaves and stems covered with a sticky sweet gum as black as coal — this ugliness is due to the presence of little green aphids, and a mould that lives on the honey. On the Spanish broom it is little black aphid. What we spray now will help keep this population away next year.

Some of you have an almond tree or so in your garden or out at the curb. Last summer do you remember how terrible that tree looked? First the blossoms came out and you had a lovely display of early spring flowers. A little later the leaves came out and your tree was dressed for the year. But pretty soon you noticed those leaves turning a sickly grey, and the first thing you knew, there stood an ugly tree in your garden in place of the attractive specimen you and the neighbors enjoyed in the first days of spring. Perhaps some of you observed this peculiar behavior of your almond tree and broke off a twig to investigate. You noticed as you rubbed the branch that a red juice came off into your hand. No doubt you wondered about this. Now what do you suppose happened out there? Well, you had company that came unannounced and uninvited. It was the almond mite, and he didn't confine himself to the almond alone, for you find him on the quince, the pear, the aspen, the apricot and the malva bush.

ALMOND MITE

The almond mite lives over in the winter in the egg stage. Those eggs are on your tree right now, and if you spray as I'll tell you in a minute, you'll find how easy it is to free your garden of this offensive intruder.

RED SPIDER

Another name for mite is red spider, and red spiders love to set up housekeeping on any plant that grows in a nice neglected warm spot. They are one of the worst enemies in the summer garden. The late E. O. Essig of the University of California, in his book Insects of Western North America, says: "Mites are of great interest not only because of their minuteness, their varied forms and adaptations for living under widely different conditions, but also because of their complex interrelationships..."

Now, let us go back into the house, and while you get your pencil and paper, I'll sum up what we want to do today to rid our gardens of enemies. It is clear now why we want to spray in the winter: to save ourselves disappointments next summer, to see our trees, shrubs and vines with clean healthy foliage in spring instead of diseased and ruined. It is clear also that each of us wants to spray our fruit trees for scale insects and eggs, also our ornamentals for these same intruders. We want, besides, to spray in order to destroy aphid eggs before new troubles come upon our trees next spring and summer — and many ornamentals are included here. Our question then is:

what shall we use and how shall we apply it?

OIL SPRAY

We must use oil sprays now. We must get what is called the Winter Oil Emulsion spray, a sticky spray which will stay put on the surface of the trees and shrubs better and longer; it also suffocates the stray enemy insect and kills her eggs. On the market there are several good sprays which will help the amateur do a good cleanup job — for that is our Opportune Task today: to clean up the garden.

Select one of the commercially prepared sprays, read the directions carefully, and apply it now. Learn to use your spray efficiently. One way to achieve this is to stick with one kind rather than trying everything on the market.

Now for our list. Peaches, nectarines, apricots, and the flowering peaches. For these trees you are going to spray for the scale insect only. Remember you do not spray now for curly leaf, brown rot, or shot hole fungus. When spring comes, I'll tell you what to do for those diseases.

On your second list put down: almond, apple, cherry, pear, plum, prune, fig, Oriental persimmon, quince and hawthorn. Spray these trees with one of the oil sprays.

Your third list is of ornamentals, the olive, myrtle, Mexican orange, the evergreen plants such as oranges, lemons, kumquats, oleanders, hollies, toyons, trailing ivy, lantana, gardenias, daphne, pittosporum, veronica and lilacs including the old-fashioned; also such ornamental vines as: trumpet vine, Virginia creeper, clematis, wisteria and roses which also suffer from scale. All of these plants have to be treated with summer oil sprays, or the leaves might be ruined. They will help to keep down the population of scale and mealy bug next summer. Of course, in spring I'll tell you again about sprays, and I'll urge you then to use them regularly, thoroughly and heavily. But today in your cleanup program, reach into the heart of these plants and spray.

HOW

How can these sprays be forced upon the plants to do the most good? They must be put on with equipment that can throw with force, so as to enable the solution to hit every part of the plant. The spray must not only hit every part, it must shoot its way in so that it can penetrate properly. When applying the spray, we musn't forget that block and tackle pile-up of aphids and the scale, and you can still see some dead ones shuffled together. It will not be enough for instance to cover the outside members; the spray must penetrate down to the very last one holding on tight to the bark of the branch. These emulsion oils do this very well because they seep in slowly, travelling down to the last individual, thus gradually destroying the colony.

SPRAYER What equipment is best to use for applying these sprays? For the amateur in the home garden, I think the most economical sprayer is the three-gallon can with pressure pump with its three feet of tubing and brass rod and nozzle gun. You can pump enough pressure to last the tankful of solution, and it will throw the material with sufficient force to provide satisfactory coverage. Some of the professionals remove the short three-foot tube and attach a longer one of from six to eight feet, at the end of which they attach the brass rod and nozzle. In this way, they can fill up their portable tank, place it on the lawn or in the path, and then work their way into the garden, under the fruit trees, and up the ladder so as to reach to the tipmost branch, and also they can get down in among the shrubbery for the nozzle shoots up as well as down. All this work without knocking over their container. Be sure and shake up the tank occasionally.

And since a best method of insect control is that which necessitates the least number of sprayings, the main object is to complete a good job. So with a strong pressure, spray the branches and twigs thoroughly; aim to get the spray on all sides, along the main trunk, in between the crotches, on the twigs, up to the tip top. Strive to get the oil spray onto the insect or eggs at every angle. This particularly for the deciduous plants; but where evergreens as thuyas, cypress trees, and junipers are to be sprayed it may be necessary to clear away first the dead, dusty brush inside the plant. One way to do this is to hose the plant down with as much pressure as your water line provides, and then a few days later apply the spray.

DON'T

In applying these winter dormant emulsion sprays, there are a few things to remember. If rain is threatening, don't spray; wait for a dry spell. You want the oil to stick, not to wash off. Never spray oils in hot spells, or in hot corners or walls of the garden; wait till a cooler day. Always spray before five in the afternoon. Another thing — don't apply these oil emulsion sprays during a windy period because the wind will carry them beyond, and when you come along with your outfit and spray, the result will be a double dose. The penalty for overspraying shows up the next year, when all the tip growth of your fruit trees will have been burned back fifteen to sixteen inches. And in the matter of dormant winter oil emulsion sprays, the most important fact of all is to follow explicitly the directions; give meticulous attention to those dilution tables that come with all spray products. Never rush into the lath house or greenhouse and shoot your protected plants with a spray of outdoor strength. Dilute it first or select a special greenhouse spray.

In going through your garden some of you may find it necessary to call in the professionals with their high-pressure equipment. Let them cover the plants thoroughly. Then later you may give the second and third spraying with your own equipment. What you do now will help, but later on towards spring we shall again discuss this subject to take care of other pests which we have not considered today, and which are better taken care of in springtime than in the winter.

CHAPTER 3

(B) PRUNING FRUIT TREES IN THE HOME GARDEN

(January: Third Week)

USE AIDS

I want to give you references to free circulars on spraying. The state through the Agricultural Extension Service of the University of California offers many free papers on agriculture and horticulture. These cover such subjects as Decidous Fruit and Nut Trees, hints on growing Dwarfed or Espalier Fruit Trees, The Home Vineyard, Rose Culture Calandar, Gladiolus Disease Control, Turfgrass, etc. And on such practical subjects Whitewash to Protect Young Trees, Staking Young Landscape Trees, and Compost Preparation. At the County Farm Advisors office papers may be selected. You can send a post card with your name and address to Agricultural Extension Service, University of California, in your county, California and make your request. Circulars on Camellias, Orchids, etc. carry a charge.

The office of the Farm Advisor is set up by us as taxpayers for our mutual benefit. We have paid for it; let's use it. The time was when the farmer and gardener went it alone, on the basis of hard-earned experience, but now the interaction between him and the departments of agriculture, both state and federal, have created something additional to personal experience and resulted in this being one of the half-dozen great places in the world for food crops and happy gardens.

This morning I invite you again to step out, armed not with spray gun, but with your pruning shears and saw. We shall look once more at those bare fruit trees standing there in your garden without a leaf. Let's step over to your apple tree. Now reach up and take hold of a little branch. You have in your hand a branch of tip growth; notice how firm it is, how fresh and

***The Circulars published by the College of Agriculture of the University of California as listed in the various chapters such as pruning, grape growing, planting, ect., are available as long as the supply lasts. They are always available however in the public libraries throughout the state; and Agricultural Commissioners often have copies in their files.**

young and new it looks in its bright reddish-gray coat. Notice too that little touch of dust all along the branch; that is called the bloom, one of nature's devices for reducing water loss in plants. This little branch you hold is called "year-old wood"; it grew last year. And observe how similar little branches are sprouting all over your apple tree, and how too in some places they are only six inches long; in other parts of the tree they have grown three- to five-foot whips, all during the past growing season. As you examine closely, you can see the end of each branch is folded into a point, and this is called a terminal bud.

Now follow along and see where that new growth comes from; it comes off of parental older wood, with no reddish color at all, only gray. That was the wood that grew in the year before last, and if you look very closely you will discover little horizontal lines at the base of the new wood, just where it started from. These horizontal lines are the old scars left by the terminal bud when growth began in the spring of last year. Now look hard at the old wood. Do you see those short little twigs, ending in a tip bud? You might find one on either side of that branch and the tip bud may end in a point, or it may be rounded. These little twigs of growth are called spurs; look at them well. They are a very important part of fruit production. They influence vitally the type of pruning you should do. They must remain on the tree because it is upon these spurs alone that first the flowers and then the fruit develop. Still again, follow back the lead-gray old wood upon which the spurs are produced, and you will see once more horizontal lines where the last year's growth developed from the grandfather wood of

SPURS

Apple on Spur

two years before. You'll see some more spurs that belong to that generation. And so on back in time and into the heart of the tree.

KINDS OF BUDS

Let us now look at the buds because knowledge of them constitutes pruning skill. They are called terminal or lateral according to whether they break out at the end of a branch or at the side. And there are two kinds of buds according to shape — pointed and rounded fat. The pointed ones are coated now for winter protection with slender scales; in the spring these scales will rain down to the ground making their contribution of humus, and the bud will burst out in leaves. The other kind are fat and rounded and their scales likewise will contribute humus in the spring. The bud, however, if it is what we call simple, as in the apricot, peach and almond, bursts out into a flower. But if it is what we call mixed, as in the pear and apple, it will burst out into a cluster of both flowers and leaves. You can tell the mixed bud from the simple bud by cutting it across with a sharp razor and examining it with a magnifying glass.

Now let's come back to the terminal and lateral buds. What do they do? They can be either pointed or fat. If the bud is pointed and terminal, it carries growth, it lengthens the branch. The lateral makes a side extension; it is what fills a tree up into a maze of sticks. If it is fat, the terminal bud bursts into flowers or flowers and leaves. The lateral bud does likewise.

As you look over your apple tree, you will see that each spur zigzags. This is because the flower bud and leaf bud come in pairs and the leaf bud which carries the stem is pushed over so that it comes off at an angle. You'll understand so long as the flower and the fruit itself are developing, usually terminally in the apple and pear, they monopolize the energy and everything else has to get out of the way.

You might put down in your notes this list: cherry, apple, pear, apricot, plum, prune and almond. These trees always produce their fruit crop on spur wood. On the apple and pear the spur can produce fruit for eight to ten years, even to twenty years; on the cherry for ten to twelve years; on the plum and prunes five to eight years; on the apricot only three years. Now here's another list that behaves differently: peach, nectarine, Oriental persimmon, fig, and Chinese quince. These have no spurs; they carry their fruit on the current year's growth, or what we call the new wood of the past season.

Before we consider actual pruning, let us think of what we aim to accomplish by pruning. I'll quote from the University circular: "1) to produce a vigorous, mechanically strong, healthy tree, 2) to secure a tree well-shaped for convenience and economy in orchard management, 3) to distribute the fruiting area well over the tree, 4) to secure fruit of good size and quality, and 5) to regulate the annual succession of crops in order to obtain the maximum average crop compatible with good fruit." *WHY*

A cardinal rule before approaching a fruit tree of any type is to stand off first and look over the tree carefully. See in your mind's eye the exact shape you want your tree to take; study your tree first, and beware of careless slashing here and there. You yourself will govern the shape of that tree. Ask yourself: What am I looking for in the shape of my tree?

Now how do you prune these trees? First the spur producers, of them the apple. Much depends upon the variety of apple; for this difference look in your circular. Much depends upon location, whether in the cool mountains, the warm valleys, the fog belt, etc. For this, too, look in your circular or study the nurserymen's catalogue. And much also depends upon location within your garden. For instance, if your tree is located where it must be kept in bounds, as near the house, against a fence, by the side of a busy walk, or in a crowded shrubbery-filled garden, you should follow the short pruning. You do this by shortening back last year's new tip growth. If this new wood on your tree is only six or eight inches long, count from the tip terminal bud, back to the last two buds, leaf buds as they now appear, and with your sharp shears make *HOW* a slanting cut. From these buds next spring will grow the fruiting spur that you now realize produces fruit.

Should your tree be growing in the open garden, you may adopt the long pruning. In this you will take your pruners and first cut out all the weak growth and thin branches. You aim to open up the tree so as to permit sunlight to reach in. All of the strong new growth of the past year you will leave untouched. Except where two or more shoots cross each other or are too close together, you cut out right to the parental branch all extras. You should cut out the big bushy ones, get rid of them unless you are extending the tree and shaping it, but if you're after fruit then cut out, favoring the less vigorous.

You will select the new wood to remain so that it is evenly placed throughout the whole tree. Then as buds develop into leaves and fruit, the branch will hang down.

In pruning the long method, you find none of your fruit will suffer from sunburn as there will be always enough foliage to provide protection. With the long pruning also you'll always have a crop never excessively heavy, but always of good quality, providing of course, you protect from enemies and provide water. And in this method you will find it necessary in alternate years to cut back old shoots even to the trunk to allow new ones to grow so as to permit your tree to be a yearly bearer. Where soil is rich and moisture is abundant, a light pruning is far better than a heavy one, and you'll get more fruit.

Now look to the pear tree; if it has been properly pruned in the past, it is the best looking tree in the garden. See its streamline effect, every scaffold

PEAR branch equidistant from its neighbor, all of them breaking from the trunk evenly on all sides. And at tip you notice new growth of dark shiny color. There are lots of new shoots; some are crowded together; we are going to prune them back to only one shoot, or one leader, to each scaffold branch. All up and down the heavy branches you see evenly placed little twigs or minute crooked and tight branches. These little twigs are where the flowers and the fruit hang. They are spurs, you saw them back there on the apple; they look similar. You prune the pear just the way you prune an apple tree.

Remember, we are still talking about the trees that bear on the spurs. Now we come to cherries. Cherries need little pruning, especially if as young trees they have been properly trained and guided into bearing. It is a well-known fact that cherry trees more readily produce fruit spurs than do apples or pear trees and consequently do not require regular pruning to encourage new wood or renewal wood. As a rule, cherries resent pruning, but there are conditions which make pruning necessary, as for instance, trees long neglected standing with a lot of dead wood and branches. Our cherry, then, will serve to illustrate the first rule for pruning the deciduous fruit tree: to cut away dead wood, to encourage new growth so that the tree once again will become vigorous with mechanically strong branches and healthy foliage. But for the very reason that cherry trees need little pruning, they often become neglected. *CHERRY*

Look now at that cherry tree near the fence there. See the neglect, with that half-dead branch, with hundreds of laterally born spurs knocked off, leaving only gaping scars and there's a limb broken and dangling in the breeze beside a stub all ragged and splintered, a danger threatening anyone who might climb that tree at harvest time. And notice how utterly lacking in vigor it is. It has no mechanical strength, and there, an unhealthy tree, it's begging for kindly attention. What can you do about it now?

One thing you can do is prune it. Take your saw and cut off that dead limb first, then cut back that broken one to clean healthy wood, and prune the jagged stub to a smooth surface close to the tree trunk. You'll be astonished how after pruning and feeding, and with a little thoughtful care next summer, that half-dead tree will grow right into a vigorous tree with new life and fine tasty fruit. Those large cuts caused by the saw you'll have to paint over with Bordeaux paste or with ordinary plumbers white lead to which add raw (not boiled) linseed oil (anything with asphaltum base burns or causes sweating) to help keep out fungus disease to give the scar a chance to heal.

What we want to do is take out the overcrowded shoots, especially the upright ones which crowd out the more desirable outward-growing shoots. This is particularly true in the Lambert and the Black Tartarian cherry trees. The Royal Anne assumes a spreading habit naturally.

Again, what can the gardener do when his tree reaches up to sixty feet tall? Naturally, he'll have to lower the branches or leave two-thirds of the crop for the birds. It is a good rule, as far as the cherry is concerned, to prune annually whatever is necessary, renewing approximately ten per cent of the fruit-bearing area each year.

Now for the plum, still in the spur-bearing group.

PLUM There are two kinds of plum trees, the Japanese and the European. If yours is the Japanese, perhaps last year you were swamped with fruit; it rained down all over the sidewalk, onto the lawn, or all over your little orchard. They always produce too much fruit on the side spurs. But notice that whip-like growth at the top. Those branches are long and smooth, twisted together, fighting for sunlight, and towards the bottom with a few spurs now carrying clusters of tight buds. Taking away branches so as to permit light and air to reach into all parts of the framework of the fruit tree is our second reason for pruning the dormant fruit tree now. Well, just try your pruning shears on this tree. The Japanese plum should be pruned so as to stimulate annual growth of the new whips. But don't worry, you can learn how to prune on this tree and you can't make any mistakes because this plum tree just laughs at blunders and dumps a ton of fruit down anyway. So, thin it out, prune the branches back to reduce the amount of the crop and still induce or encourage new growth for next year.

But if you have a French, Italian or German plum, the pruning operation is different. Mature plums that contain enough sugar to dry without fermenting are called prunes. Notice how jammed in close those inner branches are — see the brush effect in the heart of the tree. You want to reach in there and "open it up" as the professionals call it. This is not so much to keep out fungus diseases and insect enemies, though it helps, as to let in the sun to ripen the fruit. But don't let itchy fingers slash away too much. Just carefully go in and cut out all dead brush, prune out old useless spur wood which has served its time and is more dead than alive. If you butcher back, you cause the sudden development of vigorous wild whips called water shoots, which delay production and will have to be drastically cut. So just remember back the following year, each year to nibble delicately but with a purpose. Above all, use your judgment.

APRICOT

Now let's look at the apricot. It too is a spur bloomer. Perhaps yours hasn't felt the shears for half its lifetime. Notice how it has grown lopsided, and how it droops like a willow. Last spring you had a time of it underneath, spading in the insect-infested leaves — you had to get on your knees to turn the soil over. And when you harvested the crop, it was a circus for your watching neighbor; for to get that fruit, you had to jack-knife your body under those branches. And to get into the heart of the tree you fought the wild branches, tore your shirt, scratched your back, and talked to yourself in sweaty misery. And if you were an orchardist who neglected his trees, you lost money for yourself, for your pickers used more time fighting brushwood than in harvesting the crop itself, which, suited to the tree, was made up of marbles.

The apricot tree has a way of running wild for lack of your kindly guiding hand. But when it is tamed, it becomes a model of accessibility with wide open places where the ladder will fit in, and the pretty yellow fruit, properly thinned, grows plump, big and beautiful, half-hidden among the rich green leaves on the strong, orderly scaffold of branch.

Awhile ago I went down to Sunnyvale to the Losse Orchard, 340 acres of fine apricots. In my summer vacations from school I had worked there, and it felt almost like old times as I drove in. Both Austin and Weir Losse were standing there when I got out of the car, and both were very interested when I asked them to describe their way of pruning the apricot.

HOW

"Well, for one thing," said the brother who is the foreman, "don't let your tree carry a lot of useless wood. Cut out the unproductive old brush. Keep your leading branches clean. In the young small tree, which won't have much of a crop anyway, prune to encourage strong growth. You aim to bring your tree up, that is so as to get more than thirty inches of new growth. And when your young tree is a strong grower, you cut less, leaving strong shoots so as to raise the scaffold branches higher."

Walking over to a big tree he continued: "See this nice young growth with the red, smooth surface. Notice those strongly set buds. It shows that tree put out a lot of growth last summer. It didn't have much of a crop, so its strength went into new wood. We pruned that young new wood, those new shoots lightly, just a thinning here and there because on those new shoots will come the crop next summer. Those new shoots will have lots of nice clean leaves, and green leaves you must remember are fuel for developing sweet-tasting apricots. In an old tree always you must have new wood to bring on new spurs. The fruit is carried next summer on the spurs too, the older spurs which you see are placed farther back on the branch. But these keep on bearing for only three years. We prune to encourage new wood so that we keep the tree filled with new spurs. And also prune to cut out the useless old spurs, and old busy wood, that shows it won't produce fruit again because it is all worn out. Remember too, the apricot compared with other trees requires more encouragement by wise pruning to bring out spur growth.

"On these old branches then we leave from four to six inches of the new growth of last year. You prune so the leaf bud will grow in the direction you want the branch to go. It should be away from the heart of the tree. There must always be some new growth on old branches to carry the new spurs, because along that four to six inches of new growth will be three or four spurs upon which of course you get the golden apricots.

"Now look at that tree here," he said, pointing to one across the road. "It had a bumper crop last summer, you can tell now because there is hardly any new growth wood at all on the tree. We gave that tree only a light pruning because the buds are weak after the heavy job of fruit production last year. You don't want to prune a tree heavily right after it produces a big crop."

We went over to still another tree, where I called attention to long new shoots of only lead-pencil thickness. "Those," one of the brothers explained, "broke out on that branch because whoever pruned this tree last year cut off a new shoot, and the older limb getting a chance to renew itself immediately sent out a rash of whips. Expert pruners take advantage of this, and in that way they help their older trees keep up production by sending out new wood. We don't touch these except to thin out the excess. We prune down close to the main stem. If we merely shorten them as we do ordinary new wood, each one would start a spray of its own. Brush growth never amounts to anything.

"To put all this in a nutshell, we prune the apricot for healthy spur growth; you get your best fruit on it."

MUMMIES

Then they pointed to some black wrinkled balls hanging on a tree — dried up fruit that was left by the pickers because it was too small. "Those are mummies," they said, "hanging there all winter. Of course they ought to come out because they are loaded with trouble, especially the brown rot that loses us much fruit. Of course, spraying helps, but when we are pruning the tree, and come across mummies, we knock them off."

I thanked these gentlemen for their information, and as I was about to depart one of them said: "A good thing with the apricot and with the peach and other fruit trees, is to prune for an average crop. It's hard on a tree when it is pruned to throw a bumper crop. When you prune a tree too heavily one year, you have to wait over a summer for the next crop, so that the fruit comes in alternate years. Of course no two pruners can use exactly the same procedure for they have to adapt themselves to climate, soil and labor differences. A dry hot district or a poor soil will have less growth, and a man who has had his training in such a place is apt to lean toward light pruning. The point above all is to prune; don't neglect a tree."

We shall now discuss those fruit trees that do not have spurs but produce their crop on the past season's new wood. I gave you the list already, but let's repeat it: peaches, nectarines, Oriental persimmons, figs, and the Chinese quince. Now look at your peach tree; let's say it is a young tree planted six to eight years ago. It produces the flowers and the fruit on the new growth without spurs; you see nice shiny reddish-green branches, shooting up two to four feet skyward. They grew last year, and they are all ready to throw flowers and fruit next spring and summer. Peaches have to grow like that in order to produce fruit, for as you remember they do not have spurs. Let's look carefully along one of those young branches. See those buds; they come in threes, two round flower buds, flanking one flat, pointed leaf bud in the middle. They are placed up and down the long branch, and the little side branches carry them too. If you prune this branch, that is cut it down close to the main scaffold, off goes the crop. The best fruit is produced in the growth towards the base of the branch, in the heart where the sun can't cook it up. What you must do then to prune this peach tree is to take out over-crowded branches; reduce the number of branches, and prune the tree, and thus favor all the remaining ones and reduce the fruit load so that the crop will be evenly distributed and strongly supported throughout the tree.

PEACH

CAUTION

Since this tree before us wasn't pruned right for years past, it has some dead branches, and has grown tall with a few new little twiggy branches way up on top. And as the growth went up so did the crop appearing skimpily way up at the top, because, and this is important to realize in the peach, the fruiting area is carried higher and higher each year. It is clear then faulty pruning in peach trees always results in long stretches of barren branches between low scaffold and top growth. And look how burned those "leggy" scaffold branches are. That is because there were no leaves, no lower growing shoots to shield the scaffold from the torrid sun. Now what can we do for a peach tree like this?

Take one of the branches at the trunk, follow it out and up until you come to a terminal spray of new reddish-green shoots that came in last season. Cut these all off flush with the main stem except the lowest and paint the scars with Bordeaux paste or tree seal. The only purpose in leaving this little terminal shoot is to bring the sap up through and keep the old branch alive. And on this branch will come out new shoots which will renew your tree, keep it compact, and will bear peaches next year. You must never leave a stump, be sure the little branch or shoot has good buds, that will carry healthy green leaves, and the movement of sap through the scaffold from the roots will do the rest.

I have been reminded to tell you that if you have an old tree which you like, you can bring it back to the vigor of youth by lowering the scaffold a little each year, always leaving some new growth to take care of the flowing sap.

Then with the peach, more than with the apricot, there is a personal side. You want to know your peach, you must understand just what type of a peach is growing in your yard, because peaches do not all grow alike. Recently at the gardener's meeting we were discussing this very subject, and Henry Hassard, president of the club, said, "Some peaches are hard to keep low, they want to climb up into the sky, I have in mind especially the Salway. It is a late peach, it grows way up and keeps on growing that way. I have to watch my tree all the time. I keep nibbling it all the time, tipping it back here and there to keep the growth down, otherwise it gets beyond me, and when you have to lug around an eighteen to twenty foot ladder to harvest the crop you have more than you bargained for. Force the scaffold

WATCH

branches to grow out and stay low. I keep the growth low so as to shield the scaffold from the sun, but also I thin out branches too, because this tree has a tendency to overbear.

"Then take the Rio Oso Gem," he continued, "now in my garden I have found it grows weakly, it seems not to want to grow, and unless I prune it very carefully the crop is disappointing. More than that, I think this tree has to be thinned from the very beginning for the Rio Oso Gem wants to produce too much fruit, which if not thinned tastes poor. When thinned heavily, you wouldn't want a better peach."

I want to add the Rio Oso Gem has proved very successful in the Great Valley. The farmers over there are quite happy with it. So once again I recommend you consult your local authorities, for they know how a peach behaves in your district, in your soil and climate. You don't just grab any peach.

"Take the Elberta," Mr. Hassard went on, "in Los Altos in my garden I've tried that tree for five years. It did no good; an absolute failure. My new neighbor across the road told me she was planning to put one in her garden. I told her, "I've dug the Elberta peach out of my garden; it never did grow and do the wonderful things I heard about it. Perhaps it is the finest peach in Morgan Hill or in Gilroy, but in Los Altos here with me it was a failure."

CHECK All of the boys at the gardener's club agreed there was a whole lot to this business of asking your experienced neighbor or the friendly orchardist in the district about their experiences. Also you can get the same advice from your County Farm Advisor who is paid by you to know all about it. And you can ask for One-Sheet-Answers booklets etc., on what and how to do in California. Or send a postcard with your name and address to University of California, Agricultural Extension Service, in your county, California.

I cannot over-emphasize to you the importance of getting information from all these good sources. It's just as important as in cooking. In former times the good cooks worked by intuition, but without accurate measurement and weighing. Most people made all kinds of mistakes and then later with the wide distribution of printed cook books accurate measuring cups and weighing scales, thermometers for the stove, and clocks to estimate time, the art of cookery spread all over the country and anybody can cook who can read.

FLOWERING PEACH

And now one more point about peaches, you prune the flowering peach like the table peach, but wait till it is in flower so you can use the branches in the house.

Figs, as your list will inform you, produce their crop on new growth. We prune therefore to encourage new wood, but there are a few modifying factors. Do you have in your garden the Mission fig? It produces annually two crops of medium large figs, dark purple to black. Do you have the Adriatic, the White Adriatic, which produces figs of medium-size white, but the pulp is reddish inside? These two types of figs always throw out low branches. These should be removed to enable the gardener to cultivate under them. Both of these trees should be gone over annually and have all cross branches, all branches suffering from sunburn, all dead branches taken out. Top pruning is all that is required to keep the trees in new active wood.

FIGS

Do you have a Kadota fig? This is a favorite among the canning industry. The fruit is medium size, light green, and the seedless pulp is very sweet. You prune the Kadota fig tree more than the Mission because on it the new wood keeps on growing till frost. If the Kadota is unpruned then there are only two crops, but pruned heavily as many as four or five crops. At this time of year you will see new vigorous shoots, some with frosted figs. Cut these shoots of last season back to about fifteen inches, and take any inside branches out and thus permit light to reach down into the heart of the tree. Another interesting point is prune early and you'll get an early crop, prune late, that is in March, and you get a late crop.

Chapter 4

(C) STYLE THROUGH PRUNING IN THE GARDEN

(January: Fourth Week)

Style as I mean it here is not the passing fancy of this season, to be discarded in the next like the lady's hat. It is not a tricky plant rounded up like a sausage or spread like an umbrella or peaked like a campanile. It is not gigantic size, nor splendor, though those may have a place. It is not elegance, nor even neatness. Rather, it is the effect of unadorned, natural symmetry and radiance — good for a lifetime past or future. And while we are pruning for style in this sense, we shall of course be pruning also for harmony in the design; and for plant prosperity; and for blooms and fruit. Out in the native forest and meadow, where we get our inspiration, the pruning has been taking care of itself. The weather and seasons have cut back branches, and killed off millions of plants that got in the wrong places. In every big wind trees crashed whose day was done. Then pests and fire stole in. A century of all this without compensation would make a desert. But somehow from ruthlessness emerges a grand harmony between enemies and plants that can live with each other, and the result is a style unbelievably kind to the senses.

Now, in the garden we aspire to a harmony also, though it cannot be so grand. And we have to contrive it speedily, branch by branch; we are not going to kill off a hundred plants to get one that will fit — we have to make every plant count. Therefore we have to know, beforehand, where we are going, and we have to pick our way thoughtfully.

STUDY TREE FOR

Pruning for style is like sculpture. You cut away useless parts, get rid of overbearing weight and ugly edges, and release the hidden figure. If you will look with attention, you will find that the plant itself points out to you what should be done and begs you to do it.

Your trees, shrubs, and vines carry four kinds of wood, dead, old, firm, and young; and two kinds of buds, leaf and flower. You have to learn the difference before you cut anything at all. Dead wood is finished because the roots no longer support it. The leaves long ago have left the twigs, the bark has peeled or fallen away, and the passage of time has enabled decay to set in. Old wood may show scars and evidence of insect attack; it supports only meager growth, oftentimes weak and without luster, and the foliage when it drops will not be renewed. Because of interfering branches much of the inside wood no longer favored with sunlight becomes old and therefore ineffectual. Firm wood radiates with vigorous life, and is steadfastly supported by sap flow from the roots. Its branches and twigs sprout out, they develop buds, then healthy active foliage, flowers and fruit. The life processes of the plant take place in the firm wood. Young wood is still in the process of development, is moving and as in the new canes of our roses always shows a shiny bark and healthy green tone. Sometimes the young wood becomes too enthusiastic and crosses and re-crosses inside the plant body making crowded stems; it must then be controlled. The distinction between leaf buds and flower buds is simple, for usually narrow buds unfold leaves, and round fat ones unfold blooms. If you can't tell the buds apart, ask the nurseryman. He will be happy, for he is as anxious and as enthusiastic as you are to make the plants grow.

TREES

The first to think of is the dead wood. In some plants that is all you have to prune; such as the sturdy magnolia, laburnum or golden chain. And such also are some of our trees — the locust which gives the garden such rich fragrance in spring, and the catalpa, often grown for its neat clusters of white flowers skipping along the branches as spring merges into early summer. Then there are the evergreen plants; these too require only the removal of dead branches or a trimming to keep them in shape. Of course in California these may grow so fast as to make the pruning more than a trimming. But on the firs, pines or spruces, for instance, little is required. And the other evergreens like the cypress and junipers can be pruned any day of the year. Whenever you need some fragrant foliage for inside decoration, use it to trim up and shape these plants. You will find that such attention will reward you with a tidy, and what is better, a happy-looking plant the whole year through. You may get to feeling like the artist who keeps polishing his

CYPRESS & JUNIPERS

FORSYTHIA OR PERSIAN LILAC OR VIBURNUM ETC.

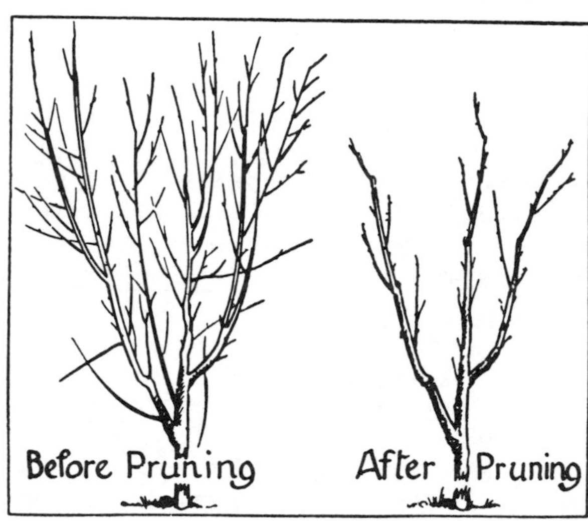

piece of bronze, long and often. Both he and you take care to stop short of glare. Along with the dead wood take out injured wood. And take out diseased wood as well. When branches are infested with disease or bugs, the best way is to cut out to the roots and burn. The roots will then send forth new growth which, with reasonable vigilance, can be made to stand as a new, hardy, clean plant in the place of one drooping in filth and weakness.

Then, you prune to maintain a balance between root and top growth; control, for instance, wild spreading branches, get rid of old surplus that is nothing more than busy wood because it gives neither flowers nor beauty. In this problem remember our rose; in the rose you look hard at any wood over three years old. So with your shrub you want it continuously to send forth new wood with fresh strength; on this your flowers appear. Therefore cut all the wood that cannot earn its way.

SHRUBS

SUMMER BLOOMER

Then again you have to prune for blooms and fruit. The plant over all is in proportion to its roots — they can only do so much. The idea is to keep blooming wood blooming, to maintain both the desired quality and the desired quantity in flowers and fruits. Keep in mind every minute the difference between spring and summer bloomers. The summer bloomers like the hydrangeas, fuchsias, summer lilac, and veronica should be pruned in the winter months, because they must first produce new growth and, later, upon it carry their flowers. If you prune these in mid-spring or early summer you will be cutting off the current year's growth; the season will not be long enough for the new growth to make flowers, and you will have none this year. These plants flower in late June, July and August; therefore, prune them well before they resume growth, and practice your sculpturing too, for you want them to grow shapely this spring.

SPRING BLOOMER

The spring bloomers on the other hand, like the weigela, bridal wreath, and Spanish broom, must be pruned within two weeks after they have finished blooming — the first two, therefore, in mid-May and the broom in June or July according to your location. The next year's flowers are formed on the new summer's growth.

On all these, whether for spring or for summer, we prune hard for a few large flowers, and lightly for an abundance. Because we want to develop new strong basal shoots, we cut out older ones when they are in full bloom or just after they have finished, as in the weigela in spring or hydrangea in late fall or winter. The roots get busy and send up new growth which, nourished during the growing season with water and fertilizer, will produce quality flowers the following year. The old rule is always good: THE NEW WOOD BEARS THE FLOWERS.

The performance cannot of course be rigid. It is bound to vary with location, shade, and what may be

HEATHER called the personal habits of plants. The heathers may be pruned right after they flower, which usually is during these winter months. And by the way, throw a handful of soil sulphur on the ground around heather too; it's good for them.

HYDRANGIA FUCHSIA Then with the hydrangeas and fuchsias — if the plants receive an abundance of sunlight you may prune hard; if they are growing under heavy shade, be more gentle. It takes so many hours of direct sunlight for the leaves to produce enough food so the flowers may be formed. In frost districts you may hold back pruning, if there is no question as to bloom, you may prune any day of the year; and sometimes in old gardens being refurbished, one must sail into the job excluding any thought of flower show.

Finally, you have to think of how you are going to formalize your hedge and some of your evergreens — that is, you have to think of it if you have to do it. I know well enough that most of the house lots, and the houses too, have straight boundaries and square corners. You are usually, from the start, limited by these features. But that is no reason why you should accent these features as by chopping off the hedge to a straight level all the way. That is the custom, not because it looks good, but because, with a line and electric clippers, you can do it with your eyes shut. I shall not scold if you do it; it isn't fatal. But it often represents a lost opportunity. There are noble effects to be gained by bushy corner anchors, by corner fillings, and by graceful swings in height and width. There is such a thing as neighbors planning their garden together, yet keeping them separate by natural-looking barriers. It is the difference between the old time bear-cages in the zoo and the present-day invisible walls. Still better — it is the difference between a fence and a running brook.

Well, we can't all go that far and we don't need to. But in our pruning for form, let us prune also for style, and let us, so far as we may, learn to resist making plants imitate fences or bedroom furniture.

However this is, we must not let the hedge run

wild; we have to keep its top down lest it thin out below and become a row of sickly trees. Light repeated pruning has the advantage of bringing out the new growth more evenly and compactly: if that is what you need, that is the way you will get it.

VINES

Now as to vines. Why do we have vines, and why do we prune them. Vines do more for the garden than cover the wall or hide the fence; they make patterns, put color where it is desired, fill empty space with graceful leaf and flower, and soften architectural lines. But these plants have sensitive feelings. They require encouragement and help in return for their kind service to the garden — in fact vines require more than shrubs, they require specific attention or else they turn against us, and do us injury in place of benefit. We must prune both the evergreen and the flowering deciduous forms. For example, have you a wisteria that refuses to bloom? Have you ever seen a jasmine that was all lanky stem and leaf with never a color or trace of perfume? Did you ever see a honeysuckle so crowded with brown, dirty twigs and leaves that the honey bees themselves buzzed it by, and the gardener gazed upon it, not in delight, but in despair? And then there is the ivy or creeping fig that covered everything in sight. Something has gone wrong. What is it? Bad pruning, or (horrible to relate!) no pruning at all.

WISTERIA

First the wisteria, an early spring bloomer. You remember the two kinds of buds, leaf bud and flower bud. These are easy to tell apart in the wisteria. The new growth of last year, 1965, that is, is straw-colored, stringy shoots of yardage length; along these, brown flat buds ending in sharp points alternate every six or so inches. They will finally unfold into the many, paired leaves. The flower buds, which come later, are plump like the breast of a robin and they appear only upon spurs — that is, upon little stems whose sole duty is to carry the flower. Older vines are already loaded with older spurs back of the straw-colored shoots: cut back every long straw-colored shoot regardless of its thickness; those of 1965 will produce spurs if you prune now. It is very simple.

SPURS

Cut them back, leaving only four to six of the leaf buds on each. Each of these remaining buds can form the spur, except the end one which either makes a spur or starts out the new growth of 1966. The remaining buds, awakened and now privileged and heartened to their new duty, immediately develop into spurs — each year they become longer, each year carry another cluster of buds. When they have become four to six inches long, they may carry as many as five of the white and purple clusters. In fact, hanging from the spur wood of old vines may be seen long, fuzzy pods which carry seeds formed after last year's flowers.

For pruning there are four kinds of vines, each requiring a distinct treatment. Wisteria, which we have discussed, is one of them. The next includes the jasmine, which resembles the wisteria in being a spring bloomer and in producing long shoots one year which will carry blooms the next. But it differs in being an evergreen which never needs spurwood. The old rule applies here again. "The new wood bears the flowers"; the harder you cut the more new wood you will have. Therefore, cut back to suit your design, whether it be for pergola, arbor or lattice, without fear that the blooms will fail. But, unlike the wisteria, the cutting is not done now, but is postponed until two weeks after the flowers have passed. The reason for the difference, though both are spring bloomers, is that jasmine makes its new growth immediately after the blooms, and that new growth is what you and I want to control for next year. The wisteria, on the other hand, follows its blooms with only yardage leaf growth; as you now understand, it has to be pruned back just before the flower-bearing spurs are due. Prune your jasmine, that is the double yellow jasmine, the Italian yellow jasmine and the jessamine, which is the common white fragrant jasmine, right after flowering from March or July depending upon the earliness or lateness of your district. If these vines are not pruned, their balance is upset and then this season and perhaps next season you can expect only a half-hearted display. By the way, the Chilean Jasmine, Mandevillea, does not

JASMINE

belong botanically to this group. It is a summer bloomer, and you get this vine ready by pruning it now, in January. Like the hydrangea or fuchsia, it must produce new shoots in the spring of 1966, and by late summer these same shoots throw out the large very fragrant white flowers. Give the Chilean Jasmine a handful of gypsum or lime, by the way. They like it once in three years.

HONEYSUCKLE

The honeysuckle, the name for the old woodbine, is a third kind of vine. Vicious, severe pruning is in order at all times. Sail into it and work it over regardless of season of bloom because new growth will spring out at you even before you have finished the job, and will bloom before you clean your tools and put them away! Once the root of a honeysuckle has become established, there's no holding it back. In some states it is a pest, and the day when, as a rare and lovely plant, it was introduced from the Orient is celebrated in reverse. But it is no pest out here, but one of the finest plants as a veil to a board fence, or as a companion to a hard rock wall. If you feel hearty, prune it to the roots as our painter did for madame's rose, and in a few weeks you will rejoice in the freshness of new growth, glowing with fragrant flowers.

IVY

And finally the fourth kind of vine is that grown for foliage, covers such as the English Ivy, and the creeping fig, the large-leaved Boston Ivy, and the Virginia Creeper. Often these are given a definite job, to cover a wall, hide a fence, screen out a tank house. With good growth they soon complete their office, and then feeling their strength and, having no discretion whatever, they carry on to absurdity. Have you ever seen a vine-clad garden and house left without a snip of the shears for five years? Talk about going back to Nature! That house wall and roof hidden under its vine blanket is fast crumbling with mould and rot.

Of course this never happens in your garden, if you have an idea just where the vine ought to go, and act with attention on that idea. The English Ivy must be cut back, severely too, lest it bring down the wall itself in its ultimate fall. The creeping fig has been guilty of picking out bricks and moving plaster and foundation in its powerful growth. When it has become overbearing, it must be laid low, not with ordinary pruners, but with an ax. The Boston Ivy and Virginia Creeper, too, may be pruned in extreme need right to the ground where they can start out again fresh, new, and under control.

TOOLS Before we finish, a word on the question — how do you cut? The tools are: a sharp blade like the one in a heavy jack knife; small hand shears; big pruning shears for reaching with handles eight feet long; a curved pruning saw; a stout ladder, and plumbers paint mixed with raw linseed oil to cover large cuts.

If an old branch is to be removed, cut it out to the ground; leave no stumps for they harbor disease and trouble which can work its way disastrously into the root. If a branch is to be pruned, cut it off even to the trunk; leave no stubs, no coat hangers. Remember the sculptor and his figures in stone; you are aiming for figures in your plants. Taking out armfuls of brush does not necessarily credit you with proper pruning technique. Don't butcher your plant unreasonably. Help it to look like a bush or a tree. Avoid the Dutch cut effect as you would the plague. But you must be decisive — you must approach the problem with fortitude and determination. You and I were talking about frost the other day. Your bougainvillea was frosted back to the ground one hard winter and you thought it was finished. The following spring, what happened? An army of new shoots, rank on rank, marched out waving glorious blooms. You need not be so drastic as that in your pruning. But you must go to it vigorously without cheating or wavering. If your skeptical neighbor says you are cutting too hard, tell him you have factual information — and make certain that you have.

You can be sure that pruning involves more than I have given you here. My purpose is, not to make an expert of you in one easy lesson, but to get you started on the track with an attitude of care and attention. As you proceed, you will find that State pamphlets on pruning are helpful. A visit right out to The

College of Agriculture, University of California, Berkeley, California, will fetch you a copy of Pruning Deciduous Fruit Trees; or Apricot Culture in California; or ten cents to the Superintendent of Documents, Washington, D. C., and get a copy of Farmers' Bulletin No. 1826, Care of Ornamental Trees and Shrubs.

The Opportune Task: Prune your summer blooming shrubs now. Prune hydrangeas, oleanders, buddleias, plumbago; prune the berry plant; including raspberries. Do not prune your Himalayan blackberries now. In your clean-up of these caneberries go after the larvae of the horntails. They are guilty of chewing and girdling the new shoots. Dust generously around the root crowns now. See page 494.

LILACS

Lilacs are now dormant. Take a good look, prune out dead wood, prune out diseased wood. Remember you want the center of the bush open so sunlight gets in. Always thin out plants in the dormant season. Now's a good time for this task. FERNS: work them over. That is, cut off old fronds, top dress with leaf mold, fertilize. Do this if the weather has warmed up and growth has begun. Especially for the Maidenhair or Fivefinger is it important to prune early. But if the weather still is cold and plants yet are truly dormant don't prune, wait till next month.

FERNS

GALL FLY EGGS

Winter storms knock off dead leaves from oak trees. Rake these from the lawn and destroy because they carry eggs of the gall fly.

HYDRANGEA

HYDRANGEAS: if you want blue flowers begin now: read pages 318-321.

TRANSVAAL DAISIES

Take a look at your clumps. If cold weather has come then proceed as follows: Shovel over the crowns of each clump old cow manure and rough leaf mold. Cover the crowns well. This top dress protects the crown shoots from frost. In spring when new shoots start up remove pile of leaf mold. The clump having been winter fed will send up strong shoots, and all leaves will be of a good green. The blooms also will appear in great numbers.

GLADIOLUS

Gladiolus: before storing corms dust with insecticide or fungicide, a good step towards thrip control.

CHAPTER 5

POINTS ON PRUNING PERSIMMONS, GRAPES AND CANEBERRIES

(February: First Week)

. . . questions and answers on pruning. We'll start with:

"My oriental persimmon was planted four years ago. It has never made a crop. Will pruning help? If so, how shall I go about it?"

PERSIMMON Oriental persimmons require about five years before they come into bearing. Planted as a whip, the tree must grow up and fill out with lateral branches. Usually when the young persimmon has put on sturdy growth, a small crop is produced, and once fruit is carried on the tree, you can expect a crop from then on. The older the tree the greater the harvest. In pruning the Oriental persimmon, you must remember the fruit is produced like the peach, nectarine and fig on the new growth wood — the new shoots that grew last summer. Therefore, pruning is more of a thinning-out of overcrowded branches, especially upper branches that take the light from inner lower ones. By thinning out unwanted branches, you enable your tree to give its strength to vigorous growth upon which, of course, the crop will appear the following year. If you have older trees, you might see right now broken branches where last year or in seasons past the crop of persimmons was so heavy that the weight destroyed the far-spreading branches. These branches unpruned bore heavy fruit out on their tips. As the fruit ripened the weight increased and the branches came smashing down with a loss of both crop and branches. By thinning out the branches, this danger is averted.

Slant the cut. Prune always close to a lateral branch, one that is going to grow out away from the tree. And as in the peach, never leave a stump and never leave a coat hanger as a punctuation point for your eyes. Clean cuts close to a lateral does away with this possibility. Persimmon trees often throw up vigorous water sprouts like those in the oriental plum. Take them out unless there is a gap, in which case you will let the new lateral growth fill in. If you have a persimmon tree as old as the hills, the kind that hasn't seen a pair of pruning shears in a lifetime, you may rejuvenate that tree by a severe pruning and cutting back of old, moss-covered scaffold branches, cutting back to a low lateral branch. By doing this, just as you did with your old favorite peach, you permit new young growth to break out along the old branch, and next year your tree will throw out good-sized fruit. Of course, asphalt will be painted over cuts larger than an inch in diameter; this is to keep out fungus enemies.

The next question deals with grapes. Here it is:

GRAPES

"In our yard we have an old grape vine, which someone told us is a Thompson Seedless. But the crop is disappointing. What can we do to correct this? How shall we prune this vine?"

To begin with, each one of us should know without a shadow of a doubt the type of vine in our garden, because the kinds have to be managed differently. There are three main kinds: Thompson Seedless, the wine grapes, and the Eastern American Slipskin.

Once a grape vine is established in the garden, the amateur gardener is primarily interested in getting a good crop. A vine has two jobs it must do each year. It must mature a crop, and it must produce new growth wood for next year's crop.

Now we'll walk over to that wide-topped arbor and take a look at the grape vine there. It's the Thompson Seedless, you can tell by the little sun-dried bunch of raisins, grapes that weren't picked last summer.

KINDS

Structurally, all the vines, including the Thompson Seedless, are alike. Up along the top of your arbor you can see long russet-colored shoots, they are the nice young new growth of last summer. Look a little farther back along the old shoot which last year you tied close to your arbor, and see where this new growth started from. You will find the new growth of last summer, the summer of 1954, started from a bud on the old shoot of 1953, and that old shoot is called a cane. You can trace this back eventually to the old and shaggy branches and trunk that bring the vine up from the root. Take hold of the new shoot that grew last summer. From the tip, follow this shoot back to eight inches of where it started from off the cane. Now if this were not Thompson Seedless but another kind which you have trained for this arbor, such as the Flame Tokay or Muscat, you would cut it there. You leave then only the basal portion of the new shoot. On that little eight inches of new growth there will be two to four buds, one right at the point of union where the shoots come off the cane, the others along the new shoot. The new growth of 1954 starts out from these buds. But since we are talking about the Thompson Seedless grape vine, instead of cutting back to eight inches you will leave three to five feet of the new shoot growth of 1965, that is, you will leave fifteen buds, because the basal buds on the Thompson Seedless grape usually do not produce any fruit at all, instead send out only skimpy growth wood. This is true also of a few other table grapes such as the Emperor.

In pruning, you do not treat all the shoots alike. If you look hard now at your Thompson Seedless grape, you see some carry old dried bunches of grapes. These were the producers of last year. Take these out, and do your pruning for this year's production on those new shoots which did not produce in 1954. A good practice each year is to prune so as to alternate the production by cutting some shoots short and others long. This is to keep your vine from getting out of control and resulting in the necessity of butchering.

Though "cane pruning" as this type is called, serves best for the Thompson Seedless, it is not appropriate for most of the other types of table or wine grapes. Vineyardists use the Cordon system of pruning, in which the trunk is encouraged up either vertically or horizontally, and the branches appear at intervals of eight to twelve inches. The new shoots are trained horizontally and are well distributed with the clusters of berries hanging at about an even distance from the ground.

And also there is the Head system. In this, the vine is given the form of an upright shrub. The trunk breaking from the roots is only one to three feet high, bearing at its top a ring of short shaggy branches opening up like an umbrella. The shoots breaking out from these branches are cut back and at pruning time enough buds are left to make the new carry the crop of this coming season and furnish the fruit wood for next season. Commercial growers for their purposes find this is the best system. After a few years a young vine will have a sturdy trunk capable of supporting a heavy load without the aid of a stake.

"How do you prune the neglected vine? I just bought a place on which nothing has been done all during the war!"

Let me tell you a story about a retired business man. In Los Altos, the foothills west of the Santa Clara Valley, this man several years ago bought up seventy acres of land, an old vineyard planted in the 80's, which in recent years had been badly neglected. As he put it, "I hardly knew a grape from a watermelon." Realizing this, he decided the wisest move to make after his purchase was to go up to the University of California, at Davis, and talk with the man who is the state authority on grape vine culture. After he told his story, the professor at Davis said:

"You have a very interesting problem. I think you can beat it. First you must remedy the neglect piled up on those poor vines, and second you must bring the vines back into bearing. All of this necessarily must be a slow process. Every cut you make on those vines with your pruning shears will have to be with concentrated attention because what you do now will count next summer and the summer to follow."

OLD GRAPE VINES CARE

The professor then said, "Why don't you visit my class this afternoon. We're going to discuss pruning the long-neglected vine."

What he saw in that outdoor classroom was much like his newly purchased vineyard. Pointing to a forest of wild shoots breaking out of the ground from an old vine, the professor said, "These willowy shoots come from the roots, below the graft. The vine above the branches is weak, scrawny, and produced very few grapes last year because the root strength was going into these wild shoots instead of being conducted up past the point of union in this grafted grape to the vine above. We must therefore clear the soil away from the base of the plant, and cut these robbers off cleanly. That is the first job in getting a neglected vine back into good production."

The professor said further, "The principle to follow now in this old neglected vine is to prune it so as to leave shoots long enough to carry buds to produce both fruit and new wood growth. There must exist always in this grape vine a balance between these requirements. If, for instance, too many buds are left and the vine gives its strength to fruit production, then the new growth for next year's crop will be skimpy. On the other hand, if too few buds are left, and the strength goes all into a new wood growth, the vine will have a hard time producing a crop, and falls far below useful production."

The retired business man continued his story: "So in an old established plant as the one he showed us and the old ones at home, I learned it is wise to leave about fifteen canes breaking out from the crown of the vine. These canes should be selected so that they are distributed throughout the vine. This permits the sun to reach in and enable the grapes to pile up the sugar. Each cane will have two buds. I learned then that the bud lowest on the cane, at the point where the shoot breaks off from the old cane or branch is never counted. Another important point brought out in this demonstration was the fact that in the wine grape you have to leave plenty of foliage on the vine because the leaves make starch which is sent down to the roots, and comes back up in the form of sugar where it is deposited in the bunches of grapes. Therefore, too severe pruning can rob a vine of its manufacturing centers, and when too few leaves are present grapes become deficient in sugar and sweetness."

My friend told me he went home with three good rules which he has held uppermost in his mind every time he set out to prune his vineyard:

GRAPE RULES

1. A well-matured vine should be pruned to leave 30 to 40 fruit buds. Remember the bud at the union of the cane and the parent stock, from last year's growth, is not counted. But you are actually leaving three buds to a cane.

2. When the last year's growths on the wine varieties of grapes are excessive in length, more than three or four feet, and large in diameter for the variety, it is pretty safe to assume that the vine had been too closely pruned in the past, and either additional shoots should be allowed to remain if they are there, or pruning back to three or four buds instead of two will then enable the vine to produce its normal load and quality of bunches. The more buds you leave in excess of those which are needed, the shorter will be the new wood growth.

3. A wine grape vine has two functions. Whenever you leave too many buds on the fruiting cane the wood growth suffers, and conversely when you cut off the fruit cane too short you get exaggerated growth of the new shoots and very little fruit. If your grape vine seems to be producing skimpy canes try pruning a little shorter to encourage strong new growth. But if you are getting very little fruit and find you have very heavy wood growth, then prune longer to allow nature to produce more.

Wine growers from the beginning of history had a craze for variation. The result is more than 8000 varieties, and a full tenth of these grow in California — that is, over 800. We shall not take the time to give you the list.

HISTORY

Beginning in 1770, at each Mission the fathers planted vineyards. From the Mission of Solano, General Vallejo transplanted old vines to his ranch which he called "Tears of the Mountain," after the stream that came trickling past his place. Colonel Agaston Haraszthy, helped by his two sons, brought to California armloads of grape cutting from the shores of the Mediterranean. At one shipment, 200,000 vine cuttings including all the important European varieties were brought here. Among them were the Zinfandel, the Muscat of Alexandria, the Black Monukka, and the Tokay. The finest dry wines of California come from the Coast areas: Napa, Sonoma, Livermore Valley. Tokay grapes have grown to heavy producers in the great Lodi area, and from Fresno come the Thompson Seedless, the Muscat, and other popular table grapes. And the worlds' largets vineyard, in which I have visited, 5,000 acres of almost desert land near Riverside at Guasti have been given over to the wine grape industry.

Grape growing in California is a big subject, and in our program, "How Does Your Garden Grow," we do not presume to present the "know-how" in so vast a field. May I suggest to the amateur a visit to his local library to look up Wickson's California Fruits. And in your county, visit your Agricultural Commissioner, who is in a position to tell you what varieties of grapes grow best in your district. Study his office copy of Pruning Grapevines by A. J. Winkler, and Grape Growing in California by H. E. Jacob.

Then there is another side to our story of grapes. The vineyards of Europe were threatened by a fatal blight and were saved only by the substitution of the hardy American wild roots upon which the choice varieties developed through so many hundred years were grafted. These wild roots were taken from our Eastern American Slipskin grapes. The whole plants too are used: Concord, Isabel, Niagara, and Pierce, commonly called "California Concord" here.

Our next question: "Do you prune the Eastern American grape as you prune wine grapes?"

ARBOR & FENCE GRAPES

Most often in our gardens these grapes are planted to decorate the arbor or are trained along the fence. They make a pretty vine and for this reason they are seldom pruned. But this is wrong. The shoots of these grapes are usually pencil thick, they are never as heavy as the wine grapes. The vigor of a vine is greatly increased by pruning. What you must do is to cut back the previous year's growth approximately one-fourth of its length each year until the arbor is covered. Then every year thin out canes less than pencil size and leave several of those larger, cut back to two or three buds.

Many people complain their Eastern grapes produce poorly. Let me suggest that you invest in two or more plants, place them near one another -- these Eastern American Slipskin grapes, unlike the European or Asian wine grapes, depend somewhat upon cross-pollination.

Our next question has to do with vines, but not of the grape.

"What shall I do with my boysenberry?"

BERRY

At this time of year, if you have established plants, take those canes sweeping along the ground and lift them up onto trellises. Some of these berry vines, such as blackberry with its many varieties and Boysen and Youngberry, grow four to twenty feet a year. You remember I told you last summer not to step on these long new canes when you were harvesting the crop. Well, now cut out all dead wood, all the old shoots that last year gave you the crop and tie back to the wire frame or posts all the new vigorous shoots that grew last year and will give you your crop this next summer. It is not necessary to cut the ends of these long canes off unless they have rooted. If they rooted, cut them off and you may do one of several things. You may give them away to your neighbor, you may start a new planting altogether, as in a new row, or you may interspace these new roots in the rows with the old plants. This looks toward the future, because plants are usually productive six or seven years and then it is best to replace them. But remember these newly rooted tip growth plants usually take about three years to come into real production.

Another thing to do now with all these cane berry vines is after pruning and tying up, give them all a top dress of strawy cow or horse or chicken manure. Make a mulch basin of these strawy materials and work them around the roots.

CHAPTER 6

GARDEN ENEMIES

(February: Second Week)

This in itself is a big subject. Our California garden is a regular culture bed for enemies. So long as the ground stays wet and cold, most of them sleep. But once it warms up, and as long as it stays moist, it teems with life. This normally would have a short season of supreme activity, and then in our long rainless summer, most would subside again. But when we make a garden, we set up an artificial oasis which prolongs the season many weeks. And into this oasis they come afoot, crawling, creeping, and flying. A teacher in China who came to this country to live said, "I thought we had pests there, but they're doubled and redoubled here!"

They carry on their attack day and night — when you are at dinner, when you are in bed, when you are at work at Richmond or San Francisco, and when you go fishing in the mountains. They never take time out — they never look up from their work; and give you a sweet smile — they are deadly serious and persistent. Some day I am going to have my electrician friend set up microphones in my garden so I can listen at night to the snails creeping out from under the board I left there last week; marching across the wet grass; and crunching their formidable jaws as they bite off the fresh green seedlings. And I might hear, too, the whirring of the owl's wings and the last squeak of the mouse. If I turned up the power, the din from all parts of the garden — the din of battle — would be terrifying and disheartening. Well, the idea is that the garden sizzles with life and death, and to this the amateur gardener must learn to pay attention. You will gain profit not only in the quality of your garden, but also in lifting the veil in a whole new world of fascinating events, hitherto unseen and unheard.

IDENTITY

Of course you have to find out first what your enemy looks like. How many of you are acquainted with the earwig? He is bound to be on the ground waiting to cut your stalks, leaves, flowers and fruit into bits with his mouth shears. If we were equipped in proportion, we could bring down oak trees with the power of our jaws. Well, you will have to know this fellow before you can catch and stop him, and you will have to know a dozen other chewers like him — the ants, the termites, and green lady bugs — politely called diabrotica — the Japanese beetle which declared war on us long before Pearl Harbor; the caterpillars and such as the oak leaf worms; the grasshopper, the snail, the slugs, and the gophers which have their own chewing skills. These are all destroyers by shearing, shredding and boring. And you have to learn to recognize also the sucking insects equipped with a hypodermic needle with which, incessantly and systematically, they probe all juice-laden plant flesh — and some of them our own human flesh — to draw out the life blood. Such, too, are the nuisance insects, mealy bug, scales, leafhopper, white fly and aphid impolitely called plant lice.

Some of these enemies are shrewd and sly beyond belief. "Toby EX," my old gardener friend, says that one spring his new grape leaves were chewed off as fast as the buds unfolded, and not one enemy in sight. He went out with a lantern after the picture show, but got nothing. Then he stayed home from the picture show, went out at the first darkness, and there they were at it — fat slick cutworms swarming out of the ground, up the vines and slashing and sawing away there. He picked off half a bucket full and in a few nights had them finished entirely.

Some of the worst enemies of your plants are other plants; the mildew which coats your plants with an unwholesome white dew is one group. Another enemy is the virus, that works inside the plant tissue and ultimately kills it.

But not all this teeming life of the garden is on the

enemy side. There is the mold, which yields Penicillin, our very great friend, who stands guard there day and night keeping back a world flood of plant diseases. And there is the neat little red ladybird or ladybug beetle, a perfect lady indeed, for she eats the aphid as well as the mealy bug. And there is the mealy bug destroyer who quite properly looks like the mealy bug himself on a bigger scale. Each of these without suspecting it is worth a million dollars, and each is a striking example of biological control. They propagate and grow with great speed; they are hardy. And they have such voracious appetites that they soon destroy the host and die for lack of food. So the State Insectary raises a supply against recurring epidemics. While they are about it they clean up the cottony cushion scale along with the mealy bug.

The earthworm is considered by some as another friend; he plows, aerates, and fertilizes the ground and contributes enormously to tilth. He also is propagated and introduced. The wire worm, on the other hand, who looks like an earthworm on a diet, is a chewer and destroyer. An astonishing quantity of the garden life is eaten daily by the birds. Watch them picking off the scales. Their appetite is never satisfied, and of course they don't know right from wrong; they will gobble one of your precious earthworms whenever they can catch him out. And at the flick of a wing, they will turn into shredders and swallowers, and get your newly planted seeds and seedlings. The gopher snake eats as many bugs as the birds and he kills rodents besides; he is your loyal friend, and if you kill him because he is a snake, you don't know right from wrong. The mole is a nuisance in the lawn and flower border because he loves to burrow just under the surface and leave a hump-ridge all the way across. He throws up the soil and lets air race through the root zone and dry it out. He dearly loves the bugs and eats them like mad, and so long as the supply lasts, he will go around the plants. We could get along without him, but he is no such menace as his companion, the gopher, who will forage the roots of a beautiful young fig tree until it falls over of its own weight, or will undermine a marigold and take the whole plant with him into the hold.

The way to get an eye on these enemies, and friends too, is to go out in the garden and recognize them, and find out all you can about their habits, their nests, their eggs, or young — what they look like at different stages, and what they do to the plants. If you need to, take along with you a copy of the new Circular 479, Ridding the Garden of Common Pests or pick it up at your county agent; or the copy of Circular 53, Home Floriculture in California. Send to the College of Agriculture, University of California, Berkeley, for your free copy of Circular 53*. And then all commercial companies offer illustrative pages on insects which are very helpful. Identify your bugs by aid of the pictures there. Just to hear about them without seeing and following them on the ground is like learning how to box by reading a book. Practice will do wonders for either one, and it's not much of a job after you get started — especially if you solemnly swear that you will never guess again. I'll guarantee that after your wise neighbor shows you snail eggs, like clusters of white tapioca in the soft earth under a rock, you will go over into your own place and find some within five minutes. And after that you will be finding and destroying them several times a week. Each cluster means a company less this year and a regiment less next.

WHERE TO CHECK

Once you learn where and what your enemy is, what do you do about it? What weapons do you use? One of the best weapons to begin with, is housekeeping. Clean up the places where your enemies breed. Those are their staging areas. Your humus pile, if kept properly moist so that it will disintegrate, will provide quite improperly a wonderful shelter and pasture for them. The wireworm may come there too, and the thick articulate and armoured grub-like milleped, a ravenous root eater. And above, at the top of the moist

*The Circulars published by the College of Agriculture of the University of California as listed in the various chapters such as pruning, grape growing, planting, ect., are available as long as the supply lasts. They are always available however in the public libraries throughout the state; and Agricultural Commissioners often have copies in their files.

leaf mold, and under the shelter of the dry, outer skin of the pile, it will swarm with pill and sow bugs; and even mealy bugs still on pieces of host plants where they have been thrown. Often, too, ants will be there. Stir it up a little once in a while and put in lime, and once in a while dust it with sulphur, where the bugs are thickest. That will discourage them. The harmful worms you can pick out and destroy.

A loose board or stepping stone on the ground will harbor snails, slugs, and ant nests. Dropped leaves and other rubbish have the same effect, and so do ground vines. Big leaves like the persimmon are especially bad. Any rank growth that keeps out the sun, any forgotten spot whatever, if it stays somewhat moist and without strict housekeeping — the garden will have such spots — will make a regular incubator. The boundary between the dry and moist ground within the garden is a favorite place — for example along the border path — and there you are likely to find a whole row of ant nests — an ant metropolis — organized with thousands of workers all ready with the first warm days to swarm all over you. Cultivate such places — the insects of most kinds will lie shallow, and if you break up the earth often enough, they can't prosper there. Weeds, too, and all surplus volunteers of any kind should be cleaned out constantly. Some of these insects will be lying in wait there for the time to come for them to get in their real work. A sloppy garden is an infested garden. And when you pull up this stuff, burn it — do not put it on your humus pile if it is suspect, or you may be merely carrying the bugs to a place they like all the better.

And here is a principle always useful. Hungry, weak plants yield to pests and disease. Strong, healthy plants outgrow crippling early attacks, and may even resist them to begin with. Potash makes the plants hard. Feed them, and, wonderful to relate, some forms of food for the plants are repulsive or even poisonous for the bugs. For example, millepedes may often be kept away from germinating peas by light dressing of superphosphate or lime applied to the drill at sowing time. Crop rotation helps with those pests such as the potato beetle which, after he has done his worst, walks down into the ground and waits for the next season. When he comes up again and looks around, the plant isn't there. And rotation makes for strong plants, too, because the soil gets tired supporting the same kind year after year. And besides all this, some kinds of plants have tough varieties — there are for example, rust resisting roses.

SPRAY & DUST

Another and more famous weapon is, of course, the spray and dust. The ideal would be a shotgun dose that would harmlessly kill everything at one broadside, as told us in the early press stories. But there is no such friendly, deadly weapon known to man. We still have to use special sprays for special purposes, and we have to use them at the right time — some once a year, some once a month during growing, and some every week. We have to take precautions not to ruin the plant. Some of the best chemicals can eat through the tender skin into the living cell as fast as grasshoppers.

What do we use? The materials are clearly and simply described in Blair's Practical Tree Surgery where they are divided into: insect killers and fungus killers. Insects require two kinds of treatment. The chewers need stomach poisons (see page 494) which you can apply before they come. Sometimes as in the oaks it will serve for the whole season. The sucking insects are given contact treatment — that is, if you fail to kill their eggs in your winter cleanup, you find them at work and then cover their bodies with contact spray, in this way either plugging the rows of breathing pores along their bodies and thus smothering them, or applying a corrosive which burns them. The usual materials are lime-sulphur, oils, Bordeaux mixture which contains some copper, and nicotine sulphate.

Then also the sprays vary according to whether your tree has leaves or is dormant. Your bare tree can take the stronger of these sprays, such as lime-sulphur or Bordeaux, and the less refined oil. Your green trees, such as the citrus all the year, and your deciduous trees when they are in leaf, mostly prefer what is called the refined summer or foliage oils. There are exceptions, for some leaves of course are tougher than others — the oak, for example — and can take a good dose. We could use these oils in winter also, but they cost more.

FUNGUS The plant parasites, which are mostly fungus, the mildew, mold and rust, are controlled by a protective coat. This is sprayed before the leaves come out as for Peach Curly Leaf, or it is sprayed on the leaf to control the mildew as on your rose. Or we use the dusts. For the virus disease, such as pear blight or aster yellows, cut all the diseased branches and burn, or uproot the whole plant. See Pear Blight, page 459.

We now shall look at some of the enemies at work and shall see how we fit our controls into their habits.

APHID First, the aphid — a sucking insect. They colonize on the tip of the new young branches of your shrubs, as the cotoneaster, Spanish Broom or honeysuckle; in fact, all shrubs in active growth in spring. The leaves curl with these busy fellows hidden on the underside; and they appear dirty because the sticky secretions attract the sooty mold fungus; and the flower buds, too, including your prize tulips, roses, stock, and snapdragons. Growers of vegetables find them on their cabbage, artichokes, tomatoes, and cherry trees. Aphids don't confine themselves to top growth alone, they invade the soil, too, around the roots of asters and pear trees, for example. They have delicate bodies dressed in green, red, or black robes. Contact oil and nicotine sprays will do for them. And some of the powders dusted on the colony, or blown upon the individuals, will work; among these is pyrethrum or dry sulphur. Those in the roots may be finished off with a solution of nicotine sulphate placed in holes around the roots of the plant.

MEALY BUG Our next is the mealy bug, also a sucking insect. He is among the most serious pests; you will recognize him by his flattened, elongate, oval body which is dressed with a cover of white, powdery wax. He may be as short as one eighth or as long as one-third of an inch. He feeds on parts of the plants above and below ground; this makes control very difficult. He prefers

Ants and aphids.

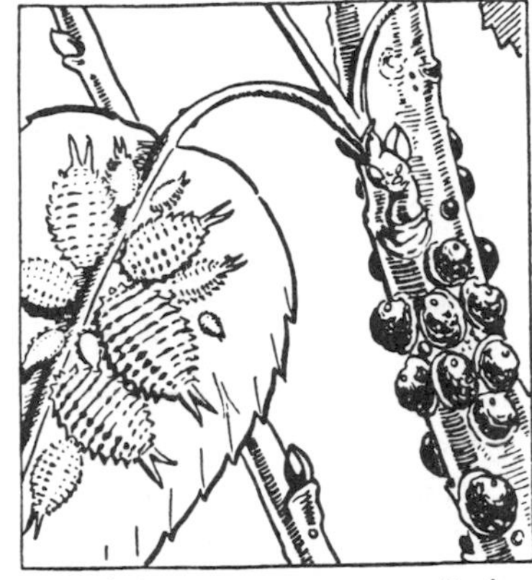

Mealy Bugs Scale

a moderate or warm, moist climate; collects in greenhouses, and in some districts in the lath house. To control the mealy bug, the gardener must manage to first control his ally the ant, which we shall consider later; this enables his parasites and predators complete freedom to work on our side. This bold bug will be far less bold and formidable then. But you and I must help the control by using sprays, especially the oil sprays which readily dissolve the protective wax covering and penetrate the bodies and eggs. Summer oils are useful. Mealy bug control must be thorough and repeated; apply sprays regularly and forcefully, and let some of them get around the roots. Another help is continued spraying with water. And don't forget your potted plants like pelargoniums where mealy bugs assemble in leaf joints and in the pot itself.

SCALES

Next, the scales — also sucking insects, and hard to see because they secrete a scaly covering which blends in with the bark. When you look at your holly tree, your oleander, or your lilac, you may see them along the stem and on both sides of the leaves as colonies of small, motionless black, red, yellow, or brown objects, flat or humped. Let us think of the black scale in particular. He comes on many plants. The females, especially the young ones, on the hemispherical hard body carry a conspicuous letter "H" made by lines and a ridge. The males are fewer and smaller. The tiny yellow louselike young crawl about for a few days, looking for a likely place, and then paying no attention to the view or other advantages insert their slender hairlike sucking mouth parts into the tissue, and remain in that position, losing their external structures and excreting a protective waxy covering. Broods overlap in a year depending on the species and climate. The well-known San Jose Scale, the most notorious member of the family, is supposed to have come into California about 1870, on some flowering peach trees brought from China by James Lick, the man who gave us also the Observatory on Mt. Hamilton. Though now the worst orchard pest in the Union, energetic, systematic attack has happily almost extinguished it in California. Its females are narrower and smaller than the males. A reason for the continued presence of this offensive intruder is that he has made hosts of many of our ornamental as well as orchard plants.

SCALE CONTROL

For control of this and other scales, go to the dormant sprays. A good one is made of equal parts of lime and sulphur mixed in nine parts of water. Several commercial dormant sprays are on the market. But between June and September, use an oil spray. To really deal with them you have to watch until the young are moving about without their protective coat. Then the oil sprays can finish them off. In some districts, they hatch in the middle of August or early in September. Remember, oil sprays always for evergreen, including citrus, and the more powerful dormant spray for deciduous, if you wait until the leaves have fallen. During the growing season spray every two weeks, or you'll be like the man who ate an apple every day except during the doctor's vacation. You can do something also with clear water; with high pressure it will pry the scale off. In many regions parasites practically control some scales; and of course the birds pick them off as fast as they can find them. Scales attack house plants too. Sit down some day during a good radio symphony and with a brush and ordinary fly spray daub the individual scale all over his oval humped body. That finishes him. Later, give the plant a good overhead watering. Repeated use of pyrethrum, rotenone, dusts or sprays of other insecticides (see page 494) are handy to use on house plants and bring excellent results. The plants are tender, and those sprays will touch nothing but the bugs, whether on garden or house plants. By selective applications, you will increase your chance of catching your insect at the stage when he is most naked and defenseless.

HOUSE PLANT SPRAYS

The Opportune Task: Use again your dormant sprays, keep down the curly leaf of the peach tree, the shot hole fungus of the apricot. Knock off those old mummified fruit pits still hanging on the branches; they carry many diseases ready to attack when the right time comes.

HELLEBORE

Helleborus, hellebore is a ranunculus, and the genus is made up of 18-20 evergreen perennials native of Southern Europe and East Asia. Low growing, long lived, these perennials grow 8-18 inches tall; all possess decorative, large, thickish, often toothed leaves divided into fans. USE: Hellebores grow best in partial, not dense shade; in groups or as specimen. The hellebore potted makes a splendid composition especially if tub is wider at the top than at the bottom; shift when plant requires larger containers. SOIL: loamy soils rich in humus best; beware of heavy soils smothering the crowns of plants; a sand top dress, especially for potted specimens keep flowers clean of soil-splash in winter. WATERING: hellebores require water in summer especially plants growing in pots; watering is recommended in dry winters. FEEDING: best in September as new growth starts; dairy fertilizer is good; commercial forms can be used. PRUNING: when new foliage starts from base of clump old torn leaves should be pruned close to ground; never pull off; cut. If pruning is completed by October bloom stalks standing high will show best during the winter blooming. ENEMIES:

(CONTINUED ON PAGE 66)

CHAPTER 7

MORE ON GARDEN ENEMIES

(February: Third Week)

We promised you more about the war on the garden enemies. The chewers, you remember, need stomach poisons; those with sucking mouthparts need smothering and corrosive contact treatment. It is indeed that kind of a treatment!

WHITE FLY

In housekeeping, or while watering your shrubs or picking your flowers, have you ever seen a cloud of flies with immaculate white wings and pale yellow bodies swarm up at you? Usually they fly out from the under surface of the leaves of such plants as your fuchsias, abutilon, lantanas, and tomatoes. This is the greenhouse white fly, common in our gardens in California. The gardener will find him during the summer and fall and will recognize his work in the fine sieves punched out of the leaves in his never-ending hunger. The young, the so-called nymphs, or larvae, hatch from dot-sized, inconspicuous eggs and, like aphids, crawl and have to stay on the underside of the leaves. Their bodies are then soft and oval like young scale. They and the adults together have a grand time sucking the goodness out of the plant. But the plant itself has a very poor time indeed, for it becomes sick and stays sick so long as the plague remains. While the enemy waxes fat, his victim dies of malnutrition, and to make the plight worse, the flies, like the aphis, secrete quantities of honeydew which attracts the sooty mold fungus.

CONTROL

You have to attack the white fly in various ways. When he is easiest to see, he is hardest to catch. Do all you can first by housekeeping. He spends the winter full of unconscious tactics, as a scarcely visible egg strewn on weeds on field plants such as the wild lettuce, and on the garden plants which were infested last summer. Wage war on the weeds — dig them in so deep that the eggs cannot germinate. Remember them when you prune and burn what you cut off. Most amateurs do not see eggs just as most people living in a house do not see dirt. But the housekeeper does, and so also does the gardener who is on his way to gaining something of professional skill, and something too, of the delight which comes from really knowing what it is all about.

In addition to housekeeping for this fly, you use contact treatments — the strong dormants to get the eggs in winter, and in summer use: either oil; or certain non-oil sprays such as nicotine sulphate; or the dusts; or mixtures of dust and oil. Like all the other pests, this fly is resourceful, and he keeps coming on. Do not let the population get ahead of you. Kill as much of him as you can in the egg stage; then as much as you can in the crawling stage, taking pains to spray the under side of the leaf. Pick an overcast day or an evening, for in the hot sunlight you will burn the leaves and have a cure as bad as the disease. And don't neglect the adults. During the daylight they are on the wing, but just before dark they settle down to rest on the leaves. Get someone to shake the plant, and while they buzz around spray them.

Now for some of our chewers. Old Toby, who is an expert chewer himself, suggested in a blithe moment that we might satisfy them with gum. But in reality, it is no joking matter; as with the sucking insects, it is war. Have you ever found holes in the petals of your zinnias, dahlias, and squash? Have you ever found jagged edges on your lemons, laurels, and privet hedge plants? This is the work of insects with jaws or mandibles, like cutting blades that mostly work sideways. They can slice through the fresh leaves, flowers, and stems with wonderful efficiency. And some can also bore their way in leaving, for example, little piles of sawdust coming from the trunk or branch of a pine or cypress tree. Well, I'll tell you about the borers when the time comes.

CHEWERS

DIABROTICA One of the worst of the chewers is the diabrotica, a pretty little green ladybug or ladybird beetle with twelve black spots on her bright coat. She not only goes after your plant above ground, but in the larva stage feeds on the roots. Fine screen wire or cheese-cloth cages will protect the young plants by keeping the adults from flying in; or several applications of one of the following sprays or dusts while the beetles are present, will either kill or repel: rotenone, pyrethrum, or any of the new, modern controls now readily available. See page 494. Any one of these applied all over the plant works wonders. But only for the time being. To keep down the population, go after it every five or seven days.

But of course this ladybug is by no means the only chewer. She has plenty of companions — on the roses, for example. Often the roses have holes chewed in them, the buds are ruined with holes, so that when the buds unfold they are riddled and bedraggled until they look like dismal slum products. When you have been anticipating clean beauty and perfume, what a shock and disappointment! Well, we can't stop to mourn. First we may blame ourselves, and then becoming more practical, we blame the ROSE SNOUT BEETLES. When it's bad, there will be hundreds of them a quarter inch long, with red-black bodies and red heads, and protruding beaks as long as the head. They attack both the cultivated and the wild rose. They not only feed on the buds and flowers, they also chew into the globe shaped fruit, which the gardeners in their special language call hips; and they carefully lay their eggs there so the larvae may find good dinners all ready when they come out of the shell with jaws already moving. When you find fruits infected, take them off. Infected fruits usually drop from a place where the beetle punctured the stem after depositing the egg. Those fruits will drop to the ground and the chrysalid winters in the soil ready to start in the spring as a new beetle. And to control the adults, get out early in the morning (get out to see the tender morning sky, and the light and shadows too) and while the beetles are

ROSE SNOUT BEETLE

still cold, shake them into a pan of kerosene. Sprays are good, and so are the dusts — rotenone, pyrethrum including also 5 per cent nicotine. The garden is a strange combination (is it not?) of pitiless war and tender feelings. And so I fear sometimes, is the whole beautiful world!

FULLER'S ROSE WEEVIL

Other plants turn up with big chunks chewed off the leaf edges — especially the lemon, camellia, hibiscus, and rhododendron. Blame here the brachyrhinus weevil, and he works on a lot more plants than I can list. He looks like the snout beetle, but gray instead, and lacking the snout. Treat him like the snout beetle, too, with certain sprays and dusts, surprising him in the morning before he is up. See page 494.

Someone said to me that it was too bad to have to dwell on these pests, which is the bad part of gardening. But as a matter of fact, it doesn't have to be the bad part of gardening; it doesn't have to be bad at all. The worse these enemies, the more worthwhile and fascinating to get the best of them, every one.

The war of course is never ended. But our words about it are ended for the present. We'd better get on with the garden itself, so it will be worth fighting for. As the season progresses, we'll come back to the ants and to other enemies. Meanwhile, if your place has special insect problems, let me know, and I will look either into my own experiences or in that of my professional friends for an answer. *

The Opportune Task: If the ground isn't too wet, turn the soil over and get as close as you can to your plant for there may be found insects wintering over there waiting for the warm days to start up the stem and devour your plant. Lots of these ugly fellows are waiting in the soil, but if you turn it over and expose them to this cold weather, they die.

TUBEROUS BEGONIA BULBS

Another opportune task. From mid-February to mid-March every few days look at your tuberous begonias which you stored away last fall. If you discover the bulbs show a pink eye, that is a tiny pink swelling

*See August: fifth week: "Insects In the Summer Garden."
See May: second week: "Tuberous Rooted Begonias

at the crown, your bulbs are ready to set in the propagating flat. Move them from storage to a porch or cool glasshouse. You have a choice of soil mixture: You can use one part leaf mold, one part peat, and one part coarse sand, the kind gardeners always use for propagating new plants. These mixtures encourage the development of thready roots which hang on to the peat and sand and make transplanting easy and sure when you move the bulbs to their permanent place in the garden or into pots. In starting your bulbs in their spring growth lay them loosely on top of the mixture, you can put in about 45 bulbs to a flat. Give them a little water, the main thing is do not soak, just keep them moist enough to tease them into growing and setting out roots. When you see the tiny pink eye has sprouted up two inches high with true leaves, then you can water your bulbs regularly. In the meantime you can prepare the place in the garden where you wish your tuberous begonias to bring color in the summer garden.

HELLEBORE *(CONTINUED FROM PAGE 61)*

aphids, snails, slugs: control: nicotine sprays, poison baits. PROPAGATION: from seed; volunteers; seedlings will bloom in 3 years. Divisions of old clumps in spring after blooming; also in September and October either take up whole plant and divide, or "steal" rosettes from sides of mother clump, thus blooms continue without interruption. VARIETIES: Helleborus niger: "Christmas rose:" leathery-thick foliage, blooms on separate stems, white, turning pinkish; some with purple coloring. September to February. H. orientalis: "Lenten Rose:" compact grower, 15-18 inches tall; foliage strong; not leathery; blooms November-January. white-purple. H. corsicus: Corsican hellebore: grows 2 1/2 - 3 1/2 feet tall, foliage distinctive, gray-green, divided into 3 leaflets, weak spines on edges; blooms creamy chartreuse, January-April. H. foetidus: Bearsfoot hellebore: handsome, dark green foliage, finely cut suggesting that of the bird's foot violet; blooms yellow green with red.

CHAPTER 8

PREPARATION FOR THE GARDEN DRAMA OF SPRING

(February: Fourth Week)

You realize of course that in cold ground seeds and roots lie motionless -- they are sleeping or, as we say with classical elegance, they are dormant. If the ground stayed all summer as cold as it is now we'd have nothing but meager, stunted, gnarly blooms and fruits shuddering in the corners. That is what our remote ancestors got when the ice advanced upon them from the north. Happily for us, as the daylight lengthens during February and March, the ground warms up degree by degree. At last it will be warmed through and at many places at once the silent wheels will begin to turn. The plants will move; they will spring joyfully from their earth beds and, continuing to mix our metaphor, we might say there will come an explosion of blooms. Then we shall find ourselves gazing with admiration and pride at our spring display as though we had done it all ourselves.

Well, we shall have had something to do with it anyway. A good deal depends in fact on what we have already done in the garden during fall and winter and it depends also on what we shall do now. In the crusade for good gardening I have been counselling you to keep the ground clean of rubbish and thickets. I have spoken of pruning and of the attack on the sleeping pests who are preparing for their own spring display. You have been learning, if you did not already know, what their eggs look like and have been finding them on the stems of the plants, in the joints, and in the ground. And you have given your trees a cleanup spray to get the eggs and to get such things as the peach tree curly leaf. You have loosened the ground on the days and in the areas that were not too soggy. In accordance with your design and timetable you have been putting in the plants, such as bulbs in the fall, new trees, vines and shrubs, as the winter progressed. You broadcast some seeds and they're already up ready to seize on any warmth to extend their roots and stalks. Readying the garden this way is of course the right procedure. And as the winter ebbs away toward spring more and more has to be done. But do not despair even if you have so far done nothing. You can start now, if you wish, and still make headway.

For the spring you must, of course, harmonize the plants which bloom together. Consider the kinds of plants; first, the annuals, which have a life of nine months from seed to seed -- for example, zinnias, marigolds, and cosmos. They die down in winter and have to be started again from new seed. Some, in this climate carry through the winter because the frost isn't hard enough to kill them, such as snapdragons. But some of these do their best the first season.

ANNUALS

BIENNIALS

Second, the biennials are two-year plants -- for example, foxglove. In the first year they send down a big root like a carrot, and in the second they throw up a bloom spike furnishing the seeds and then die. In this climate some of these also live longer but their blooms are then inferior.

PERENNIALS

Third, perennials come back year after year: for example, Japanese anemone. Now I'll assume that you have some kind of a design for your plot of ground; that you have it framed in and marked out somehow with house and shrubs, or house, shrubs, and trees; that you are satisfied with the frame; that you have put in plants that will flower some time or other; but that now you want to make certain that you will get color changing with the season.

The beginner, naturally, has the vices of amateurism. One of these is overbalanced enthusiasm for pets. He sticks a plant off by itself, a cactus here, a single rose there, and these poor things stand there eyeing each other instead of composing a picture. He would do better to put in a bed of humble annuals and get something worth seeing. *STATUES*

Another vice though is the other extreme of unplanned crowding in the zest for filling out the ground. Give every plant or every cluster of plants some room to itself. You need to get around them with your fork. *OVER CROWD*

Next take a look into the future — into spring, summer, and fall. Make a timetable schedule of when each kind of plant will be blooming. Unless you know more than most people you will find times — maybe weeks — when whole corners and areas of the blooms will go dead and you will be looking at nothing but leaves and stalks.

You may have a fine perennial border. What will it be doing this spring? It will have some blooms. But the chances are they will be spot blooms; for a real show you will need to build it out, either between its plants or in front with annuals. They are easy to transplant even when in bloom. They are the gayest and the most volcanic and dramatic. They can spring the quickest. If color is what you want it is a mistake to crowd the garden with perennials. Many of them have roots that move farther and farther like submarine marauders. Put in plenty of annuals in harmonious groups. For the spring give them the lead and give the perennials the supporting part. It's worth your while to watch an old gardener in one of our good parks getting a border ready for spring. He is busy as a bee calling curtains on perennials that have had their say and putting in annuals that are about to have theirs. He has to know a lot but it's an old story now and he does it instinctively like a cheerful self-moving machine. He was a beginner once!

CHAPTER 9

PLANTING FOR SPRING

(February: Fourth Week)

Perennials: You are transplanting established plants which you have either raised yourself, accepted as gifts from friends, or have bought at the nursery. No seeds for this group.

Delphinium: When well grown will send up a bloom spike seven feet: blues, lavenders, and whites.

Columbines: All colors — blues, creams, red, etc. — with nectar-carrying spurs.

Anchusa 'Dropmore': Stately and handsome with hairy leaves and blue blossoms.

Coral Bells: Neat growing and graceful with crimson, white and pink flowers.

Bleeding Heart: With heart-shaped pink blooms strung along a delicate stem.

Biennials: You can refer to the trade catalogues for colored pictures, realistic and helpful.

English Daisy: Growing close to the ground, with white, pink and red flowers.

Evening Primrose: Adopted from the wayside, giving us their fragrant pale yellow or white flowers as the sun goes down.

Sweet William: Of stalwart tones — good blocky colors and sweet fragrance.

Foxgloves: Majestic in shady corners, lovers of moist ground.

Annuals.

Nasturtium: Their leaves like flat umbrellas; their flowers sweet and many-colored.

Violas: Indispensable for the spring garden; shades of blue, violet, white, apricot and yellow.

Mignonette: Hardy, with green perfumed flowers.

Larkspur: The annual delphinium, grown for their old rose, shell pink, white, blue — double flowers carried along the spike.

Baby Blue Eyes: That cover the ground, and smile up at you.

Sweet Scented Tobacco: Broad leaved, tall, carrying cream, red, and white flowers, giving off powerfully their fragrance at night.

LATE WINTER PLANTING FOR LATE SPRING

Perennials: Except bulbs, use established plants only, from flats or pots. The seeds for these plants were planted in the middle of the summer of last year and you are using the established plants now. If you haven't them yourself you can get them from your nurseryman.

Linum flavum: A perennial flax with transparent yellow flowers.

Iceland Poppy: Offering on long stems sunbeams of orange, yellow, golden, pink, and white flowers.

Penstemon: The bearded tongue penstemon: robust and of many colors.

Bulbs: Such as the true lilies; and don't forget gladiolus.

Biennials:

Cup and Saucer Canterbury Bells.

Annuals: Plants started from seeds or your transplanting seedling already grown.

Clarkia: Hardy of wide color range.

Sweet Peas: Against a protected fence or wall; tall growing, blooming till hot weather.

Godetia: "Farewell to spring"; blooming late, delicate, soft, and romantic.

Pansies: Always popular; you just keep picking, and they just keep blooming.

Ageratum
Asters
Carnations
Cinerarias
Dahlias
Godetias
Lobelias
Marigolds
Nemesias
Pansies
Petunias
Phlox
Salpiglossis
Schizanthus
Snapdragons
Stocks
Verbenas
Violas

LATE WINTER PLANTING FOR SUMMER AND FALL FLOWERS*

Perennials: Young established plants, pot or field grown bulbs or rhizomes. You are transplanting established plants which you have either raised yourself or you can get from your nurseryman.

Phlox: Perennial phlox, many colored, tall stemmed; greatest success in California in sun, not in shade.

Nepeta: A form of catnip with lavender blossoms.

Aster frikartii: From Switzerland; blue petals, golden centers; flowers all summer.

Begonias: Both fibrous rooted and bulbous; fibrous, red, pink, and white; bulbous, all colors but blue.

African Daisies: Sunshine colors in bloom; white lined leaves.

Transvaal Daisies: Stately stems, rich colors — red, pink, salmon, and white.

Plumbago: Deep blue flowers, foliage frosty rich red before they drop.

Coreopsis: Gold-yellow heads, on tall stems.

Yarrow: A plate of golden blossoms, supported by lace cut leaves.

---

*See Other Fall Duties: (October: Second Week.)

Sedum spectabile: Richest of the succulents, fleshy foliage, pink flowers.

Dahlias: Rhizomes throwing up strong stalks with flowers of many colors and sizes.

Carnations: Flower in spring and in summer; fragrant.

Verbenas: Offering carpets of royal blue, soft pink, deep red, and clear white.

Pelargoniums: The Zonal Geraniums, favorites of all kinds, hardy and useful.

Annuals:

Petunias: Offering a most wonderful show of color; hard to beat; lovers of the sun.

Ageratum with soft blue flowers, and fine foliage; tames its neighbors.

Phlox: Drummond's from Texas; low, carpets along the ground.

Calliopsis: Many colored, feathery growth, tall; excellent for the summer garden.

Cosmos: Also feathery in foliage, medium or tall growing forms, shell colored, pink, rose, red, orange and white flowers.

Salpiglossis: Exotic toned blooms, gentle petaled, speckled.

Zinnias: All colors, pastel; blooming until frost time in the sun garden.

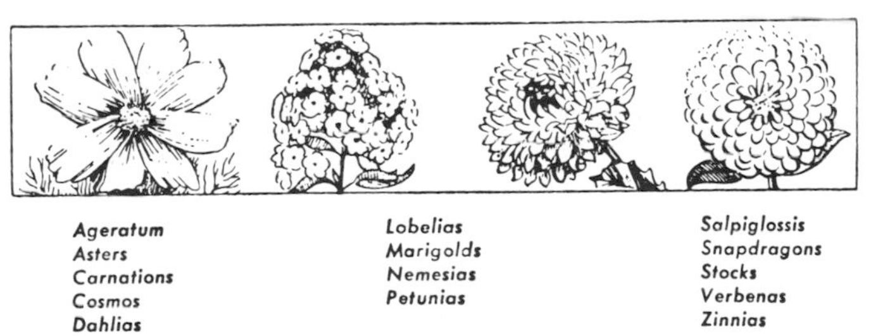

Ageratum
Asters
Carnations
Cosmos
Dahlias
Lobelias
Marigolds
Nemesias
Petunias
Salpiglossis
Snapdragons
Stocks
Verbenas
Zinnias

FALL PLANTING FOR EARLY SPRING

Perennials:

Coreopsis. Strong growing, long flowering.

Gaillardia: The blanket flower of bronze-maroon colors.

Delphiniums: When protected in winter, field grown plants grow strong and colorful.

Columbine: The native ones like shade; but your cultivated ones should be planted in good sunlight.

Geum: On tall stems, yellow, orange, and red flowers.

Violets: Always the favorite; in filtered sunlight best.

Biennials:

Canterbury Bells; The cup-and-saucer flower; blues, lavenders, pink, and white.

Foxgloves: From nests of leaves come spikes of spotted blooms.

Hollyhocks: To be grown in good sunlight; not to be watered too much in summer.

Dianthus or Sweet William: Many-colored flowers that took your breath at Treasure Island in 1939.

Annuals: Only a few that will go through the winter, With these if possible, get a good strong root growth well established in early fall, to carry them through rain and cold; otherwise they stand still, roots choked off, and blooms try to appear before they are fully developed.

Calendula: Orange or yellow flowers.

Larkspur.

Clarkia.

Snapdragons: That always grow best in cool weather.

Sweet Peas: Planted with care.

The Opportune Task: Make the flowering schedule of the plants you have in your garden. If you don't know, ask your nurseryman or look it up in a book. Then take steps to get what you want.

Now is a good time to think about the protection of peach and nectarine trees from their dreaded enemy curly leaf. Bordeaux spray is best for the control of curly leaf which attacks the leaves of your table peaches, and nectarines, and of your flowering peaches too. You may spray your trees two times a year with bordeaux to control curly leaf. Between November 15 and December 15, just as the winter is coming on, always after a good wetting rain has fallen, and then again in spring. The end of February to mid March. In spring you must apply the bordeaux at the exact time when your spray can do the most good. You must look at your trees, and when you see the flower buds are just beginning to swell, when the buds look like pearls, before the petals have opened, then you must spray your trees with bordeaux. Use one pound of bordeaux to every six gallons of water. From your nurseryman you can get prepared bordeaux mixture, follow directions explicitly. When he sells you bordeaux mixture and you see the term 5x5x50 on the container you interpret it: five pounds of copper sulphate, five pounds of lime to fifty gallons of water.* The polysulfide sprays are used also.

HOW DEEP TO PLANT

Plant decidous fruit trees with the bud union at, or slightly above the ground level. That is a good rule to always follow. As in every good rule, however, there are exceptions. Some nurseries follow the practice of topworking or budding their seedlings high, from four to eight inches above ground level in the nursery. If trees budded this high are planted with the bud union at ground level, they will be planted too deep. Mold and rots will develop in the trunk below grown. If the soil is heavy and wet, and the temperature stays below 85 degrees, the roots may not even start to grow. A close examination of the bark will usually show where the trunk was even with the ground level in the nursery. The bark is much smoother where it grows below the surface of the ground where it is exposed.

Soft shelled walnuts are often grafted very high on roots of our native black walnut which can fight the dreaded oak root fungus. The bud union of course is very high. See illustrations pages: 9, 11, 467, 468.

---

*See December: first week: "Cleaning the Garden Floor."

CHAPTER 10

MORE PREPARATION

(March: First Week)

We were looking forward to the warm days to come when the leaves would spring out of the buds, and the green plants out of the ground; and then suddenly, like lights turned on, the luminous blossoms are here, there, and everywhere. "Keep your perennials within bounds." Compact clumps are best separated by a couple of feet, at least — so that you can fill in with the swift, vivacious annuals. If you have to move perennials out, you may well provide a "workshop garden" for them and even for bulbs, so as to be ready for all seasons. Constant shifting and replanting makes a good garden — when the design is good.

Of course the perennials have to make the foundation, or you might say, background. They participate in the action, too — but their roots, if we don't take care, will silently crawl underground, as vines do on the surface, until they steal all the precious space. Each plant will suck up the moisture and drink all the goodness from the ground as far as it can reach. Well, we have to put a stop to that, for we want the lively annuals for actors too, as we have said. We must get the space for them by taking out perennials, or pruning back their roots by inserting your spade straight down eight inches away all around the plant.

This involves an additional task. That space will be covered with annuals until frost comes, and once they are planted, you won't be able to get your spade in. Get it in before they are planted. Prepare the ground; spade deep, thus at one stroke breaking it up, mixing it and cutting off the marauding roots that are already there. Add a little well-rotted cow manure, and the richness from your humus pile, where you have for months been transmuting the very rubbish which careless people burn up. Then after you plant your annuals, it will promptly, like a chrysalis, transmute still again into perfume and luminous color. But make certain, five times over, that you are not shovelling in pill bugs, millepedes and ants, too. If you find them, sterilize the humus.

Planting between now and April: first for early spring flowering. Here you put in, not seeds for which it is now too late, but established plants, whether annuals, biennials, or perennials. If you haven't plants of your own, buy them from the nurserymen. And if you do that, go to one in your neighborhood; take a sketch of your garden with you; describe to him your conditions of light, shade, and soil. Tell him what you want, and he will tell you what you can do. Nurserymen are plant growers principally, and they know what will go, and besides, a surprising proportion of them have good taste and feeling. If you do your part so as to take them on their good side, they will submerge the good job of selling into the good job of gardening.

Late spring flowering: Here you use established biennials, perennials, and what are called winter annuals. But many annuals you can start now from seeds in flats, as we shall describe later.

Summer and fall flowering: Here you may use seeds for the annuals, but the bi- and perennials must be established plants. You have decided now whether you want to raise plants from seed and cuttings; whether you want established plants from the nurserymen; or whether you want a combination. Most amateurs prefer the combination. What governs in the decision is more than the money cost. A good nurseryman improves his product by relentless culling. There is a lot of work and care involved, and the difference between a good job and a poor one is enormous. You can do that, too, once you learn how. Besides, you don't want your garden too ready-made. You will be interested in it — you will take satisfaction from it — in direct proportion to the amount of intelligent labor you put into it. You either must raise some of your plants from seeds or slips, or you'll be leaving out a whole big section of gardening. You will find your eyes being sharpened, harvesting seeds, at the same stage in your garden experience when you first recognize the eggs and cocoons of your garden enemies.

If, then, you decide to go in somewhat for seed planting this late winter, you will be sowing the annuals for the late spring, summer, and fall flowers of this year. But you will be doing more than that. You will be starting off biennials and perennials for next year.

SEED Where do you get the seed? Much failure and grief has been caused by stale or infected seeds. Some of our war gardeners can give testimony. There was a time when we used to get flower seeds from Africa, Germany, or Great Britain, and it was a gamble whether they could germinate. A goodly proportion had died on the way. We want fresh seeds. If we raise them ourselves, we make certain that they have been cured in the sun; then we label them, store them in a dry, cool place and use them at most within a few months. If we buy them from one of the well-known seed houses, we can depend on it that they have been well handled, that they will germinate under decent conditions, and that they are not swarming with some lively, ambitious virus. Until you learn the game, these seeds are likely to be better than yours. But the game is to make yours better, for your purpose, than theirs. It can be done.

What kind of seeds then, besides the annuals, do you put in? Many biennials and perennials: for example, the Transvaal Daisy. You want these to have sturdy root by next November, so they can sleep cheerfully through winter. We are getting ready, you know, not for this spring, or for this summer, or even for next spring, but for the summer and fall of next year! We'll have come to a good agreement on the atomic bomb by that happy time, and we shall wish to celebrate it in a garden which each year grows better and better.

So, in March Or April, plant in flats the seeds of the Transvaal Daisy, and of many another perennial and biennial. This you do thinking of the advantages of mid-summer growing. The three summer months are the time of year when plants feel good, grow ten times faster, grow in good proportion all over, and to the advantage of plant and man send out prospering roots which will stand being shifted without complaint. Moreover, we can replace the casualties as the season goes along. Maybe in the morning you find a blank, as though a front tooth has been pulled, where a gopher has undermined a choice plant. You have a spare all ready to fill the space. Or you find mealy bugs and aphids in the roots of your coral bells; and you can either divide the roots, wash out the bugs and eggs, looking close to make certain the job is thorough, and then, selecting the best shoots, put them back in the ground; or you can use a spare here too, and start fresh. Many a time root aphids and mealy bugs will be quite out of hand, and there is nothing to do but destroy the plant. Of course you will make certain that your spares are free from everything, too, such as sow bugs, snails and slugs.

WINTER SEED

Of course in late winter planting of seeds, we have to consider how we shall dodge the frost. There is no universal rule. It depends on where you are. Some of you live through the winter without any frost at all. Others are still being nipped every few nights and will continue to be, for all anyone knows, for two months more. If that is your case, you will have to find a place that won't be touched. Glass houses are good, except that few will have them. A sunny porch or corner of a wall opening toward south and west will sometimes serve, if the flat is set a foot or two above the ground. A cold frame will work. If your flat is not under a roof, you have to shelter it, as with a piece of glass, especially during the germinating period and for two weeks afterward. Big drops of rain would drill into your soil and lay your seeds bare. Or hot sun rays would cook the tender stem or leaves in a quarter of an hour. Thus, even if you use a lath house, you must watch out. But most people will get their flats, prepare the soil, and wait a while until the frost seems to be over. There's no great hurry until conditions become proper. How many flats do you need? Well, a good rule in gardening is to put in many times more plants than you will eventually retain. The idea is to get groups of things which you can shape and strengthen by culling. You are always taking out the weak ones and saving those which, for no apparent reason, grow lusty, strong, and beautiful. You plant many more vines, trees, and shrubs than you want. When they get under way, you will see graceful shapes and fine patterns of color and shadow which you never imagined before; and you can bring these out of the mass by removing the rest. But may I counsel you that this procedure be carried all the way through. If you plant in excess and then forget it, your garden will finally grow into a slum.

Now to come back to the flats. Have enough of them. You need many dozens established plants, and even at first in the flat they mustn't be too crowded. With elbow room, you will get a far more powerful root system, and the plants will grow and transplant better. *SOIL MIX* What kind of soil? It ought to be light, one-third sand, one-third leaf mold, one-third loam; and no fertilizer at all. Sift out all the lumps and, if you want to be certain you are not establishing a culture bed for weeds and disease, put the mixture in pans and bake it sterile in the oven. *HOW TO SEED* How do you put the seeds into the flats? There are fifty ways that are bad, and two that are good. The first is the furrow system. Get your soil ready, moisten it, and cover it up three days beforehand. Firm the soil into the flat lightly with a brick or a block of wood; make furrows two inches apart by pressing a round stick as thick as your fountain pen; use one packet of seed per flat, mix a teaspoonful of dry sand in your packet, and run the mixture gently into your furrows; then, with larger seeds such as zinnias and dahlias, cover to depth equal to twice the seed diameter with leaf mold dust or dry sand; but with fine seeds like petunias, begonias, cinerarias, and lobelias, just press into the flat, and sprinkle sand — these fine seeds must remain on the top of the soil. Cover the flat with glass, but slip a sliver of wood, lead pencil thickness, between glass and flat to provide ventilation; and cover with newspaper for darkness, until germination. But here again is an important trick. Leave the newspaper on during the daytime, but remove it about sundown. This helps to keep the seed bed fresh and free from molds. When the sun gets high the next morning be sure to replace the newspaper.

In the second method of planting in flats, after firming the soil and mixing the sand in your packet, use the balls of your fingers to roughen the surface a little, then broadcast your seeds evenly. Press lightly with a block of wood, and cover with leaf mold or dry sand and proceed as with number one method. An item to remember is that this light soil which is so good for letting delicate soft sprouts and rootlets move downward, outward and up, is equally good for letting the moisture evaporate. If you don't care, your seeds lying imbedded in dust, will throw up their hands and quit. Water them regularly, and gently with a fine misty spray. But it's no worse to leave them perishing in a desert than to wash the seedlings out of their bed. Once an old and valued friend, who had not been listening to radio lectures, came to my house for a week-end visit. Seeing me at work, he had a sudden yearning — perhaps it stemmed back to his ancestors — to put his hand in the soil. He didn't exactly do that; he grabbed the hose. He was earnest; he was persistent. On all sides he saw rugged bushes and trees, as he believed dying of thirst. Like a hydraulic miner, he played sixty pounds of water north, south, east and west. But all unnoticed were my favorite tender plants, which I had been nursing along first in primary flats, and then in the garden seed-bed — these were leaping out of the ground and flying through the air to destinations quite different from those in the design. You will excuse me — that was four years ago — and I still choke up with feeling whenever I think of it. He is still my valued friend; but when he comes now, I limit him.

CARE

In other words, irrigate your flats with a gentle rain that will settle the soil firmly around the tender roots. No pockets, you know, for specialized currents of air and water! But then, take care that your flats don't get water logged. One day, after everything is under way, you find you have a regular pygmy forest of sturdy seedlings, and you look them over with happy visions of what they'll be a month from now. You can hardly stand it to wait so long. But next day they have gone "queer"; and, the day after, they give signs of toppling over from sheer weakness — and then you know something is wrong indeed. It's the damping-off disease; the fault lies in overwatering, which encourages spores of fungus to grow at the expense of the seedlings — one of the greatest dangers of the amateur gardener. The remedy is to stop the water, permit full circulation of air over the flat, and sprinkle dry sulphur around the seedlings. You are poised delicately between too little and too much. Water in the morning and on bright days; for dull days and darkness help to make the soil soggy. And test the soil with your fingers — you'll soon learn how it ought to feel.

DAMPING OFF

TRANSPLANT

When your seedlings really get going — and they will in spite of all these perils — you must begin to think first of thinning and then of transplanting. They can't stand it there more than three weeks without help. They have suddenly used up all the food and outgrown their quarters. They are flatbound, and therefore certain to get sick. Carefully throw out all the inferior plants — all they can ever do is support feeble blooms and sickly stalks — and that means throw out three-fourths of them, and keep the beautiful sturdy ones. Then, in a few days shift and spread out the produce of one flat into two or more new flats having a soil mixture made up of two buckets of loam, to one bucket of screened cow manure to boost the eager roots, and one-half bucket of sand for drainage. And in another five or six weeks, they will be ready to shift to the garden seed-bed which has good fluffy, well-fertilized soil. Have some provision such as a lath or muslin screen for cutting off the hot sun and parching wind. And remember at this point, snails and slugs are waiting there expressly to ruin all your work. When the plants are sturdy you can put them out.

SOIL MIX

LIGUSTRUM LUCIDUM in fruit and Golden Privet.

PRUNUS YEDOENSIS 'Akebono', sometimes called 'Daybreak'.

JAPANESE FLOWERING CHERRY.

MALUS KAIDO Flowering Japanese Crab Apple.

Chrysanthemums from seed grown in containers.

Chrysanthemums by Tak Kanazawa.

PELARGONIUM DOMESTICUM used in the landscape.

DETAIL, PELARGONIUM DOMESTICUM 'Grand Slam', originator William E. Schmidt.

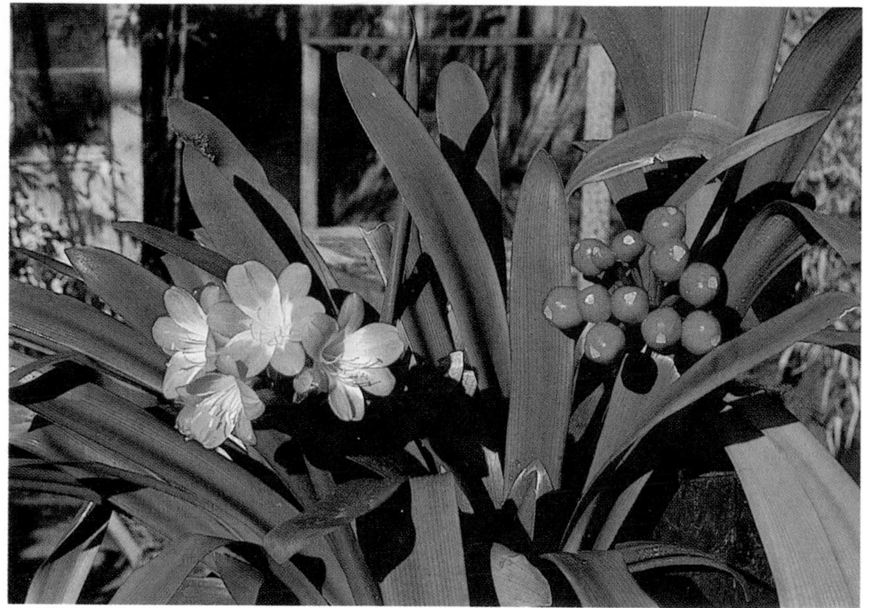

Clivia miniata, hybrid by Wally Lane

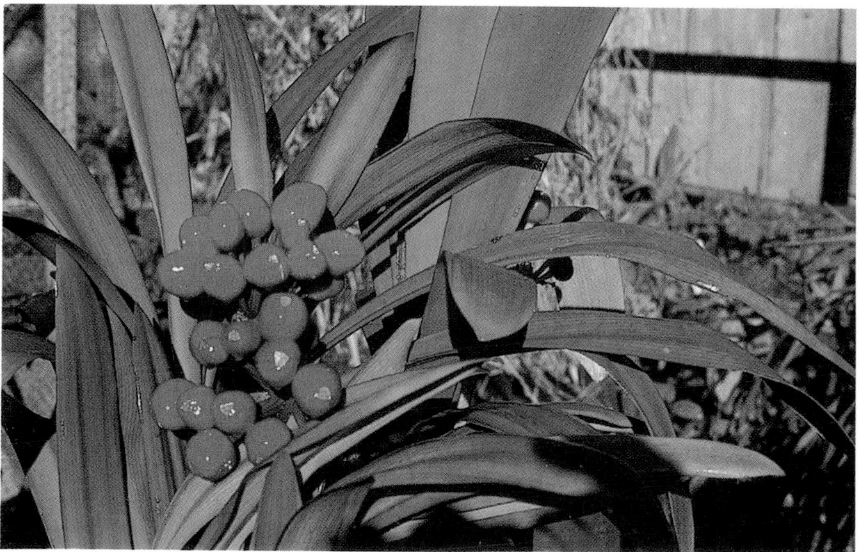

Decorative red berries of C. miniata

Tuberous begonia; "pendula" Hanging Basket

Tuberous begonia; among the "uprights"

Kiwi bloom FEMALE : note fruit

Kiwi bloom MALE

Haemanthus katherinae "Blood Lily" bloom & fruit

Successful tub culture of HAEMANTHUS katherinae

HAEMANTHUS Katherinae "Blood Lily". The Queen of flowering pot and tub plants". BULBS: usually large, thick stems up to 24" tall. Leaves apple green 14" long, 3-5" wide.

BLOOMS: usually large, thick stems up to 24" tall. Leaves apple green, 14" long, 3-5" wide. BLOOMS: brilliant red in round clusters 9" across bearing ball-shaped heads of star-like flowers with salmon petals and long coral-red stamens; when pollinated followed by decorative green, then red seeds. SOIL: sandy leaf mold, nourishing and porous; kept moist when bulb is in growing condition. WATER: frequent during growing period; after flowering gradually dry off leaving bulb in pot undisturbed. Repot only every three to four years. Annually at base of root ball replace spent soil, and replace top soil too. ENEMIES: snail and slugs. PROPAGATION: by off sets and seeds.

At all stages, from first flat to final station in the garden, you are constantly selecting and throwing away. You want health. Sweet peas, for example, if grown too tender, as will happen in too hot a glass house, will get aphid and succumb to it, while the good plants will fight them off. It is a survival of the fittest, just in the natural garden of forest and meadow, except that you are doing it consciously, with a purpose which correlates with your taste. In this way your garden becomes an extension of your own individuality — it's yours any way for good or ill, and mostly, we trust, for good. At its best, it yields living creatures, if we can call plants so, of dream-like beauty.

SEED DIRECT IN GARDEN

A task opportune for the early part of spring, summer, fall, and winter broadcasting seeds right where the flowers are to bloom. If the weather isn't too severe in your district, now is a good time, or you can wait until the end of April, or until May. Some, as in Southern California may start as early as February or March. What you sow would then bloom for you in summer. And if you broadcast seeds in mid-June and early July they will bloom in early fall, and continue to do so until cold weather. And how do you go about sowing seeds directly in the ground? It's easy. Here are the steps: 1. Wet the soil thoroughly, let it stand awhile. 2. When workable, fork over the soil, or spade deeply, break up the soil thoroughly. 3. Introduce fertilizer, or compost, some bone meal too. 4. Finish grading, but do not wet again, and, 5. When there is no blowing wind, broadcast your seeds; use an iron rake, but don't work your seeds down deep. 6. Scatter lightly a top dress of leaf mold. 7. Water later with a fine mist spray. 8. Watch the plot. I would say of these 8 steps, 2 is the most important, you interpret it to read "never sow a seed on wet ground", the soil must not stick to your shoes or to your tools. You must be able to rake down the surface to a tilth, you must grade up your plot level, you want no pockets to pool up the water and rot the seeds. Step 8 says "watch". Keep that top surface moist, especially during germination period.

HOW

DON'T

The Opportune Task: Keep referring to your design and make sure that your blooms are coming in the right places and right times. Remember your cutting garden. Make fine chicken wire frames big enough to go over the beds where you will eventually plant your seedlings in the garden. These are defense against the birds. Spade over and prepare all the spots where your design calls for flowers; have these areas ready for the seedlings which are soon going to be placed there. *

HIBISCUS Hibiscus: annual, perennial, shrub all with colorful blooms are grown in California; these include the Rose of Sharon and Hawaiian hybrids. Perennial hibiscus possess fleshy roots out of which come vigorous shoots; on them flowers as large as breakfast plates open in colors ranging from red, orange-apricot, rose and appleblossom pink and white. Shrub Hibiscus rosa-sinensis has lasting woody growth; from the firm permanent wood grow new leafy shoots on which are borne flowers. USE: In gardens all hibiscus require full day sun; in western sun they thrive handsomely. Hibiscus fail in frost and in the design positions where frost cannot touch must be reserved for them. In fall plants should be given a thick mulch, both perennial and shrub; for the latter the mulch can be mounded 8 to 12 inches above the roots close to the shrub stems. Tub grown plants can be wheeled to a protected place. SOIL: loam, enriched with leaf mold and sand. WATERING: hibiscus demand plenty. FEEDING: manure in spring; liquid commercial fertilizers occasionally in summer recommended. PRUNING: shrub can be pruned in spring after frost danger. Leggy plants require pruning to encourage new wood; blooms form on new wood. Pinch to keep plants compact. ENEMIES: insects such as ants, scale, mealybugs, mites, white flies and aphids attack plant. Control with summer oils and other controls. See page 494. PROPAGATION: soft-wood cuttings, and hard wood cuttings. VARIETIES: Hawaiian hybrids include: 'Agnes Gault' pink; 'California Gold', 'Crown of Bohemia' double, gold-yellow; 'Jiroro' coppery; 'Kamapuaa' cerise; 'Kate Sessions' amber-pink 'Peach Blow'; 'Red Monarch';

*(See "Other Fall Duties" — October: second week)

Chapter 11

THE ACID SOIL GROWERS: RHODODENDRONS, AZALEA, AND CAMELLIA

(March: Second Week)

See Illustration Pages 501, 502, 503, 504 and 505

We shall look at some special plants which amateurs buy already grown, and care for in particular, definite, though not difficult ways. These plants are shallow-rooted, and yet must not go either dry or swampy; they require sunlight, yet not the full blaze; they require shade yet not heavy gloom; they require, in the soil, acid which is continually being used up; and they take several years from seed to bloom. These special plants are the rhododendron, the azalea, and the camellia.

They were named, as most things are, according to diverse principles: rhododendron means rose-tree in Greek — someone evidently took it for a rose, or thought it was rose-like; and the thought has endured in Rose Bay, the name of our Western native; azalea means dry — the great Linnaens' believed it grew in dry soil; and the camellia was named after a Jesuit traveler, Kamle — or more likely Kamel. *HISTORY*

They all love the mountains and woods. The camellia is not native of California. The rhododendron and azalea, of course, are, but in a very limited sense, for, until we go and get them, they stay up in the wooded ravines or along the shady stream banks. The forms which we use in the garden all came originally from Asia.

The Bay region has spots that are right for these plants -- such as the canyons back of the University of California, and Muir Woods. But nine-tenths of our gardens are not what they are used to. The four rainless months, and the parching afternoon winds so dreaded by the fire chief, are precisely what they do not tolerate in nature.

Now, as we know, a time-tried amateur rule is FAVOR THE PLANTS THAT WILL FEEL AT HOME IN YOUR GROUND. Why then should we think of these strangers? One answer is that we can't help thinking of them. It's in the air; we are in a Camellia boom that is carrying the rododendron and the azalea along with it. It has been building up a long time. Eighteenth century travelers to the Himalayas, Tibet, China, and Japan kept bringing back astonishing tales of twenty thousand foot snow peaks with whole stretches of their lower slopes painted with reds and pinks. They had never seen or heard of anything like it, and they never quit talking about it. The plants were taken to Europe, developed with energy and beautiful skill, hybridized and named, and finally brought as trade goods to the United States where they spread slowly. At the 1915 exposition, E. H. (Chinese) Wilson had a great show of the so-called Kurume Azaleas which had been improved for one hundred years in Japan.

KURUME AZALEA

These Kurume Azaleas are small evergreens with small, white to scarlet flowers. After the exposition, they spread rapidly up and down our coast. More and more people got used to the acid-soil plants. And now we have our boom. We have, all over California, specialist-growers who for twenty years have been bringing these plants along. They have a beautiful array all ready to burst into bloom. The prices are high especially for the camellias. But there's a lot of work behind them. And a certain amount in front, too, in case you buy.

Another reason why we are thinking of these strangers is that, with intelligent mingling of varieties, you can have blossoms — whole plumes of them — from October through May for the rhododendrons and camellias, and from November through April for the azaleas. Each individual will bloom six weeks. Moreover, these plants, if you buy them at the right stage, give the quickest and most powerful ready-made concentrations of luminous colors — flame, pink, orange, white, purple; and for those who, as our esteemed garden writer, the late Sydney Mitchell, says, *want their color strong and thick*, there's nothing so good — or so bad. Delicacy can be gained by selection of less flamboyant varieties and by combinations with other plants and with the evergreen foliage of the acid-lovers themselves.

And still another reason why we are thinking of these strangers is that their care is now so well understood that you will: first, have no trouble at all in discovering any good natural spots that may exist on your land; and second, lacking such spots, you will be able, in a limited way, to create them. If you have to, you may even keep these plants for years in five-gallon cans made rust-proof with roofing paint; and keeping the soil acid, porous and moist, and moving the plants around with the seasons to get the proper protection from wind and sun, you will have them covered with blooms like the lights of a candelabra.

These strangers are indeed more than a seven-day wonder. They are here to stay — not on a boom basis, but as steady contributors to gardens where knowledge and attention are exercised. As for the boom part of it, it always goes beyond reason, of course. But that is how, in what might be called a beautiful rage, we get things done — that is how the varieties are multiplied until we can take our pick.

ACID SOIL

We have mentioned these as acid-soil plants. What do we mean by that? Soils, as you know are acid, neutral, or alkaline. Their tendency in this region, especially in dry soils, is to be alkaline. Our common plants need it that way, and we add lime to make it that way if we have to. Close to new houses, we don't have to add lime, for the mortar-refuse supplies it. Let us remember that when we plant the acid-lovers there. And let us remember too, that our hard tap-water which we pour onto the ground so liberally will neutralize any acid. Some gardeners claim they can tell whether soil is acid or alkaline by the look; others say by the taste. Well, when I was in school, there was a biologist who used to distinguish, by biting them, between a certain kind of ant, which contains formic acid, you know, and a certain kind of spider that looks like it. But we are wandering from our subject. We can't recommend either method to the beginner. If you are going in for acid plants, get a soil-testing outfit. A few drops of the dye, shaken up with the soil in water, will turn red for acid or blue for alkali.

And, in order to see how the acid-soil plants live, I suggest that you visit them first in the woods, next in the public parks, and only last at the places where they

VISIT are being sold. The rhododendrons and azaleas you can find in the redwoods country especially — the rhododendrons in the woods of Humboldt and Mendocino counties — and the coast road is one of the good ways to get to them; and in the rolling hills as tall shrubs with gnarled charred trunks which have come through fire. The azaleas come in the sunny pockets of the forest districts, in open moist flats, and along the stream banks. You can find both as close as Muir Woods or Tamalpais and the ravines of the Santa Cruz mountains. There is good hunting in many a charming spot even in Southern California. And take your lunch, for you'll be hungry, and fortunately in this land of plenty, you can eat!

You will, in this way, see the acid-soil plants in the woods, in the dappled shade, in the dells, and along the shadowy cathedral aisles. The rhododendron and azalea will be blooming through May, June and July on a floor of giant oxalis and wild forget-me-not, and the huckleberry, the salal, and the trilliums. These grow in woods — soil kept acid near the surface by the falling leaves that you can see (if you look closely) raining down through the long bars of sunlight all day long. Tannic and other acids are released by newly decaying stuff. The ground is like a sponge. It may be neutral down below, but up here it stays acid. It is an acid humus-manufactory; the shallow acid layer is defended against dryness by the shade and the foliage wind screen above, and by the reservoir of moisture in the sponge below.

Such soil, deepening through the centuries where-ever plants grow and accumulate — whether in forest or meadow -- is our nation's treasure, and the reason for our abundance. We may well think of it, not only in this proclaimed Conservation Week, but in all the other weeks of the year. More than half the people of the world, because they have wasted such soil into streams and rivers and oceans, are weak and hungry. Desperate to retrieve their error of stripped, bony hillsides, they are slaving to restore them with contour walls, and by putting back into the soil all the wastes which we in this country burn or run into the sea. Their toil and suffering are pitiful. We have already, in the little while since we came to this continent, used up half our own top soil, and we have seemed tto be going pell-mell toward hunger; for no grand harvesting machines — no labor-savers — can grow food in bony bed rock. It is true that power and chemistry may at some future time make rock into soil. But who would trade a bed six feet deep of black loam for any such dream-product as that? We can't be careless in a matter of life and death. If any thing on this earth is sacred, it is soil, and the plants which make it. Let us elect officers who will at all times resist their destruction and promote their enlargement. Let us not join or tolerate that Society of Royal Idiots who throw lighted matches down in tinder-dry woods; and let us not join that other less famous Order of Sterile Neatness who rake up and burn up all the good organic debris of their gardens instead of putting in a pile for humus. I do not in the least believe that this country is really going pell-mell toward hunger, for its people can read and listen, and are already taking measures. We may expect more and more soil conservation — until its principles reach all parts of the land. And we may expect a time, not so many years distant, when through intelligent control and replanting our annual crop of lumber will equal the cut; and our annual crop of humus will equal the waste. If you are thinking of putting rhododendrons, azaleas, or camellias into your garden, you can make them a lesson and everlasting reminder of the goodness of the soil; for the chances are, you will have to provide that soil where it is not.

We have so far been speaking of these three plants all together. We must look at their differences. They are, in fact, somewhat different in habit, in bloom, and in function for your garden. I'll have to confess to a personal preference. For me, the rhododendron has a vital, dignified beauty, and its blossom, though disappointing as a flower because it lacks perfume, can enliven a slope as finely in spring as the turning leaves do in autumn. The azalea is more intimate, and more graceful, and slender, and delicate perhaps — but especially with its haunting fragrance, it has flowers indeed. But the camellia, its blossom reminds me of a self-conscious wax flower on display through a glass pane. But that's exactly what some like. One lady in my garden class defended it vigorously; twenty years ago, she said, she spied in the jewelers' show-case a camellia stick pin! She was right — that was how she felt. And I am right, for this is how I feel; and you are right, too, however you feel about it. The camellia can be used intriguingly, vivaciously. But, take care you do not bore your friends with your enthusiasm for the mere curiosity. One plant, shouting all alone in a pot is nine-tenths to show off to the neighbors; it is like some strange pet that no one else *GROUP* particularly cares for. They go far better in groups, and with their companions, the other acid-lovers, such as ferns and daphne, rhododendrons, and azaleas. Try putting the camellia in the background on the same principle as you arrange a group photograph. And it is a good thing to thin the flower buds, and at the same time strengthen those that are left and reveal the fine scaffold of trunk and twig and the beautiful shining leaves.

Though camellia, rhododendron and azalea all come small and large for pot and garden, small varieties are commonest and easiest to get in the azaleas. Rhododendrons have globular heads; the evergreen azaleas are low and table-topped, the deciduous ones billowy and tall. They go well therefore with their evergreen companions, the rhododendrons. Of the camellias, one, compact and small, a dainty little thing, blossoms for the boutonniere and is fine in pot or tub. Another reaches tree size, as at the Governor's house in Sacramento, on the shady side; and in Chico, standing alone, and having to make its own shade because the house which once protected it is gone. The camellia is more independent than the rhododendron or azalea.

WHERE TO PLANT

What is the function of these acid-lovers in the garden, where do they go, and what do they do? They're better planted in rolling ground, hillside, and gulch, than in the flat. Go to Golden Gate Park, Stanyon and Fell Streets entrance, and you will see the azaleas on the southeast slope under the trees. If you have such slopes, the acid-loving plants will fit naturally in the design, though you may have to provide soil and shade. Use Japanese Maple, box elder, and other feathery plants, along with pines. In shade too blocky and dark, your acid-soil plants will grow spindly.

In level ground, your use in the design will be more limited. You can always take the shady side. Or you can make shady nooks in the hedge corners, under your oaks, or where shadows fall across the fence from your neighbor. These can become the exquisite places in your garden. Fix the soil right'. Use 2 parts each of peat, leaf mold, garden loam put through a 1/2 inch screen, and 1 part sand. Or use one part each of all these ingredients.

In the small garden, the rhododendron grows too blocky, and crowds out over your paths. But you may find a place for a small group, as in foundation or corner-planting. The azalea and camellia are perhaps easier to fit in. Use groups. Don't let them stand by themselves too much. They'll go morbid, and so will you, too.

DESIGN

Now we shall review culture and discuss items of care. First, design: Only where you have a natural place for them, or can create one. Do not try rowing up Niagara Falls. Second, time factor: Get overlapping varieties so as to give months of blossoms. Go look now or soon at the acid-soil plants in their natural homes and in the parks. Third, tilth: Test for acidity before you plant. If you have plants already, test them. The soil must be fluffy, but you may not fluff it up with a spade; the roots are too shallow for that. Test with your fingers; maintain the fluff by an annual application of peat and pine needles. Prune the submarine marauders. Roots of birches, of your neighbor's acacia under the fence, can go fifty feet, like many another heavy grower. Never permit these plants to become dry; Linneaus was mistaken, azaleas are not desert plants. Especially when these plants have finished blooming, water and feed them. Uniform watering and regular feeding is best. Use the specially prepared foods, the kinds that nourish and bring up acidity. Fourth, pests and troubles: Remember your housekeeping, when you find chunks chewed off the leaf edges of the camellia and rhododendron. This is the work of the Fuller's Rose weevil; another weevil, the brachyrhinus, will eat perfect holes in camellia leaves; the red spider, a summer visitor will come to the rhododendron if you keep it too dry; and the microscopic greenhouse thrip loves azaleas along with a whole lot of other plants, especially when they are dry. Right after the acid-soil plants finish blooming in March, April and May give them a cleanup. Use an oil spray and be sure to cover both sides of the leaves. And finally, pruning: Azaleas may be pruned and thinned, just a light cutting here and there to maintain shapeliness in your plant; rhododendrons -- well, it is almost sacrilegious to prune them, they are so slow, but, of course, remove injured branches; and camellias, they too might best be left alone until such time as your plant has attained size and girth.

CARE

PESTS

Here is a question on camellias: "What's causing the leaves of my camellias to droop? If I water them hard now (first week in December) will the plants be damaged by frost?" *CAMELLIA LEAF DROP*

A teaspoonful for the pot and half a cup to the plant out in the garden.

The drooping is caused as this questioner guesses by drought. Right in my own garden a potted specimen has drooping leaves, a direct penalty of my month-long October absence. I'm willing to wager that many of the buds are going to fall becuase the roots got no water for the whole month.

Give your plant plenty of water; first scratch lightly and see if the ground isn't dry around these roots. If so, give it a good soaking; top dress more mulch and your plant will then go through the winter encouraged to grow better in the spring. Camellias come from Japan; they can stand our California winters without frost damage. Where their trouble comes from is drought in summer and fall; people running off to see the fall colors when they should be home!

The Opportune Task: Take a good look at all of your acid-soil plants. See what their neighbors are doing to them. Prune out any intruding roots. If you find your rhododendron, azalea or camellia showing signs of poor health, dig it up, work over the soil thoroughly, line the hole with a basin of peat, reset the plant, making very sure not to replant it too deep. Top dress all your acid-soil plants with peat and pine-needle humus. Do it today; the weather is just right for that sort of exercise. Put the mulch on six inches deep. Those plants will show you they love it by their growth and their flowers next year.

DAPHNE DAPHNE odora, the Japanese bush common in California gardens blooms in winter months. That is the time to prune for picking flowers is pruning. The idea is to really prune, picking tiny twigs of flowers is not pruning. Prune into the heavy branches. Then the bud will break out and put forth strong new shoots. Just look under the whirl of leaves on a stem; there will be found tiny green buds all along the branch. Select one of these buds, cut one half inch above it. Make cut on a slant. The bud will rush into growth and become a new strong shoot, and will be able to carry good fragrant flowers. A newly purchased plant does not require pruning, just the older specimen. WATERING: Does your daphne bush have yellowish leaves, that droop? Often this is an indication of bad watering. Usually too much. For the yellowish green sickly daphne plant withhold water, let soil dry out. For gardens in summer fog areas withhold water entirely from about mid-July till October. This enables the plant to form bloom buds. Daphne ordora grows best in morning sun, afternoon shade.

Chapter 12

LAWNS

(March: Third Week)

Last time we took a look at the acid-soil growers, the rhododendron, azalea, and camellia, and stopped for a minute at that first-class natural resource, the top soil — a subject to which we shall often turn because it is basic both to garden and to food. This time, the start of a new quarter's series, we shall look at lawns — opportunely both because they demand work at this season; and because also this is the day of St. Patrick, who will not be displeased if we import a fragment of his beloved emerald to place in our own beloved gardens. But before we think of this, let us look at our radio treatment of gardening, and consider again what we are undertaking to do. My work in past years was both on the lecture platform and on the less formal platform of the garden itself. It was the method of question and answer. The radio, of course, did not permit this method. When first my diffident words went into this microphone, and then, through old habit, I stopped and listened, and not even an echo came back, I got the feeling of talking to myself alone. But this feeling didn't last, for people, both acquaintances and strangers, soon began coming to me. They showed me what I had left out; they asked questions, and gave me the answers, too. Some of these listeners are making their living in gardens, and they have what it takes, for they know how to sell their services and goods. Others spend all their leisure time in gardens, and they have what it takes also. You might expect each of them to recommend his own department of interest. But they took a bigger view, and they encouraged me to take a bigger view myself. How was this?

With a touch of pretense, I had named my effort a Crusade for Good Gardening. Some of my hearers, professional and amateur too, now give that phrase more meaning than I expected it to have. They say I must look at little gardens in a big way. They say that in the next few years, with houses spreading along the arteries of quick transportation, little gardens will spring up by the hundreds of thousands. These must be not bad gardens, but good gardens —

For the benefit of many
And the injury of none.

The shortening work week and the lengthening span of life — will men and women spend these released hours in deadly acrobatics on the grim highway? Or will they doze like slugs on their front porches, puffing out with fatness as the years creep by? "NEITHER", my friends all shout in chorus, "they'll work it off delightfully in their gardens!" Well, gardening is my favorite among all. There's bound to be truth in their prophesies, and I'll go along with them to the limit of my ability. We'll have to keep on thinking of the plants — we can't afford, in looking for wider meaning, to neglect the thing itself. But we'll stop at intervals to inquire how our enthusiastic subject, which we enjoy so much at close range, fits into this sometimes scowling world.

Now lawns. What are they for? How do we make them? How do we keep them? What do we do about them now? There's hardly a house without a lawn. Why? First, we need a floor to walk on and rest on out-of-doors — an extension of the porch, for children, for dogs, too, and for yourself. Second, we need a viewing-place from which to enjoy the nearby borders of luminous color and green foliage; and the lace-work of the trees against the sky; and, between the tree trunks, the vista of fields and house-tops sweeping to the distant mountains. The finest lawn I ever saw was a little high meadow near Sierra City. It came out from under big, scattered pine trees. It sloped down to a wandering, sunken brook that was crowded with alders and giant ferns, brightened by the lavender bog

FUNCTIONS

violet, the blue penstemon, and the large-leaved herb with yellow flowers; it was glistening with half-hidden pools, and along the meadow you could see far-off, huddled mountains. That was indeed a viewing place. And it had another, or third quality of the good lawn; it was a resting-place of quiet and seclusion, for idle or serious talk with companions who share your mood. Fourth, your lawn makes the keystone for the arch of your whole garden, however big or little. You can't form or place the lawn without forming and placing all the rest.

To get these results you don't push the lawn out, nor set it naked and unbordered against the street. Nor, if you live on a slope, do you merely dig a level shelf. These rows of houses all placed evenly back from the curb are designed on the abominable principal of uniformity, and make a good lawn hard to get. Here's an idea, then, for the builders — when they design the house, let them realize that the garden, which is no less important, must be designed at the same time. Before they set a stake in the ground, the decision must already have been made how every part of the land will be treated. The house and the garden, by rights are a firm co-partnership. Take care, or your lawn, coming last, will be squeezed into the worst quarters like a poor relation. Find the best place for it, and it will serve you well. And then see that it is not cluttered up — keep it free — never let it be cut in two — defend it against that persistent defilement of a walk running down the middle, or a spot garden bed like a hole in the ground. Even if you have the right location, where the lawn can lead and beckon you out-of-doors — even if you contrive a beautiful bright green carpet — you can make it into a bad lawn in a minute, you can make it worried and little, by cutting it up with beds and walks. The garden designer will take two equal areas and merely by arrangement shrink one of them down to look only half as spacious as the other. If you clutter your lawn, you can almost stop it from being a lawn. You want the cushion turf underfoot, not pavement blocks; walks should take you,

LOCATE

not through it, but around it. And flowers, if their full beauties are to be seen, need to stand against a background, and they need the dramatic relief of the emerald foreground, too.

After doing our best to find the right place, how do we make the lawn there? The lawn is to be a permanent carpet, and if it's not to wear threadbare, the foundation must be made ready. Working the ground a foot down is not too much. All piratical roots, as of poplar, birch, acacia, and eucalyptus, must be ripped out, and later must be kept out; the bed must be cleared of all junk, the sticks that bring termites, broken glass that could cut roots, bricks that rob a spot of its moisture, chunks of tar and pitch and cement that no root can penetrate. Only materials that belong in a cushion — leaf mold, peat, well-rotted manure with a lot of straw — can serve in the foundation of a lawn. If your soil is sandy or clay, as in San Francisco and in many places in Southern California, you must pour in the humus to provide easier runways for the fibrous roots of the grass. If the ground balls up when it's wet and cracks when it's dry, use peat, a convenient form of humus; use lots of it, a 3- or 4-inch layer — chop it in, keeping it more to the surface rather than spading it too deeply. Should your ground be underlain with rock, as with the sandstone or serpentine which in the Bay region so often stops us cold a foot down, you must provide drainage. The top soil will have to be pulled away, the rock chipped or cut so that its surface takes an even slope. Then the top soil is returned and thickened to at least one foot. Lawns do not prosper when their roots rest in cups of still water. The idea is to make the roots go down six inches at least — twelve is much better — and to have the sponge there water-soaked but not water-logged. Drain tiles are used only when the ground is hopelessly soggy and should be introduced only upon the recommendation of an expert. Generally our ground drains well without them. Should new soil be brought in? In nine cases out of ten — NO; for with work you can manufacture your own soil right there;

PREPARE

you don't need to bring in a lot of stuff that you know nothing about. All black soil is not garden loam, and because it comes from another district is no reason for putting it on your land. If you spade over your ground, work in manure that is somewhat rotted, but not old (about one year old is best); you can get it loamy, mellow, and friable. Humus, including manure and peat, is best to improve soils. Why is the deep soil cushion needed? Grasses after rains all over the world go to hay and straw. But we want them to stay green in the lawn during our parching summer months. On a hot day, if you could see evaporating moisture on the lawn, each blade of grass all day long like a mimic chimney would fly a little banner of vapor from its tip. In this way a barrel of water is lost into the air in no time, and if your soil is thin your roots will be shallow, and you will have to water every day, even twice in some districts, to keep your carpet of little green plants from withering. But with deep soil and roots, you can get by with filling up your soil reservoir once a week. The necessity, of course, varies in different places within reach of my voice. San Francisco and Berkeley have more moisture in the air than Menlo Park — but not enough more to make shallow roots safe.

WHEN TO SEED

But is this the time of year to make a lawn? Some gardeners say early fall because that is Nature's time for planting seeds when the ground is still warm and there's a chance to build sturdy roots before they go too far in surface growth; and because the sticky soils work up better after the summer's sun has vitalized them. Others say spring and some like even summer. They say that is the time for quick germination and rapid growth. They all succeed — because they know how to deal with the troubles peculiar to each season — frost in fall, extremes from hot to cold in spring, and especially parching in summer. If you learn how, you can make a lawn any time. Now is one of the good times.

After digging, finish the grading: level the area, rake it with a heavy iron rake, get rid of all depressions, leave no humps nor hollows; and rake out all rocks and pebbles the size of marbles. Leave fallow for two weeks to let weeds germinate. Water to encourage the weeds. Hoe the weeds off after they have germinated and level the surface again. Next, sow the grass seed. Do this early in the morning when there is no wind; never sow grass seed on a blustery day for you don't want the fitful wind to broadcast your seed for you on the sidewalk where it will do no good, or in the shrub border where the grass will become troublesome in years to come. Cover the seeds with a veneer of peat dust. Roll the area with a roller only partly filled with water — you are not making a roadbed — you don't want to pack the seeds in so they can't germinate.

But, what kind of seed? Why use grass anyway? Because everybody agrees there's nothing else as good. What do you want — a lawn for service for the family to enjoy, or a lawn for the picture that isn't going to get hard wear? All of us want a lawn that will not condemn us to slaving work — a lawn that is lush with grass able to choke out most weeds, that will do well in partial shade, and able to stand some drought if you have to go to Los Angeles, or even better, to the mountains, for a few days!

For amateurs, the most serviceable seeds are shot-gun mixtures, "all-purpose mixtures"; one of them, for example, is made up of:

SEED

Rye: annual for immediate growth and perennial whose roots strike down, drink deep, and tolerate some dryness.

Kentucky Blue: long lived, used for fairways and airports.

Rough Blue: that fills in the shady spots.

Dwarf Clover: that stands a lot of drought and blends in color with the blue grass.

Red Top: that fills in the moist spots.

Astoria Bent: that sends the roots down first and then creeps; and other grasses including the Fescues.

But here is a mixture for a service lawn that has turned out better yet because it gives a more even coverage; it stands up better under use and retains its sword-like appearance; it flourishes under good care; and it looks good even in winter. It is made up of the following proportions: four parts of Paces Rye; four parts of Kentucky Blue; two parts of Astoria Bent; all by weight. But, of course, differences are required by variety of sub-climates around the Bay. In San Francisco you have moisture floating in the air, and therefore the moisture-loving Fescues thrive best. And in the hot valleys a lawn of pure Blue Grass is unexcelled if it gets plenty of water.

CARE

Caring for the seed bed. Stay with it until you have a turf. By all means take your trip to Los Angeles some other time. Keep it moist morning, noon, and night; don't be so theoretical as to think that it can't be dry because summer hasn't come yet. Once you turn the water on you can't quit. A fish out of water is no worse off than a tender new grass shoot.

Weeding. There will be weeds after you have planted your new lawn no matter how careful you've been. Pull them out as soon as the ground will bear your weight without leaving footprints. One demon-weeder whom I know uses a fence board to walk on. For the first cuttings, use only a very sharp mower, and one inch high.

When you get your lawn, how do you keep it? The weather and you will struggle against each other, one to keep it dried up and the other to keep it wet down. The best lawns of all are in such places as Old and New England, where the weather and the lawn work together. Even in those places, lawns want attention, and because of their old traditions, the gardeners there take more pains than we do out here where we need it so much more.

RULES

Here are items for the established lawn:

1. Rake thoroughly to get rid of twigs, bones, and other refuse.

2. Weed out both the annuals, the carrot-root perennials, plantain, and dandelion, and the sprawling

chickweed. The new selective weed spray kills weeds (including clover) but won't touch grass. Don't wait for it. It's function is especially for big lawns, golf links, etc. It's not much of a job to weed a small lawn. If you find yourself reluctant, offer your family an incentive reward, such an an ice-cream all around for a basketful; they will be delighted and so will you.

3. Cut the grass both ways at right angles; set the blade one inch high.

4. Your grass catcher will take away the long clippings.

5. With a spade, sharpen up the lawn edges; leave them neatly trimmed.

6. For a spring top dress use a humus builder like mushroom manure if you can get it, or use one of the well-known trade mixtures of barnyard manures and humus. A fine dress of peat will help. Screened rotted cow manure is good though some weeds will always come with it. Be sure to screen manures, for you don't want to throw rocks back onto the lawn after having cleared them from it. Spread any of these materials over the lawn to provide a humus build up. It is best to apply now the fertilizers that provide the humus sponge; later in the season we'll recommend the fertilizers to use.

7. Reseed bare spots in the lawn; then protect the seed with a fine cover of peat. Remember, your lawn has to be repaired every year.

8. And finally, give the lawn water. Top sprinkling is not enough; the water must trickle well down to the lowest root, for if it fails to, as the summer comes on your lawn will turn brown. The marvel of the Santa Clara valley in the 70's was the old Barron estate lawn. It stood there like a beautiful green oasis and visitors from the great city greeted it with ahs and ohs. The secret was, Mr. Barron had flooded it like a field of alfalfa, to get it ready for them.

COMPOST What should be done with grass clippings? Put them on the compost pile. Do you know what a compost pile is and why you should have one? Compost is the green and dead organic materials gathered from your garden at "house cleaning" periods. This is piled in a convenient and if possible in a sunny place, and is alternately soaked, dried out, and turned to aid in its decomposition. Mould and bacteria break it down into small particles. Now we speak of this as humus, the store house of essential plant food. Humus is nature's own plant food. Thus your pile of plant refuse makes the compost, the compost returns to humus, the humus to plant food, and so we have the perennial cycle. Your aim is to continually put back into the soil that which is taken out. (See page 244.)

CYCLAMEN

Cyclamen persicum has variegated leaves, small flowers white with prominent purple blotch. Hybrids include bright flowers red-purple, rose crimson-pink, white and splotched. USE: In California with proper planning Cyclamen grow outdoors and prosper under high branching deciduous trees where winter sun and summer shade reach. Avoid frosty places. SOIL: loose, enriched with leaf mold, peat, sand. Never spade around cyclamen; never bury corm; half way out of soil best. WATER: plenty while growing August till May; when dormant June-August keep corms just moist, never desert dry. FEEDING: cow manure. ENEMIES: mites, thrips: summer oils; weevils: Sevin. PROPAGATION: seed sown from July-November cool green house, soil mixture 4 parts peat or leaf mold, 1 part well rotted cow manure; sow in rows three inches apart, firm, cover with 1/2 inch of sand, water thoroughly. Prick into second flat; shift into 2 1/2 inch pots in soil mix of 1 part cow manure, 2 parts peat or leaf mold and 2 parts sandy loam; from 2 1/2 inch pot gradually shift up to 6 depending upon size. SPECIES: Cyclamen europaeum foliage heart-shape, bright green marbled with silver; almost evergreen; flowers rose, fragrant. C. coum album white flowers, red at base. Bloom in spring; foliage round, deep green; no marbling, glossy. Cyclamen neapolitanum leaf ribboned white, flowers small, August-September, miniature plants; good ground cover.

Chapter 13

FOOD PLANTS, ANNUAL AND PERENNIAL VEGETABLES

(March: Fourth Week)

See Illustration Page 508

Today we talk of food plants. Why food plants? What plants shall we select? When shall we put them in, and how shall we manage them in the garden?

There are good reasons for food plants. The first and biggest is that food is more precious than gold and more precious now, than flowers. Did you ever think of the difference between hunger and appetite? Appetite is the word we use in this country. It is a pleasant, warm desire for food. Hunger is the word they use in Europe, in India, in China, in the Philippines, and in parts of Russia too. There is nothing pleasant about that. Have you ever seen a truly hungry child — feeble, slow, dizzy, convulsive with knife-stab pains, and face twisted in ugly agony? This country has little hunger. When a man is caught stealing a loaf of bread we are shocked. What should we think of men fighting in the mud for a crust? Such men, in their passion for life, will kill if they have the strength. Hunger is what they have in countries that hold more than half of mankind. Talk of a sometimes-scowling world. It scowls there all day long. To those shivering people, hunger is the great brutal fact above all — bigger than the atomic bomb. It stands like a monster between them and the blessed sun. Even those who are fed cannot escape the shadow. Everything precious fades away — all the delicate, accumulated decency of centuries — cleanliness even — and nothing is left but miserable life, base and brutal. I have thought until lately that we, so far away in this country, could escape this shadow. But in the blunt words of a friend of mine, "EVENTS SAY NO! The shadow is already on us. Everybody is beginning to feel it. The way to judge people's actions honestly is to imagine what we'd be doing in their places. That's practical sympathy. We're not going to make the foolish error of forgetting that we, here, enjoy appetite, while they there are suffering the agonies of hunger."

Thus speaks my blunt friend. For us thinking of amateur gardens the inference is that we have a plain common-sense task, opportune in the extreme of growing food at home; because the more we grow, the more our government will have of wheat and other staples for the comfort of suffering people in other lands that there may be plenty in a world of want.

WHY

But of course this is by no means the only reason for food plants in our garden. There are others which urge us happily onward in the same direction. The fact is that home-grown foods are good for the house, too. The house is more than a place to stay. It is a place to live. A garden of food plants arranged so something will be coming along all through the year enriches the house and makes it a home indeed. When industry takes a down dip and jobs go scarce for awhile — or when the job is over and you retire — your skill with food plants will give you a refuge and you will go back there, not with dread but with eagerness.

If you select and grow home-grown food right, they taste good, are good. Commercial handling requires varieties that can take a beating after they are harvested. It puts a premium on durability and appearance and it often requires premature harvesting. What's best for keeping is far from being best for eating. If you plant your own you can have the most tender, crisp varieties; in all their delicate aroma, sweetness, and flavor, they will come to your table.

What we have been used to from mass production is quantity, hoarded up and then released to take the peaks and dips out of the market. That is necessary; the processors are even improving quality, and quick freezing is especially promising. But let us not wait for all that machinery when we can learn quite simply how to take our dinner, not out of a can or carton, but out of the good, black, vitamin-rich earth.

So much for the why of food plants. Next, what kinds of food plants do we introduce into our gardens? Thousands of wild plants yield leaves, fruits, or roots that we can eat. In remote times our forebears harvested them wild in big wicker baskets. Later they got to tending them and developing the good varieties. And now with food coming by train and truck we scarcely know where it comes from — some vague farm, no doubt, which we see only as a blur when we speed by it. We don't know even what the plants look like. Well, we're going to find out.

KIND Classify the plants according to what part we eat — roots, leaves, or fruit. Not all are necessarily better home-grown — potatoes, for example, or wheat. Some take up too much room, such as pumpkins, but are fine if you have the area to fill up. Corn takes room, too, but I can tell you it is good. Many plants grow a lot in a little — such as parsnips, carrots, beets, beans, peas, radishes, onions, Swiss Chard, and parsley. A few of the lesser-known vegetables will prove worth while. Those unable to grow cabbage should consider the kohlrabi; it will give greens for the soup, besides a tasty dish for the table. A few leeks in the garden will serve for a year's supply. They can be topped regularly and like the Swiss Chard keep coming. Yellow turnips are better because they will stay in the ground longer and keep free of worms. They can grow from fall to spring. White turnips are not profitable. Two plants of the New Zealand Spinach are plenty and may even be put over in the rock garden. Endives are excellent food plants but require tying up a week before cutting to blanch them and reduce the tendency toward bitterness. The plants are very hardy and a fall planting will go through the winter.

Select the good varieties. Seeds looking exactly alike carry dark secrets in their germs and the product will differ as a race horse from a donkey. Ask among people who have experimented. And don't try raising something that won't go in your soil and sub-climate. The root vegetables, as they swell, have to move the soil out of the way and they can do this well only if the soil is mellow and fluffy. The artichoke prospers where the air carries floating droplets of moisture. There is no reason why anyone should misplace plants. Talk with your local nurseryman especially if he has been there for some years; and with some wise neighbor who has had seasons of experience. They'll tell you. A superlative feature of gardening is that everyone wants to share his success with everyone else.

PLAN CROP

Provide for the timetable. You don't want one hundred ears of corn and eleven quarts of parsnips in one month in the year even in the depth of winter, but it takes foresight both in selection and in successive plantings of the same thing to prolong the harvest. This all means that you have to have a schedule — a design before you plant a seed. And of course you have to decide how big your garden is to be — not too big certainly. A small garden may be as productive as a larger one; even a 5 by 10-foot plot if worked to the limit can produce surprising amounts of food. This would be intensive gardening and most of us will have more room. Let us consider some figures of production. An adult can consume with a rounded meal three or four carrots. A row ten feet long will contain forty carrots if placed three inches apart. By planting at intervals, two or three short rows can take care of the table demands for a long period. And a wise practice is to pull alternately so that the carrots remaining may benefit by less competition.

Other vegetables may be planted similarly and in a small plot one can grow beets, chard, lettuce, radishes, and yellow turnips. Cabbage and cauliflower demand more room and in the small garden may not prove profitable. Fast growing vegetables such as lettuce and radishes may be placed in one section of the plot, while the permanent crops, as asparagus, rhubarb, artichoke, and horseradish can be given a place by themselves. Wait until May and June when the weather is settled for the tomato, pepper, corn, eggplant, bush and pole beans and squash; but many crops may be planted several times a year. You can plant beets and carrots at any time; radishes six times a year; bush beans, corn, lettuce and onions twice, three or four weeks apart during April and May; and squash twice druing the summer. Peas classified "early", "mid-season", and "late" will fit the planting time. Here's a list but before I give you the list, here are some reading references: Send to the College of Agriculture, University of California, Berkeley 4, California, for a free copy of Tomatoes in Your Home Garden or any pamphlet on beans, corn, etc. Many one subject pamphlets are available. You may also send to the Superintendent of Documents, Washington 25, D.C., for Controlling Insects on Flowers, Agriculture Information Bulletin No. 237. It costs .40 a copy.

WHEN TO PLANT

Now for the list. You can plant now the leafy vegetables: chard, beets, cabbage, peas, sprouts, lettuce, endives, spinach, parsley, carrots, potatoes (if you want them) radishes, onions, rhubarb, artichokes and asparagus. And here again let me caution you to spend time in selecting the kinds. Get only varieties known to grow in your district. You can do everything in the world for your food plants to get them growing, the seeds will germinate beautifully, but if the variety is wrong your time and labor are lost. For the colder parts of the state, start with the early varieties "Early Blood Turnip Beet" or the "Early Jersey Cabbage". You must absolutely use an early variety for an early season, not an early variety for a late season. Remember — the early varieties mature faster.

Later in May or June will come all the sun-lovers; the tomato, pumpkins, squash, corn and beans, eggplants, peppers, cucumbers, and melons. The hard-shelled pumpkins, zucchini, and squash will keep into winter; carrots, beets, parsnips can be kept in the ground; the Swiss Chard, parsley, also may be grown then.

LOCATION

Where will you put your food plants in the garden? To mature, a tomato takes 800 to 900 hours of sunshine or 130 to 150 six-hour days. An ear of corn takes from 65 to 100 days, depending on whether it is an early, a mid-season or a late variety. These have to have full sun. A lasting house shadow falls like a blight across the garden and in its track all is pygmy. Have you ever eaten bitter lettuce? That is where it came from. You may find trouble fitting the plot in where the sunlight will be good enough. That prompts another advice to builders — the design for the use of all land should include not only lawn, borders, and all the rest but food plant gardens also. Any placing is bound to be a compromise of various interests. One rule is if you are short of room, make a small very fine garden. Whatever you do, do not now go and mutilate a good garden design for the food plants. Do not disfigure it with patches here and there. If you have to do so, appropriate frankly and boldly a good-sized rectangle. Though rows and square corners look about as natural as square eggs, still a well-tended plot has the kind of beauty that comes from neatness and freshness. Besides you can use some of the plants in borders such as parsley, radishes, beets, and Swiss Chard, if the sun is right there. And in the background you can use the permanents such as artichokes, rhubarb, Jerusalem artichoke (which is a kind of sunflower, with edible roots good for soup and salad) and the berry plants, youngberry, loganberry and the improved forms of blackberry.

PREPARE

Next, how do you prepare the ground? The answer is, you do a thorough job, for a "jerry built" garden will be a burden all through the whole growing season. Seldom is the ground ready without a good spell of work. Often the weeds are thin in the very place you have chosen. If the weeds won't grow, neither will your lettuce. My old friend Toby says, "Tell them to make all along the side of the plot a trench two spades deep and move the soil you took in a wheelbarrow over beyond the other side of the plot and dump it. Now," continued Toby, "tell them to make a second trench alongside the first so the top soil goes to the bottom and at the same time work in six inches of fresh cow manure. Keep on until the whole plot is done." I told Toby my hearers wouldn't dig so deep as that. "Yes they will, too," he answered, "if only you tell them that for every lick of work on the foundation, they'll save five on the super-structure. And," he added, they want their vegetables big and handsome don't they? Tell them if the carrot can't spear its way through the ground, it will knot up and come out a freak!" After this the ground by rights should lie two or three weeks before you plant to sunbathe and rest, and let in the air. But in a pinch you can plant in a few days. Wet down thoroughly two or three days beforehand. Start now to give your food plant every advantage. Vegetables have to grow fast to get sweet.

Before Planting. For the protection of your seeds and tiny plants dust the soil as is necessary. See page 494 — just a light dusting. This to get the insect and fungus pests before they get your plants.

Planting. Use flats for seeds of eggplants, peppers, celery, and tomatoes. But beets, carrots, peas, beans and radishes can be planted in the ground in rows; press the rake handle down and it leaves a nice groove; spread your seeds in this groove. Take carrots as an example: their seeds can be covered with fine sand, or even a strip of burlap. This insures the presence of moisture and helps in the germination. The seeds take a long time to germinate and they're easy to lose if they once dry out.

Watchfulness. Stick by it! Early in the morning take a look; late in the afternoon have another; and at night go out with flashlight and see what's happening. Slugs and snails can march down the row with deadly accuracy and leave only chewed-off stem stubs for you; or birds can take it away before your eyes. Try celluloid windmills, bright colored ones to scare birds off!

Warning. Many chemicals are residual, remaining affective over a long period. Therefore on food plants especially 30 days before harvest is the last time to apply. Read directions carefully. On food plants rotenone and pyrethrum are safest.

Weeding. There'll be a little to do. And of course you'll follow up with cultivation. Beets and carrots will require thinning. Use the beet tops for greens, the carrots for soup.

Watering. Watering is one of the gardening arts where skill makes all the difference. Last summer I saw two amateur vegetable gardens of similar size separated by a white picket fence. They had about the same number of rows. Both were shipshape. But the two owners had contrary theories of watering. Number 1 was an overhead sprinkler enthusiast, and he kept worrying for fear that some spot wouldn't have water enough and kept moving his sprinklers around. Number 2 went for irrigation of the most careful kind for he had no money to waste. He meant business. He had rows raised a little with trenches in between. His ground had been prepared many weeks in advance and every scrap of spare humus on the place had gone into it. He knew where his water went to — it soaked into the soil sponge — and he noticed carefully when that sponge got full. For about twenty of his plants he had pieces of pipe pushed down eight inches to carry the water deep and as he said, aim it like a rifle at the mark. In addition, after every irrigation he cultivated the surface breaking the hair-like tubes which otherwise would pump water up to be lost by evaporation; and in this way he kept the water coming up through the plants where he wanted it. With good-natured amusement Number 1 confessed to me the end of the season that he had averaged three thousand cubic feet of water per month and that his wise neighbor had used only one thousand and had gotten twice the crop!

The Opportune Task of the world is more food, and our part is to prepare the garden for food plants.

CHAPTER 14

PEONIES

(April: First Week)

See Illustration Page 507

HISTORY We speak of the peony, which comes from the word meaning the god of healing, and has been cultivated in gardens since the time of Pliny the Elder, the Roman naturalist who perished in the destruction of Pompeii. What sort of plants are peonies, where do they come from, how long have they been used in our gardens; and what should be done for these plants to succeed with them here in California? These plants are members of the crowfoot family. You know them by their large-petalled flowers. Some with satiny texture have a single row of petals and standing above them are golden stamens; in others the flowers are many-petalled, crowded into a ball of folded parts. *KINDS* There are two kinds of peony that grow with astonishingly different habits. First those with fleshy clubs of roots known as the herbaceous peony; the leaves and flowers sprouting out from the crowns. Second the tree peony which grow upon ordinary roots a firm woody stem as high as eight feet. The leaves and flowers run all the way up the stem. We will discuss the herbaceous forms first, and come to the tree peony later. There are twenty-two herbaceous species altogether and you'll be relieved to learn that we have to speak of only three of them.

There is one form in Siberia, Paeonia albiflora or white-flowered, which is fragrant. There is another wild one in Europe, Paeonia officinalis, the official peony which offers only a disagreeable odor. And the third is a native California form, Paeonia brownii, the "Western Peony" which grows on the hill slopes 600 feet to 5400 feet in the Sierras and reaches as far north as Washington State, as far east as Utah and the Rocky Mountains. This one which I studied long ago when I was a student I am not at present acquainted with. I looked in book after book and couldn't find out whether it smells sweet or sour. By the way, I'm reminded of an incident in my garden class. One day I passed around a big specimen of the flower called "Jack in the Pulpit". A woman, a stranger whom I'd never seen before when it came her turn to look at it buried her nose up to the hilt; after a long sniff she threw the flower toward me, and shrieked "Why didn't you tell me". So don't tell me I didn't warn you.

HYBRID

Our garden herbaceous peonies are derived from the Siberian and European forms. Much labor has been devoted to the peony. As long ago as 1580, gardeners were growing many varieties around London. Then in France in 1824 Lemoine, a gardener of scholarly reputation, made important hybrid crosses in peonies. In England in 1840 Parker and others worked intensively toward imporving the quality of herbaceous peonies. And in this country as early as 1826 the single white flowered peony was exhibited in the New York Horticultural Society. Today most of the herbaceous types are progeny of Paeonia albiflora; identified with its white satiny-textured, cup-shaped flowers measuring four to five inches across and resting in the center a cluster of yellow stamens. This has been crossed with forms of the European, Paeonia officinalis, whose flowers appear very early. Other forms of course were used to develop our peony of quality and today our gardens abound in peonies of strong growth, sending out each spring huge globular single and double-flower heads, their colors varying from deep purple-crimson to white.

From Japan there has come by improved hybridization the Chrysanthemum-flowered Peony; these have a different petal arrangement in the individual flower. The flowers are large, with broad shell-like outer petals, while the inner petals are narrow and incurved like those of the large-flowered Chrysanthemum. In all of the improved double-flowered peonies the flower lasts longer than does that of the single-petalled type.

TOICHI DOMOTO

Now that we have answered the questions about the sort of plant the peony is, and where it comes from, let's answer the remaining question -- what should be done for these plants to succeed with them in the California garden? I have invited Mr. Toichi Domoto of the Domoto Nursery in Hayward, California, to answer your questions on the peony. Under the guidance of his late father, Tom, and through study at both Stanford and the University of Illinois, Mr. Domoto has gained a commanding knowledge of tree and shrub culture in Central California. With his interesting bonsai he has truly worked with and studied the peony; we are fortunate to have him with us today. Mr. Domoto, I know you are an expert flower grower; and I know you are as much a flower lover as any of us; tell us why you like the peony and what it looks like to you.

Domoto: My father imported all kinds of plants from Europe and Asia previous to Quarantine 37 in 1917. Bay trees, rhododendrons, and azaleas from Belgium; camellias, dwarfed trees, and tree peonies from Japan were just a few of the plants he imported. The manner in which the huge satiny flowers emerged from what looked like dried-up sticks with the roots tied up in sphagnum moss and rice straw intrigued me then, and my seedlings fascinate me now.

Wilson: We often hear amateurs complain that peonies are difficult plants to grow in California. Do you feel that criticism is correct, Mr. Domoto?

Domoto: No. I do not. If the Eastener starting his garden here will remember that we have no summer showers, and if the Californian will remember that it rains during the summer in the East and Middle West, he will appreciate the position of the peony in this country. Use the garden hose accordingly. Select the early and early midseason flowering varieties of Paeonia albiflora. Avoid the very full double late-flowering ones. Plant them in good rich soil, well drained.

Wilson: You feel then that the amateur should give special attention to the way he places the root of the peony in the soil?

ROOTS HOW TO PLANT

Domoto: Yes, I do. The herbaceous peony has fleshy roots suggesting long sweet potatoes jointed together at one end. This is the important end. The rose-colored eyes which are the dormant shoots must be covered just so. Not so shallow that the sun's ray will blind it; nor so deep that the moles will run into it; but just two inches below the level of the soil. A good root division contains three to five strong eyes. These start growing in early spring. First the leaves unfold on the stems, then the round buds develop at the tip, and then the flowers.

Wilson: I've told our audience to make the soil loose and dig the holes big enough, providing for drainage in those districts where drainage is known to be slow and sluggish, but have you any special suggestions for placing peony roots in the ground?

Domoto: Yes, a hole two feet in diameter and one and one-half feet deep is recommended. Place the division in a bucket of water while digging the hole. This is to give the division a good drink after a dry journey from the nursery. It encourages the sleepy eyes to awaken and start pushing the rootlets into a new foothold in your garden. Second, take off the copper-wired label and attach to a stake before the name gets spattered with mud. This also prevents the wire from cutting into the roots.

Wilson: In planting peony roots, do you use any fertilizer?

Domoto: It is not necessary, but a good handful of bone meal thoroughly mixed with the loose soil in the bottom of the hole is a good booster for the new roots, as they reach down into it.

Wilson: Then you throw in the soil over the roots.

Domoto: Just hold the division firmly in place in the hole; the idea of building a mound in the hole and draping the roots over it is a good one. Work the soil in slowly so that it settles in between the fingers of the root system.

Wilson: Do you tramp the soil in, or do you prefer to let the water settle the soil?

Domoto: I prefer to wash the soil in. Have the

water slowly running from the hose; poke it like a stick into the hole until it fills up with water.

Wilson: Well, that takes care of planting the new peony. We have been talking about placing bare roots of the herbaceous peony, but, Mr. Domoto, is there any advantage in buying these plants already established in containers or pots?

Domoto: The only advantage that I can see is that the purchaser can select the particular plant in bloom. But if he has confidence in his nurseryman, he will be further ahead if he orders bare root divisions for fall planting. These roots may look severely cut back, but don't let this worry you. The large plump eyes are what count. The shortness of the old roots makes the division throw out young fresh roots to support the division.

NO BLOOM

Wilson: What is your advice to those whose herbaceous peony fails to bloom?

Domoto: Let him go look at the plant right away. First, see if the plant is getting enough sunlight. It needs at least six hours of sunlight during the growing season. Having satisfied this point, dig carefully around the crown with a sharp stick or pronged hand cultivator and determine if the plant hasn't settled down below the two-inch mark.

Wilson: And if spring growth has already begun, what would you advise?

Domoto: In that case, scrape away the excess soil, and then in September replant to the correct depth. Meanwhile be sure to give it ample water during this summer.

FEED

Wilson: Would you recommend a manure mulch?

Domoto: Yes, apply it in the fall and scrape away before the new growth starts in spring.

Wilson: Should wood ashes be cultivated into the soil around peonies?

Domoto: Some people intend wood ashes as a source of potash to stimulate the development of flower buds, but a handful of superphosphate or steamed bone meal is better. Scatter over the plants early in spring before growth starts. Scratch it in.

Do not feed oftener than once in every two years.

USE

Wilson: What are the uses of the peony in the garden?

Domoto: I'm glad you asked that one. Peonies are best used in the perennial border. Mixed in with other plants, they take the spotlight when they come into flower, and rightfully too. When they have finished blooming, their glossy green leaves serve as support for the other seasonal plants in the border. For example, peonies are excellent with lilies. They protect with their foliage the tender stems of these taller plants. In the perennial border too they usually are watered properly. And that is a very important thing about growing peonies. Give them water, plenty of water, and then every year you can expect a lot of flowers from your clump of peonies.

SEED PODS

Wilson: Do you recommend picking off the seed pods after the blooms have faded?

Domoto: Yes, I do; in this respect they resemble the rhododendrons; if seeds are allowed to develop they rob the plant of strength that otherwise would remain to build up the plant for the flowers of next year.

Wilson: Mr. Domoto has given me a little list of types good in Central California. We are still talking about the herbaceous type of peony. First the double-flowered types:

VARIETIES

Festiva Maxima, a white
Madame Jules Elie, large rose pink
Walter Faxon, the only "real pink"
Richard Carvel, red
Reine Hortense, hydrangea-pink

Now for the single and Japanese types of herbaceous peony:

King of England, early midseason, dark red shade
Laciniata, red
Mischief, soft uniform pink
Isani Gidui, a beautiful white Japanese variety
Amano-no-sode, rose pink with immense center of long yellow staminoids

Domoto: I'd like to add when your peony flowers,

and the urge is to cut the bloom for use, do not cut all of them; leave at least a third of them. Leave at least three leaves at the base of each stem. These leaves are the source of food for next season's flowers.

DON'T

TREE

Wilson: The second type is the Tree Peony. That is, the stem above the ground is a permanent wood stock; it supports the foliage which breaks out from lateral and tip buds where also the flowers are borne. These plants, like the herbaceous, are deciduous, dropping their leaves in fall, carrying dormant buds all winter, which buds in spring burst out into new leafy growth. Tree Peonies grow wild in China and Japan. Sir Joseph Banks in 1787 took specimens to London from China, among them Paeonia moutan, the wild spicy form; and our old friend the missionary, Abbe Delavay, discovered in Yunnan, China, a fragrant large-flowered yellow one. In the gardens of Europe and later in our gardens here, tree peonies have been as favorites, usually as specimens. Success here and abroad in past years has been uncertain. In one garden plants would die back a foot for every six inches they went ahead. It was discovered at this rate instead of growing taller they grew shorter. In others, after growing well for a time would suddenly go off altogether; while in some gardens one would see immense bushes eight feet in diameter and bearing hundreds of huge blooms, each as large as a cantaloupe. Where tree peonies thrive they have few equals. But why am I talking about tree peonies with Mr. Domoto here? Mr. Domoto, will you tell us something about their habit of growth?

HISTORY

Domoto: Tree peonies like herbaceous peonies are long-lived. Once the plants are established they will produce flowers in increasing numbers. Have patience; it takes them two seasons to get started, and the third season for good large blooms. There are three methods of propagation: seeds, divisions, and grafts, either on herbaceous roots or on Moutan tree peony. Seedlings and divisions continually send up new shoots when they are established. Plants grafted on herbaceous roots must be planted deeper to encourage root formation and consequent new shoots from the base. Plants grafted on Moutan must be constantly watched to remove the suckers before they take over the entire plant.

Wilson: What are your special recommendations to grow the tree peony in the home garden?

Domoto: I am sure there is no secret; happy roots, happy growth.

Wilson: And what is your idea of happy roots?

Domoto: Roots that can move through the soil easily. Tree peonies do not like to be baked hard and dry. The roots must be able to move out freely into the soil. In Japan and China where these plants have their original home they grow under plenty of light in a natural rich soil. I grow them in rows between the apricot trees, which provide shade and also a windbreak.

Wilson: Then you recommend ordinary good soil, not an excess of moisture.

Domoto: I recommend a generous treatment. The tree peony extends itself much further than the herbaceous. Though the tops may be only two or three feet, the roots will extend out four or five feet and down as deep as you have prepared the hole. The plant makes only one growth a year. The eyes in the axil of the leaves of the flowerstalks are next season's flowers. These must be nourished during the summer to prepare for next spring's burst of growth. Don't give them the air during the hot summer; give them water. SOIL

Wilson: What do you advise is the best time to move tree peonies?

Domoto: Just like the herbaceous, move them in September and October; only under emergency conditions move them as late as December. At our nursery we have learned tree peonies are best moved at resting time; the roots seem to be at rest by October even though the leaves are still attached. Then the newly established plant has all winter to become well anchored and in spring the strong fibrous roots start out and the plant is ready to go ahead. MOVE

Wilson: You have made it clear then the best time to move peonies is when they are entering the dormant period. And your answer does away with that question that came in the mail: How often should I transplant a peony?

Domoto: Select the proper spot in the beginning. Don't transplant them.

ENEMIES

Wilson: How about enemies of the peony, both herbaceous and tree kinds?

Domoto: Sometimes scale and thrip bother the tree peony. An oil spray combined with bordeaux in the spring before new growth starts will eliminate the scale and help prevent "die-back". The thrip can be prevented by spraying the plants overhead with water at least two times a week during the summer. If it attacks, use sprays. See page 494. Dilute according to directions. Watch out for snails; they are very fond of the new shoots.

Wilson: What is this "die-back" that you just mentioned?

Domoto: Die-back is a fungus disease. It usually attacks the new soft growth near the ground with herbaceous peonies and on the soft shoots as they grow out from the old wood with the tree peonies. The shoots look wilted, then dry up.

Wilson: What would you recommend for its control?

Domoto: Besides the bordeaux, the new effective fungicides are now being tried. Clean culture; cut herbaceous peony stems clean to ground level in fall, not the tree peonies. Gather up and burn all old leaves and dead twigs. Cut off wilted branches sufficiently below to insure clean wood. Sterilize your shears or knife before making next cut. Should the plant get old and woody-looking, don't be afraid to prune back severely in the spring when in flower. The dormant eyes near the ground will grow out again. You may lose a few flowers for a season, but will be rewarded with a more vigorous bushy plant.

Wilson: Tree peonies in your garden are beautiful, but it is only in a nursery where they are grown by the acres that the full effectiveness of their massive flowers may be seen. An acre of these plants in flower, though regimented in nursery rows, makes a wonderful glow of color on a bright day. I remember last year on a tour of the nurseries when I dropped into your place at Hayward, Mr. Domoto, I saw tree peonies that really started this talk today. One purpose of discussing peonies now is to make sure you realize that for the next four to five weeks peonies will be coming into full bloom. Go out and see them; select the types and colors you like; then in October when the proper time to move and transplant comes, you'll be all prepared.* I heard about a fine old specimen growing in the same spot for 45 years and still blooming and doing its best every year. And now that we have Mr. Domoto here in the studio, let's use him to get acquainted with the different kinds of tree peonies so we can select them to be planted next fall.

VARIETIES

Domoto: They are all beautiful.

Souvenir de Professor Maxime Cornu; a double yellow with orange suffusion. This is a lutea hybrid.

Le Esperance; a single deep yellow with bright red anthers. Also a lutea hybrid.

Reine Elizabeth; a full double pink European type.

Moutan; single purple, the wild variety, a good one to use as a test if your locality has none growing.

The difficulties of propagation make the named grafted varieties more costly than those raised from seed. If you can select a seedling at your nurseryman's in bloom, they will give you satisfaction. If ordering a named variety from a list, be sure to make a second choice or else leave it to the discretion of the dealer to substitute.

Wilson: We want to thank you kindly, Mr. Domoto, for telling us so many hard facts about the right way to grow peonies.

---

*See Opportune Task for October: Second Week

CHAPTER 15

CHRYSANTHEMUMS

(April: Second Week)

We shall treat a garden plant which came from a wild Siberian ancestor in the dawn of history; it was described five centuries B. C. by Confucius for its "yellow glory"; carried to Japan like so many other Chinese valuables; celebrated in the Emperor's flower show there one thousand years ago; seized by traders and taken to Europe, in both single and double forms, *HISTORY* two hundred years ago; soon a window-box and sheltered-corner flower for the humble cottages of England; and after that over here. But though it was long famous in the past, its biggest time is now. In place of a few simple daisies which everyone understands, we see kinds, kinds, and more kinds, doubled and redoubled; pygmies with silver reverse, to vivid red with gold markings; and three hundred names, from Granny Scovil to September Cloud. Most of these kinds have been developed in the last twenty years, in a regular fury of excitement, enthusiasm and driving work.

As everyone knows, the chrysanthemum is the fall flower; its pungent fragrance brings to the seasoned gardener vivid memories of sparkling days getting shorter and shorter, the lively show of colors after all the summer flowers have quit, and the preparations all through the garden for the rainy cold months ahead. We think of it at this time because now is the time to start it.

SELECT FOR We must think what we want it for — we have designs on it, or we make a design including it, for a specific purpose. And it must of course fit into a specific place. A few of us will want it for size, or for the latest thing in varieties. Most of us will want, first, composition, which means good grouping within the garden. There are a variety of forms from low, bushy dwarfs to strong, branchy, heavy, which go well against a background of evergreens; to thin-stemmed, daisy-like, which can make a mass effect, supporting each other in crowds, and rippling and sparkling in the breeze; to the top-lofty exhibitionists whose heads have to be held up by stakes and must stand apart from each other and from everything else. When you select, you must have a picture in your mind of what the plant will look like next September. Second, you will want some cut flowers and chrysanthemums make good cut flowers. Third, you are likely to want some plants in pots, to move about for experimental effects and for continuation of blooming after the outdoor weather grows harsh. Fourth, whatever you do, color will guide you. And here's another fact about chrysanthemums — whatever kind you have, and wherever you put them, that place will thereafter bear the character of herby fragrance. An arbor, so perfumed, takes on new meaning in the design — I say this seriously. We forget our noses, but if we were suddenly deprived of them we'd find an instant change in the whole garden. It would become a different and quite inferior place.

What, in a few words, are the kinds? The late Alex Cumming said: the cushion types, dense and low branching, compact, which need to be divided every second year; and the Korean hybrids, which have been developed so amazingly in recent years and include most of those you see in the catalogues — varying from the small pompons to large single flowers, and to the great nodding balls of yarn. *KINDS*

But the kinds cannot by any means be covered in a few words. For wise selection, study the plants where they are growing, and get advice from those who know both the plants and your sub-climate. Chrysanthemums adore the sun and follow it with their faces from morning to night. They take most genially in the Bay region to the middle peninsula. Farther south the summer is too burning; farther north it is too tempered by fog. In these places you will have to work harder to make them comfortable, though it can be done, and for those who like garden tricks, it is worth while. Wherever you live, let me counsel you to start with only a few plants. Then, next season, having learned much of their nature and management, you can proceed with assurance.

You can raise your plants from seeds if you want to, though the time is getting late, and you'll not know in advance what colors you will get. Or you can divide old plants, and select the outer rooted suckers which creep under surface away from the central cushion. Or the beginner can buy rooted nicely-branched cuttings in three-inch pots. But the gardener's method of getting new plants is to start them himself, through tip cuttings. You proceed as follows. Water the old established clump the night before you make the cuttings, to supply moisture throughout the young stem and leaves to the very tip. Take four inches of the new tip growth; it will have four or five leaves. Use a razor to make clean cuts. Place the cuttings in sharp sand. Firm the sand around them. Place each cutting one inch away from its neighbor, and settle the sand by watering. Though the chrysanthemum flower is a sun lover, the cuttings resent the hot sun or warmth of any kind; shield the rooting bed with newspaper, supported above the cuttings. This is especially needed where they are under glass. Your water schedule is arranged to keep the sand bed moist while the cuttings are producing their new roots. But watch out for damping off which we have discussed before.

HOW TO MAKE CUTTINGS

You will have plenty of time to prepare the ground, for the plants won't go in for six to eight weeks. The soil must be rich and must be kept rich. However dainty to look at, chrysanthemums reach for everything in sight; and after a year or two will sulk because the soil, out of which they have squeezed all the life, can no longer offer them the food to which they are accustomed. The rule is, either remove to a new location, or add large amounts of food.

SOIL

To grow chrysanthemums, then, you start out by developing a first-class reservoir of soil food — a first-class sustaining soil sponge. It must be mellow and it must be deep — eighteen inches is none too much. Rich, sandy loam is good, but make certain that it is rich and not merely painted black with mulch. If the soil is sticky, pile on the manure or other humus and work it all together until it will crumble even when moist. Peat moss helps, because these plants like to be slightly acid. Most ground, whether sandy or muddy, will need manure; it can go in fresh because you will work it in thoroughly, and because the planting is some weeks in the future. In addition put in commercial fertilizer such as bone meal; it is well balanced and has super-phosphate which chrysanthemums need.

Before the planting, which will not come until the latter half of May, you will begin one of the practices essential to good culture. When the plant gets six inches high, you have to pinch off an inch or two of each growth to make the side branches grow, and develop bushiness. Later you will continue pinching every time a foot of growth has been added, until the flower buds form. *PINCH OFF*

Put the plants in the ground fifteen to eighteen inches apart, in groups of two or three with free spaces between them. Firm to the depth of the root — you don't want channels there for bypassing torrents of water and air. *PLANT*

Then you water. You may sprinkle enough to keep the leaves clean until the buds start to come. But too much sprinkling makes the rootlets gallop along just under the surface. Moreover, with any cloudiness, you might get mildew. Do most of your watering by irrigation. Afterward, cultivate to create a dust mulch. How often water will be needed will depend on: first, the depth of the soil-sponge; second, the depth of the root-cushion. A main reason for having the soil deep is that the root-cushion may swell down deep also, and so make available to the plant a reservoir, not only of food, but of water also. The soil should be kept, not soggy, but moist at all times; you can test it by cutting out a cylinder with the trowel. Don't make a swamp for your plant, but if your soil is *WATER* properly prepared and you have drainage, and especially if you take proper notice of the condition of the soil, you will miss this danger. Frequent but shallow cultivation will provide air to the roots and will keep moss carpets and swamps away.

Before you know it, the plants may begin to starve and slow up in their growth. Give each one a handful *FEED* of commercial fertilizer and wash it in with water. Alternate with liquid manure. Usually you can postpone this until the end of July when the buds of the earliest varieties will begin to show. The late bloomers will need another feeding in late August or September.

STAKE All except the low, bushy plants will need to be held up by wires, strings, or stakes. They have to stay up in the sun — that is where they prosper. Nothing is more hideous than stems flopping in a mat, and flowers sweeping the floor upside down. Their wild ancestors grew along with other stiffer-stemmed plants which gave them support; but we now are specializing them in certain features, like the dogs we breed for exhibition, and they are individually weak and in need of support. Support is a simple mechanical matter in which the main danger is spoiling the looks of the garden. Look at other gardens, several of them and find out which system they use to stake their plants. While you are about it, take a look at the graceful, dainty cascades made with particular kinds *CASCADE* of plants in pots. How do we get cascade chrysanthemums? You root them in the same manner as you root cuttings of the regular chrysanthemums. Then put each one in a pot, two to four inch pot, later transfer to four to six inch, and from the six inch pot to the finishing pot. To this last one be sure and dust the bottom with bone meal. When your plant gets up to one foot high, pinch it, taking out the leader, that means you only take one half inch of the tip. Then you start to bend the shoot, you bend it over a wire, keep on depressing the wire every few days, you are training your plant to obey your design. The wire frames are slanted up toward the sun, and later you train the plant by bending the frame down toward the ground, and thus you create the cascade. The point you have to think about is that you want your plant to grow downward, the plant on the other hand always has a desire to come back, you have to keep it down against its will, so tie the tip down, and all the time you will be getting laterals, branches breaking out; you'll be getting also sub-laterals and tri-laterals. You keep inching these laterals until you have the shape you want. All of this depressing is finished by the first week of September, that's when the plant will show bloom buds. You must remember always that your precious plant must never go thirsty once during this entire training period, give it plenty of water, and when color begins to show then feed your plant every two weeks alternating with a fast commercial fertilizer; that is feed it the slow acting liquid cow manure one week, and the following week feed it some commercial fertilizer. One of our listeners with whom I discussed cascades said, "It sounds like a lot of work. But you're always working with time, and as you do jobs around the garden, you do this one piece by piece."

Now to return to our regular garden forms. All the time until the buds begin to show, you continue pinching off the tips of the shoots. Then you quit that and start pinching off some of the buds where they are bunching — that is, you do if you are looking for size and lustiness. The gardeners have some more lingo here — when they tell you they take a bud, they mean they leave it on the plant! How many you take on and how many you take off depends on how far you want to go. If you have one of those exhibition plants, and you want a giant, you remove all the buds but one at the topmost tip — this must be an absolutely perfect bud — or perhaps for safety you leave one more for a while to serve like an alternate delegate should the other fail. If you have the more modest plants you remove the buds from the sides and leave those at the tips, making six or eight in all.

The insects, perhaps, sensing that pyrethrum comes from a chrysanthemum, are less fierce in their

ENEMIES & CONTROL

attack than on many other plants. Yet they do attack, it is especially in wall corners or anywhere the circulation of air is impeded. If you have old plants in your garden, the chances are that the aphids are already there in the tender tips of the new leaves; they, and the thrips also, can be easily handled with nicotine or pyrethum, with soap, and for the thrips you can use Diazinon, or see pages 494–500. The red spider, when hot weather comes, gets on the under side of the leaf, makes a gray webbing there, and causes blotches and yellowing. He is a little bigger than the thrip. A well-balanced oil spray containing nicotine and soap will fix him; and dusts are good if applied lightly and evenly — a big puff in one spot and none in another part of the plant is poor treatment. Caterpillars and other chewers may show up, and they need poison. The young plants, especially; will need protection from them for they are relished even by the snails and slugs if there isn't something nearby that they like better. The cutworm, who also steals out at night when no one is there to see him, is the worst. If he is around, you will have to hunt him with a flashlight, for, as Cumming says, he prefers the young plant to any poison bait that you leave out there. Or, you may be able to turn him up in the daytime from his hiding place in the soil nearby. Whatever the pest, regular inspection and spraying is the thing. Once a week is a good interval, and your plant will take on an odor repulsive to the insects. Because the leaf cups at the end, strong spray collecting there will burn it. Strong spray will also callous both tips, veins, and wood, making the plant inflexible, and hard to train. For these reasons, you spray frequently and mildly. Six o'clock in the evening is a good time — when the white fly has settled, and the dew is still to come. Spray the under sides of the leaves, and follow the stems up to the place where the bloom bud shows color, in this way keeping the aphid from entering and defiling your flower.

HOW STRONG SPRAY

But the worst enemy of the chrysanthemum is not the insect at all. The worst enemy is moisture on the

MILDEW

foliage, and the prone position which many of the plants take when they are not properly held up. With these comes mildew and other troubles. Keep the foliage dry and up in the sun, and these troubles will never touch it.

The difference between plants carelessly grown and those attended persistently, intelligently, and with good taste is almost unbelievable. On the one side you get scraggly little, dull growths matted together, and on the other, wide, graceful, sparkling rainbows of foliage and color for both garden and house.

The professionals, of course, have many methods additional to those I have mentioned. They control temperature, shields from wind, and keep out the green ladybug; they use a cheesecloth canopy. As you know from your attendance at football games, they have to meet a particular date in the fall with carloads of blooms all brought to the precise condition at the same time. To stimulate the blooming, if that becomes necessary, they shorten the daylight by a housing of opaque paper cloth — in this way imitating the shorter days of fall in which the blooms naturally develop. The amateur will find no need of such devices.

Even if I knew it all, which I do not, for I am not a grower, I could not tell you one-tenth of what you need to know about chrysanthemums. Go to those who have spent their lives with these plants. One such was the late Alex Cumming, Jr., whose book, The Hardy Chrysanthemum I have mentioned, and use Bailey who has written the great Encyclopedia on plants, or go to the growers hereabouts.

The Opportune Task: Prepare the ground for your chrysanthemum plants. Spade it deeply, work bone meal down there, and above all, select a sunny spot.

PEACH LEAF CURL

Did you miss spraying your peach trees with bordeaux in late February or in mid March? Do you see the leaves of your trees covered with blisters, or do you see the young leaves wavy and inflamed with pink or yellow spots all over? That is curly leaf (Taphrina deformans) and by summer every one of those leaves now being attacked will turn fiery red, dry up, and drop off. Well if you failed to spray your tree, you can resort to a heavy pruning now, cut back the branches which carried the blooms, leave a few inches of the base, and from the buds in the lower part of the stem new shoots will spring out and the leaves will be free of the disease because warm weather is unfavorable for the development of the spores of curly leaf. Every year, of course, you wouldn't resort to this severe pruning. It is, however, a method for keeping your peach tree, especially the flowering form, looking healthy.

MAGNOLIA TREES Evergreen trees native in United States, and deciduous forms native of forest lands of the Himalayas, India, China, Japan. USE: let each plant become an eminant individual in the garden! Give the magnolia room, plenty of light, but not the scorching sun of the hot valley, where filtered light best. Greedy feeders such as acacia or eucalyptus keep away, magnolia roots can't stand the competition. At margin of lawn, end of glade, near corner of house are good places in the design. Avoid windy places. SOIL: loose, rich in humus inclined toward the moist is best —never desert dry soil; soil can be top dressed in spring especially for newly planted young specimens. Once tree is established mulching will not be necessary. A mulch of strawy cow manure, decomposed leaf mold, and humus mixed with river sand is good top dress for the crown roots of magnolias. PLANTING: most deciduous magnolias and the evergreen are grafted plants. Make sure when you set out newly purchased magnolia the grafted union is above ground level. Union is easily discernable for the scar divides the two kinds of wood— never bury the scar though humus mulch can come up to it. WATERING: magnolias must have water the year round because of their shallow roots. Water thoroughly. making sure the water reaches down through mulch. FEEDING: strawy manure can be used in the top dress for young plants; later trees get vigor from the soil without fertilizer of any type. PRUNING: wild suckers

(CONTINUED ON PAGE 150)

CHAPTER 16

FUCHSIAS

(April: Third Week)

We consider the fuchsias — whence in wild forms they came to us; their hybridization; the habits of the hybrids through the year;what climate and sub-climate they require; how we can use them among our other flowers to serve the ideal of the garden; how we can find the plants; what soil they need; what planting, watering, feeding, pruning, and defense against enemies; what winter care; and, last we can find a printed discussion of the whole, big, inspiring subject.

Where, then did the fuchsia come from, and how did it get here? Like the chrysanthemum, the fuchsia is a world traveler which has come to California after long, devious, and exciting journeys. We can scarcely realize how many voyagers and gardeners, over how many generations, have worked together to bring us what we now have. The originals grew in the damp of the mountains and in the interiors of the forests; all the way from the cool uplands of Mexico and Central America; past the equator; and thence down along the coast of Chile where they were defended from frost by ocean currents; and even as far south as the Straits of Magellan. In addition, a few originals grew in New

HISTORY

Zealand -- and I should like to know how they made it across that wide, Pacific water! For all, the dormant season was frostless or close to it, and the blooming season rainy and cool. Already in their wildness, they had a charming variety; from the Mexican, with drooping, apical clusters of scarlet and green flowers; to Peruvian, with long terminal scarlet clusters; to Bolivian, rich crimson trumpet tubes; to Chilean, graceful with scarlet calyx; to New Zealand, a pretty little creeper, with oval reddish berries which last for months. Among these the two extremes later blended in the hybrids were: first, the upland tropical, tender; and second, the coastal-temperate, hardy.

One hundred and fifty years ago, the story is that a sailor brought home plants to his mother in England; that she raised them in her window; that passers-by stopped to admire the strange and graceful flowers; that slips went to Kew gardens; that a nurseryman propagated hundreds of plants and sold them for a guinea apiece; that Church-of-England clergymen grew so entranced that on Sunday the sexton had to hunt them out of their glass houses; and that, by one hundred years ago, crosses between the long and globe-flowered kinds had yielded astonishing effects, and the varieties which already included some with white sepals exceeded five hundred.

This all had to go with plentiful, good, low-cost labor, in the artificial climate of the glass house; and it made a rare and joyous life for those who preferred it to the more rackety fox-hunting. Thus it went on and flourished through all Victorian time, until the golden dreamy days exploded into the First World War. The pieces were never put together again. We can understand why, and why these plants cannot quickly revive in the Old World.

The fuchsia had meanwhile migrated to California, and had come upon golden days here also. For a long while it was cultivated in the English mood. Our rich families had their glass houses, too; and, in their sincere search for what was good, they had their English gardeners and sometimes, even their imported English soil! Can you see the good ship wallowing gallantly around the Horn to bring compost to the fresh, new millionaires? It seems impossible, just as some of our favored practices will seem impossible fifty years hence. But it looked correct to them, and it was correct, for it got them their flowers, their very beautiful flowers — just as ours look correct to us.

It seems impossible because we realize now that a big part of their trouble was wasted in this coast climate. Though the wild forms bloom in the rainy season, and ours in the dry season so that we must provide an artificial rain, this is more like their original home than any other the fuchsias have found in all their journeys. In large areas they do not even have to be taken indoors for the winter.

Toward the end of the last century, after a strong vogue, they went out of fashion here. The faddist deserted and for two decades you could scarcely buy a plant from a nurseryman. Only a few of the true believers preserved the precious kinds from total loss. But, after the First World War, they came back with a rush;from the choice Europeans, new hybrids emerged, of charming quality, increasingly fitting the climate, and have since then continued to emerge. We are now the fuchsia center of the world. As would be expected, the American Fuchsia Society was started and is principally supported here.

HYBRID

How do the experts get a hybrid fuchsia? Much as they get the hybrid tomato. When the flower opens, it is artificially fertilized with the pollen from another flower; and then it is protected from other pollens. The ideal is to gain hardiness against the frost; drought and sun resistance for the interior valleys; pest and disease resistance; beauty or novelty in form habit and color combination. No new variety which the experts accept as genuine can be mistaken for any other. The variations between the extremes are endless; the ardent hybridizer can go on making new combinations all day and all night, for months at a time. One grower whom I know had many hundreds in one season.The experts agree to pass out to the public only what, by current opinion, has value. The new plants must have something. Some are curiosities and salable because they are hard to produce. Others are beauties of grace and color that will long survive their season of novelty. When I was somewhat younger, I was enormously pleased when one of these varieties was named Professor Wilson — though all I was professor of was a W. P. A. class. But before the season started, my pride, and the flower along with one thousand other attempts utterly faded away. Three of the famous hybridizers are the late Mr. Niederholzer, and Messrs. Reiter and Schmidt. They are, as we say, headquarters, and much that I tell you has come out of their experience. Mr. Niederholzer, who always was an amateur, was a beginner, as he said, in 1938, That was in my so-called professor days and he came to my lectures. I had an idea which I hoped someone else would act on because I knew it was good — namely, that each one take a particular plant; work on it; find out all about it; learn by trial for several years what it will do in our ground and climate; and then end up perhaps knowing more on that subject than anyone else. Mr. Niederholzer was in the position and mood to do this very thing, and he did it and made and gave out, as an amateur, a succession of fuchsias which everyone cherishes, including "Blue Moon", "Sunset", "Lucky Strike", "Fritz Kreisler" and "Wonderblue". It was in one of his discards that my name, for one brief moment, was celebrated.

HABITS What are the habits of the hybrid fuchsias, through the year? As Mr. Reiter says, it rests during the winter unless it is forced in the glass house to continue growing and blooming. Out of doors in heavy frost it will be killed back nearly or quite to the roots, but the roots will not die. As soon as the ground warms up it sends out green shoots and leaves, it grows violently if the warmth continues and food and water are available.

Next, from May to October, flowers come out like stars in the summer sky. The plant continues to grow; its flowers wither and go to seed. As Mr. Schmidt says, here is where you and the plant for the first time disagree, for your purpose is flowers and the plant's purpose is seeds. You thwart it — you pick off the seeds as soon as they show; and the plant goes on making more flowers so it can get more seeds. Last, to come back to Mr. Reiter, the plant goes into a decline. Do not try then to keep it awake. Leave it alone and let it sink again to rest.

On climate you already have suggestions in what I have said. However far the fuchsia has been adapted, it has never relinquished its yearning for the coolness, partial shade, humidity and frostlessness in which its wild ancestors were nurtured. You will remember that the chrysanthemum is a sun-worshiper, and that it languishes in San Francisco with its coolness and droplets of fog. But the fuchsia on the other hand takes its sun in moderation — a few hours a day, especially in the morning, suit it best.

Does your location, like so many in the Bay region, have an afternoon sweep of northeast wind called lightly the "firemen's fright"? It ought to be the gardener's fright also, for that wind, which comes on many a hot day in the blooming season, has close to zero humidity, and it will make tinder out of a wet sponge in no time. We don't see it; it looks like any other breeze. But our fuchsias know all about it, and almost at its first touch they fold up their tents like the Arabs. You who live in the interior valleys will be wise either to omit fuchsias altogether, or to provide with real care and attention spots of sub-climate where you can reproduce these conditions — as in the CARE barred shade of a narrow-slitted lathhouse; keeping its roots mulched deeply with moist peat, and strawy cow-manure; cooled with sprays; and cloaked in a halo of moisture against drying winds. Except for the few varieties which have been inured to sunlight, the ideal temperature for blooming is neither above 60 nor below 50 degrees. If you have winter frosts, as I have at my home in Menlo Park, and burning summer sun, you can still have some fuchsias, and in choosing varieties the first thing to do, as with all plants, is to find out what thrives around you. If you haven't the coast type of climate, you must either create it artificially or limit yourself to the varieties of plant which have been adapted to what you have. Ascertain the reason for your neighbor's successes. He may have used, with real cunning, the most favorable spots of a kind your garden does not possess. Or he may have brought in the better adjusted type of fuchsia. Or what is more likely he may have done both at once. To duplicate his results you will have to repeat his favorable factors.

USE The fuchsia hybrids vary in habit and function. For example: a climber can be trained formally tree-like, six to eight feet tall, and set in a tub, with a spreading head and bare trunk. Others may ramble up a wall, or be used to make an espalier design on the wall, or grow in a pyramid, or in bushy forms as specimens or as a hedge, or trailing in hanging pots.

Though fuchsias are most often planted in groups all of one kind, unmixed with other plants, they go well with rhododendrons and azaleas either in the background or in the foreground according to relative size. And they go well also with hydrangeas and woodwardia ferns.

When you know what you want, where do you get the plants? For the beginner, the easiest source is nursery plants, already well rooted in three-inch pots. These will be a month ahead of anything you can get ready yourself, if you start now. Of course those who have had plants have already taken cuttings and have them in sand taking root, or have them rooted and in pots. The best procedure here is to use two inches of newly grown green tips. They root with remarkable ease with ordinary care, and that is one reason why the fuchsia has multiplied so fast.

SOIL What kind of soil do they want? In a measure they are accommodating — that is, if they get set in a soil that is too heavy, they don't exactly sulk as the chrysanthemums do. But they don't like it either. That was good deep forest mold where they developed to begin with, and they'll thank you to get them something like it. Make certain the subsoil will carry away the surplus water. If it is stickier than average, test it with a hole two feet down, fill it with water, and time how long it takes to go dry. If free water stays in that hole overnight you have suspiciously little drainage. One way to fix it is to take off the top soil, save it to one side, and then fly at the subsoil — ruffle it up with the fork or shovel, work organic rubbish into it, and let it lie exposed to the sun for a few days. Then put your top soil back and unless you are down in one of those pockets the water will drain.

TOP SOIL

What you want for top soil is the moist sponge again, like that for the rhododendrons and azaleas, with less emphasis on the acid side. It should be crumbly; make it so with rotted cow manure. Soften the lumps, cut them up, and mix them in. In other words, you want soil in good tilth, eight to twelve inches deep. Excuse my repeated reference to soil — it is as much for my benefit as yours — it is for the benefit of everyone. Let the soil aerate for a week anyway — a month would have been better yet, for dug up, with all the weeds off, it sweetens and gets altogether more wholesome for the summer's job. Keep this fact in mind throughout your garden, and prepare ahead of time for the plantings you will make later.

ENEMIES

Soon you will put your fuchsias out in the garden. The individuals should be two and a half to three feet apart. The roots are shallow and will race through most soil reaching six feet away. Firm the ground around them — and you have taken on the job, not by any means hard if your location and soil are right, of keeping them moist from now until October. One way of doing this is to put above the roots a mulch two inches thick. Sprinkling is what they are used to. Directed upward against the undersides of the leaves, it will clean off aphids and some other abominations. Many gardeners wash the leaves daily during the hot weather. But I am happy to say that fuchsias keep wonderfully free of trouble if they have half a chance. I've had them in my garden for seventeen years with very little trouble indeed. In some districts ground mealy bugs, white flies and aphid attack fuchsias. In other gardens green house thrip, two spotted mite, and red spider bother. Control them with any multipurpose spray. Use what your local nurseryman uses!

SUMMARY Let us list the things we want for our fuchsias:

First: good drainage is imperative.

Second: partial shade.

Third: moisture at all times; they like water inside and outside.

Fourth: provide plenty of food because their work in the garden is to provide masses of flowers.

Fifth: in the coast districts the dormant pruning was finished a month ago. Where the frost departs late, however, it may still be done. As the new shoots grow you will pinch them back to make them branch freely and take the desired shape.

For the fuchsia references look in the Fuchsia Book in the public library, or buy from the Fuchsia Society, Academy of Sciences, Golden Gate Park, San Francisco.

Propagation By Cuttings: Hardwood Cuttings: The easiest winter multiplication of one's stock (October-December). Water plant thoroughly twenty-four hours before selecting wood.

Method: Select healthy, plump branches of a quarter to three-eighths inch thickness; take these in the brownish bark area of the branch wood (eight months to eighteen months old), cut into lengths six to twelve inches. Make the lower cut just below a node (eye), the upper immediately above a node. Even half-way between the nodes is good, in fact, it is better. Insert the defoliated hardwood cuttings for half their length in loamy, light soil in a section of the garden which is well drained and where there is the least danger from frost. The cuttings root in the winter and may be transplanted the following Spring. Cuttings protected with a glass bell, inverted mason jar, or similar device make roots much earlier. It is helpful if these protected cuttings can be placed where they are sheltered, during the winter, by a fence or a wall, etc.

Criticism: This method is most successful only when the fuchsia is dormant (winter) and it requires too much of the mother plant framework to get a few cuttings. Rooting is slow and resulting plants are inferior to tip grown materials. Practicable only in our milder coastal regions.

Ripe Wood Cuttings: The best method for the amateur and it can be practised throughout the growing season although most successful in early summer.

Method: Select leafy cuttings on which the foliage is completely mature (firm and dark green) and from which the growing tip has been removed when chosen from actively growing wood. The bark of these cuttings should be at least partly green but may be brownish toward the base. Select cuttings of lateral branches from three to six inches long in their entirety so that the base of the branch, where it forks from the parent stem becomes part of the cutting. This "heel" is known as a slip. Leave foliage, never let it wilt.

Put this cutting at least one inch deep in sand or sandy loam; keep moist; cover with glass jar, cold frame, etc. Dipping the rooting stems in hormone powder before inserting them in the sand accelerates rooting.

When the dormant buds begin to break into growth your cutting is thoroughly rooted; transplant it.

Criticism: Experts say this is the best method for the amateur since ripe wood cuttings produce good plants. It succeeds best before the cuttings have flower buds. It is not recommended in the fall or when the selected branches have just completed flowering.

Soft Wood Cuttings: This is the method used by nurserymen and advanced amateurs possessing glass-house facilities.

Method: Choose green, soft leafy branches three inches in length. Dip cut end in hormone powder. Place cutting an inch and a quarter deep in gritty sand, top gravel, or moistened peat in cold frame or cutting box. Keep moist and warm. For those cuttings placed in the glasshouse an electric cable is recommended although cuttings taken in summer do not need artificial heat.

Criticism: This is the best method and produces the best plants. It is particularly desirable where speed is needed. Best plants for exhibit work come from soft wood and soft tip cuttings.

Soft Tip Cuttings: This method is also used by nurserymen and advanced amateurs possessing glasshouse facilities.

Method: Select wood from the most actively growing leafy tip branches. Use sharp knife in cut through the soft, green, immature stems. Proceed in similar manner as in the soft wood cuttings.

The Opportune Task: For your garden choose varieties of fuchsia that are worthy, that are known to grow well in your district. Consult a nurseryman who specializes in fuchsias.

TUBEROSE

TUBEROSE: Polianthes tuberosa is a member of the Amaryllidaceae family and native of Mexico. It grows very well in our California gardens. The following treatment is recommended: Place in the full sun, in open ground. SOIL: loamy, inclined toward heavy; clayey also. In these soils bulbs grow exceptionally well. Loosen soil thoroughly at time of planting. Add considerable peat to soil to assure a constant supply of moisture for the growing roots. Single bulbs of course may be planted, but if possible select rootstock in clusters; the production of flowers is usually better. Set bulbs four inches deep, for large bulbs, less for the smaller ones. A rosette of foliage grows first, then the bloom stalks 1 1/2 to 2 1/2 feet tall. On these spikes the very fragrant flowers appear toward the crown. Some are single, and some are double flowering forms. Permit bulbs to remain in place for two years, then divide, and spread bulbs around. WATER: provide plenty during growing season. In frost areas protect bulbs in winter. VARIETIES or named forms; Mexican Everblooming is single; Double Pearl is the popular double form.

CHAPTER 17

GARDEN DUTIES PECULIAR TO THE MONTH OF APRIL

(April: Fourth Week)*

The garden emergencies for April — and we might call them Opportune Tasks — are weeding, soil preparation, the first crop of pests, attention to the lawn and tying and staking up new growth. First, the weeds. During February and March, seeds of many wild annuals have germinated and roots of perennials have started to sprout. The cool rainy weather favors them, and everywhere you look from seashore to

mountaintop, you see lush velvety green growth, one of the charms of the California spring. But it somehow contrives to clash with our desires in the garden. The weed has no charm there. April is the very time to get rid of it. For you can pull it up by the roots even if it is as long as a parsnip, or you can turn it under in the soft ground so that it may return to the soil what it has taken. A month and a half hence this job will break your back, but now you can easily push in your fork with a minimum of effort. A big part of the difference between a good farmer and a poor one comes from doing things at the right time and that goes for gardeners too. Weeding in April is quite as

WEED

*For the purpose of our book, several months will have two fourth weeks or two third weeks in order to incorporate the opportune tasks for this season.

timely as pruning fruit trees and roses in January and February.

Equally timely is the second item, that of soil preparation. Many of you know something about soil, and have seen what comes forth from it. Others are going to have their first experience, like a friend on whom I called one day. I found him sick in bed, leading me to the window and pointing to thirteen tulips he had received for Christmas. He had at that time come to me and I had told him what to do with them. This was the first time in his forty-five years of life he had ever put his hand in the soil. As he pointed to the swelling buds, his eyes glistened (he had been sent to bed merely to rest a sore throat) and he said to me, "Albert, it works! Look, they're up! They are going to bloom!"

SOIL

He had to prepare his soil last December because that was when those bulbs had to go into the ground. But the main bulk of plants and seeds have to go in from now on, and this happens to be the best time of the year to get the soil into the right condition. While your soil is so willing, as it is in April, for it will never be in this fine mood again, either in the month of May, June or July, put in plenty of work on it, and your little piece of earth will return to you far more than you ever gave.

Of course, experienced gardeners are always doing something for their soil, but you beginners and near-beginners whom we want especially to help in How Does Your Garden Grow must learn to get your soil into condition and you must learn to feed it. Dig around in among the established trees and shrubs, turn over the soil, let it fall loose, throw out any dead or decaying rotting roots. But remember many roots run like a mole close to the surface of the ground, such as fuchsias, hydrangeas and the feeder roots of orange trees. Many plants go sick if their roots are chopped off. Find out where your roots are; go gingerly. When you come close to a shrub or tree, better use a pronged cultivator instead of a spade. This goes for the roses too — when you feel the roots with your cultivator, stop! You have also to prepare your plots for new annuals and perennials;these I'll discuss later.

INSECTS

Another April emergency is the first crop of insects. There are the aphids, they are little but they are mighty. Remember that every seventy hours you will get a new batch of these pestiferous fellows who in their voracity will punch holes and make ruinous spots in the leaves of your most choice plants. Or they wither away tender tip growth of your roses, honeysuckle vines, stocks and many others. Keep yourself alerted to their presence.

Slugs and snails.

I was talking the other day to an experienced gardener who lives on a beautiful hill in San Francisco. She said, "Now is the time I go after snails and slugs. They move through a plot of choice annuals just like lawn mowers." The first crop of snails and slugs are moving out. Look in among the tall grassy weeds, look under the protecting leaves, the saxifragas, the ivy, in among the tall blades of your iris, and look around the rocks, under bricks and similar hiding places for those slimy slugs. Gather up the ones you find, put out poison baits to get those still hiding from you. An old fable tells of a race between a snail and a man which by some strange maneuvering the snail won. That race is still going on, and the snail is still winning. But you in your garden, warned by the magic of radio which brings you How Does Your Garden Grow, get up early and give yourself an even start and finish late in the evening with a flashlight, triumphantly in the lead. And that you may get even a greater head-start on your competitor, take notice that those little pearls of tapioca you spade up in the soil are snail or slugs eggs. When you find them, always destroy.

SPRAY

And this is the time to give your evergreen oak trees and elm trees a spraying to keep away the worms that eat tender leaves. Start around April tenth. You might get in touch with your professional with high-power equipment.

ROSE MILDEW

It is in early April when the bright days of sun compete with the overcast mist days that mildew appears first on your roses. Look closely at your bushes and climbers. You may discover the young tender leaves are taking on a powdery whiteness, the unmistakeable sign of mildew. Or you might spy on the under-surface of these leaves little red spots; they are rust. The moment you discover those enemies get busy. As I glance at the clock I fear it might be already five minutes late! A good way is to start spraying your roses right now so as to provide those tender leaves with a protective coat that the ever-present spores of mildew or rust can't unbutton. Make up a mixture, stir it up thoroughly, of 10 per cent fermate and 90 per cent dusting sulphur. When there is absolutely no wind, then with a bellows blow this mixture into your roses. The fermate in the mixture checks the rust; the sulphur dust checks the mildew. Do it every ten days and your roses will prosper this month. And mulch your roses in April; it helps the feeder roots. Use compost, peat, leaf mold. Those feeder roots are like fish; they stay up at the surface for air, and mulch always enables the air to get to the roots.

FRUIT & NUT TREES

During the month of April, spraying your pear trees is an essential job. Just as soon as the last petals have dropped from the old flowers, you should spray. You do it to control pear blight and scab which are fungus diseases, and to control the worms of the codling moth. Use the following mixture: a spray that includes a fungicide and an insecticide. See page 494. The fungicide stops the scab, the insecticide stops the moth worms. You may use this same mixture for your apples. Those of you with the early varieties of walnuts may spray with the same combination, or you may use the bordeaux mixture 8-4-50. If you have an apricot or peach tree, you can go ahead, just as soon as you are sure the frost is over in your district, with the thinning out of crowded bunches of fruit. The sooner this is done the larger the individual crop, and the surer you are of freeing your tree of brown rot and other ugly enemies. Leave three or four fruits instead of heavy clusters of seven or nine to a group. It is quality not quantity that counts.

I might add in this group of emergencies that the wild suckers in your trellis berry vines, such as boysenberry, blackberry, youngberry, should be grubbed out. Don't let them send up volunteers in the middle of the rows. Only keep the new shoots at the crowns of your plants. Do this job now too.

The fourth April emergency is the lawn. If it is under evergreen oaks these have been sending down a rain of dead leaves as they develop new ones. And these, if allowed to pile up, will kill your grass. Be dutiful and keep them raked off, and of course you can do a better job if you mow the lawn regularly. I must certainly remember to do it myself. The rains have been doing a wonderful job of keeping it in condition for you, but like many a faithful hired man, they will soon quit the job. Four out of five lawns go dry in DON'T April. Between rain squalls real warm weather comes and lawns will dry hard and start cracking. Don't permit this to happen to your lawn. Look at those grand stretches of lawn you see in Golden Gate Park. They know when to turn on the hose; and you never see dried-out lawns there.

And the last April emergency is tying and staking up new growth. During this month of April you will marvel how the new growth springs out at you. You will see new strong shoots from your delphiniums, climbing roses, on your wisteria vine and on your cotoneaster. Guide them while they are young and pliable. Keep them from slopping all around the garden. During April, watch all the new mild growth, keep it under control, place it where you want to keep it. Later, it will rather break than bend to your will.

The Opportune Task this week concerns the dahlia. Select a sunny place, always away from roots of trees and shrubs. Work up the soil thoroughly in April, get it fluffy. Set out tubers in early May. Always have the soil well worked beforehand. Dig the hole deep enough so that the tuber can be covered four or five inches, and leave a wide basin two or three inches deep for watering. Lay the tuber flat, never on end, be sure never to break the neck of the tuber because at the opposite end of the fat tuber past the neck is the eye from which new growth starts. Out of the tuber come the new roots, out of the eye comes the new spring growth. As you set out the tuber, place a stake immediately at the eye end. Never crowd your dahlias, the spacing of two and a half to three feet is best. Water well as soon as planted and about once a week until new shoots are well above ground. Irrigate thoroughly about twice a week when plants are growing vigorously and blooming. When your plants have grown a foot high you may top the new growth, this will cause more branching and make a sturdier new growth. Disbudding will encourage larger blooms and better stems. You take off small side buds and sprouts above leaves for two or three joints, the larger center bud remains. Use fertilizer sparingly. The time to fertilize is when plants are topped. Spray to prevent pests ruining your plants. Beware of the ant, keep him away. Dust with sulphur to control mildew. For a long season of bloom keep old flowers with foliage cut off and be sure to keep plants well watered at all times. Do not dig clumps until about the first of the year, leave soil on them, and store in a dry, frost-proof shed. Cut off dry stalks, stack together with their labels attached, and cover with old bags or burlap. Wash and divide at planting time.

DAHLIA CARE

CHAPTER 18

AFRICAN VIOLETS

(April: Fourth Week)

"How can I grow African Violets? Mine never bloom, the leaves become limp, turn a yellowish sickly brown and often rot off." To answer this question I propose to give a full account of the proper culture of the African Violet because many people have expressed interest in this house plant.

To begin with let us understand this plant is not a member of the true violet family, all of which come from the cooler regions of the world. This plant is called Saintpaulia after the family of the young man who discovered it. The African Violet grows wild in two places so widely separated and under such varied conditions that this fact might account for the peculiar success and failure amateurs have in growing the plant in their homes. At Tanga, East Africa, at a place only 50 to 150 feet above sea level in a rich soil under a forest canopy this plant grows a luxuriant native; and then a primeval forest 2,500 feet above sea level is the second location. At the lower station the natural soil is derived from limestone and in the fissures chuck full of rich soil it grows well; while in the higher station in the forests of Usambara in shady situations, on soil derived from granite rocks, the second stand grows. This plant still retains some of the delicacy that would be expected of a tropical product; it cannot be grown casually out-of-doors in this temperate climate but has to have an artificial indoor condition somewhat like that of its ancestors.

HISTORY

Saintpaulia or African Violet is a stemless perennial herb and if rightly handled grows easily; the most important condition is an even temperature. The plants do poorly in rooms where the temperature is allowed to become hot and then permitted to cool down. A fairly even temperature at all times must prevail. Drafts are poison! The professionals even hate to open the door to the greenhouse. Keep plants away from an opening and closing door or window.

SOIL

The only soil requirement is that it should be rich and loose. Use equal parts of good loam, screened leaf mold, sand, and some very old manure mixed in. Let me quote a letter sent in by a lady who has been raising African Violets for over ten years. "I use a soil mixture as follows: one-third good loam, one-third sand, (and I get Number 4 Monterey sand), one-third peat moss and oakleaf mold. I often put a little charcoal in the bottom of the pot to assure good drainage but this is not necessary." Always gritty river sand.

WATER

Watering properly is another secret of success in the growing of African Violets in the house. A good rule to follow is to feel the soil; when it is dry on top, give water. Another important point in this matter is to allow no water to come into contact with the hairy foliage. It is not wise for instance, for the amateur to water his plant overhead. A better way is to allow the water to reach up from a pan in which the pot is sitting. I want to read another paragraph from this same letter. "I place three little baby plants in a six-inch pot in a soup plate as no water must come from the top of the pot — only sub-irrigation. I use only luke warm water, never cold, with balanced plant food standard strength once a week using plain warm water as often as necessary to keep the surface of the ground moist." The temperature must imitate that of the tropics, that is to say, the chill must always be taken off. The nurserymen have water standing in basins in the glass-house and this water comes to the temperature of the air before they use it. And I even know an amateur who uses water as hot as it will draw from the tap. But this, of course, cools down as it climbs up through the soil in the pot. Of course, let me caution, the potted plant should never be left in a pan of water after it has become saturated. Understand that drainage must be insured; though the plants should be moist at all times they must never be kept soaked. Many times when people write in telling me their potted plants show only poor growth I can point my finger at too much water, very seldom is it too little water. And when I am shown a plant whose leaves are marred with spots I know that it has been splashed from overhead watering.

LIGHT

Now what about light? The African Violet was born in the filtered light of the tropical forest. It does not want the blazing sun. The plants like light but keep them away from the full bright sunshine. Sunshine filtering through curtains of lace or split bamboo is good; a north-east window is good, too. In the commercial house there is plenty of light but never a streak of sun. Home owners must provide good light.

PROPAGATE

Now for methods of propagation. You may start plants with care at any time, but they root more quickly in spring and summer than in fall and winter. Select a healthy leaf with a strong stem and cut it off with a sharp razor blade. Insert the stem down to the base of the leaf in sharp sand mixed with peat moss. Keep the sand moderately moist during the process of rooting which takes from four to six weeks. After the stems are well rooted, plant in small pots and grow on and when the pot fills up, shift the plant into a larger pot. But let me quote again from our letter which, by the way, comes from a woman who lives in Berkeley, and who, though confined to a wheelchair, has kept herself busy and happy raising African Violets to give to her friends. "I have enjoyed the African Violets so much that I am more than glad to tell others." About propagation she continues, "In recent years I have taken a saucer partially filled it with water in which I put a half teaspoonful of chemical food (full strength). Then I have left the leaves lying on the side of the saucer with the stem reaching into the water. There they remain not only until they form roots but until the new little leaves have fully developed to about an inch tall. I have found these leaf rooted plants are much more certain to grow fast than those rooted in sand alone. I shift them later into a sandy soil with the roots kept right on the surface; and once a week, in watering, I apply the chemical food. As the plants develop, of course, they are shifted into the regular soil mixture in shallow four-inch pots." Shallow pots are called "pans" by the nurserymen and the pans are ideal for the African Violet because they have shallow spreading roots.

Propagation is also achieved through divisions. When a plant becomes too large, divisions can be taken off the mother plants, they make roots quickly in sand and throw blooms much earlier than those from leaf cuttings.

Commercial fertilizers may be given established plants when bloom buds appear, and large flowers will unfold.

(CONTINUED FROM PAGE 130)

MAGNOLIA TREES

coming from seedling roots below the graft must be pruned off especially the deciduous kinds. Branches that sweep out into paths, etc., can be pruned; best cut close to trunk – never leave "coat hanger" stubs. ENEMIES: wind is the worst; select places in the design where wind can't blow boisterously over magnolia to tear leaves or destroy fresh blooms. Scale insects occasionally infest trees; control with summer oils. PROPAGATION: seeds, layering, grafting. VARIETIES: M. acuminata: Cucumber tree; deciduous, tall growing large thin leaves; yellowish cup-shaped green-flowers, 4 inches across, appear May or June; fruit pod cucumber shaped. M. campbellii, Campbell magnolia: deciduous; flowers rose-pink outside, lighter pink or rose inside; blooms 6-10 inches across, appear in February, occasionally first bloom buds frost injured. M. liliflora; Lily magnolia: erect growing tree up to 12 feet; deciduous; leaves unfold same time as blooms open; blooms remain half open, come about April until June. M. grandiflora: Bull Bay evergreen, large tree, slow, but erect up to 80 ft. leave large leathery, glossy, blooms in summer, flowers 10 inches across, lemon-scented, waxen white; fruit, cone-shaped out of which red seeds on strings appear. M.

(CONTINUED ON PAGE 158)

Chapter 19

PETUNIAS

(May: First Week)

Our subject is the petunia. You know it by its blossoms, long-tubed trumpets like the old gramophone horn. Rather, the horn was like the petunia, for that had flourished down in South America for ages before Edison had made his talking machine. A sun-lover, from dawn to evening twilight, it knows and tells us when summer has come to the air, and to the soil, for then it starts instantly to flourish. Blooms soon appear. The cool breeze of evening and morning floats their divine fragrance all over the garden. Drawn by the scent, the night sphinx moth scatters the pollen. The color is flashed gaily about as though by an energetic painter with two brushes and seven pots of paint.

Like an annual weed not sulking for the rights of its ancestors, but keeping alive in any old soil; blooming away all season and tossing seeds to the wind; spreading and rampaging around toward the end, sending out long, weak, bare, sprawling stalks with the blooms at the tips; still there after your vacation with no one left to attend it; resistant to most of the enemies; coming through the frostless winter and even blooming then a little; and cut down by frost but ready to spring up again from the seed, and often from the roots.

HISTORY

This is the common or garden petunia. It might sound like the ideal of all indolent gardeners. But even this plant, acting so much like a wild thing, has had much artificial culture; to reach its present stage, it has a long development;and the finer, rarer forms — not the common or garden variety, but often compact with flowers four to five inches across, rivaling the carnation, and as beautiful as the orchid — have required some of the most skilled and devoted work in all horticulture. They are costly, per plant, but to the gardener who appreciates them they are worth it.

The experts believe that our forms, both common and rare, came from two South American originals. The first one produces white trumpet-shaped flowers and starts growth as an upright plant, but ends the season by sprawling over everywhere. The second original produces purplish-violet flowers, which are fragrant like the white form, but the flower has a broad throat and a short tube, having lost the true trumpet shape. Neither of these ever gave much promise of their rainbow offspring. Anyway, some traveler brought them home to Europe, for more than a century ago colored hybrids of them were cheerfully prospering in many gardens and in many forms there. The petunia came here too; escaped and became native — it has run along the sandy stream bottoms from Santa Clara and Sacramento counties through Southern California to Texas, and even as far as Florida, making an annual ground covering mat with tiny rounded leaves and purplish flowers which you scarcely would pay attention to. This is what happens to the petunia when it is neglected altogether. Petunias like pelargoniums and fuchsias are now in a boom. California and the East are both strongly interested in them.

HABIT

What about the habit of growth? The first garden hybrids were high growing and scraggly, and were single-flowered. Then from these scraggly singles a sport appeared and this was more compact, had short growth and short stems. The gardeners by using the pollen from the flowers of these compact sports crossed them back and forth, back and forth — for it takes a long time to establish a character in new plants — until now you and I can grow from seed petunias of compact habit. Remember a new character may appear once and then the chances are thereafter it will fail. The experts tell me it may require six years before a desirable character is established and dependable. Now our hybrids do not sprawl but grow bunchy and compact. But still, some of the plants of the new generation will revert to the habits of their ancestors.

But there was more to it than this. The gardeners were anxious to make the flowers not only compact, but more interesting. They early noticed a sport on an ordinary scraggly garden plant which carried a big blossom with beautifully fringed petals. And this, after long labor, they developed into permanent form. Similarly they developed giant flowers with ruffled petals. At the same time they dwarfed plants to neat compact forms, and they magnified the blossoms of the blooms up to four to six inches in diameter with ruffled petals and shallow throats.

Finally the petunia reached its greatest development in forms that were semi-double, double and even what is called double-double with petals full and many-skirted. And some of these choice flowers were on plants so compact that they were called dwarfs and extreme dwarfs.

And so in our gardens today we have petunias that sprawl, others that grow compact, still others that trail and are used for hanging pots. Then we have the single flowers and the double flowers. What about the colors? The rainbow is complete except for yellow and orange. 'You may select petunias with clear pink flowers, pale-rose, velvety-purple, and one that is called balcony blue, like the sky; then there is one a deep wine red, another mauve, and all kinds of white forms from ivory to lily white. Further, you may have fringed flowers with sharp edges to the petals; the ruffled types with petals smooth and wavy; and the

COLORS

frilled types which are ruffled double, with tightly folded petals. Many of the common garden flowering types have flowers with wide open petals of smooth edges. And many of these like the chrysanthemums and fuchsias have been baptised with lovely names — *NAMES* Old Lace, of a purple hue; Rose Jade, with a deep rose color; Snowball, fringed petals of pure white; Shasta, as white as the mountain itself; and recently one named Commentator Wilson.

What are the uses of the petunias in the garden? The singles are bedding types (bedding in the garden language is a term used to denote the massing of plants for show effects); and the fringed big flowers are used as annuals. A few plants may carry over the winter or may seed themselves and appear the following spring *USE* as volunteers. As annuals, they are planted like great carpets in the full sun; such a mass effect gives a strong effect in the summer garden. Here the painter sometimes throws away his brush for awhile and goes splashing the paint around directly. They go in front of the shrub border, down the garden path, and into blocks of vivid color, sweeping onward into the partial shade. And single colors, as the Rose of Heaven, carry a long driveway or grass path into brilliant life when planted as a border. The use of single colors can give the garden a new tool to bring out the design. But beds of jangled colors surprise us often by creating, not discord, but a kind of brilliant harmony. The bloom crop is so heavy that for weeks you can't see the foliage. The singles are often planted in window boxes with individual colors planted to each box. Long stemmed ones which are called "balcony petunias" serve well here and in porch boxes, in the hanging pots, and urns. And I can tell you, filled with bright color, they will lift the architecture.

The giant ruffles and the doubles are used as perennials; in our frostless areas they winter out of doors, but in colder climates are taken indoors. These plants too are selected for bedding planting, and many times for the specimen. They have individuality in shape, type, and color of bloom, and have become true favorites. Petunias are so generous with their flowers, especially if given a happy home, that they serve well as cut flowers for the house, and they last a long time then. You can pick all day, you can give every guest an armful, and not miss them at all. Cut the petunia back and it grows more readily and keeps throwing blooms.

Give your petunias sun all day if you can, or at least for the morning hours. Keep them out of the middle of the garden. Don't let them steal the show by distracting attention from everything else. Tame them with other plants; put them where they will blend in with trees, shrubs, perennials and other summer-flowering annuals. Petunias combine well with the blue flowers and delphiniums make a lovely background.

Where do you get your petunias? Seeds primarily, but note they often give you many reversions. Your packet said "pink" or "select rose", and when the seedlings bloomed you discovered a menagerie of plebians and aristocrats all living cheerfully together. This can happen even if you paid a big price for the packet. When the growers plant their seeds, they have to rogue out their seedlings — that is, they detect the rogue in its infancy and "put it away". Perhaps at some wonderful future time, we shall be able to follow this idea in disposing of infant Hitlers and other ambitious bomb droppers and throat-cutters. The seeds are tiny; one ounce yields two hundred thousand. (Someone, it seems, has counted them!) You can plant first in flats. Or, you can start in the open ground by broadcasting when the weather becomes settled. Then you can get plants from the nurseryman. You can buy them in flats or in pots. But when you get plants from the nurseryman, find out how he got them.

In the Hall of Flowers at Treasure Island in 1939, you and I had our eyes opened to the petunia. There we saw flowers of every description, but it was always at the fuchsia exhibit and the petunia exhibit that we had trouble seeing them at all because of the great crowds at the tables. Why was this? We know already about the fuchsias, but in the petunias it was the effort of one man. Like his favorite plants, he came to California from afar. Otto Meerly first looked upon a petunia in a glass house in the Swiss Alps; he was fascinated with the flower. When he came to America he landed in an estate in the East, and there he worked with this interesting group of plants; but when he reached California, he really got down to business. Mr. Meerly started hybridizing petunias in 1932, and he has produced some fine types. One with large rosy pink flowers he's named for his daughter, Susan. He lives a few blocks from me in Menlo Park and last summer I went out to his place, and there was a petunia carpet that covered an acre of land. He was on his knees pollenating the many petticoated doubles with a camel's hair brush. He cut the ends of the petals off, so he could reach inside. From one flower he had cut off the anthers, and now he was brushing the pollen from another flower to the pistils. Then he enclosed the flower in a cellophane sack so no other pollen could get in. He tagged his plant, and later in the year he harvested the seed of a new hybrid. Of course elsewhere in the world other hybridizers have been working, as Mrs. Theodosia Shepherd of Ventura, California, Geo. J. Ball of West Chicago, and T. Sakata, a Japanese student who sent us excellent forms just before the war started.

I asked Mr. Meerly, what are the hybridizers struggling for? What is their goal? "First," he said, "toward low-growing, compact habit; second, still larger flowers; third, richer color with distinct tones, and with less fading in the California sun; and finally, to increase the percentage of doubles from seed."

CUTTINGS But petunias are not always propagated directly from seeds — you can take cuttings. These are made in late August and September. The cuttings are from the new growth, never from the woody stock. Rooted in sand, potted later in a neutral soil, the young plants are carried through the winter in moist, not wet, soil; in the glass house handle them as you would a geranium keeping them on the dry side in winter, only watering them occasionally.

What kind of soil do petunias want? If you start seeds in flats, use a neutral soil, one with absolutely no manure or fertilizer. Use a mixture of one-third top soil, one-third sand, one-third leaf mold, and the top soil and leaf mold screened. Cover the seeds slightly with sand, never with peat or leaf mold. Sand checks packing and drying. This is important because the delicate seedling shoots are not prepared for foundry work and can't hammer their way through a crust. Sand here doesn't pack so that the germinating seeds can get through easily. In the garden, when it's time to set the petunia out, have a well-prepared spot ready. The growing petunia can take a rich soil, richer in fact, than any other annual. Thus you work in a lot of good well-rotted cow manure or even horse manure if you have it. And above all, make the ground fluffy. Later on when your plants are coming into bloom, feed them with a quick acting, well-balanced commercial fertilizer. If the petunia has to grow on a starvation diet, expect only small flowers. Watering: keep them moist, especially after planting them, and while the plants are growing.

SOIL

Enemies: only sow bugs and snails attack them. Plenty of poison baits will defend them.

How do you keep them flowering? Just keep picking!

The Opportune Task: You and I will have to pay for this glorious weather. First by watering freely. Don't let the lawn dry out; once cracks get in, once the root crown becomes brown, you will have a job on your hands getting water down. So watch it now. Water so the soil doesn't bake; this goes for the flower beds and rose garden, too. March and April are months the evergreen oak drops its old leaves. Rake them up. I raked off my lawn twenty wheelbarrows of these just yesterday; they went to the compost pile, and my lawn was relieved of a messy covering which would have packed and killed out many grass crowns. Get after those snails and slugs that are moving out in armies from the ivy covered fences, from under the protecting leaves of the acanthus, from under the agapanthus where they multiply but never eat the leaves. Get your baits around now. Don't overlook those aphids that are sucking the life out of your stock, honeysuckle, roses, and even your spireas. And worst of all on the cherry tree. These are just reminders.

(CONTINUED FROM PAGE 150)

MAGNOLIA soulangiana: hybrid, large shrub or tree; deciduous, blooms purplish, occasionally white; in fact there are several forms of this one of the most favorite of deciduous magnolias. Flowers appear late February-March.

The Play of Shadows.

CHAPTER 20

TUBEROUS ROOTED BEGONIAS

(May: Second Week)

In December I told you how to store tuberous begonias. (See December, Third Week.) This year I told you to take your bulbs out of storage and start them off. (See February, Third Week.)* But I have never really given you a full talk on these popular plants, I want to do just that. We talk about tuberous begonias because now is the time to put these bulbs out

into the garden; and now is the time for seedlings to go out into the garden if you grew them yourself. Another good reason for selecting this subject is that we have in the studio Mrs. Verna Schath of Redwood City. Both she and her husband have devoted twenty years to growing these plants professionally and they have learned the answers. Before I start the questions, however, I want to paint the background.

HISTORY

There are 400 to 500 species of begonias; the beautiful leaved froms are found in the lofty rain forests of equatorial Africa where they grow wild among tree ferns, orchids, and coleus, those patterned leaved plants you saw at the California Spring Garden Show in Oakland two weeks ago, and among the graceful club mosses and delicate liverworts living in trees.

*See (January Second Week: Opportune Task Growing Tuberous Begonias from seed).

They grow in the wet forests of the Malay Peninsula, the Southernmost point of continental Asia; they are found also in Borneo and up in the Philippines where certain forms grow up as high as a man's head. But today we confine our attention to one type of begonia, the tuberous rooted, which comes from Mexico, Central and South America. The name begonia honors a Frenchman, Michel Begon, superintendent of the botanical gardens at Santo Domingo.

Mrs. Schath, let us discuss planting the established bulb; what is your recommendation for soil preparation for tuberous begonias?

SOIL Schath: That all depends; if you have never grown begonias before then first study your soil. If you find clay or adobe, remove from six to twelve inches and replace with two parts leaf mold, one part well-rotted cow manure; manure that is at least six months old; one part propagating sand, this is Marysville River sand; and one part peat to hold moisture.

Wilson: And of course you have a recommendation on drainage.

Schath: Be sure drainage is good; if you find water stands or drains slowly, place two or three inches of broken crocks or coarse gravel in the plot before dumping in the good soil.

Wilson: That gives the beginner the right idea for proper soil preparation; what do you recommend for the more experienced?

Schath: To them I caution: beware of packed soil. Recondition the soil in the old beds — that is, spade over; if you find it heavy, add generously coarse leaf mold; and add also a little manure for food; do this every year; these provide food and fluff up the ground; and fluffy soil, as I have heard you tell over the radio, is necessary for the fibrous roots.

Wilson: You mentioned peat a moment ago. What is your rule for placing peat around tuberous begonias?

Schath: Peat is used only for holding moisture. If you applied it last year to the plot, then this year all you need is a light sprinkling on the top of the bed which may be raked into the top inch. Too much peat sours the soil and rots the bulbs.

Wilson: How do you go about planting the established bulb?

Schath: First the sprouts on the bulbs should be at least two inches high before they are taken out of the starting flat and planted in the garden. You have already told how easy it is to start these bulbs in flats;* and they should never be rushed, or taken out of the flats too soon. Begonias don't belong out in the garden till the chill of spring is gone.

Wilson: Then when the new growth is two inches high and the evenings are warm you proceed.

Schath: Just lift the bulb from the flat, keeping all the soil that sticks to the roots.

Wilson: How should those roots look when the bulb is first removed from the flat?

Schath: You'll find dozens of delicate white, thready roots clinging to the particles of leaf mold and sand. Everyone of those roots is valuable to the plant, and they should not be destroyed or rubbed off when the bulb is being lifted from the starting flat.

Wilson: Out in the garden, how deep do you have to plant these bulbs with all their new white thready roots.

Schath: Plant them no deeper than they were in the flat.

Wilson: Then you don't push the bulb down into the fluffed-up soil after all? (Some experts do just that!)

Schath: No, all you do is make a hole large enough to receive the bulbs; just rest the bulb and firm the soil around. I have found this method will result in your bulb showing a little above the soil level and that is where it should be. I found large bulbs had rotted in summer, and this I learned was due to water lying in the cavity of the bulb.

Wilson: Where is this cavity?

Schath: Where the stem joins the bulb; it rests in the pocket.

Wilson: Do all begonias have pocketed bulbs?

*See (February Third Week: Opportune Task.)

Schath: Yes, practically all; I have also found that bulbs of frilled varieties, such as "Fascination", are flat with no cavity.

Wilson: Now, Mrs. Schath, do you want to tell the amateur how he can make dead sure his flowers will face him instead of the wall?

Schath: It's not a secret, it's just how nature has ruled for the tuberous begonia. If the gardener will look closely at the leaves atop the two-inch growth, he will find them pointed at one end; at the other they are rounded. When putting the growing plant in the garden, just make sure the points face you; the flowers of the tuberous begonias always face toward the points of the leaves.

Wilson: So far we have been discussing bulbs that have been started in flats. Let us shift now to the seedlings, the new little plants from seeds started last January. How should the amateur proceed with them now?

SEEDLING

Schath: Go out to the lath house or place where you have grown the seedlings. Take a ruler and measure; if the young plant stands up two inches high, it is ready to plant out.

Wilson: You take care in moving the seedlings of course.

Schath: Yes, even more care than for the established bulb because all you have is a small amount of thready roots clinging to the soil. I might say that the biggest cause for failure with seedlings is the robbing of the soil from the delicate fibrous roots; when these youngsters are being shifted, let every fiber hang on to every bit of soil and leaf mold.

Wilson: Then you proceed with planting the seedlings just as you do with the established tuberous roots?

Schath: Yes.

Wilson: Where in the garden have you found is the best exposure for tuberous begonias?

LOCATION

Schath: That all depends upon where your garden is located. In San Francisco, around Monterey and Santa Cruz, the plants can be grown in open gardens because of the overcast filtered sunlight. But down the Peninsula district to 35 miles south of San Francisco, and over in Marin County north of San Francisco, they grow best under oak trees, in lath houses or in the garden with sun up to 10 o'clock and shade the rest of the day; or shade all day till 3 o'clock after which direct sun is all right. Tuberous begonias can't stand direct midday sun.

Wilson: What do you recommend for begonias in the Great Valley; or inland Southern California?

Schath: There they can be grown in shade. In the shade tuberous begonias incline toward leggy growth. They must be staked. In the shade they will get light but no direct sun. And to these gardeners of the Great Valley I want to say add plenty of peat in the original soil mixture, and with a top dress of peat in the plot or in the pot if the begonias are being grown in pots. In the warm air, this additional peat holds moisture.

Wilson: We haven't said a word about water; what schedule do you recommend? *WATER*

Schath: Be sure and get the watering done early in the morning; before 10:30 is the best time. Because by doing so you give the ground a chance to warm up and keep this warmth during the night. Cold soggy ground at night brings disaster to the blooms, especially the large showy male blossoms. At night they drop every time if the ground stays cold and moist. And if they or the lower leaves drop, they rot, causing a fungus mold which first infects the stem of the plant and then works down to kill the bulb.

Wilson: Can you sprinkle overhead safely?

Schath: You can when the sun is not shining directly on the plants. Big drops standing on flowers with hot sun shining result in ugly brown burns.

Wilson: When should you start feeding tuberous begonias? *FEED*

Schath: Start feeding when the first flower bud appears. On a seedling this will be about the middle of June, on the established bulb this can be as early as the last week of April or the beginning of May, depending upon the time you started the bulb.

Wilson: What fertilizers have you used?

Schath: To answer this question I'd like to make a suggestion. The items of all commercial plant foods are labelled. Select one high in phospheric acid, which always develops blooms. Follow directions on the package. Fishmeal has been the old standby. For a seven-inch pot a tablespoon given once every six weeks does the trick.

Wilson: Of course you just don't throw it down on the begonia.

Schath: I always put it two inches away from the bulb, and two inches deep; the active roots don't get burned though they get the benefit. And I might add the one tablespoon to a seven-inch pot every six weeks goes for bloodmeal, and cottonseed meal too. I've found that if any of these foods is placed too close to the bulb you can tell immediately by the leaves; they will turn brown and crumple upon touch.

Wilson: You haven't mentioned sheep manure.

Schath: Sheep manure is OK, a little every two weeks is all right. First wet the ground, then apply lightly on the soil.

Wilson: What about liquid fertilizers? You know they have a lot of them on the market now.

Schath: Liquids from the animal manures should be used about the color of weak tea, once a week. The commercial liquid fertilizers give their own recommendations.

Wilson: How long do you keep on feeding tuberous begonias?

DON'T Schath: Never feed begonias after September 15; later than that date makes the plant leggy.

Wilson: And now what have you learned about the enemies of tuberous begonias. How many real enemies have they?

ENEMIES Schath: Nematodes in the soil attack the bulbs. See page 494 for controls. The worm of the oak moth chews the top tip growth of the begonia plant. When you discover him pick by hand and destroy him. Control ants, keep them away from your tuberous begonias. Keep also the mites from attacking the leaves. They cause the leaves to curl. Summer oil sprays discourage mites, so does sulphur dust.

Wilson: And now a final question: what is your opinion about pinching off the flowers?

Schath: That duty is reserved only for the hanging basket forms. These plants must be pinched back to make large specimens. The first flower bud appears; all that has to be done is to pinch out the center in each shoot; this is done just once; if, however, a fuller plant is wanted, then a second pinching can be given. *

Wilson: Let us outline what should be done for tuberous begonias in the late fall. All summer we enjoy the beautiful flowers, but as the season comes to a close we see the leaves turn yellow and some of the lower ones have fallen to the ground; what about those fallen leaves?

Schath: Fallen leaves, even the fallen flowers lying on the ground, decay and cause fungus, in addition to the other agents of decay. All fallen leaves and blooms from now on must be picked up and destroyed. It is very dangerous to permit this to go on around healthy begonia plants. My system is to go through the bed and pick up every fallen leaf and flower; in fact, I do this all summer long because I want to keep that fungus out.

Wilson: Will half-decayed leaves lying against a stem or lying on another leaf do any harm?

Schath: Definitely yes. It works this way; in the cells of the leaf is an acid sap. This sap, in direct contact with other leaves, especially moist ones at night, eats through and creates a mucous brown spot, and acting like a poison eats its way rapidly right down into the bulb. Once it starts, there's no cure.

Wilson: What does this decay look like; will it destroy the bulb?

Schath: It is a thick brown slime; it hastens down the stem and I've found it does kill the bulb. I've dug up the bulbs, and every time when I neglected to keep out decaying leaves and blooms I have found a rotten bulb instead of a firm one that should have been there.

Wilson: How about the soil; do these rotting leaves contaminate it?

Schath: Again I answer, indeed they do — leave them there and your fungus will be waiting for your new bulbs in spring.

Wilson: I believe you have made that part clear, but back again to the yellowing leaves; the more leaves turning yellow, the smaller the flowers become.

Schath: Yes, that's just it, and sometimes more singles than doubles appear and then you know the tuberous begonia season is over. However, I will say I have had people on January 2nd call me on the phone and tell me they are sitting at the window looking upon their tuberous begonia under the oak tree and still have color there. They say the plants just won't go to sleep and they ask what they should do.

Wilson: But of course that is unusual isn't it? Don't tuberous begonia bulbs go to sleep by early December?

Schath: Ordinarily that is the case. In a very well protected location, and if we have a mild winter, they don't want to go to sleep.

Wilson: Then in October shouldn't we take up opportune tasks for our tuberous begonias?

Schath: We must get ready to dig the bulbs up; we must first get them to slow down, the bulb must prepare itself for the long rest that's coming.

Wilson: And how do you proceed.

Schath: First, realize that there is a whole lot of food in the healthy leaves and healthy stem that must go down into the bulb where it can be stored for next year's use. And the way to get that food down is to withhold the water. This takes time; it must be done gradually.

CARE AFTER BLOOM

Wilson: What's the best method?

Schath: Instead of daily watering so necessary in the summer, give water only about twice a week and sparingly, put it on of course with a fine spray.

Wilson: Explain what that does.

Schath: The bulb not getting its accustomed water from the ground draws the sap down from above and brings the food with it.

Wilson: What sign tells you the tuberous begonia bulb is ready to be dug, especially in middle California.

Schath: Just look at your plant, notice if most of the leaves have dropped; all that is left is a stem; that is a pretty good sign.

Wilson: But if your plant stays green, I mean a few green leaves are still on the top, then what?

Schath: You can safely break off the top as long as you leave ten to twelve inches of the stem standing. Now the important point is to tell if the bulb is ready to be dug up, gently tap the standing stem; if it falls over, the bulb below is ready; but never break the stem off. DON'T

Wilson: Then the stem falls down of its own weight when the bulb is ready, and why must you never break the stem off?

Schath: Breaking the stem off robs the bulb of its only chance to properly seal. When a friend brings me a tuberous begonia bulb and I see it is shriveled up like a dried prune I know at once the stem was broken by force. The bulb had no chance to store up the food or to seal the bud.

Wilson: And what happens when a tuberous begonia bulb looks shrivelled up like a prune?

Schath: In the first place in spring when the sprouts come they are more or less dried looking, weak and oftentimes wither up altogether. Nine times out of ten if the plant does sprout it will be so weak it dies and should it go on to flowering the blooms are mediocre because in the beginning there was no reserve food.

Wilson: What do you look for in a properly sealed bulb?

Schath: It is round and feels very firm.

Wilson: We're a little ahead of our story in a way — we haven't yet taken the bulbs out of the ground. How do you do that; how do you dig up the bulbs?

Schath: I generally use a trowel. Shove it under the bulb and gently pry up.

Wilson: When the bulb is out of the ground how do you dry it?

SURE BULBS

Schath: There are two methods. In the first, wash off all the soil from the bulb and place in a flat, put the flat in the sun to dry. Of course I had thousands of bulbs so I placed them on a screen and ran water over from the hose. With a few bulbs you can just wash them in a basin.

Wilson: You don't scrub them, do you?

Schath: No! Heavens no! You must very carefully wash them, get rid of the dirt, leave the roots clean, and above all do not break the skin.

Wilson: How do you dry them?

Schath: All day long right in the hot sun I leave the flat. A couple of times a day I run out there and roll the bulbs around so a new surface gets the hot sun. At night I bring all the flats indoors. If the flat is wet, then I transfer the bulbs to a new bone-dry flat.

Wilson: How long does it take to thoroughly dry a bulb?

Schath: Approximately seven days if the weather is sunny.

Wilson: That was your first method, what is your second method of drying bulbs for winter storage?

Schath: In the second method there is no washing. I lift the bulbs, shake off as much dirt as possible and then I lay them in the flat out in the sun, of course. Each evening I take the flats in, for fear of dew or rain. I remove whatever soil has dried that day by gently rubbing my hand over them.

Wilson: And what if it keeps on raining?

Schath: Then I recommend the second method; all that is necessary is to take them into a good ventilated place and keep the bulbs away from heat, furnace, gas or stove. The air automatically dries the soil. Later, after all the soil is removed, at the first opportunity after the sun shines again, I take those bulbs out and leave them in the sun two or three days longer.

Wilson: Do you dust the bulbs with anything before storing?

Schath: I have never done so.

Wilson: How do you store the bulbs? STORE

Schath: I place them in the flat, singly, not piled upon one another. I select a cool dark dry place, one that gets lots of fresh air. Every two weeks I take a look; I search for mold in particular; it attacks usually from the outside or at the sealed bud points. Whenever I discover a moldy bulb I throw it out; I don't believe in taking a chance.

Wilson: Supposing, Mrs. Schath, before the begonia bulbs are mature enough to take out of the ground you want the place for your winter cinerarias? Cinerarias can't wait, you know.

Schath: Lift the begonias just as they are growing; take up with each about four inches of soil around the bulb. Place in a flat or in a box; and move to another shady place. Then you proceed just as I've already described; continuing watering lightly watching the foliage. When the stems drop off, lift the bulb, put in the sun to dry and store for the winter.

Wilson: I remember in one of your guest talks you gave some ideas of how to prepare the soil for next year; that is, if cinerarias are not going to be planted in the begonia place. Don't you want to repeat that?

Schath: First of all, I like to give a generous sprinkling of bone meal; just make the ground dusty white, and work it in well. I also spread out fresh manure, which can be fresh because it will have all winter to be washed down. The ground is left rough; and this is far better than waiting till spring.

Wilson: What about potted tuberous begonias? POTTED CARE

Schath: You lay the pot on its side in a dry airy place. Proceed just as with the plants in the open ground; that is, watch for rotting leaves; wait till the stem drops off. You can leave the bulb in the pot in a dry airy place.*

Opportune Task: For planting outdoor carnations, review chapter, "Carnations" — October: Third Week.

*See Questions and Answers — Can tuberous begonias be left out in the garden in winter? December: Third Week.

Chapter 21

FORM AND COLOR

(May: Third Week)

We consider here form and color; what we take away from the flower show is a memory of these features. It has no meaning otherwise, for the garden is precisely equivalent to the impression it makes on our senses. A blind person is handicapped, as we say. But through his delicately trained touch, smell, and hearing, the part he gets may nevertheless become exquisitely real to him. The total value, the amount of garden, varies with the quantity and quality of sensory impression; what is left to the blind man can carry him miles beyond the man with two good eyes who notices nothing.

Now, what we take notice of depends on our interests. A man hiding from enemies in the mountains back of Manila would be sniffing the air all day and all night, and would learn the scent of his enemy — he would taste him at a distance in that game of life and death along the alleyways of the forest. But that same man could drive his car down Market Street every day for ten years without once sniffing the air. In fact, our senses go dim if we don't have to use them.

Well, for the sharpest garden delights we must wake up these senses, no matter how long they have been dead to the world. We must go to the garden directly, along the paths of sight, smell and touch — we must use those paths in the sharpest possible way. Our first impulse is of course the opposite of this. We may work away merely calling plants by their names. We may accept the base rumor that all foliage is green, and not once use our eyes to see that it runs all the way through silver gray, gray green, olive green, cypress green, to wood brown, red and yellow; or to see that the upper and lower leaf surfaces are of quite different tones; and that the aspens for that reason tremble and twinkle in a breath of air. Or, nothing counts for us but flowers alone; and we forget the pleasure of a cool twilight glen of fern fronds, moss, trunks, leaves; with a little glistening, dark pool half hidden in the midst of it; and in the midst, too, the tiny voice of water trickling down the rocks to keep it all moist. Or we forget all else and put our minds on perfection of growth. Let me give you an example. You know the perfume of the petunia in evening and morning. At these times of day, the particles of scent ride in droplets of moisture. In the Flower Show a freshly watered petunia bed looked just right and I advanced toward it all expectation, like a honey bee stuck my nose eagerly into a lovely four inch bloom, and drew a long, ecstatic breath. But something was suddenly wrong. I was in full retreat backward, gasping and clawing the air. A little girl cried out, "What did you say, mister?" I answered as best I could, "Fish meal!"

What it comes down to is that we need a just balance in our gardens between the departments of form, color and perfume. Let us look at these departments one by one.

Form and, of course, size along with it govern the place of the individual tree, shrub, or plant in the design. Here is a list of the more common forms, with examples. The experienced listener will recognize at once in what parts of the garden each can go. The spire -- the birch and the Monterey Pine. (In this pine the lower limbs are modestly hidden in a skirt of foliage.) The spire, without the skirt — the Italian Cypress used at house corners. The spike — the acanthus, the leaves of which the Greeks used to embellish their columns; issuing from a skirt of dark, shiny, deeply divided, beautifully veined leaves. The artichoke with its spray of leaves dividing and spread out like fingers — silver-blue-gray-veined, well groomed; sending up its spikes to bear the flowers which are eaten green, or which left to mature become big, cobalt-blue, thistle blossoms; at any stage, unless they are sprayed,the aphid's happy home. Other spikes are hollyhocks, delphiniums, and foxgloves — all good to back up the perennial border.

TYPES The pyramid: juvenile giant sequoia and the incense cedar.

Vase-shaped, as the elm.

Open to the sky, as the apricot and peach.

Umbrella or saucer-headed: the Italian Stone Pine that some of our boys saw in Southern Europe; and the Bunyabunya tree that others saw in Australia.

Arching, tumbling like a waterfall: the weeping willow, the Chinese Cotoneaster pannosa.

Ball or head, hoisted in the air: oak, maple and the buckeye.

Ball low down near the ground: many potted plants, hebes, boxwood used for hedges, ageratum, and marguerite.

Gnarled, knobby, corkscrew: table quince, pepper, some old oaks, and old Mother Lode rose bushes.

Prostrate, hugging the ground, weather beaten: horizontal cotoneaster; seacoast plants beaten into the bank; junipers and pines at the high mountain divides weighted to the ground by the winter snow blanket, and holding the pose all the year through.

Bunchy, branches breaking from root crown holding flowers at tips: oleander, and hibiscus.

Forest of stems or sticks standing straight up, each sending out branches with flowers at tips: Japanese Rose (Kerria) and privet.

Sprawling, climbing, attached, blanketing, moving, curtaining, rampaging: Banksia rose, grapes, bougainvillea.

The individual leaf blades are: heart-shaped, spear-shaped, round, oval, oblong, bulging outward, long and narrow. The margins of the leaves are: smooth, toothed, notched, and cut or, as they say, incised. The stem holds up the leaf sometimes at the center, as a waiter holds a tray on his hand; but more often in an incision in the base, sometimes slight, sometimes deep. The blooms occur on the plant either around the outside, on the tips of the new wood, as in the fuchsias and flax. Or they come all through the foliage as in the broom.

FLOWER FORMS

The blooms themselves have as many forms as the plants have dispositions and tastes. One of the commonest is the daisy-form — the central disc bordered by ray petals. The petals may stand stiffly out; or as in some of the most prized chrysanthemums, they may make a droopy fringe.

Other bloom forms are the tube as in some fuchsias; the bell, as in the campanula and canterbury bell; two lobes — the salvia; star shaped — the forget-me-not; trumpet — the morning glory; lipped sack — the snapdragon; overlapping petals in a whorl — the rose; and the cup with a spur like the nasturtium.

Now for color. This we certainly take for granted and don't half use. The world is full of it from great blotches as big as a mountain, to the steel-blue glint on a beetle's wing. What wouldn't a blind soldier give for just one glint a day! Yet we waste a million glints an hour, we have so many of them. That's perfectly natural and perfectly natural too is the fact that, as we have more gardens in this country, we are getting more interested and seeing more color.

SELECT COLOR WITH CARE

To see color, we have to distinguish it, and to distinguish it, we have to name it. Fortunately the names, of which there are thousands, can be simplified. The physicists, who know their color, say that all you have to do is pitch them out the window and let in the rainbow. The meaning is that all the colors are in the rainbow. They can be arranged around a circle grading continuously from yellow to orange, to red, to green, to violet, to blue, and back to yellow again. You can put any hue, which is the name for the pure color, somewhere in this circle — for example, a particular fuchsia blossom lies between red and violet, and it can therefore be called violet-red. Or it might be a tint of violet-red, that is, it might be diluted with white. Or it might be a shade, diluted with black. Furthermore, keeping the same hue and the same tint or shade, it might be either a strong or a weak dose of color. Precisely the same hue could have all these variations according to light, shade and intensity.

The idea is that unless you are an expert the usual color names slip vaguely around your tongue. But, by using this simple scheme, in no time anyone not color-blind can learn to see his colors precisely. A color circle, which you can get at any art store, will prove a tireless friend.

For if you don't see the colors precisely, you're as badly off as a tone-deaf man trying to put together notes of the musical scale. What you want in your gardens is not a jangle, not a yelping menagerie of plants which can't live together or let anyone else live, but a harmony. There are short cuts to this result by means of the color circle. The complementary hues such as orange and blue which come opposite to each other in the circle, do well together especially if they are not in equal quantity. The softer-tinted are the easiest to fit in. Also the hues lying alongside each other in the circle go well together — such as orange-yellow, orange and orange-red. But if you try to stick a strong orange next, not to its complementary opposite, but to a hue only a quarter way around the circle such as a violet-red, you get something to pain the eye. Out in the woods the plants get on well with one another in a group, partly because the foliage tones them down, and partly because they are climate-controlled, and somehow, climates create a wild natural harmony. For example, the flowers tend toward the quiet tones from blue through violet to red, with a good proportion also of white and yellow. In the tropics the flowers are more flamboyant from red through orange to yellow. The members naturally harmonize well enough within each group. But when we bring cool temperates and tropicals together, as we have done here in California, we have to take care.

I went out to see Professor Mendelowitz of the Stanford Art Department and he said: "In all this go in for good massing and in this way create a good strong color sensation. And remember that contrast creates color emphasis. For example, if you put a row of red geraniums against a red brick wall, the colors kill each other, and all you have of interest is your green foliage. But if you use white geraniums, everything comes to life. The greater the color the greater the contrast. The very strong red must have with it other strong colors. One can't just put red and blue together, for instance, without considering their brilliancy." Another thing Professor Mendelowitz said was, "Some of the very brilliant oranges are difficult to combine harmoniously with the other garden flowers. They are apt to be so strong and harsh that they overpower the more delicately tinted blossoms." But the orange Gazania so often used in the sunny parking strip is softened beautifully with the gray foliaged white flowering creeper, called "Snow in Summer."

COLOR IN SHADE

The following is a simple list of combinations that will do in partial shade:

1. Fuchsias background; white fibrous rooted begonias border.

2. Tall fuchsias background; multicolored tuberous rooted begonia foreground.

3. Tall pastel fuchsias background; hybrid, white, blue, lavender, pink on to red hydrangeas, foreground. Any blues and lavenders can go with fuchsias and conversely yellow and orange are likely to be bad.

4. Ferns background; variegated ivy foreground. Here and there white, lavender, and rose foxglove.

5. Mass planting multicolored begonia background, lobelia foreground. But if the deep red begonias prevail, then use the deep blue lobelia; if pastels are dominant, use the light blue lobelia. You don't want the borders to overpower the rest.

6. Meadow rue and foxglove in the background, and in front mass planting of Canterbury Bells, white, pink, and lavender and the blue lace flower.

7. Other plants that will go in the shade are forget-me-nots, the white tobacco so sweet at night time, the bleeding heart.

8. In addition you can cajole into the shade

petunias, violas, iris, and some of the lovely calceolaria called "lady's purses", that we saw at the Flower Show.

COLOR IN SUN

These we've been speaking of are for partial shade; now for summer combinations for the sunny spots:

1. Tall French Marigolds, lemon to gold, with the medium ageratum, Zinnia linearis and a border of the low light blue lobelia.

2. Hybrid cosmos in mixed colors for the background; then for medium height blue Aster frikartii; with a foreground of the long blooming white Esther Read shasta daisies. Or even red salvia background with Esther Read foreground.

3. For a mixture standing lower; in back, deep purple petunias; next the very dwarf French Marigold, which is called Tagetes; and next a border of lobelia.

4. For two-toned combinations of low plants, use Zinnia linearis, with ageratum; or phlox and ageratum, or pink geraniums with ageratum.

5. Or white phlox with blue campanula; or violet blue with red, as columbines with coral bells; and with deep violet or white iris on the side.

6. And yellow coreopsis with deep blue delphiniums.

7. Or for a strong effect, use red or yellow coxcomb for center and a border of ageratum. The men, you know, go for the reds and yellows.

8. There are of course a thousand and one other good ones. You seasoned gardeners will remember from some past year a combination which was good above everything. Let us hear about it so we can pass it around.

And now for the Opportune Task: Spring is coming to a close, the daffodils have finished long ago; tie up their old leaves, do not cut them off, but make braids or knots of them and fork in the ends, so that you can get ready to put in other plants there. Ranunculus too are through; unless these plants are in a bed of their own you will want to get them out of the way. Some of you may want to collect seeds, but those who are not going to do so might clear up the space and prepare the soil afresh. In fact, clear out all spent annuals; winter stock, forget-me-nots, and calendulas. Get the sun-lovers in the ground now — zinnias, petunias, French and African marigolds, phlox — all should be planted now for summer and early fall flowers. Prune back the spring-flowering shrubs, that are through; tie up flopping rose branches, the climbers especially.

CLIVIA

CLIVIA: long time favourite in California gardens; ideal house plant. Leaves dagger-like, upright, arching, wide, dark green. Outdoors plants do best in good light under high shade, never under direct sun. SOIL must be rich in leaf mold, organic material like compost is ideal for the thick fleshy absorbant roots. Depth is important in which root crown is even with soil level, somewhat like the garden cyclamen. POTTED PLANTS : soil similar; roots like crowded conditions and prefer to be set high, the crown above soil level, actually exposed. WATER: during growing season water regularly. In October no water; November begin again and plant soon will be on way toward throwing up strong stalks supporting red-orange, delightfully fragrant blooms in umbel arrangement. FRUIT: decorative plump red berries also in umble arrangement; SEEDS: develop within a year, and new plants grow. FERTILIZER: feed potted plant at each watering using fertilizer half strength. ENEMIES: snails, mealy bugs. Vigilence. Clivia miniata, C. nobilis and hybrids available.

GARDENIA

Provide the gardenia with warm sunshine, afternoon is best. In the hot valley modify that sun with high shade. Provide roots with plenty of water. Follow these instructions there is little or no bloom bud drop.

CHAPTER 22

MESEMBRYANTHEMUM—THE ICE PLANT

(May: Fourth Week)

We have the mesembryanthemum. Even that ponderous name is an abbreviation. What it means is noon-flower, because some of its species open after the sun is well up and clap their petals shut at sundown.

The mesembryanthemum along with the cactus, the sedum, and many others is one of the succulents. Succulents, like camels, thrive where water is scarce. They make a virtue of necessity. They are trained to hardship until they prefer it to all else. For sheer contentment they need not the good damp humus but rock, gravel, and only a dash of food and rain. They climb mountain slopes where the air is wrung dry by the cold; they cling to the meager rocky soil of California road cuts; they survive scorching sunshine, trade winds and the salt spray on a sea cliff; and in greatest abundance of all, they spread far over the wide dry plateaus of South Africa and our own West.

HABIT This the succulents do by being astonishingly prudent, self-restrained and patient. They know how to lie low and wait. They want little; they have no tap root to draw up deep water and food, but only a shallow, slight mat. What they get they use as though it were the most rare of all sparkling fluids. They accomplish more with a little than any other class of creatures. They are the truest of all conservers. How do the succulents do it? They do it through reservoirs in their stems and leaves. When the rains come they fill these up with water and then bloom; and then closing tight their valves and gates they guard it all through the thirsty weeks against evaporation. In some, a leaf, detached from the ground for two years, has been known to take root again and spring into life. Some have their seeds in a capsule of tightly closed valves each of which has inside ridges contracted by the dryness. In a heavy dew or rain these ridges expand, throw the valves open like an umbrella, and fling out the seeds to seek for life in the precious interval of wetness.

What are these reservoirs and how are they protected? The whole plant is made for them. As you know, the leaves of other plants are thin membranes hanging from the branches like wet muslin handkerchiefs. But for the supply from below they would dry out in no time. But these succulent leaves are more like a tight wad of wet handkerchiefs. They are shaped more like French-fried potatoes, and clusters of fingers. They vary in a thousand ways but have the common characteristics that they are thick. Furthermore, they have their evaporation pores, not close as so usual, but wide apart, and they often carry a thick skin armed with wax for better measure and inside they are fat and juicy with a kind of watery flesh. The stems, if any, often have this same flesh. Because in a thickened leaf the inside volume can increase many times over with little increase in the evaporation area, the leaves are fine devices for holding water. And the marvel is that it was worked out in various plants of wholly different ancestors. There are succulent vines even, and ferns; there are succulent geraniums, daisies, wood sorrel, and milkweed, for example. Many divergent kinds through dire necessity altered their ancestral habits to meet new troubles, just as our ancestors did when they came down out of the trees. And which has made the better adjustment — those speechless plants, or we who talk so glibly and so much?

Our succulent for today, the mesembryanthemum, is native here in only a few of the quieter forms which you have seen up and down the coast. One of them has tough wiry stems and meaty leaves of triangular cross section, hanging over the cliffs or making a close mat to hold the drifting dune sand, and throwing up a few rose-purple, fragrant flowers. Another is the low, broad, wavy-leaved ice plant covered with crystal-like projections which glitter in the sunshine like hoar frost found above high tide, especially between Santa Barbara and San Diego. With age and in drought the foliage turns from tender green to ruby, filling the pockets of the cliffs with rich color.

However, the mesembryanthemums which astounded the world at our Expositions of 1915 and 1939 all came from South Africa. It must have been a black man who first climbed up to the interior plateau called the Great Karroo, and saw the dull sand explode into bright colors all over. Though we have no record of what he did we may suppose that he and his wife and children rejoiced as ours do today at the sight of the carpet of weeds set so thrillingly with jewels. What we do know is that Europeans were down there in Shakespeare's time and that they soon came running back, all excitement about what they called the Cape Plants. In 1679 a book described a mesembryanthemum in a Dutch garden. By 1750 in both Holland and England were gardens of Cape Plants including freesias, pelargoniums, lion's tail, and several of the

HISTORY mesembryanthemums. These two nations, competitors for mastery, had each carried home from Africa that kind of treasure whose removal was no loss. And in this — I suppose without conscious purpose — they bound the world closer together, for if you or I ever go traveling to see the place where the Cape Plants came from it will be like seeing again the familiar stars and we shall feel at home there.

Dr. W. A. Cannon, who studied South Africa for the Carnegie Institution, told me at Stanford once that the Karoo plateau is on open, windy, sunny country, like much of ours here. The sun is dominant, but this is not Sahara for the succulents have to drink now and then.

The African mesembryanthemums were going strongly in California sixty years ago. The one called Hottentot Fig escaped and promptly went to work binding the sand dunes from Santa Barbara south. Also it was quite willingly led for its higher education to the Berkeley Campus where the merry students named its fruit "faculty onion". Miss Kate Sessions of honored memory came back from European gardens to her home in San Diego with vials full of seeds, and soon she had her own garden of Cape Plants to the wonder of all. Theodosia Shepherd of Ventura created a hybrid from Roseum which has pink flowers and Coccinea which has red. Also Charlie Abraham, San Francisco's apostle of gardens, worked with the mesembryanthemums. And so did William Hammet Hall, first Superintendent of Golden Gate Park, and John McLaren.

This history I got from Eric Walther, Botanist of Golden Gate Park and Director of the Strybing Arbortum there. He told me also about the mesembryanthemum in the 1915 Exposition. They had a problem then, he said, of making a great windbreak on the water side. They piled boxes covered with wire netting to the height of fifty feet, and many blocks long. It took an immense number of mesembryanthemum plants and the result was the famous hanging tapestry. I can tell you that was something! Of course the gardeners stimulated these plants beyond their natural dry climate gait. It wouldn't do in an exposition for them to imagine they were home on the veldt and go dormant and turn pale and brown and look neglected. So with perfect drainage so as not to rot them, they were given extra food and water and made to put on an extra show of blooms. But of course nothing equalled the first unforgettable, flaming curtain of spring.

It was Mr. Walther who suggested their use in the 1939 Exposition. There the windbreak was made by the buildings. Between them and the water five hundred feet wide and nearly the length of Treasure Island on the side toward the windy Golden Gate was a great area which was seized by the mesembryanthemum lovers. The hanging gardens were nothing to this as to size. They needed plants by the hundreds of thousands. But they knew just how to get them, and the plants themselves, which have a genial helpful spirit, knew just how to take root in fourteen or twenty-one days. All that was needed was hand work and organization. The gardeners snipped off tips and rooted them — and so on until they had enough.

It was an assembly line; and while their work was going on you could look far along the dwindling perspective and see the mounds of raw plant material dumped on the floor and the workers making the cuttings, setting them into flats, and sending them off to the warm forcing tables of the glasshouse.

Though it was nothing to what a few years later these same workers did in the war, it was at that time a giant's job of work. And when all those plants had been taken to their bed on Treasure Island — not the sand and rocks of their ancestors, but the accurate mixture which would drain and feed at the same time — and when at last their blossoms began to flash out it was worth many times the work. It was called the Magic Carpet and twenty-one different colors were there. Most people, as is natural, looked, said "Oh!" and hurried on through the portals to the brash machine magic of the modern age. But some, of longer memory, lingered to watch again that pageant of effect, invented one hundred thousand years ago and first seen in wonder by that humble man on the African plain. For it was indeed a pageant. Strong-colored flowers of red, pink, yellow, copper, and purple opened in silent chorus near noontime when the sun was strong.

But of course the Expositions of 1915 and 1939 made only temporary, forcing use of the mesembryanthemums. With little help they fit big areas of California to a marvel. Mostly they are perennials not too fond of frost. In cold weather they recede and become dormant. They abound increasingly southward from San Francisco through Santa Barbara, Los Angeles, and San Diego into Mexico. The State Highway department has done a great job with them healing the ugly, raw scars made by road cuts in our rounded hills. Here in these cuts the mesembryanthemum is at home. Whatever rain falls from above runs instantly away except for what the prudent plant grabs for its reservoirs. Here you will find the cumbersome leaved mesembryanthemum with large cream flowers which turn pink later in cut after cut, like the bright lining of a coat as you drive by. Another mesembryanthemum used is the Floribundum that makes a fine-mesh, close mat of gray foliage later completely hidden under its rose-pink bloom.

And along with these is combined the accidental charm of the nodding wild oats, the poppy, the waving wild radish, and the lupins whose different varieties overlap to bloom through the season. All this together breaks the fall of rain and stops gullying. And the shallow intertwined roots are so coherent that any slide has to go down in big chunks.

In the highway dividing-strips a ground cover is made of the pink Floribundum with here and there diagonal bars planted to the low-bush rock rose. The white or pink blossoms of this bush come in clusters in which a single rose puts forth each day, disuniting and falling apart by nightfall. Yet by coming in relays the blossoms continue for months.

The function of the mesembryanthemum in tying down sand becomes something real when you find one of these free-wheeling dunes shouldering across the pavement, or into the window of your beach cabin. The plants lay down a heavy dead weight network. They are here to stay, for they enjoy their work, and the restless dune at last lies still like a fettered giant. You can see a fine succession of these giants thus fettered along the Great Beach Highway from the Cliff House to the zoo in San Francisco.

How can you use the mesembryanthemum around the house? The kinds are: first, shrubby; second, prostrate, creeping mat-forming; third, small tufts or clusters; and fourth, distinct individual little plants including those which imitate rubble or stones. From these kinds you can select for pots, hanging baskets and window boxes; or outdoors for a rock garden, a sunny wall, a slope too severe to mow, or a park-strip between sidewalk and street, so hot and dry and teeming with rocks that nothing else would grow there. Here your plants with memories of the rocks of their African kopje will gratefully put down their roots. They even thrive on that great gray rock we call Alcatraz and send back from it rays of color.

KINDS

How do you get the plants? You can plant seeds. But cuttings are no trouble at all. You take new tender growth like the tip growth in fuchsias and chrysanthemums; let it dry in the sun for two days, and then stick it in a flat or in the ground where you want it to grow. It must be kept slightly damp; but there is one danger — it may rot because it is too damp. It should root in a few days. A good soil is half coarse sand, and the other half good garden soil and leaf mold. But it must have drainage. Better lean to the side of drainage, dryness, and starvation. Pots should have broken brick and a very coarse gravel mixed in.

CUTTINGS

The worst enemy is too much water. Birds get after the more tender small forms; sow bugs collect under the matted growth; snails hide there too. If bugs infest the roots of potted plants you can plunge pot and all in a pyrethrum solution.

I hate to leave these plants; it is a pleasure to admire the sturdy character which wins out against such odds. But meanwhile enemies have been stealing up on our other plants.

Succulents other than mesembryanthemum worthy of your inspection: I know a garden in San Francisco which faces the Pacific ocean and 90 per cent of the plants growing there are succulents. They have been planted to fit the design and throughout the year that garden is a living picture because of the varied shapes of the plants in it, and their seasonal flower display. I have seen similar gardens in Santa Barbara, San Diego, and in San Bernardino which is closer to the desert than to the ocean. Then in Salt Lake City with snow everywhere last Thanksgiving I saw an indoor plant display which contained many similar to those of the seashore garden of San Francisco. And on a recent trip to the Shaw Botanical Gardens, of St. Louis, Missouri, and to the New York Botanical Gardens I saw more of these plants growing happily under glasshouse culture. You understand of course these plants prosper under the blasting wind of the Pacific, and under the broiling sun of Southern California, but seek protection from the winter cold inland and in gardens everywhere in the Eastern United States. Succulents are distinguished by having their stems and leaves (if they grow leaves) made up of large water holding cells. Many kinds of these fleshy plants have been collected from all over the world, Africa, Japan, Mexico, California, etc. The following is a list of representative forms of succulents.

Aeonium canariense
Aeonium arboreum
Aloe distans
Aloe aristata
Aloe spinosissima
Ceropegia woodii
Cotyledon undulata
Crassula falcata
Crassula multicava
Dudleya candida
Dudleya injens
Echeveria elegans
Echeveria pulvinata
Euphorbia abyssinica
Euphorbia splendens
Gasteria brevifolia
Kalanchoe beharensis
Kleinia tomentosa
Oliveranthus elegans
Rochea coccinea
Sansevieria
Sedum adolphii
Sedum guatamalense
Sedum morganianum
Sempervivum calcareum
Sempervivum arachnoideum

For the Opportune Task: get acquainted with sulphur as ammunition against plant enemies. Learn what it will do for the garden and how to use it. Remember there are different kinds: first, a heavy sulphur, broadcast as around the heathers, to loosen the soil and improve water penetration; then there is dusting sulphur, excellent to keep down mildew on grape vines and on such garden shrubs as euonymus, lilacs, and of course on the roses, and on perennial phlox and dahlias too. The principal use of this sulphur is to control powdery mildew which can ruin rose, disfigure many shrubs, and spoil grapes. Resting on the foliage the sulphur will give off a vapor when the temperature is high and this does the trick. And of course sulphur will control thrip, especially on young citrus trees; it checks red spider too, and beetles on the vegetable plants. Get out your dusters and study the uses of sulphur, and be sure and get acquainted with soil sulphur; farmers use it, and experienced gardeners too. Soil sulphur is heavier than dusting sulphur; it can do much to improve heavy, tricky soils.

CHAPTER 23

PELARGONIUMS—THE LADY WASHINGTON GERANIUMS

(June: First Week)

We look at the most familiar of all house and garden plants — the gay, good-natured geranium, or pelargonium. We shall consider what it is; where it came from; its original and adopted climate; its use in California; where we get plants for our own use; and how we plant and care for them.

What are geraniums and pelargoniums? Why do we have two names? Both names came from the fruit which is long like the beak of a crane or stork; and the two names are in fact the names of these two birds in Greek. By such simpleminded devices is our language compiled! For everyday use we divide the

KINDS forms into: first, the common or garden geranium, a somewhat succulent mongrel, having regular, single or double flowers, which develop strong colors, most often scarlet, under the sunny skies of California, some with zone shadings in the leaves, and in many sizes and habits including small compact dwarfs. This is what the gardener means when he says geranium. Second, the scented-leaved geraniums known mostly as rose-geraniums. These also are mongrels. And like mongrels they vary from giants near tree size to pygmies that live in a pot; from little crinkled or round flat leaves, to big fleshy ones, and leaves that vary so in shape and color — from lacy to oak-like to deeply cut, and from darkly marked to silvery — that, as with dogs we ask how they can all belong in the same group? They have, however, one characteristic in common — the leaves, not the flowers, have strong scents which according to Ralph G. Cahn the nose interprets as: mint, lemon, citronella, lime, apple, rose, apricot, nutmeg, and when in doubt, pungent.

As pot plants these used to be an old fashioned feature of the home, the scent of which in later years recalled powerfully the childhood scene. They were part of the kitchen garden for food flavoring. Their oils were extracted for home-made and factory-made perfumes. The flowers in soft shades of lavender to rose, are small.

The third kind, the colored-leaved geraniums, are pretty curiosities for house use, with strangely colored leaves of green, purple, white, silver, gold, and bronze, or green and black zones.

The fourth kind is the Ivy Geranium, a vine-like form with thick shiny foliage, and plenty of single or double, pink, white, lavender purple, or reddish blossoms.

The fifth kind is the show or Regal type, called the Lady Washington or Martha Washington. It is what the gardener means by pelargonium. Its flowers are less regular and more varied than those of the garden geranium for the two upper petals of each flower often differ from the other petals, in size, shape and color. It is the product of long, selective hybridization and comes in single flowers, and what some people call semidouble flowers; for unlike the common garden geranium, the Lady Washington has no double flowers. The Lady Washington pelargoniums could be called cultivated elaborations; they have been bred for a combination, sometimes incongruous, of delicacy and ostentation. The colors appearing in various tones include pink, red, purple, coral, violet, lavender, salmon pink, light orange red, dark crimson, rose pink, and white with blotches in the petals. The variations are many, the colors develop well in our climate.

Most of these plants, geraniums and pelargoniums, are evergreen. Only one, a night bloomer with very small flowers, has bloom fragrance.

Our present geraniums and pelargoniums are descended like the mesembryanthemums from South African forms, and like them, too, they landed in Holland and England two hundred and fifty years ago and spread at great speed from garden to garden. New varieties appeared, and by the early 1880's there was

HISTORY

something of a geranium craze; it was all by accidental hybridization until a century ago, and all the forms stayed single (poor fellows) until 1860. Then among the garden geraniums an accidental double showed up in France, a new variable was therefore introduced, and the interest of the collector — a tangible factor in plant breeding — was correspondingly heightened.

PELARGONIUM We shall now confine our attention to the Lady Washington pelargoniums, the show or Regal geraniums. Everything I say about position in the garden, soil, water, enemies, and care is for this particular group. In the next chapter we shall consider the others.

Like the fuchsia, the pelargonium found itself at home here. It had a great vogue and after reaching a climax, declined in favor, and many kinds were lost. Lately, again it has been returning. The International Geranium Society of Santa Barbara (1413 Shoreline Dr., Santa Barbara, California, 93105), which publishes an illustrated journal, has recently been quite active. Mr. William E. Schmidt, a speciailst, tells me that the present aim in hybridizing is: more compact growth; larger-blooming Lady Washingtons; clearer white, red and pink, especially free of under tones such as violet; the search even for that breath-taking result, the new color; and an unmistakable double-flowered Lady Washington pelargonium.

Now, before we discuss the use of pelargoniums in California, let us think how this climate compares with that of the original home of its ancestors.

What they had was bright skies, a long dry season, and little winter frost. In northern Europe and in most parts of England, they were planted in the spring, killed off in the fall, and therefore behaved as annuals. Or, they were nursed along indoors. Pot culture and the plants that look well to pots were emphasized. Only in warm sunny gardens as of Spain did they come heartily out of doors and become perennials as they do so familiarly in many parts of California.

Lady Washingtons do well in the full blaze, in *PLANT* coastal gardens from San Diego to San Francisco, but for the interior valley partial shade is recommended.

They want a well-drained soil, with moderate nourishment, and if the temperature falls below 28 degrees the Lady Washington will not last long. Therefore if your plants are to go untouched through the winter, pick your spot, remembering that any garden has spots of sub-climate varying strongly though close together. The sheltered corner of wall may even stay semi-tropical in the midst of the frost belt, even in places of Southern California.

In many places they can be perennials and keep on growing from year to year. In other places, even around the Bay, they will be frosted back part way or to the roots, and then will come up again. What you do with them will of course vary with your place.

Variously, then, according to your private brand of weather, you can use them for borders if you so desire and in beds. Or you can use them in window boxes, and especially if you have to outwit the frost, in pots. USE

To get the best from the most delicate of the Lady Washington pelargoniums, look at them closely, flower by flower, and leaf by leaf. In pots you will see them nearer and, in one sense, know them better. These pots can also be taken to the garden itself. They can be moved about for trial effects, to make splashes of brilliance on the roof garden, on the porch, on the steps, and around the patio. Or they can be sunk in the ground and for the time become real garden plants.

They go well with other Africans — they blend in with succulents — you can see a fine joint planting of pelargoniums and mesembryanthemums at the east end of the Yerba Buena tunnel, San Francisco Bay Bridge. Transvaal Daisies are good also and the blue creeping campanula, the bushy marguerite, and many others. Fuchsias make excellent neighbors.

Now having decided to use them, where do you get these Lady Washington pelargoniums? From seeds, if you want the excitement of uncertainty; for as with petunias you won't know just what you'll get. The usual way is from cuttings. You can take them at any time you go by a plant you like. All that is necessary is a good sprig of growth three to five inches long. And CUTTINGS here is a point. Many amateurs complain the show geraniums grow too scraggly and leggy. Taking cuttings is your opportunity to check this tendency in your plant. By pruning, you at the same time keep your plant compact and bushy and you get sprigs for cuttings. The kitchen sink procedure is to root the cutting in a glass of water exposed to partial sun, the glass itself hidden by black paper. The more formal is to root in coarse sand, and later shift to a pot with soil enriched — not by manure but by leaf mold — and later shift again to a larger pot or into the garden itself.

The professionals always make their cuttings in WHEN August and September because then the new growth will be no longer sappy and watery but will have become firm and stocky. They ignore any flower buds present and prune their plants back for the cutting wood.

The rooted plants will grow in your soil whether adobe or sand, so long as it is well drained, though they prosper best in loam.

What of watering? If it's blooms you want, keep CARE them on the dry side and they will think they're at home in Africa, and will throw out their blooms. But, though it is true they will grow with less water than some plants, for shapely specimen the plant should be given water regularly. If they become distressed for lack of water, they will drop their lower foliage, and take on a scraggly look. And any blooms the plant may be carrying in this dry stage will blow off in no time; whereas a plant given even moisture is kept soft and is kept going at all times, and of course the flowers are longer-lived.

What of enemies? The Lady Washington pelargonium suffers from the same enemies as the fuchsias; aphids, for instance, mealy bugs, and white flies. Use a multipurpose spray to rid yourself of these troublesome pests.*

The Opportune Task: You can have your last chance to put out tomatoes, butter lettuce, and squash, and zucchini for the summer table. While you're about it plant some more beets and carrots; from each packet,

*See August: Third Week: "How To Make Cuttings of Pelargoniums."

sow part of the seeds every ten days so they won't ripen all the same week. And then there are the cucumbers, lima beans, and bell peppers that can go in now. These vegetables along with tomatoes do best when the ground is warmed and now we can already begin to see the heat waves boiling up. Even more corn can go in, but this time make for it a little planting trench, and make basins for the squash, and cucumbers. First dig up the soil — it's still willing — churn it up, work down fresh soil so that the roots will have something good to reach into and feed on later. Then plant your seeds, plant them a little deeper than the first planting because of the warm weather. Later, as the plants grow up, you will cultivate or fill the trench or basin with mulch and that will bring up the soil to the proper grade, and your roots will be far down and thus won't burn in the summer heat. There is nothing like a basin for planting tomatoes, squash and peppers, or a trench for the corn. Remember the need of fluffiness — that is, good tilth — for all of the garden plants. We can't stand those cracks that come after the watering and now we must cultivate. Cultivate around the roses, the fruit trees you just planted this spring, around the shrubs, especially the spring flowers which have just finished and are now putting out new growth for next year. Cultivate around any tree or permanent plant newly placed in the garden. Get the fibrous roots working, for they act like knives, forks, and spoons to gather in the food; and of course cultivation gets the air to them.

CARE OF THE NEWLY PLANTED

For your old established plants, now is a good time too to put out compost and mulch material in the basins. A basin three feet around a redwood, a pine, a walnut, or a magnolia, should be made right now before the top soil bakes or becomes any harder. What is needed most of all for a plant trying to become established in a new spot, and for the continued good health of an established one, is water, cultivation, and a mulch. For filling a basin with mulch material nothing beats pulling the heavy weeds and dropping them right in the basin; it builds up a natural mulch.

CARE OF THE ESTABLISHED PLANT

The winds that come in early summer often play havoc with the new young growth on the plants and trees. Remove all broken or torn branches; if they are big ones paint the scar over with garden wax or asphalt to keep water and fungus attack out. Perhaps there are some trees needing stakes; flopping trees always get into trouble, and they look bad. Tie the stake to the tree so there is no rubbing.

The Ivy Geranium
". . . how sweetly flows
That liquification . . ."

Maybe some of you will want to gather seeds from flowers that were particularly good this year. Now is a good time to collect calendula, stock, ranunculus, forget-me-nots, snapdragon, and pansy too — do it now before you clear out the batch. Cineraria seeds and those of columbine are ready now. And in a week or so seeds from the early delphiniums will be ripe. Remember the early seeds of delphiniums are the best. Before the seed vessels open, cut the main stalk just above the side branches. Stand the stalk up in the garage away from the wind, but not out of the air, because you don't want to wet the seeds when they're freed from the little vessels.

Again I'd like to call to your attention the particular climbing roses that are to be pruned at this time. All the one time blooming roses should be pruned heavily now. In this group are the Belle of Portugal, the Banksias, Silvermoon, Baby Rose, the Cecile Brunner, Cherokee, Ramona, Rosa multiflora from Japan, and the Paul Scarlet. Take as an example the Belle of Portugal; prune back all the old stalks that gave you a big display this spring; get rid of old branches because you want now to encourage new growth for the show to come next spring. And always follow up a heavy pruning with a heavy watering.

And one last job: give the azalea, rhododendron and camellia another tablespoonful of acid food now, and follow this feeding too with copious watering. Remember these plants are beginning their growth for the season to come.

CLEMATIS: Give established plants a summer mulch to keep roots cool. Did you purchase a new vine this season? Remember when you set out a new Clematis in its permanent home to pack the soil firmly. Even potted plants must have their roots set firmly in the soil. PEONIES: Now remove old blooms and green pods. Let new growth-strength go into next years bud development. ROSES: Water roses well once every 7 to 10 days. You can water them overhead if you do so in the morning. Stems dry off in the warm day and no mildew develops. Its when roses have water standing on them more than five hours that mildew takes over. VEGETABLES: Sow crop plants now to be harvested in fall: carrots, endives, dwarf beans, beets, and lettuce. Sow celery seeds now.

CHAPTER 24

THE COMMON OR GARDEN GERANIUM

(June: Second Week)

A week ago we were thinking about the pelargonium — that is the show or fancy geranium called Lady or Martha Washington. Today we turn to the common or garden geranium. This is well named for in gardens everywhere it is of all the most common flower. When your eye catches a flash of color along the highway in some well-kept little garden with its strip of lawn and side walk, or a vacant lot or wind blown gas station, it is the common geranium that you see there. It bravely smiles in draught and neglect; and in the drab unhappy rubble-cities across the sea it is the first brightness to reappear among the chunks.

How does the common geranium differ from the pelargonium or Lady Washington? It is more hardy against the frost. But the difference that affects us most is time and length of bloom. The Lady Washington opens its big clusters all at once in a spring flush of bloom. It is at its height now and will soon be done for the season. The common geranium, on the other hand, starts blooming in the spring, reaches its peak in August or September, but in the coast climate as in San Francisco, Los Angeles, Long Beach and San Diego, keeps on blooming even in the winter. Its flower head called the umbel, with the same idea as the umbrella, is made up on a spray of little stems from five to several dozen, each at first carrying a pendulous bud. These buds open, not all at once but in succession, so that you have at the same time a bright ball of full blown flowers, stems where the petals have dropped and the seed is forming, and buds which have not yet opened. In this way the flower is constantly being renewed.

Then of course these plants have quite different

habits in flowers and overall shape. While the heads of the geranium are carried on main stems often a foot long which hoist them well out above the leaves, the pelargonium main stems are short and the flower heads set on top of the leaves. The geranium flower is usually round about an inch and one-half across but can be as much as two and one-half, and it is either single as are many of the more delicate colored varieties — or double, sometimes becoming so full and close clustered that it has all the charm improved out of it. The pelargonium flowers are much larger, shaped like a nasturtium or a loose-petalled lily, and have strongly contrasting dark lines and blotches which give extra value to the clear hue.

The common garden geranium has been called also zonal because its leaves often are prettily zoned in light and olive shades of green; horseshoe, because the zone markings are in the shape of a horseshoe; fish, because of the unmistakable odor of fish in the foliage of a few of the early varieties hybridized a century ago; and bedding, because they have been much used out in the garden.

In the old times the common geranium had small loose flower heads with the petals of the individual flowers separate. The breeders in time contrived to gain more delicacy and at the same time to close up the petals and achieve the rounded flowers which we now know. That was more than a century ago. In recent years there have been further changes in both color and form. For example, fine compact dwarfs eight inches in diameter have begun to emerge and the aim is to keep the blooms proportionately large. These will be just what we want for pots and they will fit finely for bedding and massing.

When did these plants get to California? It must have been in the Spanish and Mexican days. They *HISTORY* certainly were brought in also along with shovels, sawmills, books, and mahogany bar furniture. In 1854 a San Francisco flower show had fifteen kinds including one scented-leaved. A double white made in Europe from a single white and double red was sold there for ten dollars per plant; and an Oakland nurseryman bought one and by 1874 was selling them for one dollar and fifty cents. Because they were so easy to grow and yielded so much color we went in for quantity. The common single flowers have something of the charm and grace of the wild rose. But in our zest for improvement we went to extremes; by doubling and redoubling we bred these qualities out until in the worst forms we had what that fine old describer, L. H. Bailey, calls "little better than balls of colored paper." Another trouble was the jangle of coarse colors to which California planters seemed for a long time insensitive. And above all we overplanted. In Berkeley twenty-five years ago exuberant residents used to take visitors out to admire exuberant banks of the red or pink flowers standing there week after week like a painted stage set.

Of course our taste revolted, we ripped up those hedges and banks, and we went so far that any geranium even one as dainty as an Indian azalea became unfashionable. One after another of the choicest kinds stole away into the night. But a few independent souls — bless them — who go not by fad but by principle, kept the geranium going through the lean years. They stressed the name pelargonium to make us forget the chrome effect and now we are back in the golden mean where we can see them for their very genuine value.

We have discussed propagation for the pelargonium. For the garden geranium it is much the same. I called on Mr. Ernest Matthews, Superintendent of an Atherton estate, and asked him to tell me something of the practice he used to follow in England. He said that there they follow this practice: In spring when the geraniums are set out, the entire old plant of the previous year which had been wintered over indoors is laid on its side and its roots covered. Then as the new growth begins the shoots "break" and as they come up they naturally reach and pull toward the sun and light. What happens is that because the old leaders are out of commission, new ones from the side shoot forward, each ambitious to become itself a leader. It is what happens with many kinds of plants. The result is in a full-growing plant of heavy mass spring growth. The whole plant fills out with a strong vegetative growth and on the new growth a mass of blooms appear.

With this practice the gardener will have such abundant growth that he can pinch his plant and keep it shaped to suit him; he can hold it down where he wants it.

On one of the larger English estates where Mr. Matthews worked they used the Madame Salleray, a low dwarf with pink flowers and variegated leaves. In winter they took the old stock plants and heeled them in for protection because their weather is unlike ours in California. Then these plants, fifty thousand on each side of a driveway two and one-half miles long, were laid on their sides as described a moment ago; the growth, full, compact, and heavy, made an unbroken line of variegated leaves and guiding feature for night driving and strolling which is practiced much in England. With the background of azalea molle, rhododendrons, hawthorns, peonies, and other plants of clean and colorful foliage, it was breath-taking. The blossoms of the geraniums, the azaleas and rhododendrons opened in the early spring about the same time and when the azaleas and rhododendrons were finished the geraniums continued. Years later on visiting this estate Mr. Matthews was surprised, and we may suppose not displeased, to learn they called this the Matthews Drive.

PROPAGATION

Now a word about propagation. If you wish to use cuttings, the practice in California is to take them from pot plants rather than directly from the garden; for you will there find them shorter jointed and better shaped. Make sure that your pot or flat used for rooting the cutting stays well drained. Coarse, gritty sand will do. Like the pelargoniums the geranium, after it is rooted, may be shifted into soil enriched not by manure but by leaf mold. A good mixture is two parts loam, one part coarse top sand, and one part leaf mold.

POT SOIL

You will find that pots need a system of care of

their own. I'll never forget the garden geranium which Mr. Wallace Brown brought to a meeting of the American Pelargonium Society. It was a burst of bloom tumbling all over a beautifully glazed pot. Mr. Brown showed us that the roots were jammed into a little tin vegetable can which was hiding inside. But the space between the two was filled with loam chuck full of humus. This he explained served two purposes; to insulate the roots from the hot sun and defend them from evaporation. The idea of the small container is to force out the blooms by confining the roots. Remember this: in transferring to a bigger pot you select only a little bigger -- you add only a little more room. You feed too with a little balanced fertilizer at intervals when you find the plant is standing still or its leaves turning yellow. Though the geranium must not be over-fed, in a pot it needs something to keep it interested at all times. Plants in pots require watering more often than those growing in the ground. The pot-within-the pot method lessens the frequency; but drainage should be perfect. Let the pot drain, never let the plant stand in a bowl of water. And we must not forget for one moment that frequent pinching will give us a well-balanced plant with abundant flowering heads.

CARE

Always to be remembered is the principle that out in the garden these plants can be put in difficult spots. But that does not mean they should be thrown in there and forgotten; for the difference between careless neglect and energetic good taste makes all the difference between a bad garden and a good one.

What about soil for the common garden geranium? It's the same as for the pelargonium; they'll grow in sand and adobe but will prosper best in loam.

What about water? Once they get well rooted their requirements are not so urgent. If it's blooms you want, keep them on the dry side and they will think they are at home in Africa; they will survive in the full blazing sunlight. This does not mean, however, that they can't make use of some water; nine times out of ten the amateurs fail to water the plant enough. And give your plant some shade as well in your garden.

For if they follow their natural gait with neither shade nor water the blossoms will burn up when the hottest days come, the leaves too will dry out toward the end of summer, especially the lower ones, and the plants will go ragged. Ugliness means poor attention.

But take care not to overwater. The symptoms are lush, lanky, translucent, sappy, watery growth, with very few flowers.

Feeding goes with watering and like watering must FEED neither be too much nor too little. Potted plants need food to encourage new wood, because as we already know upon the new wood the blooms appear. The garden geranium survives starvation but will do better when fed. Just a teaspoonful of a balanced fertilizer thrown at the roots and watered in well will do the trick. Stop feeding the last of August. Be persistent but moderate. If you give too much the growth will skyrocket, the blooms will be feeble; sickly yellow, curling leaves widely spaced up and down the stems. Such a plant is structurally weak.

Put the geraniums in the garden where they will get plenty of light and air; and remember that to stay in good condition the blooms need part day shade on the hottest, brightest days.

I'm including the ivy geranium here because like IVY the common geranium it is commonly used out in the gardens. The ivy geranium, less formal and more graceful than the others, is especially attractive covering walls and fences. It is somewhat hardier than the garden geranium but a good severe frost will get it. With short, stubby, firm growth better flowers appear. These plants serve on banks and look well in garden vases, window boxes, and hanging baskets and balconies. The most striking geranium effect I ever saw was an upstairs window box in San Francisco planted to pink ivy geranium cascading over the front door.

The common geranium, like any other plant, should be harmonized with its surroundings; and the persis- USE tence from months of its strongly-colored blooms makes this all the more necessary. It goes well with blue lobelia and ageratum, the many-colored annual phlox and other Africans; it goes well against the evergreen background of the foundation planting; in the perennial border grouped with whites and blues;against the yellowish, celery-colored leaf of the feverfew; and against brick walls. But there are places where the geranium does well by itself as in a hedge.

ENEMIES So long as it is in hearty good health, the garden geranium does a good job repelling its enemies. A penalty of this quality is that the gardener trusts it too much — he takes for granted that his plant is safe and the enemies in spite of all get a foothold. Look now and then for aphids and mealy bugs; and for holes chewed in the leaves and blooms by caterpillars. Snails too attack the tender growth.

Following is inserted from a letter of comment received from one of our listeners, Mrs. G. W. Stuart of Carmel, California:

"I have good luck rooting geraniums from tips. And with pink ivy geraniums growing up to the ridge pole of the house, each winter I have the vines clipped down to the roof gutters and away they go in the spring showering the place with beauty." Further, she writes: "Recently I have devised the scheme of planting my garden geraniums in pots and setting them about the place well sunk in the earth. This tallies with your suggestion that we constrict the roots." And let me interject, remember in the potted plant don't be afraid to pinch in order to hold balance, shape and beauty in your plant. This is particularly helpful to you in the city with window boxes, and with sunporches where you grow the potted geranium so much. And Mr. Matthews urged when I visited him the second time in the climate of Carmel and San Francisco you can really shape plants in pots because the general growth in the plant is slowed down by the coolness. Now back to Mrs. Stuart; she writes, "Geraniums do the oddest things.
KINDS I have one variety that will only go up; another variety that will only go down. This latter is a delicate lavender that drips from high window boxes, but I never mix my colors. Each has a definite place all by itself. Then I have a mammoth variety that is supposed to

listen to reason and remain on the ground. It has no relation to a climber, but lo and behold, on the north of the house it too rises in its glory straight to the roof. The leaf is enormous; the bloom is deep salmon on stems a foot long and beautiful for house flowers. Then I have the nutmeg geranium and the cinnamon variety. But best of all is the spearmint, with its hairy fragrant leaves which appear on my dinner table to embellish my salads. On the west of the house I have orange geraniums and never in my life have I seen such luxurious flowers. Your reference to 'great balls of colored paper' was apt for these orange things burst into balls the size of two fists. This orange can be very trying if thrust in with other colors, so I keep it free from conflicting arrangements." Perhaps it is Maxime Kovalevsky that Mrs. Stuart means. Our friend Mr. Matthews asks, "Have you ever tried planting near Maxime Kovalevsky the lavender blue Campanula muralis?"

CARE

Mrs. Stuart continues, "I have learned the benefit of grooming and tipping my plants. They must be disciplined. I am a very 'young gardener'. My experience with flowers has been in Borneo, Siam, and the Orient at large. There one does not struggle; one merely sticks something in the ground and it goes to town. But I find I love the garden best that calls for personal attention — but, my heavens, the things I have yet to learn!

"It makes me see red when I hear someone say contemptuously that geraniums will grow anywhere without care. Sure they will; long, scraggly, leggy, half-dead plants. Without care they go to weeds and why shouldn't they, may I ask? I deplore the way geraniums fall dead at the center before the entire head has matured. I have a trick when I bring them in the house for vases. I pull out the dead center and interject a small blooming flower at the heart. This keeps the great balls intact, but why do they go dead at the heart before they really get going?"

I may answer that this is their nature. The individual flowers of the head mature progressively, yet, says Mr. Matthews, the condition is hastened through faulty growth methods.

And now for the Opportune Task: I shall give you what Mr. Matthews told me on summer pruning and shaping of the new fruit tree. Now is the time, he told me, to work over the newly planted tree. Many people are afraid to cut these trees back. A naval commander said to him once, "I'd think nothing of turning a battleship but to handle one of your plants, oh ho, that's another thing!" But the plants have to be handled nevertheless. It is a mistake to permit a young tree to grow wildly. It needs at the beginning a proper all-time basic scaffold and habit of growth. Once a man called him to shape his trees. "I want to get them started off right," he said. Mr. Matthews pruned the trees heavily, selecting outside buds, removing cross branches that though vigorous were starting off in the wrong direction. He removed two-thirds of the tree and left branches that were low, close to the main trunk and mechanically sturdy. "Oh my, you have ruined the tree," cried the man's wife when she saw what was left of the tall, scraggly, soft-stemmed, big tree she had bought. "I paid two dollars and a half for that tree, the best one they had in the nursery, and now you have ruined it," she complained. But a year later she was both reassured and delighted when she saw how her neighbor's tree stood like a scarecrow with flapping branches and carried only one or two peaches, while her tree had sturdy branches loaded with fruit. We have to see a tree not only for today, but for the future.

To put this in my own words — it is a matter of the architecture of the plant. Its whole life will depend upon this original pruning for shape. Don't expect rich fruit the first year, or the second, any more than you expect work from your little children. To bear fruit in future years it must now begin to develop sturdy arms, sturdy branches. Pinch them back right now; if you don't know what pinching is ask your nurseryman. This is a summer trimming and summer trimming or pinching is necessary to young newly planted fruit trees. You are going to make basins, put compost in the basin, you are going to cultivate, maybe with a small tractor. Therefore the scaffold for your tree should be a little higher up so that you'll not have to roll on the ground to do your work. Look into this possibility now and don't be afraid also to top your apricot, plum, peach, pear, quince, or apple if you just planted them this spring.

TIGRIDIA: The Tiger-flower or Mexican Shell-flower (Tigridia pavonia) loves a place in the full sunlight. Plant corms in groups for the mass effect, place each corm two inches deep. Loosen soil thoroughly before setting out corms. Out of the corm grows foliage similar to the gladiolus but creased. In mid-season the flowers appear in succession. They are shell-like in appearance, and on older corms will open five to six inches across. The colors run from white to various forms of red, orange, yellow, and buff. A bloom lasts one day, rolls up like a hibiscus flower that has finished. New blooms open on successive days. WATER: give Tigridia plants plenty during summer. Corms are long lived and may be permitted to remain in the ground or they can be taken up before cold winter sets in. Propagation by corm and seed.

Mr. Wallace Brown's Way with the Pelargonium.

CHAPTER 25

TRANSVAAL DAISIES

(June: Third Week)

For this chapter we have the assistance of Mr. Henry Hassard who agreed to answer questions on a perennial that's become popular over the years throughout the United States and especially in California; the Transvaal Daisy, known as the Barberton daisy and botanically referred to as Gerbera jamesonii. This perennial grows wild in the province Natal, also Transvaal, an inland province of the Union of South Africa. Political disturbances brought the Transvaal Daisy from its far distant home; this beautiful plant honors the name of Dr. Jameson, who by a good many people was roundly abused for starting the Boer war. Gardeners serving in the British army were impressed with this brilliant red flowered daisy; they gathered seed, sent them home to friends who tried to grow the new-found plants. It was something different; and the earliest attempts failed. At the close of the war soldiers returned to England, bringing with them living plants which they nursed aboard ship on the long trip back. A Professor Lynch of a botanical garden undertook to grow these newcomers. In 1896, an insignificant white form was discovered and this presumably was the beginning of a new race of hybrids.

HISTORY

The climate of England was none too favorable and plants were tried out in a warmer climate in Southern France. Adnet, a French hybridizer, was very successful in producing improved colors and perhaps larger flowers, and he became an authority. Growing these plants in California has proved to be a study problem; those who wished to succeed have been challenged by the Transvaal Daisy. Sometime ago in this field professionally, I met the late Mr. William Metzner, then 93 years old, who was one of the first Californians to work with this plant. Later on, I met Mr. Henry Hassard, who is well known as a Gerbera grower, and before I start questions I want him to tell how he became interested in this field of endeavor. Mr. Hassard, just what was your introduction?

Hassard: I first started growing flowers as an amateur; and I took up the Transvaal Daisy early since it was new and many gardeners were talking about it. I experimented with raising seeds, I crossed plants and watched what happened in the seedling. As time passed along, I found my hobby cost so much that I had to set to work to get something back and in that way it led to the cut flower business. I began with 400 plants. I first raised Transvaal Daisies in Carmel and had good results; I now raise them in Los Altos. I sent to other growers who offered seed for sale and I have planted seed as old as two years and have had as good results as with fresh seed. Just the other day I sent to India for some seed of new colors, and I'm waiting their arrival. In spite of all this, I still classify myself as a hobbiest.

Wilson: We have selected the Transvaal Daisy to discuss because this is the time to work with these plants. Mr. Hassard, what do you consider is the time limit for transplanting and for the sowing of seed?

WHEN TO SEED

Hassard: When the ground has warmed up; that is the time to begin work on the Transvaal Daisy. Seeds do better when sown in warm soil, and the gardener should never touch his old plants while the soil is cold and stiff. I have moved Transvaal Daisies in all times of the year, but in the Bay Region I have found that after the first of May is the best; the subdivisions will not get started in cold ground and by May the ground has warmed up.

Wilson: Suppose we start with the work of subdivision first and discuss seed sowing later.

Hassard: Let's make it clear; this is one perennial that you never want to dig up and move unless you absolutely have to. The only real reason for moving a clump of Transvaal Daisies is to break it up and replant the subdivisions so as to increase the number of stock plants. Subdividing of poor-blooming types is an absolute waste of time. Select only the good types for increase.

Wilson: Do you advise moving young clumps, or must you wait till the plant is fourteen years old?

Hassard: You can move young clumps all right; but do not start too soon. Wait till you've had a couple of blooms on the plant. In that way you can select the type of bloom you want, as to color for instance, and build up your stock of favorites.

Wilson: How do you proceed with moving old clumps that you want to subdivide?

DIVIDE Hassard: First water the plant thoroughly; do this several days ahead; never dig into dry hard ground because you're sure to tear. When you've conditioned the soil then go down as deep as possible with your shovel or spade. I like the shovel because it gives greater lifting power. Dig all around the clump, then lift up the clump, shake off as much of the loose soil as possible. I always take the clump over to a dry spot in the garden, some place that needs water. Then I turn the clump upside-down, resting it gently on the crowns with the roots sticking up in the air. I take the nozzled hose and soak the clump thoroughly; I wash off all the soil. It takes a lot of water to accomplish this, and that's why I move over to a dry spot.

Wilson: Could you use a bucket or big tub to wash off the soil?

Hassard: Yes you can, but be sure to get the soil off; then you can see the roots and you are ready to proceed with the next step which is to examine closely the arrangement of the root system, and how the crown eyes are attached to the root system. If you have a large old clump you will see as you do in the iris that the central part is crowded with dead eyes, and on the outside edges you will find the strong new eyes. Transvaal Daisy plants grow variously; some are compact and the eyes grow in tight; others grow more loosely, they spread out with old growth in between as for example in a five-year-old plant.

Wilson: How many eyes can you divide from a clump; that is, divide them safely without weakening the clump.

Hassard: Each little new clump to be separated from the mother clump must have at least three eyes. Some plants will break up into only three pieces;others will break up into twenty. Some plants multiply slowly and it's best to leave them untouched. And the flower production follows the same; that is, from some plants you'll get 15 to 20 flowers from one eye; others will require a new eye to form before a new blossom. All these points should be considered in the selection of clumps to subdivide.

Wilson: What kind of an eye must the gardener look for when he is ready to subdivide?

Hassard: He must be careful to select an eye that shows the new leaves beginning to unfold; dormant eyes seldom develop into living plants after they are disturbed. Each subdivision must have a living eye.

Wilson: I read that someone used a hatchet to cut off the new eyes; what is your method of separating from a mother clump?

Hassard: I use a 12-inch screw driver and an old bread knife. The screw driver I use for a center leverage, for a turner; the bread knife I use to make clean cuts. I push the knife in between the eyes; with the roots cleared of soil I can see where to cut. It depends upon the individual plant; some have a firm crown just as you find in the iris and it demands pressure in cutting through; with others I can simply pull them apart.

Wilson: So far you have shown us how to separate a young eye from the mother crown; but what do you recommend as the best thing to do with the roots of your new plant?

Hassard: After separating your plant, look closely at the root system. Look for any black and soft roots; *CHECK* cut them out cleanly. Secondly, clean off with a sharp cut all the roots that you find were broken or cut in the subdividing. This does not mean cutting the root back to the base of the crown. A healthy cutback will heal, and will send out a new root which will go down into the cool ground.

Wilson: Then you're ready to plant.

Hassard: Yes; and go about it as you have explained the procedure for planting the rose. Make a good deep hole, put in the bottom of it a cone of soil. Mix up half loam, half sand. Then over the cone spread the roots. Fill in the rest of the hole with this mixed soil.

HOW TO PLANT

Wilson: How would you finish the planting operation?

Hassard: When it comes to completing the moving of the soil around the crown, it is important to make sure the soil doesn't cover the crown. The crown should just rest at soil level. In fact this part of the planting should end just like that of strawberries. Not too deep, nor too shallow; this precaution is for drainage.

Wilson: Would you mulch the Transvaals as you do the strawberry?

Hassard: Yes, use peat or any loose material which will help to shade the crowns and hold the moisture. And of course, as I have heard you say many times, finish the job off with a good soaking.

Wilson: So far, Mr. Hassard, you have told us about what to do when breaking up an old clump and how to reset the new young eyes. But what do you do for your old clumps; those you are not going to lift and break up?

Hassard: I keep them clean; that is I watch and pull any weed I see growing in the clump. Intruding wiry grasses are the worst. I keep them out of there.

Wilson: But that isn't all you do.

CARE

Hassard: Oh no! Established clumps of Transvaal Daisies require just as much attention as other perennials. I keep working on them all the time. I keep them mulched. I irrigate them when they are thirsty, I cultivate around the clump after each irrigation; I keep the soil loose around my Transvaals. Another thing, I take a bucket of gypsum and scratch it into the soil around the clumps. My soil at Los Altos tends to pack tight, and this keeps it loose. Transvaal Daisies won't grow if the ground gets hard around them.

Wilson: Of course the best part about these perennials is the flower; have you a special method of gathering them?

Hassard: I have learned the best way to pick flowers of the Transvaal Daisy is to pull them. I reach down to the crown, grab hold of the flower stem as low to the ground as possible, then with a slight twist I pull the stem; and off it comes easily. Remember the stem of this perennial is hollow, so be sure and pull it from the top of the crown, for if you bruise the stem, you upset circulation and the flower droops and fades immediately.

Wilson: Then Mr. Hassard you rather pull the stems than cut them.

Hassard: I never cut them. The reason for pulling is that you save time and you have one operation instead of two. When you cut you can't help leaving a stump; as the stump dries it hardens, and the sharp edge will cut your finger later when you reach down to get another flower. You later will have to clear the stump out, whereas if you pull the flower stem, the point of attachment heals readily and a new bloom takes its place. You may pull a young crown; don't worry, another will appear as the wound is below the surface and it will heal.

Wilson: What's your method of fertilizing the established clumps?

Hassard: I have found in the spring around February when more rains are still to come, and again in August when it is possible to give a heavy irrigation, that if you apply a dress of chicken manure the clumps spring up with a good crop of flowers. The winter rains will work down the fertilizer; but in the summer when I irrigate I find it best to wet down the ground, then pile on the fertilizer, then wet it down again. This takes out the burn during the heat. FEED

Wilson: Do you use any commercial fertilizer?

Hassard: Occasionally in the summer with a lot of water.

Wilson: And before we go on to the seedlings, what

have you learned about the enemies of the Transvaal Daisy?

ENEMIES Hassard: Crown rot is bad wherever drainage is faulty and too much water stagnates.

Wilson: I had in mind insects particularly.

Hassard: Diabroticas go after the blooms; they eat holes in them and change a beautiful flower to rags in no time. But Diazinon gets them. Then there are the ants. Ants love to nest in the crowns; they are the worst and they bring aphids to the plant. For getting rid of them I use nicotine sulphate. And Malathion will work too. I have a power sprayer and with it I go after the nests.

Wilson: I imagine it's possible for the home gardener with a smaller sprayer to use the same material.

Hassard: Yes, in fact, all the home gardener has to do is take two ounces of nicotine sulphate to a pint of water, put it in one of those bottle containers that can be attached to a hose; fill that bottle with water and attach to the hose; and you know how that works.

Wilson: Yes, as the water runs through the bottle it takes along the nicotine sulphate.

Hassard: That's it, and with a good force directed right into the crown of the daisy where the ants are nesting you'll soon get them out.

HOW TO SEED Wilson: Now, Mr. Hassard, what about seedling Transvaal Daisies?

Hassard: Right now I'm getting my soil ready to sow the seed. I use the same mixture, half sand and half loose loam; I sow the seeds right after the first of May. I sow them outside in an open frame or bed. They germinate quickly, in fact I get much better returns from my seeds than if I sowed them in January, in a greenhouse. There I leave my plants growing until they are ready to move. I shift them into pots; grow them there for a while and then set them out in the garden the following spring when the climate is settled and frost is gone.

Wilson: What do you do with them that first winter when they are still in the seed bed?

Hassard: I top-dress them with peat; I give them

a mulch — in fact, any place where the winter temperature gets down to 32 degrees, these plants should be mulched. Older plants adjust themselves to the winter climate but the seedling need protection.

SEED CARE

Wilson: We haven't said a word about Transvaal Daisies in the garden design. What about that, Mr. Hassard?

Hassard: One rule goes for every use in the garden. The Transvaal Daisy must have full sun; in full sun they bloom; in shade the plants go all to leaf, they look then like a prosperous rhubarb clump but they never give you a flower. I might say in the hot valleys they can be given sunny shade and they will bloom; but in our coast districts, especially in foggy places, plant them in all the sun you possibly can. And I've heard in Golden Gate Park they often sprinkle gravel around the crowns of the Transvaals. This they have found helps to keep the ground warmer and more flowers unfold as a result.

LAWN MOTH CONTROL

Opportune task: Get ahead of the lawn moth with a preventative treatment. Use Dibrom, it kills soil insect pests. Dibrom kills the grub of the lawn moth if applied early enough. Late May, early June is right. In the life cycle of the lawn moth, the grub stage is dominant in June. Dust the lawn with Dibrom; in granular form it dusts right into the soil surface of the lawn. Dibrom is long lasting and watering does not lessen its efficiency. Follow directions given on the container. Apply twice in the summer; result, less injury to your grass from lawn moth pests.

POISON OAK

POISON OAK may be attacked with Ammate of Aminotriazole in equal parts during hot months of June till September. The idea is to spray the weedicides on the foliage when the hot sun is actually shining on the plant. Drench the leaves, new growth, tip, etc. soak down thoroughly all of the woody plant. It might require two treatments. Prepare yourself for the attack by bathing all exposed parts of your body in a strong soapy wash; let dry without towel. Wash again on the hour if task is long.

Chapter 26

DELPHINIUMS

(June: Fourth Week)

I'm anxious to tell you about delphiniums, favorite of all the spires, because of their graceful tallness and their lovely blue and whites, and because too they are so easily grown that everybody can have them. Up north, while I was calling on a stranger some one asked him over the phone to play golf that afternoon and he replied, "Why I can't play golf; my delphiniums are in bloom."

The spire can reach ten feet high but the average gardener should not strive for anything like this. Too tall, the plants are difficult to stake, storms play havoc by toppling them over.

The spire makes the show but the floret, that is the individual flower, yields delicacy. The hybridizers have been working for color; they have sought depth, brilliancy, clearness and purity. Color affects harmony — the little pure white central florets contrast with their background of large petals of deep burning sapphire or glistening royal purple. The florets which may be pure white, cream, or lavender combine well with almost any hue, add much to the garden picture and to a flower arrangement. The beautifully angelic pure white semi-double and double delphinium of good substance, size and vigor is now a reality from the hybridizers. And they do much to build up the floral show. The delphinium flowers are classified single, semi-double, and double. The semi-double type are popular because their fullness looms out in the delphinium spire.

Delphiniums are blooming now: Rudolph Kempf, *CARE* professional gardener of Los Altos who was given a medal one year by the American Delphinium Society (Ridgefield, Connecticut) says it's a good thing after the first flush of spring bloom to cut the flowering spike back six to eight inches above the ground; let the clumps rest for two weeks, then water heavily and the roots will send skyward new spires which will provide a second crop of blooms in September.

What kinds of delphiniums can we grow in our gardens? California is particularly fortunate in having a native called cardinale, the "Scarlet Delphinium." A hybridizer whom I've known for years, Frank Reinelt, now of Capitola and Santa Cruz, took this wild one of ours and crossed it with the English Wrexham (developed by Samuel Watkins of Wrexham, Wales) and originated four strains of marvelous delphiniums which he has called:

KINDS

The King Arthur Series, true royal blue with a white bee,

Guinevere Series, clear pink-lavender with a white bee,

Summer Skies Series as the name indicates, and the

Galahad Series, his greatest achievement in giant white.

You can see in the foliage of these lovely hybrids the unmistakable character of our native delphinium. These hybrids are superior for another reason besides color. They were developed also to provide the seedlings with strong stems; they are flexible and under ordinary conditions stakes are not required to hold them up.

Mr. George Barber of Troutdale, Oregon, who is credited with the first white delphinium says, "I woke up one morning, went out to the garden, and there was a white one." That man really gave the gardening world something when he brought out of his back yard the first clear white delphiniums, Interesting new forms in the modern delphinium too have been developed by Mrs. Claire Franklin of Santa Maria, in a compact spire every floret from end to end opening; and the cylindrical spire can be shipped easily and there is no undeveloped tip to break off. And from England delphiniums known as the Improved Strain are available from Blackmore and Langdon's.

Where do the seeds come from? You may purchase your seeds, a practice followed by most gardeners who grow their plants for cut flowers. But some gardeners choose to permit their plants to produce seeds. Pointed capsules are found along the tall stems. A succession of blooms throughout the growing season follows pruning, and each flower along the spire is followed with a seed capsule. But the best seeds are *SEED* always found at the lower part of the spire, because they are usually completely filled out and, from them, strong plants will come. The seeds will be ready the last of June: gather and prepare to sow them in July. It is of interest to note the English strain of delphiniums develops better in the clump each year, but in our Pacific Strain it is better to start each year with fresh seed. That's what the professionals do. As Mr. Kempf says, "One year or one season is enough"; the hybrids usually go out or if they do carry over they are very slow in coming back. And too many bugs get them in winter especially if only a mild coldness prevails.

How do you start off with delphinium seeds? The *SOIL* soil for the flat should be equal parts of good garden loam, sand, and leaf mold. A good method is to scatter the seeds in the flat thinly and evenly. Press them into the loose soil and barely cover with screened leaf mold. The soil is never firmed over the seed, because you want the seedlings to easily push their way up after germination. Good germination requires moisture, aeration, and a steady low temperature; not burial under the soil because, as you know, all seeds require light soil conditions, they refuse to grow in soil packed tight.

And at this point there is damping-off disease that you should know about. Damping-off in the seedlings is often troublesome. This dying of the little plants is usually brought about through overwatering and the persistence of moisture in the flat or soil. Meticulous attention to watering, disinfectants, and use of Morsodren or Dexon will help in the control.

Plenty of air passing over the flat is another easy measure to keep damping-off from your seedlings.

Never put your flat or pot of delphinium seed in a hot-house, because the seeds just roll over and die. Keep them cool as by covering the flat or pot with a sheet of paper resting on the glass; and be sure to provide ventilation by slipping a sliver of wood such as a plant label between the glass and the flat. DON'T

What about transplanting? When your seedlings have produced the second leaves — that is, the true delphinium leaves — and before the plants are too crowded, prick in flats three inches apart; use a light mixture of two-thirds sandy loam and one-third leaf mold, but no manure because delphiniums do best in a slow steady growth rather than a quick sappy one inspired by fertilizer during their young stage. Let me interject that delphiniums all through their lives prefer the light sandy loam, they're not so happy in heavy soils. After transplanting into flats your seedlings must be kept shaded for several days; remember it's coolness they want; then gradually give them more light to harden the little plants off before setting them out in the open garden.

LOVE BEST LIGHT LOAM

In the meantime select a spot in the garden where these seedlings are to go. Pick out one providing more hours of sun than shade. Spade deep; introduce lime — delphiniums like it; and put bone meal down in the bottom to provide food when the roots of the new sturdy plants are ready for it. After the seedlings have grown a bit and the plants show they are on their way, pinch the leader out. This encourages bottom breaks and stronger flowering crowns. Seeds sown in July may be set out in September; and then the little plants will develop a nice root system in the winter. You'll be surprised how much cold they will stand. Mr. Kempf usually throws a shovel of manure over each clump as the winter begins. The plants will produce glorious spires in April, May, and June.

What about enemies of the delphiniums? Snails and slugs eat the young shoots as they grow, and deform the stems. The remedy is poison bait. Cutworms; the larvae after the eggs hatch remain below ground; at night they work just at the ground surface and eat the

ENEMIES

young shoots. The remedy again is poison bait. Wireworms eat the roots. Good drainage helps, and still again poison bait. Cyclamen mites ruin flower buds; they may be controlled with nicotine sulphate or pyrethrum extracts. And red spiders, who busy themselves on the foliage, may be controlled with sulphur and petroleum oil or Diazinon sprays.

Then there are the diseases of the delphinium. Leaf spots distort and eventually blacken the whole leaf. Systematic spraying with bordeaux is best. Crown rot is troublesome in some gardens, especially in the cool fog belt. A soft spot in the stem can spread to rot the whole plant and make it wilt and die overnight. The remedy is precaution. Vigor resulting from good culture keeps crown rot away. Drainage, especially in the winter, must prevail where delphiniums are grown. Powdery mildew is controlled with sulphur sprays. Delphiniums planted too close with no ventilation always suffer from mildew.

The Opportune Task: Cut back about one-third the old blooming wood on your bush roses; this will encourage new shoots for your second crop of roses this fall. Any dead wood, easily recognized at this time of year, should be removed because bugs and disease will always lodge in them. If you find any change in the shape and size of the foliage coming up from the ground, if you see there foreign foliage on canes, it is from the wild rose root stock upon which your choice one was grafted. Prune this out right to the ground. Clear the soil away from the root. Take your knife and with clockwise movement cut out the wild branches leaving a conical cavity which permanently destroys the growing point. This is a ticklish job for some — if in doubt ask your nurseryman. Another point, don't let your summer annuals or fall chrysanthemums suffer from lack of water during this hot weather. Be generous with the water.

CHAPTER 27

SUMMER CARE OF THE LAWN

(July: First Week)

We are concerned with the established lawn; we speak to you, the lawn enthusiast. What should you do for the lawn in warm weather? Just three things: prevent annual weeds from seeding, water, and mow. The weed job, except in the new lawn, we are inclined to overlook because someone has told us the lawn mower takes care of it. But the lawn mower won't necessarily take care of crab grass which starts with two leaves, purple at the base, that by the end of the season grow as big as your hat; and it won't take care of burr clover that can become quite troublesome. How do you get rid of these weeds?

I asked Mr. Charles Gamblin, whose beautiful flawless grass carpet in Palo Alto proves he's an expert to give us his prescription.

WEED CONTROL

"So you want to get rid of weeds in the lawn, do you?" he said. "If they are annual weeds just water a lot and feed often; every ten days this summer give your lawn a light application of ammonium sulphate; and while your Kentucky Blue lawn or fescue or Golden Gate Mixture lawn will grow like fire, the annual weeds will be burned and crowded out for they can't take all that food and heavy watering. When you give your lawn the water it wants, the food it needs, the grass being the most dominant of the earth's vegetation will crowd out the weeds."

Then there are the perennial weeds; they do not die each winter but live for several years. Oxalis (Wood Sorrel) in sun or shade with its persistent root system will walk away with a lawn and worse still has seed pods fixed up with a mechanism for artillery firing that can shoot a foot and a half away. Lawn pennywort; lies flat on the ground with creeping root stock and round shiny leaves that possess the place; this too can walk away with your lawn. White Clover: has a way of "sneaking up on your lawn" as the gardeners say, especially if you do not want white clover in the grass. Some people object to clover because it shows every mark of a foot step when the lawn is walked on. Others claim slugs hide under the cool green leaves. Clover in the lawn unwanted is a weed. Then the best known of all perennial weeds is the dandelion called facetiously the lawn orchid. New weedicides control them.

On perennial weeds Mr. Gamblin said, "For oxalis anytime this warm summer weather spread over the lawn ammonium sulphate mixed with sand for better distribution; then water generously but do not mow for three weeks; just let it grow. The Oxalis competing for light will be stimulated to grow also but the competition is too much, the plants become exhausted from over stimulation and this slows them down.

"As for dandelions you know they grow with their leaves flat on the ground but with feeding they throw up their leaves. Get onto these leaves a good top dress of a modern weedicide. Apply strictly according to directions. Apply always when the sun shines right on the dandelion leaf--the results are excellent. Where there are only a few dandelions in the lawn a teaspoonful of straight ammonium sulphate dropped into the crown of the dandelion will work too. The fertilizer burns its way right down to the very tip of the root and it's good-bye dandelion. The lawn in the immediate region may also die back from this burning chemical fertilizer but it will come back strong and rich green.

"The mouse-ear chickweed with the sticky leaves," continued Mr. Gamblin, "You will find prefers shady-moist lawns; it always burns in the sun. For getting it out of the lawn cut down the amount of water if possible; keep it on the dry side and use a coarse rake to pull runners, roots and all; that gets rid of chickweed."

These are Mr. Gamblin's methods proved by long experience to work. Now there is a new method of weed control through chemical sprays. From the laboratory comes 2-4-D. What does this do to the weeds? 2-4-D is a growth regulator, a hormone, and it immediately stimulates the growing points and centers of the plant, and literally "tickles it to death." Every point, every part of the plant is tortured into growing and twisting at a furious rate, until it uses completely all of its strength, goes to pieces, starves, and dies. One of our gardeners in Palo Alto experimented with his ten-year-old lawn and this is what he observed: First, he cut the grass close; then sprayed 2-4-D according to directions all over the lawn. For two days afterwards he gave the lawn no water; on the third day the effects of the spray began to show and each day afterwards for ten days the weeds looked worse. "The whole lawn looked rotten for about twelve days," as he put it; then "I top dressed with fertilizer and watered heavily and you see how nice the lawn is now. I got rid of 95 per cent of the weeds; daisies, plantain, dandelions, chickweed, and a lot of broad-leaved stuff. But it doesn't kill seeds, so a little later I'll try again to catch any weeds that I missed this time."

2-4-D does not injure your grass; it gets only the broad-leafed plants — but that unfortunately includes clover. You can use it for getting rid of poison oak as I did last summer. Spray it on the foliage in mid-June when the sun is bright and hot. And it works for wild carrot. Some gardeners have used it successfully on morning glory. Of course it is new. 2-4-D may not work so perfectly in your district or on your particular lawn. It kills clover and it isn't successful with creeping Bent Grass which often runs in among the roots of shrubs and perennials. Ask your neighbors and nurseryman about their experience.

The second important office for summer care of the lawn is watering. You know the Pueblo Indians express a beautiful thought in their prayer: "That we may walk fittingly where birds sing. That we may walk fittingly where the grass is green." To the desert Indian in his rain-hungry adobe green grass is a paradise.

The need for water is affected by top dressing.

TOP DRESS

Last spring you top dressed your lawn with a humus compost; you spread evenly over the grass compost which you had accumulated yourself or which you had bought. These materials helped then; they will still help in the hot weather because they provide a buildup cover to the root crowns. It isn't too late now for another top dress. Use a mixture of one-half compost material (or weed-free manure if you can get it) and one-half sand. The compost will hold the moisture and the sand will filter down through to the root crowns. It acts as a mulch without which no amount of watering can take care of the hard dry spots that often develop during hot weather. If you notice your lawn has lost its even greenness, investigate these spots with a screw driver. Nine times out of ten it will bounce back at you, and nine times out of ten the lawn is not getting enough water. Actually you might even find dust down there. Water hard dry spots individually; punch in the spading fork or the sod spiker; the water will go down these little holes and reach the thirsty roots. The sand, if you sprinkle it there, will wash down into the holes and keep them open so that more water will go in. Remember in adobe, cracks appear when the soil dries out, but in more loamy soils this cracking does not take place. Mulching helps to check cracking.

WATERING

How much water should I give my lawn? Differences often exist on the same property. The front lawn may demand more than the rear lawn. If one area is open to the winds it will require more than an enclosed area. What kind of soil is the lawn growing on; is it flat or is it sloping? What district are you in? In cool San Francisco there is no summer watering problem, whereas in Stockton and San Diego watering is a must from May until early fall rains. In the warm valley we have to remember to keep the grass green; the roots must get down eight inches and one foot is safer. Kentucky Blue Grass roots have been found three feet down. Top sprinkling encourages top roots; deep watering, deep roots. The marvel of the Santa Clara valley in the 'seventies was the Barron estate lawn. It stood there like a beautiful green oasis and visitors from the great city greeted it with ahs and ohs. The secret was that Mr. Barron had flooded it like a field of alfalfa to get it ready for them. Of course you and I will not irrigate, but we can run our sprinklers by the half hour instead of by the minute so as to put the water down there. The idea is to give enough to take care of normal evaporation, to replace what is being transpired through the grass blades, to provide for the thirsty roots, and to break down the humus you put on the lawn.

FEED

Commercial fertilizers may be applied from April to late August. Apply in the early morning and water immediately. Fertilizers move in one way only, straight down, not laterally; thus apply or distribute the material evenly over the grass. Too heavy or spotty, or left in lumps, these materials will burn the grass or may excite too lush a growth which later might get the lawn into trouble. Lawns of Kentucky Blue grass, fescue, etc., are fed successfully at this time of year with ammonium sulphate, or with commercial fertilizers.

BROWN SPOT

What are those brown spots in my lawn? That is a frequent question asked of the nurseryman. There are two different causes for brown spots; fungus or insect. Mr. L. R. Cody, for twenty-five years agricultural commissioner of Santa Clara County, told me fungus spots occur more frequently on lawns that get watered in late evening. So water yours in the morning, especially if you live near the coast; and in the fall do so no matter where you live. The grass in the fungus spot is a light yellow color; and control requires a fungicide. Several good ones are on the market, all you have to do is follow the directions. Or you can use clorox, or the regular hard clorox from the kitchen — four tablespoonsful to a gallon of water. But you can't apply clorox all of the time. That is not as a constant watering agent. Fresh water must be used upon the lawn between treatments.

CONTROL

SODWORM

The insect which causes brown spots is the sodworm. He feeds on the roots. Once I saw a gardener take a hose, open the valve wide, soak the brown spot heavily, and the worms came out a running. He told me he has swept them up by the shovelfuls. The blackbirds and robins go after them too. Mr. Cody says, "Several years of trial have taught me to make up a solution of one ounce of pyrethrum extract in four gallons of water; then put this solution into a sprinkling can; thoroughly saturate each brown spot to some twenty inches beyond the edge. This brings quick death. On larger lawns where a duster is available, pyrethrum dust and sulphur can be used; of two and one-half pounds to the 100 square foot or by spot dusting; then water lightly." Dibrom is a good control.

The third duty for the summer lawn is mowing.

MOW Mow the lawn as often as is necessary to keep it looking neat and to keep the grass from becoming wiry. This may mean once a week or even twice where the lawn is growing in full sun, but less often for the lawn growing in shade. Bent grass has to be cropped close as will be later explained. But for other grass keep the blade one and one-half to two inches above the ground. A plant needs both roots and leaves and the effect of shaving it off at the ground level, especially in summer, is to starve the root system because food reserves for the roots are manufactured in the green growth above ground. The more this green growth is limited, the less extensive and lusty will be the root system.

During the war when the gardeners were building ships and slogging through the European mud, I called one day on an old friend, a woman of eighty-three years. As she opened the door her face broke into a beautiful smile and she said, "Oh, you're just the one I want to see." This pleased me and I thought, "Isn't it nice, I can make my friend so happy with so little effort. That good turn a day of the Boy Scouts is something." It was summertime, the apricots were ripe; I said cheerfully to myself, "She wants me to pick her a couple of boxes and while I'm about it of course there'll be a bucket for me." And so in my most gallant voice I said. "What can I do for you?" "Mow my lawn," was her prompt reply. "MOW YOUR LAWN!" I cried in a strange-sounding falsetto. My eye swept the grass and around the hedge boundaries. It measured a complete acre! "That is just what I'd like you to do," she continued. The good turn idea retreated and looked dim.

I said, "It's beneath my dignity to mow people's lawns." But here I learned that age and experience brings with it knowing ways and my dear friend said right back at me, "It will do you good, Mr. Wilson, to get off your dignity." And so the lawn was mowed. But why am I telling you this story? It took the rest of that day; it was foundry work, pushing, shoving and grunting. The blades of the mower were lost in a thicket of wiry, tough grass; some of it was long enough to catch in the wheels. To make any kind of a job at all I had to go over it twice at right angles. That was something! My joints were like rusty hinges, my muscles knotted and cramped. I drank a gallon of water under the hot sun. The lesson is: neglect other things if you have to; pruning and maybe cultivating can wait; but NEVER THE LAWN. Now that the war's over — CUT IT REGULARLY.

MERION BLUE GRASS

MERION BLUE GRASS is a good lawn either dress or service-play. Merion, a green grass with a blue cast, grows thickly becoming a solid turf, yet retains dress appearance. It grows equally well in sun or in shade. Sow seed at rate of 2 1/2 pounds to 1000 square feet. WATERING: Merion requires less than most grasses; it does not demand frequent watering. FEEDING: use fertilizer regularly. ENEMIES: rust attacks blades when lawn is kept too moist. Control: the combination of 1 pound copper sulphate to 40 pounds fertilizer is good.

The Opportune Task: On July 4th some of you may want to get in a few extra licks. How about planting a tree to commemorate the day — a pink flowering chestnut, a sweet fragrant linden, a true English holly, a fir, maybe a redwood spire? Then there are annuals; for example, phlox drummondii planted in July will give flowers in October. You can also broadcast more salpiglossis; scatter the seeds right in the open ground and they will grow fast with this summer weather. Turn over the compost pile; help it on its way; air, water, and sun and barnyard or commercial fertilizer, if you add it, will break it down to leaf soil in two months. How about going over the chrysanthemums; give them the first or second pinching.

Look around; water those trees in the background, don't let them grow scraggly in an agony of thirst during the summer months. Specimens, those precious trees stationed in the lawn or at the margin of the border, in particular must be watched. And on all the new growth of your evergreen plants such as the strawberry tree, Portugal Laurel, and Viburnum, watch *THRIP* particularly now for thrip; don't let thrip get started. Water the plants overhead once in a while, make sure plenty of moisture is at the root zone. Spray a light summer oil now on these plants; try Diazinon to kill thrip. Transvaal Daisies want deep watering too; too much overhead sprinkling encourages crown rot. Remember roots of the Transvaal Daisies reach eighteen inches down; irrigate around them in the summer; it takes lots of water to get down there. All the Shasta Daisies have about finished their first bloom, as the Esther Read. Cut them back to two inches above ground; water generously to encourage the good new growth which will mean fine blooms later in the summer and in the fall. Don't let them get weak, flop, or go to pieces.

Give your blackberries a mid-summer watering. *DON'T* Your Boysenberries have long runners now. Do not cut them off for these runners bring next year's crop. Don't step on them while you're harvesting this season's crop. If you either injure them or cut them off you force the stumps to make hard wood; and that will produce no fruit or poor hard fruit. Keep the runners single, that is, no branching or forking along the stems. Some will grow 20 feet; tie them back to the canes which have fruited and favor the new ones. On these new runners is active foliage; spray them vigorously to clean off dust and mud, but it is best to let the new canes sprawl until the first good rains (December to January) then you may pull them out and arrange on the frames.

CHAPTER 28

BENT GRASS LAWNS

(July: Second Week)

What should you do for the Bent Grass lawn? The late Tony Tavares, an expert and an enthusiast always says, "Give me a Bent lawn in preference to any other type of grass. If cared for it will last a lifetime." Where he works a Bent lawn covers one-half acre and it is without exception the best lawn I've ever seen; deep green all over, it looks like a picture out of a book. So I gave Tony the third degree and here are his answers.

First of all, "We have selected Rhode Island Bent grass because those oak trees there make partial shade. In shade Rhode Island Bent doesn't want much water. I find," he said, "with too much water it gets thin and ragged. I water this lawn every other day; the sprinklers go for ten minutes only. But every spring, three or four times I spike the lawn with a spike roller. This punches little holes in the turf and the water gets down easily to the roots," he said. By the way, you can get a spiker with a spade handle for the small lawn.

There wasn't a brown spot nor a weed in Tony's whole lawn — well, I'll modify that one, for when we got down on our knees we found a difficult spot where a few weeds had crept in. Tony explained that that spot was not covered by the sprinkler. "It is always getting dried out," he said, "I have to run the hose there especially to make sure the water goes down. Never let the Bent lawn, nor any other lawn for that matter, get thirsty or hungry, don't let the grass become weak, because as sure as day follows night the weeds will walk right in." DON'T

I asked him to explain how after the winter had passed he starts off Bent grass for the coming season.

"If dead stuff built up in the turf the year before, I rake the lawn hard with the special rake which cuts in and pulls out. But if there is no dead stuff I start right in with regular watering and give the spring feeding,' was Tony's answer. "Of course all of the commercial fertilizers are good; I've used them all. But in the spring I use one sack of ammonium sulphate to seven sacks of Milorganite, one of those fertilizers prepared from municipal waste factories, mixed thoroughly together. Twenty-five pounds of this mixture to one thousand square feet is all right. The ammonium sulphate is the pusher, it gives the quick acid food that Bent grasses like; the Milorganite fertilizer is the feeder that provides a steady diet for the grass." Tony continued, "I mow in the summer twice a week. If you want a nice looking job cut in straight lines not in curves; this week cut north and south, next week cut east and west, and you have always a pretty job when you finish. I use a mower with seven blades," he continued, "but Bent lawns may be cut with the regular five- or six-blade mower, if the reel travels fast. The mower is set for a three-eighths cut of the grass. And remember to warn our friends on the radio that Bent grass if not cut close will send out long runners or stolons which turn yellow and are weak green only out near their ends."

FEED

"And one more question, Tony, what about mulching Bent in the summer?" "In August I broadcast sandy loam all over. There is the stuff," he said as we walked over to a big pile. I ran some through my fingers; it was sandy, but rich in humus. Tony took a couple of handfuls and flipped it onto the lawn; it disappeared among the grass blades. He said, "I usually apply it in the morning; then in the afternoon when the sun has dried the lawn I work it in with the back of a rake. For big lawns we have a regular spreader that moves this loam into the grass. The dividend comes next year for I use less water and the grass crowns have a humus build-up."

HOW TO MOW

Mr. Charles Gamblin, another expert said, "In spring first adjust your lawn mower with the blade high enough so that it runs easily and it doesn't jam. Just as soon as you have good traction start to cut the grass, setting the blade so as to get closer and closer to the ground itself. You are doing this to shear the grass real close; then you do not have to go in for all that hard raking and pulling to get the long stolons out. Stay with this process all spring while the weather is cool. At that season give a first feeding using bone meal, something that is slow but sure; bone meal spread on the lawn in the cool moist season just puts heart into the grass for the whole year. All this time the new shoots of the creeping grass will be breaking out from the root crowns while the old ones will die out. Now mowing in the summer with its warm weather is just the opposite of that in spring. You let the grass grow longer because you do not want the hot winds to dry out the roots. You no longer want to cut close; set the blades at one and one-half inches. Then, always water your Bent grass lawn with the rise of the sun, never send it to bed wet. Follow these suggestions and your Bent lawn will not only look right, it will resist fungus and other disease. And one more recommendation," he said, "adjust the blade up again in winter and stay off the lawn when it is wet because you don't want your mower to skid or to gouge in." FEED

Mr. Ernest Matthews says, "Keep the lawn spongy; see to it that a resilience under foot is maintained; permit no hard spots; investigate and work them over. Bent grass is a delta grass and delta grass is water-loving. Make sure it has water at all times, especially in the summer, because once a Bent grass lawn dries out you have a job getting color into the dead carpet."

"I feel," continued Matthews, "the best idea is to start on the Bent grass lawn during the winter rains. At that time give the lawn a heavy top dress of humus from your compost heap mixed with peat; sometimes I use manure which was wet down in mid-summer so that weed seeds inside would have time to be burned and those near the surface would germinate. With the back of the rake I work it into the grass. When the rains fall, I stand back and look out the window and see CARE the rains pound the goodness into the lawn. Then in spring the new growth breaks out from new roots that build up from the top dress. The lawn then has a spongy resilience under foot."

Mr. Charles McDonald of Los Altos who has an extensive Bent grass lawn told me he waters his lawn regularly, he turns the sprinklers for an hour at a time in the one place, he said he "just soaks the grass." Besides he said, "I feed my Bent lawn with plant food. This, with the soaking, has freed it of all brown spots." And we all know one of the greatest enemies of the Bent grass lawn is brown spot.

Mr. E. W. Van Gorder, of the Stanford University Golf Course says, "The Bent lawn takes work; it requires more attention than any other grass but the rewards are ample. If one is not prepared to give this care he should plant something else. Astoria Bent is the type suitable for lawns. Do not use Seaside Bent; its place is on the putting green only."

What do you do with the cuttings after mowing the lawn? Mr. Otto Meerly, the Petunia expert has some good ideas here. He says, "Place the cuttings on the compost pile. Work them into humus soil just as you do all your old leaves. Or you may place them in the basins around shrub and trees; scatter them thinly as

DON'T you sow seed in the open ground but under no condition ever put grass cuttings in the flower beds. In the flower beds," he said, "the cuttings always pack, the direct sun heats them up and they rot and go sour and later when you try to cultivate them into the soil the packed cuttings come up in sheets. Under the sheet the ground has become slimy because air could not circulate through." Otto went on to say, "Don't leave the cuttings on the lawn either; they become hay, dry up, look bad, and leave the lawn untidy because the new grass blades push up these old cuttings instead of hiding them. The sprinkler water does not fall hard enough to push the hay cuttings into the grass crowns. Or if the grass makes a lush lawn and you leave the cuttings then there is a danger of choking and rotting the grass below and making the lawn thin out as it does under trees. Perhaps in the East it is all right to leave cuttings on the lawn but this is bad practice in California." However, I might report that some gardeners leave the cuttings on their Bent lawns because in hot weather the grass is cut twice or three times a week and the cuttings are so very small they easily work into the turf.

The Opportune Task: Just as in the winter garden there is a cleanup time in the summer garden. Get ready for the fall by cutting out and taking away all the dead leaves and grass in the bulb beds; the foliage of the daffodils, the Belladonna Amaryllis; clean them up in mid-summer. We've mentioned summer pruning. Go after the flopping branches of your evergreen plants. Prune the thuyas, for example. Yew trees need to be tied up — not like a sausage, but straight; use cotton string to tie the loose branches in; do not wind wire around. Clear out the dead foliage inside the yew tree, a good forceful stream of water will wash it out. Formal plants are enjoyed best when kept in good condition. Get rid of dried paper-like flowers on the geraniums; pull up dried sweet pea vines. *

TOMATO pests active now in warm weather. They include horn worms, army worms, corn earworms, and tomato mites. Apply dusts or sprays regularly to discourage these pests. Use sulphur; handpick worms. Do a thorough job, both sides of foliage. Sometimes two and three applications are needed. *PESTS*

CHRISTMAS trees: watch that tree you planted last winter. Has a gopher gotten under the plant. Have you watered it regularly; that is are you sure the water has penetrated down into the ball of soil. Hot winds, sloping ground, and insufficient watering often cause the needles to drop heavily. Mulch your specimen; water it generously. *TREES*

CHRYSANTHEMUMS: if it is necessary to pinch for the second time, you had better be sure this task is done by the third week of July. Do not pinch after that time. Review chapter on Chrysanthemums.

---

*See Iris (September: Third Week) Iris stylosa.

CHAPTER 29

LAWN SUBSTITUTES

(July: Third Week)

We will begin our discussion with the question: Why substitute for a grass lawn? Ground covers are used in place of grass lawns for convenience as in the case of the week-end gardener who wishes to be free of as much work as possible while down on the ranch. Again another gardener elects the ground cover because of acreage to cover; many consider that lawns demand too much work and attention and believe that ground covers save them from this punishment; and there are those who feel lawns are expensive both in water and in material. But let us look into these opinions.

KINDS What plants are suitable as substitutes for a grass lawn? To serve as a lawn these plants must be creepers, a kind that stays to the ground. In this group are: Dichondra with small leaves; Lippia that flowers all summer; Chamomile that loves the sun; Angel's Tears that loves the shade; Ajuga with copper-toned leaves and deep blue blossoms; Mesembryanthemums that made the "Magic Carpet"; and "Irish or Japanese Moss" neither name of which is correct. Then there are plants which can serve as simple ground covers filling space, keeping down dust, hiding scarred banks, and providing color. In this class is English Ivy, of dark foliage; Periwinkle called by many, "Myrtle"; St. Johnswort so free with its large golden flowers; ivy geraniums for months ladened with showy flowers; wild strawberry with runners that help cover ground; prostrate cotoneasters; and creeping junipers. If one wants to cover a piece of ground each season providing color en mass, verbena, phlox, petunias, and annual portulaca may be selected.

Much, however, depends upon the climate of the garden. Dichondra does well in most climates for it is found wild in the Sierra foothills, San Diego, San Bernardino, and has prospered long in Golden Gate Park and on Alcatraz Island. Lippia isn't at its best in moist climate nor is Chamomile, while Angel's Tears must have a cool coastal one as must also the "Irish or Japanese Moss." Periwinkle folds up in hot weather but comes out in fine new foliage in the wet spring. St. Johnswort often suffers in fall with an ugly infestation of red spider or thrip. Ivy geraniums do not prosper in heavy frost; though, of course, prostrate cotoneasters and creeping junipers grow anywhere in the state.

DICHONDRA

Let us discuss a few of the true creepers often used as substitute for the grass lawn. I hunted up Mr. E. R. Booker of San Jose; he has had a Dichondra lawn for five years; in fact he planted it himself. He's a business man but gardening is his hobby; the Dichondra lawn is his specialty. I asked Mr. Booker how he planted Dichondra and he said, "I prepared the ground thoroughly, spaded up the area, got rid of the junk and plaster, leveled it, where necessary I added loam. I used a two by four to guide me and in a straight line planted little chunks about the size of a silver dollar. These were placed one foot apart and each line alternated with the one before. I pounded in each chunk to make sure the roots were down. Peat makes a good cover after the job is in but I wouldn't recommend manure because of the weed liability." "How long did it take to fill in?" I asked. "At Easter time I planted it, by July the area was completely covered," was his reply. "But while it was filling in, I cultivated regularly because once the ground packs, Dichondra roots stand still, the runners or stolons don't move out, then the weeds come in and they can simply ruin a lawn of Dichondra," he stressed. "I have observed," he said, "people expect Dichondra to grow by itself but that is not the case. The ground must not be allowed to pack, cultivation is necessary to get the area covered right." His "lawn" looked fine; rich green all over, lush and vigorous in the shady parts. "How often do you water your Dichondra?" "Once a week I run the sprinklers for half an hour." "Do you fertilize a Dichondra 'lawn'?" His answer to this question was, "I fertilize the Dichondra twice a year, first in spring about April and the second time in August. As a matter of fact, just as soon as the leaves turn yellow it's O.K. to apply fertilizer." "How do you spread it?" "Well in August when the brown leaves appear I take an old stable broom and sweep the lawn pulling the broom toward me. I never push the broom because it is inclined to dig in and tear out; in this way I clear the 'lawn' of dead leaves. Then with an ordinary kitchen colander I sprinkle a commercial fertilizer. My neighbor uses a liquid fish fertilizer and gets excellent results too. I get an even distribution with the colander but of course I move along fast when applying the stuff because it isn't safe to leave commercial fertilizer lie in lumps on Dichondra," he said. "Then, I finish off the job with a heavy watering and in no time the leaves have returned a rich dark green. In August, after the feeding and when new growth has developed, I give the lawn its annual cutting with an ordinary lawn mower."

ENEMIES

"What are the enemies of Dichondra," I asked Mr. Booker next. "Weeds, if you don't watch out will actually crowd out the lawn. Dichondra won't fight back, especially when Oxalis comes into the lawn. Oxalis has a tap root and gets in to stay — Dichondra has a running stolon. But I keep Oxalis down by cutting the lawn three or four times; this makes the Dichondra send out more stolon roots; they crowd out the Oxalis. Then too, by applying a light top dress fertilizer the Dichondra is further encouraged while the Oxalis gets none. And of course, one can dig out big clumps of Oxalis when he finds any," he said.

Another enemy of Dichondra is the slug; he loves to eat the leaves; he'll get away with the whole leaf which, by the way, is round, heart-shaped as a violet and the plant produces a little purple-white flower hidden below the foliage. But if you don't fight the slugs they will eat the whole lawn. "I just broadcast prepared poisons; that gets rid of slugs," he said. "Frost will hold Dichondra back" he volunteered, "and cold weather will turn the leaves brown in fall. But I feel Dichondra holds up under wear better than a grass lawn because if you or the children scuff it, it comes right back. On the other hand, near flower borders and along the sidewalk I can take a heavy paring knife and cut along the margins and thus keep Dichondra where I want it." As I was about to drive off, Mr. Booker held me a minute to say, with a twinkle in his eye, "Tell them never pour on salt water from the ice cream freezer," pointing to the only bad spot on the place.

But all gardeners are not so satisfied with Dichondra. Mr. Gunar Ernst who has gardened up and down this state says, "I will agree Dichondra is excellent between stepping stones, confined and in contrast with stone it makes a picture, but Dichondra is like clover, you can't lie on it because the juice will stain your clothes as it does also white shoes. And since you have invited me to say something let me add there is no substitute for a lawn; if you have a large area put it in grass and then get a power driven lawn mower. I don't care what ground cover you select — it gets bugs, weeds and volunteers such as little oak and hawthorn trees work their way into it and you have just as much effort keeping the ground cover looking right as you would a grass lawn. But I will agree to one ground cover." continued Mr. Ernst, "and that is wild strawberry, especially if you have a bank or slope where mowing and care would be difficult. Then the strawberry is good because the plants color up so well, in spring with bloom, all summer with shiny leaves, and fruit that are eatable, while in fall and in cold weather the foliage of the wild strawberry turns a rich color." About those weeds he speaks of, you cannot use 2-4-D on Dichondra; that spray injures this ground cover.

Other professionals report dismal failure with Dichondra. One gardener, Mr. Rudolph Kempf, whom we have quoted elsewhere in these pages, tells about his Dichondra lawn which became so unsatisfactory that he had to reseed the area to grass. "In certain seasons," he said, "the Dichondra looked beautiful. It spread over the entire area, stood out a rich black green, not a weed would be in evidence, and the very sight of it cheered you as you gazed down upon it. And then before two months had passed this same beautiful green carpet became mangy with great dead blotches showing dust or mud; weeds crept in, and the color then became a brown sickly yellow. Nor would fertilizer of any sort or rivers of water bring it back into good health. We were far from satisfied with Dichondra," he said.

LIPPIA Perhaps the most commonly used substitute for lawn is Lippia grass. It does particularly well in a sunny place; getting a good start and with proper care Lippia makes a fine "lawn" and for the parking strip, especially wide ones, it is grand. "What do you mean by 'good care'," I asked the boys at the gardeners meeting the other night. Once a year top dress it with compost material or even with screened loam, was the consensus of opinion. "Are there any objections to Lippia," I asked. It blooms all summer and the pinkish flowers attract the bees and that's bad for the children or anyone who wants to use the "lawn". And when you sit on Lippia grass you have lots of company in spiders, sow bugs, and insects; and if a gopher or mole gets under Lippia you have an uneven area bumpy all over and you might as well kiss goodbye the sward idea of your substitute. Then Lippia turns brown in winter and you have no lawn. But one gardener maintained if you'll mow Lippia regularly the bees aren't so bad and you have a nice ground cover. Yet not everyone likes Lippia. Take Albert Wilson for instance. One summer in a moment of weakness when his grass lawn in the rear garden was discouraged and doing poorly he thought of Lippia and planted some pieces in the bare spots. Now the Lippia possesses the place climbing into the lily garden, slipping into the pool, running into the hedge and up into the peach tree, squeezing under the brick walk over by the rose garden, and even crowding onto the driveway. Albert used to call his home "Happy Hours" but ever since bringing Lippia into the garden, it's been "Busy Years".

The other day in a sidewalk consultation with Mr. Charles McDonald of Los Altos I asked him if he ever got rid of the Lippia planted fifteen years ago for the previous owner of his place. "No, I suppose you never can get rid of Lippia once it is planted," he said. "But we keep it down by feeding the lawn strong doses of commercial fertilizer that burns it up and the grass crowds it. It's an unending battle because the roots of Lippia go nine inches deep; in one place we had to take it out."

What about Chamomile? Chamomile has a strong pungent fragrance attractive to some folks; it has a lead grey-green color and produces little yellow flowers. I called up Mrs. Silvey who gardens in the Los Altos hills, and this is what she says about Chamomile: I'm disgusted with it; for five years we have worked hard with Chamomile and all we have is a volunteer moss in its stead. In spring it shows some promise; my husband and I feel we've been unfair in our criticism but as soon as hot weather comes, it goes blah; weeds get in, becomes patchy, and the 'lawn' just isn't." But Mrs. Silvey parted on a more cheerful note by telling me her neighbor with richer soil, not rocky as hers is, likes Chamomile. *CHAMOMILE*

"Carpet Bugle" is another creeping perennial often used — Ajuga is its Latin name. This plant possesses lush leaves, green in summer, bronze, copper-toned in fall and winter; one variety always has copper-toned leaves. It hugs the ground and in spring makes a sea of blue flowers covering as I have seen it as much as 15,000 square feet. On banks and in partial shade this plant is particularly fine. Ajuga does well in almost any soil; if neglected it will look ratty, get bumpy and lumpy, but turn on the water and mow it with a regular lawn mower say once a year, and you have a good ground cover. *AJUGA*

From the fernery Angel's Tears; or Baby's Tears, is often taken into the garden. Helxine soleirolii is its botanical name. It is a moss-like plant possessing tiny light green shiny leaves that grow into a compact mat in the presence of shade and getting loose and free *HELXINE* where abundant moisture predominates. In sunlight the plant becomes a pest in all cool coastal gardens, especially in San Francisco and Carmel; if once it creeps among the azaleas and rhododendrons or any of the permanent plants it is impossible to get rid of. Angel's Tears, is purely for show; you can't step on it because the leaves are succulent and full of water. And quite similar is "Coralbead", a creeper forming a dense mat of mossy foliage producing showy orange-red berries. In Japanese gardens and in shady places it is popular.

ARENARIA "Sandwort" is the name you'll find in the books, but amateurs insist upon calling it erroneously "Irish moss, Japanese moss", but botanically it is known as Arenaria balearica coming from the Balearic Islands and Corsica in the Mediterranean. In some districts of California as in San Francisco, Santa Cruz, and Long Beach, "Sandwort" makes a very attractive lawn substitute. This plant is characterized by its dark green, fine, needle-like leaves produced in mats never more than three inches thick. Myriads of miniature, angelic pure white blossoms lift this dark carpet into starry greeting in the light of the July and August sun. But all do not succeed with "Sandwort". In Palo Alto its beauty is only seasonal. I have seen this ground cover puff up, develop a permanent wave that no rolling could settle. I've observed how spongy it has become in moist cool weather and have seen how the first blast of warm weather has cooked and burned it so that actual dead spots appeared all over the carpet. Besides high temperature its greatest enemy is the sow bug which feel it has come to heaven when it finds "Sandwort". Slugs, why they dance over this ground cover in the moonlight.

Let us now summarize. The professional gardeners hate lawn substitutes. They feel it takes just as much time, some say more, to keep a substitute lawn in proper shape; it requires almost as much water, perhaps not quite as much fertilizer, depending of course upon soil type and location; and many feel the initial investment of establishing a substitute is as great as establishing a regular grass lawn. The amateurs, on the other hand, less interested in generalizing their work into a practice, have found substitutes here and there to fit admirably though they, too, still rely principally on grass.

Last summer I was called in to design a sitting area in a shady spot near the entrance way of a nice country home. Grass lawn was out of the question because of deep shade. My plan called for a brick platform to occupy the open area with flower beds around the margins to provide seasonal color. "Could you suggest any material other than brick for the ground cover," asked the gentleman. "You could use slate but sometimes under weight it will crack," I responded. "Anything else?" he asked. "There is gravel but you track it into the house, and the ladies with open-toe shoes hate gravel." "What else?" he pushed. "Spanish tile are all right but often they show a rather tough surface; then alkali will work through the surface even if you shellac it," was my answer to that one. But still my client was not satisfied and he again asked, "Is there anything else?" "Yes, there is, the area could be covered with oak tanbark; it gives a good color, lasts long, doesn't stick to the shoe, you can roll it once a month and if it gets thin, add some more. Tanbark," I went on to say, "looks natural, leaves falling upon it blend into the picture, though of course you can rake them out." "Well, what about cement?" asked the gentleman. "CEMENT! My goodness no, not at your front door; they use that to pave streets with; brick is what we want to use here." "Oh well," he said, "I only asked! I happen to be president of the Cement Company." *STORY*

And now for the Opportune Task: You may still carry on your succession of vegetables in the garden. Beans, corn, lettuce, spinach, and squash; select the squash called "Delicious". And it is still time for a late batch of summer squash. Think now about starting the seeds of the perennials and biennials for next year's garden. Plants started from seeds now in July can be in bloom next spring. There is a whole raft of them: hollyhocks, cup and saucer campanulas, coreopsis, delphiniums, foxgloves, columbine, sweet william, geums, penstemons, Siberian wall flowers, gaillardia, and scabiosa. We'll have more to say about these flowers later but start thinking about them now.

LILACS

LILACS: For the old fashion lilac in California always give the full sun, good air circulation, and space to grow. When possible select the grafted or budded specimen. It grows vigorously and usually produces a large, free flowering plant in a few years. Privet is employed as the rootstock, and lilacs grafted on privet should be placed deep so that the bud-union is about four inches below the surface of the soil, and the grafted lilacs then will form its own roots which break out from the stem below ground. (Usually in two years.) Suckers that appear will be those of the grafted hybrid. All new suckers that first appear should be allowed to remain, as they feed back strength to the roots. After two or three years they bloom as freely as the original part of the plant. Old established plants that send up "a million" suckers, should have some removed; remove them in spring. Pull them from the socket below, they never come up there again.

WHEN GRAFTED

CUTTINGS

CUTTINGS: may be rooted, but these often fail to send up suckers and occasionally or finally die out. WATERING: stop watering the lilac in late July. Bushes then get rest early enough to complete the dormant cycle by time spring returns. Lilacs make all of the years growth in six weeks of spring. A light watering afterwards is alright, but no heavy irrigation. Newly set out plants get water the first year right up till fall rains. PRUNING: newly set out plants get none till the third year. Let shrub become adjusted to its new location. After that time try to keep center of plant open. Best time to thin out center growth is when plant is dormant; you can see then what you do. Here too only the strongest suckers up in the center of the plant should be retained. Get rid of the remaining ones, especially those on the outside of the plant. They cause plants to grow out of bounds. For old established plants remember each year to prune out some old wood; favor the

(CONTINUED ON PAGE 247)

Chapter 30

SUMMER CARE OF THE CITRUS TREES

(July: Fourth Week)

We speak of the citrus, a useful group of plants with a long history; what a fascinating story they tell from their original home to the prize tree in your own garden. Whence come the citrus? They have been grown in California for one hundred and fifty years; they are natives of tropical and subtropical regions of Asia. The Mandarin of small fruit are said to have been found on the coast of Africa in 1487 by the Portuguese on their first trip around the Cape. Later upon reaching India and China these travelers found them already there. And the Mandarin was taken to England by Sir Walter Raleigh. *HISTORY*

The Arabs were the great distributors of the citrus in the East and they took the lemon to Europe in the 13th century. The Crusaders off to Syria and Palestine found the lemon had been delivered there before them, introduced centuries ago from India. Today refugees resettling in the Holy Land have planted great groves of oranges. Even now Italy on the Mediterranean grows thirty varieties of lemons, France has twelve varieties. California since the beginning of the citrus "dynasty" in 1870 had the Lisbon lemon, and old introduction from Spain, and the bane of the pickers because of its thorns, the Villa Franca without bitterness, though *KINDS*

strong in acid, brought from the Riviera; the Eureka which should be grown in every garden; the Meyer or Chinese lemon from China given to the California gardens by our Department of Agriculture and now offered for sale by every nursery throughout the state; and Ponderosa, "The American Wonder Lemon", with skin never thin enough, nor juice rich enough, yet a gorgeous ornamental in the garden.

California's commercial industry is based upon five important varieties of citrus: Washington navel orange, originating in Brazil, brought to this country by the United States Department of Agriculture, and planted first at Riverside, California; Valencia orange from Spain possessing rich color in fruit that ripens late, developing into trees of great vigor and hardiness to our weather; Eureka lemon, the most important lemon of all, is popular because you can pick one every day in the year and a sweet rind covers the fruit. It was originated here in California; the trees are almost thornless.

Then there is the Marsh grapefruit, botanically known as Pomelo, and grown in the desert areas of California and Arizona. Grapefruit is popular at all breakfast tables; it is true the skin is thick, and though also the fruit is not sweet yet it is juicy and is of good flavor. The landscape gardeners use the grapefruit trees in their work because they possess a decorative form in growth. And there is, of course, the pink grapefruit,* the Thompson grown in a great scale in the Rio Grande Valley of Texas. But we have it here, too, though the fruit will not get pink in our climate; the quality is like the Marsh, but it takes more heat to color up. Then there is the Chinese grapefruit, a most beautiful ornamental tree; the fruit too is attractive and prized by the Chinese for their New Year festivities. A close relative of the grapefruit is the Tangelo which is a hybrid between the grapefruit and the Tangerine. This is a new citrus but can be recommended for our gardens of Central California. The Tangelo really gets sweet, like a Navel orange, with the mixed flavor of the parent fruit and the experts

*See page 415

even suspect the trees may become everbearing; that is they might produce more than one crop a year. This fact is not yet known, but they have hopes.

Then there are other citrus in this large family which have become popular in our California gardens. Among the limes we grow Bearss' seedless from Tahiti, largest and finest of them all. From India, Rangpur, hardiest of the limes, bearer of heavy crops of small fruit of a beautiful deep orange color with the fruit being extremely acid. The Rangpur lime is a wonderful citrus; anyone can grow it, you'll find it loaded with fruit at all seasons of the year; and as espalier, trained flat against a warm wall on the south or west side of the house, they can't be beat. Mexican lime, an old standard, semi-dwarf and excellent for tub culture. And the little sweet lime so valuable for beverage purpose because of quality and flavor; excellent for tea.

In some gardens I've seen beautiful Tangerines and Mandarins, known as Kid Glove Oranges because the rind is thin and peels off readily. The rind is exceedingly aromatic and this quality imparts a spicy flavor which is not obtained in other citrus fruits. There are many others, the list is long: Algerian Tangerine, Willow Leaf Mandarin, Citron of commerce, a large conical fruit with an exceedingly thick rough furrowed rind; the fruit from which the candied citron peel of commerce is made; the Ruby Blood orange with delicious bright red juice that fails to color up in the Bay region as is true also with the pink lemon; and the Kumquat, the smallest citrus fruit, a favorite for marmalade.

What do we do for the citrus in our gardens? Is growing an orange harder than growing a lemon tree or any other citrus? We must know their habits through the year. First, let us review our talk "Planting the New Fruit Tree", because unlike the bare root deciduous tree, citrus may be planted any time in the year. "Dig a big hole — twice the size of the container or balled up root; dig deep; loosen the soil in the bottom, use a fork, or spade or shovel; chop up, break loose, make

CARE

the soil down there friable. Especially for the citrus dig that hole three by three by three feet (there's lots of room underground), the roots go deep, we must prepare for them, use a crowbar if necessary to explore the hole and make it ready for the roots to come. Drainage for the citrus must be good because they have deep penetrating roots. Prepare for them by throwing into the bottom of the hole a little bone meal, work this into the soil down there, don't leave it in one lumpy cake. If your citrus comes with its roots tied up in a ball of burlap, set the roots in the hole, throw in one part peat and two parts of the good top soil that you piled to one side when digging the hole." With the citrus it is best that you do not cut the strings nor open up the burlap covering because often the soil around the roots is sandy and you do not want it to break away or fall apart. As the plant grows the roots will come through the burlap. Sometimes when you buy a new citrus tree you find the roots already have come through the burlap; handle them carefully because, "rough handling might break off the little new adventurous roots and you do not want to cripple your plant at the beginning. Then you fill in the hole with the rest of the good top soil. When the job is finished the neck of the ball should be just at ground level. Let me repeat this, this is important because some trees are budded higher than others; so when your planting job is done the bud scar should be at ground level or just above ground level, one or one and a half inches up, never under the soil.

"Should your specimen come in a can — simply cut the opposite sides and pull apart. You can lift the plant out with its cake of soil and put it in the ground. Should your specimen be in a tub or a box, because you have dug the hole three feet by three feet by three feet, you set the box and all in the hole, then completely remove the sides. Always set the plant in the hole one and a half to two inches deeper than it was in the container, but remember again with the citrus that the bud scar must be above the ground floor. The operation of planting a new tree in the garden is completed with a basin ground level filled with compost through which the water is poured. Fill the basin three times; let it seep down past the compost each time; then fill it once again for me and your plant will go singing on its way."

Study the citrus and questions will arise; so I cooked up a batch and went to see Mr. Joseph Grimshaw who has specialized in citrus for fourteen years. He used to grow them in Southern California, then up in Oroville, and now he's at Hayward. I asked him, "What climate suits the citrus best?" "The warmer the spot the better they grow," he said as a starter. "Plant them on the south or west side of the building or provide some sort of a windbreak to shelter the tree from the north-east winds, especially while the tree is young because those winds generally are the freezing winds."

"What about those who already have citrus growing in the garden. What should they do now?" I asked Mr. Grimshaw next. "Keep the soil in good condition; the best soil is none too good. And the worst thing a gardener can do to a citrus is to spade up the ground under the low branches. The tap root goes deep but the feeder roots of these trees are most active only about one foot under the ground surface. Instead of spading under the weeds there, water and pull them out, throw them down, and then cover the area completely with mulch materials. Right now is a good time to mulch under the orange, lemon, grapefruit, all of the citrus in fact," he said.

What do you recommend for mulch materials?" *MULCH* "Barnyard manure with lots of straw; bean straw is excellent; and put it on three or four inches deep; peat and leaf mold are good too. You know," he went on, "heavy soils like adobe crack in the summer; this can tear the roots apart but a good mulch will check cracking especially under trees where you don't want to cultivate or can't cultivate, or, as in the case of all the citrus, you shouldn't cultivate, so put on the mulch; cow manure is good but go easy with the chicken manure," he cautioned.

"What is the water schedule for citrus trees in

WATER summer time?" "Water them every two or three weeks; down in Southern California they follow a system of irrigating every twenty-one days. But don't plant your orange in the lawn, for too often the lawn grows on heavy soil and water doesn't evaporate too quickly; then in such a place the citrus become unhappy," answered Mr. Grimshaw. "What about apply-
FEED ing fertilizer now?" He said, "Citrus need plenty of fertilizer. Start applying it in spring, March and April, and in the early summer; animal manure is good if you can get it, especially for the top dress mulch. Chilean nitrate, commercial ammonia, superphosphate — that helps to set the fruit — blood meal; commercial fertilizers used very carefully and early in the summer will help. Citrus trees fed with these foods will have lush foliage, firm leaves instead of sickly looking sagging ones. But of course don't give them the gout; you can tell it by the leaves becoming bumpy and curling in wavy fashion. Feed the citrus moderately.

We might go back again to our words of last spring. Remember then we suggested, "first soak up the ground; then with the strength of a Samson drive a crowbar down. Make those crowbar holes all around the tree just inside the leaf-drop edge — make the hole deep and then fill them up with bone meal; and soak it in with lots of water." The deep roots will find strength in this feeding and later strong growth will result in your tree. Feed them in June, July, and early August. But remember no fertilizer must be applied in the fall or winter months because late feeding tends to soften the growth and for winter you want hard wood, not watery, sappy stuff that will burn in the lightest frost.

"Why do oranges taste bitter?" I asked. "They pick them at the wrong time," he replied. "Take the Valencia for example; it starts to color up about Christmas time, but the actual picking of the fruit
WHEN should not commence until the following August. Then
PICK you can keep picking until Christmas. The gardener must not get too anxious to pick just because he sees a

little color. The Washington Navel orange up in Oroville begins to give color in November, but the fruit is not tree ripe until the following February. Perhaps in the Bay region they may have to wait until April, then the fruit can be picked through the summer. And if one has a Washington Navel and a Valencia orange they can have fruit all year long. Tree-ripe oranges are usually sweeter than those from the counter.

FLOWER FRUIT DROP

"Why do oranges and lemons drop before they ripen?" He answered this one by saying, "Often carelessness in watering, mostly too much water." And there is another answer, perhaps you have noticed flower buds dropping off. Many times the gardener will spray his tree when the flowers are open and in full bloom; this washes the pollen, fertilization fails to carry and the undeveloped fruit drops off.

ENEMIES

Of course spraying is tied up with insect infestation and a good idea is to watch for aphid, mealy bug and scale before the bloom appear;spray then or only when the flowers are in the pearl stage, unopened, or best of all wait until the little fruit are the size of marbles; then it is safe to use the oil sprays. Among the enemies the aphid, mealy bug, and scale are the worst in summer time; they with their friends the ants will go after any orange, or lemon, or kumquat, or lime that is kept dry and hungry. So water your plants overhead once in a while, especially in the evening when the leaves have cooled after a hot day. The summer oil sprays are effective in controlling aphid, mealy bug, and scale. But what do you suppose is the greatest enemy of the citrus? "The gopher is the worst," said Mr. Grimshaw. "There are more trees lost through not controlling gophers than any other cause."

Do you know about the free circulars? No. 79, Control of Injurious Rodents in California, it tells all about getting rid of gophers the easy way; and circular No. 114, Citrus Culture in California. Send to the University of California, Berkeley 4, California. Upon leaving, Mr. Grimshaw said, "Everybody likes some type of citrus around the place; a lemon, orange or grapefruit, and I feel," he said modestly, "I'm doing the people a favor by inducing them to grow citrus in the garden because they are easy to grow and certainly the plants are among the most decorative and satisfactory of the fruit trees; as long as they prune out the water sprouts from the center of the tree as it grows; thin out so as to let in the sunshine and air; and as long as they control a few of the insects; then the garden will have something."

WATER SPROUTS

Three years ago a newcomer to California bought a place in Cupertino where orange trees were growing. She was telling her friend, the gardener, about it. "I have a lot of oranges and all they give me is a corky fruit, no juice, no sweetness at all and I bought the place because of these trees too," she said.

"What! in the rich soil of Cupertino; under the bright sun of our Santa Clara Valley, and only corky, tasteless orange," her friend exclaimed. "Shame on somebody. Now I'll go down there one of these days and see what's happening."

"And so I went down," he said, as he told me this story. "And there they were, neglected, scrawny, half-starved, dead branches inside and out, insects galore; I'll tell you," he said, "it was a mess."

But there is one thing about the citrus family;those plants can take a beating, actually they can be neglected for two or three years and then if given proper attention will come back.

"So I sailed into that row of trees," he went on to tell. "I pruned out the dead wood, trimmed back the scraggly branches; I sprayed all the trees hard — three good doses. It was summer time but I gave them a top dressing of compost and I slipped them a little commercial fertilizer; I soaked the water to them; besides I whitewashed all the trunks; and before I left that day, I read the riot act and boy! did those trees come back! She was in the other day and what do you suppose, right off the bat she said, 'I'm citrus-minded now. Those trees are covered with strong shoots and new leaves; the fragrance of the flowers this spring, oh! And now there is a load of little oranges coming; the place is heaven itself."

The Opportune Task: Go after the dry spots in the garden. You'll find them in the flower borders around the shrub areas, and of course in the lawn. It's the sun and wind that cause dry spots. Give them water, use a sprinkler because it will spread the water better than a running hose. The spray of water sinks in all over and it gets to the high spots; so often water running from the hose falls into a gopher hole or into a low spot. Let the dry spot soak up the water sponge fashion and the sprinkler does it. Then all this month (July) use lots of water.

(CONTINUED FROM PAGE 238)

LILACS

shoots. Diseased and dead wood is always pruned off. Get rid of seed pods, clip faded blooms. Watch out not to injure the new wood which always surrounds the bloom. Picking blooms in spring is a kind of pruning.

FEEDING: Never feed lilacs with strong fertilizer; do not give them lime; in California give them bone meal, two cups to a four year old plant, scatter around the bush. Apply every third year. A mulch of manure thrown down at the roots during the rainy winter or early spring is good; don't dig it in, for fibrous top feeding roots might be injured.

ENEMIES: Oyster shell scale; in May the young ones hatch; control; use a summer oil spray, or in January use a strong dormant spray. VARIETIES: Among the popular Clarke hybrids the following are recommended for the California garden. CLARKE'S GIANT: immense flower clusters; individual bloom 1 1/4 – 1 1/2 inches across; soft gentian blue when fully open; fragrant. BLUE HYACINTH: individual flowers like blue hyacinth. ALICE EASTWOOD: with dark claret-purple buds that turn to bluish-purple, finally to pink. KATE SESSIONS: with single flowers which open purple, changing to blue. MISSIMO: tremendous blooms, cyclamen-purple flower clusters.

Examine every new lilac, tree, shrub, or vine; are wires of the labels girdling? Branches often die when wire girdles, cutting into bark. Remove.

CHAPTER 31

ANNUAL SEEDS FOR THE NEXT SEASON'S GARDEN

(July: Fourth Week)

We deal with planting seeds of the annuals. Certain kinds of annuals thrive especially well in certain parts of the world. You can see snapdragons by the acre in the Philippines; asters by the mile in China; valleys brimfull with bachelor buttons in Central Europe; snapdragons decorating the rocky hills of Spain. Though these flowers are special to these places, they and one hundred others all thrive with a little help in California. And the first item of that help is to get their seeds in the ground at the right time.

Now, mid-July, is the right time for many of them; that is, the hardy annuals which can go through the winter. Everything — warm soil, warm air, bright sunlight — is in your favor and in theirs too. So let's consider the steps you and I must take to sow seeds of hardy annuals.

How can you get good seeds? Two weeks ago in my own back yard I collected the seed pods from my old plants of white stock. Each straw-colored pod was filled inside with straw-colored flat disc-shaped small seeds. I shook the seeds out into a bag, left the bag in the warm sunlight so that the coats would dry out, and that is where my fresh seed of white stock came from this year. I did the same with my rust-proof snapdragons, and some larkspur which I've put away till next fall. But you can buy fresh seed from your nurseryman if you have none of your own.

Prepare your flat, select one in good condition with no rotted wood or nails out to tear the skin when being handled, provide drainage and avoid air pockets. A consistently successful gardener friend said to me, "I throw into the bottom of the flat a layer of coarse soil. This rough material provides drainage. Some gardeners use gravel for the same purpose. Then I put over this rough material the good top soil that I have already mixed and screened; it is made up of equal parts of loam, sand and leaf mold. And then instead of using the wooden block or brick, I take my fingers and knead the soil down all over the flat, and finish off by leveling the surface. I give it a good soaking so that the water settles down the soil thoroughly as it passes through it. I let the flat stand for a day before I sow the seeds." *HOW TO SEED*

Many gardeners put newspaper in the bottom of the flat to retain moisture. I have several times noticed that the favorite part of the paper was the colored cartoons in the Sunday supplement. I am told that the inks discourage the pests, especially the ants, from nesting. Although I am sure these same inks sometimes discourage the people, I can't guarantee them for the ants.

Be especially careful with annuals to sterilize the soil before you scatter any seeds. Annuals seem to suffer more than perennials and loss can be greater from damping-off disease killing the seedling or fungus rotting the seed, destroying the germ cell after it has pushed its way through the seed coat. What is damping-off disease? Your seed germinates, in your anxiety to help you keep pouring on the water. Soon you have broken the balance, so that the fungus can get going. This, a ravenous parasite, sends its roots boring into the delicate stem and robs it of its nourishing sap. Then, instead of standing up like soldiers, they begin to bend over like old men, and the next day they are down and done for. Sterilize the soil. An *DAMP OFF* easy way for the home gardener to do this is to pour boiling water over the flat; when dried off, saturate again with cold water. The commercial growers find the hot water takes into solution such chemicals as nitrate, which later on burn the delicate roots of the seedlings; they leach them out with plenty of cold water. Let the flat dry, and then level up the soil again and you are ready to scatter the seeds.

Another precaution you have to take with annual seeds is that many of them are finer than the average perennial. Pansies, for example, are as fine as pepper. With this in mind, Charles Gamblin, the well-known professional gardener, says, "I always make sure the soil is firmed and fills the flat, but isn't packed in tight. I want the top surface loose enough, yet close enough so that the soil particles come into direct contact with every seed I sow. What I am after is a surface that allows each germinating root to get between and attached to the soil particles as soon as it leaves the seed. In other words, the finer the seed the more care you take."

After the seeds have been sown in the flat — and a good way is to drop dry sand in the packet, shake well and then scatter over flat — and a fine loose cover of dry soil put over them, they may be lightly watered

CARE

with a fine spray. "We must watch out not to wash the seed or get them floating," said Mr. Gamblin. "The big point is to stick by those flats after you have sown the seeds." And he told me of another gardener who stays right by when he has started off his annual seeds. "If necessary," he said, "I sprinkle the flat two or three times a day on hot days to make sure the moisture is present continually for those germinating seeds. Just as soon as I see the new green leaves, I know the seeds have germinated, and I immediately cut down the amount of water so as not to tempt damping-off disease to come in and kill off my new plants."

Another system for either annual or perennial is to place the flat in a pan with one inch of water. Slowly the soil will draw up the water, becoming saturated, leaving the pan dry. Lift the flat out, and as a rule there will be enough moisture for the germination period. But even so, you can't count on it. A little deficiency in water absorbant in the soil will let it dry out.

Mr. Gamblin said, "I like to sow the larger seeds in rows — such as calendulas and stock. Here are my reasons. First, I can add a little more soil if it's necessary. I make rows by drawing my finger along the prepared soil. I make them far enough apart so I can work among the seedlings and do things there that would be impossible if the seeds are scattered in the flat. Second, I can water right down the rows making sure the water gets to the seeds, and they won't dry out. Third, should trouble come, in the form of mildew or any of the soil-borne enemies such as damping-off disease, I can treat the rows with mercury — even sulphur dust helps — and the rows also keep the disease from spreading. There is enough space to drop in a little sand after each watering, to take up the excess moisture. Take stock for example; sometimes stock gets the yellows in the flat, and become sickly. In the rows I can drop a little lime, and right away arrest that trouble. Fourth and finally, when time to transplant comes, I work down the rows. The seedlings fall apart easily as I transplant them to the next flat." The yellows which Mr. Gamblin refers to is a mosaic disease supposed to be caused by a virus, a mysterious germ which is too small to see.

TRANSPLANT

So far, we have been talking of the management of seeds in the flat. The next step is to transplant for the first time, either into a new flat or into a nursery bed under a lath frame. Handle exactly like the perennials. Don't crowd them into the flat; give each plant plenty of room. But be very sure you put the roots well down into the soil and firm well. Don't let these delicate seedlings flop around when you sprinkle them; press them firmly.

OUTDOOR SEEDING

"And I have another system," said Mr. Gamblin. "It's like Arthur Taylor's* system for sowing perennial seeds outdoors — the more hardy annuals like stock, forget-me-nots, and calendula. First, I select

*See(August Second Week: Planting Perennial Seeds for Next Year's Garden.)

a spot that gets the full sun. I set a sprinkler that throws the water around over a circle, and soak the spot well. After it dries a bit, I get my spading fork and I fluff up the soil, make it loose, then grade it and it's ready for the seed. When this is all done," he continued, "I make circular grooves inside that circle and in them sow the hardy annuals that keep on growing this fall and winter. I cover the rows with a light dusting of peat; this is to check caking. I keep a weather eye out for sow bugs and pill bugs. I place a wire screened frame over the plot to exclude the birds. The idea is with all this room outdoors, I can sow a lot of seeds and after I can transplant the seedlings easily, with very few losses indeed."

All of these plants, both perennials and annuals, you will be moving out into the garden sometime in September when we'll have another discussion on this subject. When seedlings have been transplanted in the second flat or nursery bed, or when first put out into the garden, it is safest for both amateur and professional to water them always with a fine spray. Do not irrigate by flooding. Flooding a flat brings moss; flooding newly planted seedlings brings damping-off, a lurking uninvited guest wherever wet conditions prevail. Instead, sprinkle overhead with a fine spray and be sure the seedlings get enough so that they won't dry up.

DON'T

ENEMIES

What about insect enemies of your little plant? Aphids are the worst; they will go after stock, even the rugged calendula. But there is a way to get the best of them. Keep the flat of seedlings cool, be sure air circulates freely over them. Under stuffy conditions the soil is sure to become hard, and to delicate roots just out of a protecting seed coat hard soil is like the rock of Gibraltar. A little trick is to give the seedlings sunlight in the early morning hours, and shade in the afternoon, but at all times plenty of air. Insect enemies are less likely to be troublesome because the plants are sturdy. The essentials of success are plenty of air and cool treatment. Too much heat, or coddling, produces weak, lanky, insect-infested plants from which a mass of flowers such as you planned for never can be obtained. But don't forget the birds; they too love your seedlings.

Here is a list for your selection:

ANNUALS FOR EARLY FLOWERING (that is, if weather is good, around Christmas)

Calendula, satisfactory and easiest of them all. Orange King and Lemon Queen, among the best of the double varieties.

Violas and pansies can be the glory of your gardens early and late in the year.

Cineraria, whose flowers are known for their brilliant indigos, blues, purples, crimsons, some delightfully colored in patterns. Try any of them for a wonderful corner of bloom.

Schizanthus, "Poor Man's Orchid," likes good soil and can be grown in pots or in the open garden. They delight in moist atmosphere and enjoy low temperatures.

Wallflowers, plant them now so they will be ready to go out into the garden when the rains start. And don't forget the Siberian Wallflower; next to forget-me-nots you can have a bright effect.

Mignonette, old-fashioned and sweet-scented. To get good results, dress the ground first with lime, and firm the ground tight when you sow the seed.

Stocks, the rich odor and colors of this annual will tempt any gardener to try growing them in his yard. Keep an eye on the young seedlings; any that show up with narrow curled leaves are diseased; yank them out, for they can be only trouble makers later on.

But a word more about stock. Sow the seed thinly *STOCK* so that the young plants may have abundant room, for a little extra space will be repaid by stout and vigorous growth at the outset. But do not condemn stock seedlings that start out with weak stems. A lady, speaking to her gardener, said "I want this and this and this one," pointing to all the vigorous strong-growing plants in the flat. On second thought she said, "Now, you can have all the rest." These were weak looking unpromising stock plants. The gardener thanked her. When the plants bloomed, she had all the singles, the gardener had all the beautiful double flowers.

PRIMULA Primroses are another favorite annual. Sow the seeds of Primula malacoides; some people call it the "baby primrose." We grow it as an annual, but in China, it's home, botanists have classified it a perennial. Since 1908, gardeners in England, Germany, Switzerland and the United States have worked on these plants so that today you can select varieties that suit your particular color scheme. In Chicago in 1915, Ernst Eriksson, brooding in bed over an itchy rash from that other Chinese primrose, Primula obconica, resolved to create a primrose that would equal this one in beauty and charm, but without the itch, and he finally hybridized a fine strain of Baby Primulas. Select seeds of Erikssons deep red, Erikssons white, or Erikssons special mixture.

And one more annual that Ernest Matthews asked me particularly to call to your attention: Gypsophila elegans, the annual Baby's Breath. Be sure and give it a well-drained and not overly enriched soil. Consult your catalogues; there are several fine varieties.

Now let's go on to another list:

ANNUALS TO BLOOM A LITTLE LATER (that is, early spring)

Viscaria, the compact form; one of our brightest annuals, producing masses of flowers which withstand frost.

Nemesias, bushy plants covered with abundant flowers. Perhaps these are new to you. Essential needs for success are a cool soil and plenty of moisture. Once let the plants go dry and they come into flower too soon, get leggy, and run to seed. It is important that they should suffer no set-back before being put into their flowering positions. The time of sowing should be so arranged that the plants are ready for putting out in the garden when they are wanted. If they have to be kept waiting in the flat after they have reached the stage for transplanting, they will quickly become starved and suffer a check from which they cannot recover. Nemesias do wonderfully when they get a good root hold, they will give a splash of many colors, and if kept watered and not allowed to go to seed they last for weeks.

Candytuft, the Hyacinth Candytuft. This annual sends up a stem twelve inches tall and opens up an umbrella of white flowers. Some plants branch out with many umbrellas. Give it a rich soil, and it will give you back a rich show and a sweet-smelling one, too.

Forget-me-nots, remember the mass of forget-me-nots at Treasure Island? Try to duplicate that in your garden. These forget-me-nots have nice names, like "Blue Bird" and "Blue Eyes," and while this flower is pleading with you not to forget it, don't forget the Chinese forget-me-nots.

And finally, snapdragons. They have been hybridized so much that now you can select any color you want. Afterglow, an all-round orange bronze; Klondike Supreme, a deep, large flowered yellow; White Wonder Improved; Mary Louise, a light shell pink; and Windmiller's Lilac. Again, I invite you to study the catalogues.

The Opportune Task: prepare for the annuals that you sow now and are going to put out in the fall. Go through your box of seeds. The only way to get seeds you can depend upon is to use those not over two years old. Whether you collect your own seeds or buy them, you can't be sure of the quality or color. You are almost certain to get variations.

CHAPTER 32

ROOF GARDENS

(July: Fifth Week)

Roof gardens. This isn't a new idea at all, for the Greeks and Syrians had them, while the Romans had literally roof forests with plants in boxes, pots and lead urns while the floor was often of mosaic, that supported in some instances pergolas of stone over which grape vines grew. Today the roof garden is not only for the city, for suburbans may have them too. In fact there is an advantage in the suburban district as it is not likely to suffer so much wind, for often in the city sharper winds with a bellow effect blow daily. We speak of roof but this doesn't limit us to the house itself. There is the deck above a proch, the flat roof over a low wing connecting two parts of the house, and even the flat top of a garage may serve as a roof garden as is often seen in Palm Springs on the desert.

We must be practical in this matter. If I were to build a roof garden I'd first consult the architect or the builder who put up the house itself. A garden on a roof with yards of soil, a ton of gravel, heavy boxes, pots of all kinds, and plants of many types, means lots of extra weight. Not to mention the people who will be invited to enjoy it from time to time and who will be walking around on the flooring and sitting in the furniture. The architect could investigate also the drainage problems, as it would be a great convenience to wash the floor off once in a while and of course that rain water must leave no puddles on the roof. The architect can help also in the selection of a good floor to be put over the roof; to be sure this is a detail, but done right, especially on the almost level roof, the flooring adds strength to the design and provides comfort for walking and using the roof garden and will help to keep things dry and keep everyone healthy. There are various ways of making the roof waterproof and putting the floor above it. Gravel and tar is the most commonly used. A grating of wood is needed here because it is definitely not wise to establish a garden directly on a roof of gravel and tar. The gratings can be painted slate color to keep down reflection; and the pieces spaced wide for better circulation of air. And in this detail also the more space between the roof and the floor the better. Then tile or slate make excellent floor coverings in a roof garden, and with these no wooden grates are required.

Along with the flooring the problem of safeguards at the edge of the roof must be given attention. Railings or parapets two or three feet high serve very well especially for protection and privacy. Of course where the parapet is not possible then the use of boxes of heavy plants will help.

Where is this roof garden to be? Will the wind come from the north or west? Will the sunshine be upon it all day, just in the morning hours, or all afternoon? Indeed we must take into consideration every condition of weather. Walls you know are climate makers; an adjoining tall building can reflect light and may lend shelter to your roof garden; or guided by your architect you may construct glass walls which will let in the sunlight but keep out the wind. These glass walls too may be graded so that the tall sections of glass will stand where needed most and paneled down to floor level. Glass, however, must not be allowed to burn the plants. *STUDY*

My own experience in developing a roof garden has been limited to a few in San Francisco and Palo Alto; so when a listener wrote inviting me to discuss the subject over "How Does Your Garden Grow" I remembered Mr. George Kelley in San Francisco has put in hundreds of roof gardens. He's our man; let's tackle him for I know he will hand out the information graciously. Imagine my delight when he said, "The plan's the thing; make up your mind what you want; get the picture and work for it." Why those words are like preparing for the garden itself. The plan's the thing; *PLAN* what a simple truth. Of course that roof garden can't grow all over everywhere;there must be a background, there must be a margin, there must be an open area because the situation, the purpose of this roof garden, and the character determines the dimensions. I remember when a student drawing plant cells I saw through the microscope but drawing them as big as cobblestones all over the paper, my late professor Douglas Houghton Campbell telling me time and time again, "watch your proportions". The roof garden more than the garden outdoors must give the effect of calmness to the place. Time of course can soften the newness of the materials, but the open area in the design, being level and as wide as possible providing an intimate foreground for the distant view offered from the roof, must be considered a complete garden unit in itself.

USE But for what is the roof garden to be used? If seclusion and rest -- none but the best in furniture should be used; furniture which can take any weather which would not require a dash to the roof with every cloud that floats by. Perhaps it is to be an outdoor living room. But let us say you have determined to have it a real garden with life for all year round. In this there is the question of the effect desired; shall it be formal? An advantage of the formal design is you can plan for the color and effects during the seasons. In the formal roof garden there may be little hedges of boxwood or plants trimmed to globes and pyramids with flower beds laid out in geometric patterns with good straight lines because the area is usually so small. Formal gardens tolerate no spotty effects. In this formal roof garden advantage may be taken of all walls by stepping up the boxes with the shallow ones in front, the high boxes in the rear: and along high walls interesting effects may be established by a pattern of trellises. The stepping up of the boxes as well as the trellises create an illusion of perspective. Trellises lend height, covered with a ravishing mantle of bloom they take away severity; in fact, the only solution for a wall is a pattern; the wall is there for a purpose, it should be ornamented. Remember the quick-growing Boston Ivy with its abundant foliage — it will completely annihilate a wall and do the job beautifully too.

Then some roof gardens will be for display; a show of quick fancy color; in this it is best to select plants that can take it both as to drought and heavy weather. What beats cineraries or calendulas in winter or violas and pansies in spring; petunias and lobelia in summer and chrysanthemums in fall?

Those expressing themselves in a roof garden as in the conservatory must indeed be lovers of flowers and plants. The roof garden requires lots of fuss and regular changing; perhaps not much weeding but certainly a daily routine of care must be followed. Best of all, know that roof for sunlight, shadows and wind. But when one's home is the roof, what could give greater joy than to walk right out into the garden there.

CARE

All containers must be of durable materials. And it is best they rest on wooden slats in order that air may circulate freely underneath. Boxes and tubs should be tarred inside especially up to the soil line for it is along this line where rotting takes place so readily. Careful attention to size of containers is important because more nursing is required if too small; greater drying out takes place; boxes therefore should be eighteen inches to two feet deep and two feet wide. Of course for the annuals, low boxes in front may be only six inches to one foot deep because their roots are shallow. If cost is not a serious item, it serves best for the picture to use containers of one kind; better unity may be had with graded sizes of containers made of similar materials. Be suspicious of outlandish, garishly painted pots, of baby's old bath tub, or cracked pickle jars, and those kitchen water tanks of a generation ago that, having burst, rightfully belong to the junkman instead of being given a place in the roof garden. Especially be careful of trashy souvenirs thrown out into the roof garden.

Drainage is our next problem; just as the roof itself must carry away the water, so in each box, pot, and container ample drainage must be provided and as mentioned already, keep the boxes up off the roof floor. For large boxes and tubs use large size gravel, in some cases as big as chunks of coal, this covered with a layer of sphagnum moss, so the soil won't go out into the drain pipes; for shallow boxes and pots regular pea-size gravel will be all right. In all cases, of course, use it thick enough -- at least one inch deep.

SOIL Then we must consider the soil. This is important all around. To begin with, use the finest available, good fresh soil, soil that's been purified by the sun, soil that's full of humus, because when it goes into these boxes and containers something happens to it and it loses its sweetness. Every year the professionals follow a system of lifting out the permanent plants replacing the soil in the shallow boxes and small pots and resetting the plants. In the large containers they usually fish around and take out as much of the old soil as they can without tearing roots to pieces and replace with a fresh well-mixed compost. This is to get away from the constant packing and souring of the soil due to the system of watering. Then of course fertilizer must

FEED be applied each season; not the rough smelly stuff, but well-rotted, chopped up cow manure for bulk and humus build up and then of course the old standbys in the commercial fertilizers. Mr. Kelley says, "For summer time a good old manure mulch is fine because it provides food and cuts down the water problem as the humus material, like a sponge, holds on to moisture." But those of you who are planting a new roof garden will not have to feed your plants for the first six months, maybe not for a year, but following this period a regular program of fertilizing the plants must be established. I like the way he put it when he said, "Those plants are going to live from these boxes and tubs, they can't send out their roots to get more food as they can in the garden." You remember our talk on the pelargonium when I told you their roots will travel six feet away, and fuchsias — why they'll run down the block if they have to.

WATER "What about the watering?" I asked Mr. Kelley,

"You can't establish a rule for that. Go best by the feel and the looks for the soil. You can't say once a week nor twice a week, the conditions of weather, sun reflection from the hot roof, wind and exposure all modify the moisture requirements of your plants in the roof garden. But when you apply water," he went on, "be generous, thoroughly saturate the soil, for drainage will take care of excess and the normal requirements of the plant at hand will use the rest of the water."

Of course you and I know insects and bugs fly up in the air as well as low down in the garden. When I was at Berkeley some butterflies flew into the roof garden and a humming bird came to the fuchsia. So the roof garden has its animal population too. But one thing — they don't have the gophers; and snails, slugs and ants can be kept out by vigilance. But aphid, mealy bug, scale, and flies will reach the roof garden. And if one is not careful the whole picture may be ruined by these offensive intruders. Mr. Kelley had a fine suggestion there, he said, "Don't wait until the insects come, be Johnny-on-the-spot ahead of them. Clean house regularly, spray every six weeks. Use an oil soap, summer oil, your favorite insecticide, whether you see bugs or not, and you'll find there won't be any because even the odor of these sprays will keep them away." More than that we must realize up on the roof we are in the zone of chimney smoke and of course in dust too. So with a fine nozzle spray water overhead once in a while; the fine misty spray will do wonders to keep off dust and soot; it will discourage insects in the bargain. Ivy in particular can become actually black with dust and soot. With some of the larger plants like aralia and aspidistra use summer oil, freshly mixed up in your tank and spray it with force on both sides of the leaves, douse them, do a good job and make them shine. But don't use any of the oil sprays on the succulent plants (if you do not know what a succulent is, ask your nurseryman) because the oil discolors them and may even burn too. A carton placed over them will protect them during housecleaning.

ENEMIES

DON'T

What plants are best for the roof garden? First of

all stay away from the fliers; magnolias, loquats; large leaved plants susceptible to wind injury are not good up there. Evergreens are much better, and against heavy walls and panels Lawson Cypress, Hinoki Cypress, Podocarpus, feather duster palms, and eugenia serve excellently. And for the trellises the Star Jasmine, Burmese Honeysuckle, and climbing roses; Hoya Carnosa, where protected somewhat, blooms faithfully every year and the sweet smelling Mandevilla, along with other favorites provide color, fragrance and interest throughout the seasons. Then for plants of a smaller stature, ones providing atmosphere to the roof garden picture; there are elaeagnus, sacred bamboo, (Nandina domestica) and genista; but change to new ones every second or third year because the plants get ragged looking. Try a poinsettia against a warm wall; and there are the heathers for strong color in winter. For the shady places there are fuchsias, hydrangeas, the gold dust plant; abutilons — some people call them Chinese Lanterns; and for the spring season there are the camellias; rhododendrons and azaleas; the fragrant Viburnum carlesii; and let's not overlook the Japanese Maple, with its wine-colored leaves unfolding in spring and turning red and gold in the autumn. But with these plants particularly keep the soil in good condition, maintain the proper tilth with peat and leaf mold because all of them become bedraggled and unhappy if the soil packs and gets bad.

PLANTS FOR COLOR

Then there are the perennials like Penstemons, blue natives, or hybrid red, white, lavender or pink flowers, Marguerites, both white and cream colored, coreopsis with bright yellow flowers for summer, blue salvias to stand up tall in the background, sweet williams always attractive, carnations the favorite of many, even Valeriana which you can depend will establish itself anywhere and bloom for evermore. The garden geraniums of all colors and the trailing ivy geranium that particularly serve so well in boxes, get them young, pinch them back, keep them from getting leggy, and up on the roof or in the window box they can't be beat.

And the flowers which do so much to bring the seasons to the roof garden: For example, begonias, lobelias, marigolds, French and African; petunias, ageratum, zinnias, and hybrid dahlias all for summer. In cool San Francisco cyclamen may be used. And as the year moves along there are pansies, snapdragons, violas, nasturtiums, all of the bulbs, as daffodils, hyacinths, and gladiolus, too; and a mesembryanthemum may be tucked in to give its bright color to the roof. And cosmos and pincushion can be grown along with tomatoes and beans as I saw in Berkeley on a roof there.

Mrs. Eileen Gill who has a roof garden in San Francisco and who used to attend my garden class long ago wrote a letter expressing her ideas on this subject and I'm going to read it to you. She says: "First think of protection: protect your plant with lath — glass — any sort of windbreak. Second, right kind of plants: Do you want color in your life? Do it with annuals (the landlord may move the rent up if it's perennials). Get something gay: nasturtiums, lobelias, violas, pansies may be planted around the base of tubs to add color. Third, you cannot afford to experiment in a small space. Buy the best. Each flower and each bloom is seen by you over and over. In a ten-acre tract you don't look so often. Fourth, do not use painted pots. Pictorially interesting but from a gardener's viewpoint detrimental. (Let me interject here: the terra cotta, the glazed, the Chinese porcelain, and Mexican pots are all good.) Fifth, soil; keep it light. Aerate. Use leaf mold and good fertilizers. Sixth, keep yourself interested. Go to garden shows; buy a new plant, be selective, throw out the weakies. (And here again let me add — forget this economy business. I'll save that to grow it on for next year. Many times Christmas gifts and Easter plants are through when the season is over; you take them out to the roof garden, or plunge them into the window box and the first thing you know you have out there a jungle of second rate messy foliage plants. Better economy by using less and nicer plants rather than keeping

DON'T

yourself busy doctoring along a spent plant.) Don't try to grow lemon trees on a roof in San Francisco. Seventh, your roof garden can be a conversation piece. You can make your roof garden work for you. Succulents can come down from your roof garden, be on your dinner table and return the next morning having added conversation. Eighth, you can lie in the sun, surrounded by plants that you have worked with and loved and tell, "How does your garden grow'."

And now for the Opportune Task: Keep all of your potted plants that you have in good condition; potted begonias, hydrangeas, pelargoniums, potted specimens as boxwood, arborvitae, rare Japanese plants; give them all plenty of water and a little fertilizer too will encourage them. Watering overhead once in a while ties with our recommendations above; it's good for them. Out in the garden too give your fuchsias lots of water; just soak them, keep them moist and you will have flowers in numbers and of color you never dreamed of. Don't forget your ferns at this time either, when kept too dry the summer scale and enemies move in on them and then its good night; keep them clean, keep them cool.

CALIFORNIA NATIVE PLANTS

Vacation months are good to consider California native plants. The following list includes kinds willing to grow and useful in the cultivated home garden.

Acer macrophyllum
"Bigleaf Maple"

Acer negundo californicum
"California Box Elder"

Adiatum jordani
"California Maidenhair"

Aesculus californica
"California Buckeye"

Aquilegia formosa
"Western Columbine"

Arbutus menziesii
"Madrone"

Dryopteris arguta
"Wood Fern"

Azalea, see
Rhododendron

Baeria chrysostoma
"goldfields"

Mahonia nevinii
"Nevin Mahonia"

Mahonia pinnata
"California Holly Grape"

Calycanthus occidentalis
"Western Sweet Shrub"

Carpenteria californica
"Bush Anemone"
Ceanothus arboreus
Ceanothus cyaneus
Ceanothus thyrsiflorus
Cercis occidentalis
"Western Redbud"
Chamaecyparis lawsoniana
"Lawson Cypress"
Clarkia elegans "Clarkia"
Cornus californica
"Creek Dogwood"
Cupressus macrocarpa
"Monterey Cypress"
Delphinium cardinale
"Scarlet Larkspur"
D. parryi "Blue Larkspur"
Dendromecon rigida
"Bush Poppy"
Eschscholzia californica
"California Poppy"
Fremontodendron mexicanum
Garrya elliptica
"Silktassel Bush"
Leptodactylon californicum
"Prickly Phlox"
Godetia bottae
"Farewell to Spring"
Helianthus annuus "Sunflower"
Heteromeles arbutifolia
"California Holly; Toyon"
Juniperus californica
"California Juniper"
Lavatera assurgentiflora
"Tree Mallow"
Calocedrus decurrens
"Incense Cedar"
Liliums, Lilies in variety
Lithocarpus densiflora
"Tanbark Oak"
Lupinus arboreus
"Yellow Tree Lupine"
Lyonothamnus floribundus
asplenifolius "Catalina
Ironwood"
Mimulus, variety of
Nemophila insignis
"Baby Blue Eyes"
Nicotiana glauca
"Tree Tobacco"
Oenothera hookeri "Yellow Evening Primrose"
Palm "California Fan Palm"
Papaver californicum
"Western Poppy"
See Lithocarpus

Penstemon cordifolius
"Scarlet Honeysuckle"
P. heterophyllus
"Violet Beard Tongue"
P. spectabilis
"Notable Pentstemon"
Pinus radiata
"Monterey Pine"
Pinus coulteri
"Bigcone Pine"
Pinus muricata
"Bishop Pine"
Rhododendron macrophyllum
"California Rose Bay"
R. occidentale
"Western Azalea"
Rhus ovata "Sugar Bush"
Romneya coulteri
"Matilija Poppy"
Rosa californica
"California Wild Rose"
Ribes sanguineum
"Flowering Currant"

Sequoiadendron giganteum "California Big Tree"
Sequoia sempervirens "Coast Redwood"
Sambucus caerulea
Pinus sabiniana "Digger Pine"
Pinus torreyana "Torrey Pine"
Platanus racemosa "California Sycamore"
Populus fremontii "Fremont's Cottonwood"
Prunus ilicifolia "Hollyleaf Cherry"
Prunuslyonii "Catalina Cherry"
Pteridium aquilinum pubescens "Western Bracken Fern"
Pseudotsuga menziesii "Douglas Fir"
Quercus agrifolia "California Live Oak"
Quercus lobata "Valley Oak"
Quercus kelloggii "California Black Oak"
Rhamnus crocea "Redberry"
Rhamnus "Coffee Berry" "California Elder"
Symphoricarpos albus "Snowberry"
Torreya californica "California Nutmeg"
Toyon, Heteromeles arbutifolia
Umbellularia californica "California Laurel or Bay"
Verbascum virgatum "Wand Mullein"
Vitis californica "Wild Grape"
Yucca whipplei "Our Lord's Candle"
Washingtonia filifera "California Fan Palm"
Woodwardia fimbriata "Giant Chain Fern"
Zauschneria cana "California Fuchsia"

MELON IN GARDEN PATCH Mites attacking melons? Red spider mites do this; evidence first shows up in yellow spots in the leaves near the center of the plant. On closer examination the spiders can be located by their fine webs which they spin usually on the underside of the leaves. Now it is too late to use sulphur because sulphur might burn the plants. Instead use a vegetable dust, use it at 2 week intervals. Dust must reach both sides of the leaves for complete control.

DAHLIAS Are the dahlia leaves getting mildew? Often the lower leaves will show attack. Cut off those leaves particularly badly infected. Then dust sulphur through the plant, over the leaves, under, all around; this will stop the mildew.

CHAPTER 33

WINDOW BOXES

(August: First Week)

What materials can a window box be made of? Good redwood lasts for a decade. Use screws instead of nails and metal angles at the corners. Decorative terra cotta boxes and cement ones with fancy glazed tiles are likewise serviceable.

The inside measurements for a window box should be six to eight inches deep and ten to twelve inches wide. This allows depth for the roots to explore the available soil. The outside measurements may be fourteen inches wide and one inch shorter than the window space. For very large windows the boxes may be in sections. To make the boxes really last, line them with galvanized iron, sealed tight with solder.

All boxes must provide ample drainage. In the bottom near both ends make holes. Small boxes will get along with one hole, best in the middle. Drill holes as big as a good sized cork, insert a pipe, and solder it to the lining, then lay flat over each hole a piece of coarse galvanized screen. Then with some of this same galvanized screen make two cylinders five inches in diameter and five inches high like a carton without top or bottom. Fill these with coarse crushed rock; then place them resting one end over the screens above the holes; and the drain will never stop up.

Just what kind of soil is best for the window box? *SOIL* Mix two parts fresh soil, one part leaf mold, one part sand, and a dash of peat to act as a sponge. Mix with this one-half pound of bone meal. Use no bulky manure because it is not bulk, but richness that you want here. Some professionals prefer a well-balanced commercial fertilizer and to the average box would add one-half pound, especially if annuals are to be grown.

Window boxes have special climates, according to the compass. Therefore plants must be selected with a definite knowledge of the varying exposures of sunlight, or the varying trials of wind and cold. For example: on the windy side a good aid to the plants is to press down the soil and use a deeper box so that the roots can have a firmer anchorage and a mulch top dress will stop drying out. Thus aided, any of the plants, annuals or perennials, can take whatever the sun throws at them.

WATER What is the schedule for watering a window box? It's windy up around those boxes on all sides of the house, and if we don't keep watch everything will dry out. Soak thoroughly and then be vigilant for dry soil, especially when the box has been newly planted. Once in a while water overhead to keep down soot and dust and to discourage insects too. What about insect infestation? Merely remember what we have said before.

FEED What about fertilizer? You don't have to fertilize annuals because their soil was prepared with fertilizer to begin with. The permanents, such as boxwood, dwarf junipers and ivy need an annual application of bone meal or commercial fertilizer. To make sure the fertilizer gets down to the lowest roots, punch holes with a spike down to the bottom and then fill them with fertilizer and soak immediately with plenty of water. Or use a good soupy cow manure. Just soak it with water for three or four days, thin it down, and pour it all over the soil. This is particularly good for the evergreens and flowering perennials.

CARE Of course the day comes when the box fills up with roots, just as they do in a pot, and then the thing to do is pitch in, pull out, prune back roots, provide clean drainage material, and new soil, and reset the plants. While you are doing this you may of course have plants in pots which you may wish to plunge into the box firming them outside in a cushion of peat or humus.

I have saved the selection of plants to the last, though of course in the work it has come before these other matters. Not all plants can grow in the window box. Some plants lose their foliage too early in the season. Some can only grow big. Some have marauding roots which will not be confined. Examples are privet, eucalyptus and acacias. We have to leave out all of these and many more.

We have to think of blooms, foliage, shape and size. Some plants hang like the A. sprengeri Fern and should be put in the front of the box. Some stand up rigid like the boxwood and should be put in the back; and others bush out giving the feeling of fatness and sparkle like Genista and belong in the middle.

PLANTS TO USE

Window boxes may serve as the whole garden to an apartment; they must move with the seasons. For color, now, summer use masses of annuals with a long flowering period, like petunias, ageratum, lobelias, perhaps a white Chiffon Daisy, a bronze calceolaria, and sweet peas for a curtain. And dwarf sweet peas called by some "Cupid" make a uniform growth of about eight inches high and each plant about one foot in diameter go well in window boxes as they both droop and intertwine with their neighbors. Fall can have its contribution too with chrysanthemums, grown in pots and plunged in the box. In frost free districts the dwarf salvia can be carried almost into the very heart of winter. And for winter you can have little spruces, holly trees, and berry plants. For next spring you can get daffodils, grape hyacinths, the showy ranunculus, tulips, primroses, forget-me-nots mixed with anemones, and pansies; in fact there are dozens of these bright spring flowers.

Last Sunday after the broadcast I went up to the roof of the National Broadcasting Building and in niches along the roof line saw boxwood growing there. The effect is plain for there is no color, but kept trimmed and in good growth it is excellent for window boxes. Along Lake Street in San Francisco since my childhood I've enjoyed a window box with dwarf grown cedars of Lebanon; they always look attractive; another window box I've known for years has nothing but the prostrate Chinese Juniper. It's like a little gray-green carpet out in front of the window. As I drove around San Francisco last Sunday I saw a fine box planted to nothing but pink and white fibrous-rooted begonias. And everywhere were the trailing ivy geraniums, pink, rose, and lavender, tumbling over the boxes, or solid colors of the various common garden geraniums. These are the easiest and simplest. Then there were several facing the afternoon sun filled with petunias. I can't tell you how those windows stood out along the block; they were like lights in a dark night and as you passed by you couldn't keep your eyes away from them. But in my own city, for I am a native-born here, house after house stood with barren window boxes; just painted and left empty. That shouldn't be. It's not what they do in some cities. I've heard that in Switzerland window boxes are the pride of every house so I called on my friend Otto Meerly who hails from there. The light of happy memories came into his eyes. "Everybody has window boxes at home," he said. "Every house, every store, apartment, hotel, even schools and churches have them." There were not only flowers but beautiful boxes of strawberries, lettuce, radishes, and the decorative kohlrabi. For Otto reminded me not everyone could afford the luxury of flowers. Then there's the window box of the English cottage; in Germany, Austria, Scandinavia, even in South Africa and in South America, homes have window boxes.

I used to take my garden class up to Russian Hill to the little home of the late Arthur Francis Lundberg. He had come back from a European sojourn thrilled with window box ideas. It was just the thing for him because his house stood on bare rock not a bucketful of soil there, only what he brought up himself. Well he built window boxes on all sides. On the north he planted ferns, just ferns alone. On the west under a pepper tree he had seasonal things — tuberous rooted begonias in summer, primroses in spring; on the south and east he elaborated into miniature gardens. With dwarf plants, succulents, little cypress trees, and scraggly veronicas, he built up miniature Chinese and Japanese gardens and bits of Venice and Naples — with pools for gold fish, little bridges, garden lamps; and at night especially the effect was enchanting. One window showed you the beautiful Danube with tiny castle, drawbridge, mounted soldiers, and miniature valley and forest.

The Opportune Task: Those of you who have already harvested the apricots should rake up all the unwanted fruit that fell to the ground. Dry them in the sun and then burn them; or move them to the compost pile. If you place them in the compost pile be sure and sprinkle lime over them so as to get rid of any worms or borers from maturing. At any rate I think it is bad practice to bury the mess because of the borer population. Then some branches might have been broken down with the weight of the ripening fruit, or blown down in a strong wind. These fallen branches should be cut off with a nice clean cut leaving no jagged edges. The cut surface should be painted with a thick paste of white lead and oil, something that will be sure to cover the surface and stick; this to keep out borers and keep out spores of harmful fungi sure to come in damp weather.

Another job for the apricot is to get rid of some of the unwanted wood; not a heavy pruning, just a light thinning of the new wood that's growing wildly in every direction but where you want it. This light pruning helps to strengthen and to fill out the fruit spurs now already on the tree for your next year's crop because by thinning out you permit the sun to reach in. Then your next job especially if no water has already been given is to irrigate the trees after the harvest. All during August up until the middle of September you may give water to the apricots. At the same time feed them with a well-balanced commercial fertilizer (one containing 6 parts nitrogen, 9 parts phosphoric acid, and 6 parts potash). Remember these fruit trees are forming their fruit wood now for next year; we want to help them keep growing nicely.

Pears will soon be ready for harvest. If the crop is heavy get rid of some of those little crowded pears, you won't lose anything by thinning because then you are directing into the remaining desirable fruit, the rich natural sugar that is now forming in this warm sunny weather. Should your crop be heavy be sure to support the branches with props to keep them from blowing and breaking in the wind, thus destroying years of growth.

Remember those boysenberry vines? I told you a short while ago not to step all over the new shoots while you harvested your crop. Well, the crop is gone now so prune off the old canes; of course there may be a few berries still on — I'll let you eat them as you prune. But do not touch those new canes, leave them alone, leave them just where they are until cold weather unless you see insects or scale developing on any of the inside wood. Then give them a spraying with some light summer oil or oil soap to keep down the scale. And with the boysenberries, too, after pruning give the roots a good drink; this is to encourage the length to the new canes which in turn bring the fruit. For that matter water all berry plants now — blackberries, loganberries, and youngberries.

Those of you who have artichokes in the garden have a job to do. The harvest of spring is over, some of your artichokes have produced blooms, some even seeds. Your plants are now resting; they look ragged. Cut these old stalks right down to the ground; this is called "stumping"; and you cut four to seven inches below the soil level. Let the plant rest for several weeks; the artichoke being a true perennial will send out new cycle shoots from the old crowns. Usually when cool moist weather comes the new shoots will develop — though after a six weeks' rest you may irrigate the plants and hasten the new cycle growth. Now, however, you prepared for them by cutting away the old stems and leaves. Remove these parts to the compost pile, or bury them deep in the soil.

Another mid-summer job is to look at the grape vines; if they seem to be crowding, cut back the tips of the vines not into the hard wood — you don't want them to bleed — but just the active tips. By cutting back the wild growth you permit more sun to reach into and sweeten the grapes.

CHAPTER 34

PLANTING PERENNIAL SEEDS FOR NEXT YEAR'S GARDEN

(August: Second Week)

July and August are good months for sowing seeds of the perennials.

One of the real pleasures of gardening is to plan for next year's garden — we want to make it better than this year's. You know there's a poem about gardening and the refrain goes something like this: "but next year it will be different; wait till next year." People realize as they garden through the year what is the matter so they plan and that's how gardens get better and better.

We have said in our previous talks that after plan and design, timetable comes next. This is the season to plant seeds of perennials. Why do we want to plant seeds now? Because we want to have strong plants to set out in the garden this fall; or we won't have good flowers for next summer.

Where do you get the seeds? Many of you have already harvested seeds from your delphiniums, coreopsis, meadow rue, columbine, and lupins, all true perennials; while some of you collected seeds of hollyhocks, foxgloves, cup and saucer canterbury bells, iceland poppies, sweet williams, and perhaps mullein, all biennials; this is the time to plant their seeds also. No doubt you dried them in the sun and stored them awhile in a cool place because all seeds must go through a ripening process when the starch and fats are converted into sugars. The seeds are fresh and are now ready to plant in the soil. Of course you may buy them from your nurseryman and specialists, in particular, know what seeds to sell you and can tell you how many are right for your garden space. There exists any number of hardy perennials which may be grown by seed; in fact through seeds gardeners may enrich their collection, especially among the class of perennials that are best grown from seed. By growing perennials from seed, with knowledge of variety, habit of growth, and period of bloom, a gardener can prepare for a long-time display of flowers. But there are some disadvantages with seed culture among some of the perennials; for example, in phlox, iris, and peonies, seedlings often turn up uglier than the parent. One summer I remember admiring in a lady's garden a beautiful bed of pink penstemons; they were next to a sandstone wall and growing in full sun. My friend was planning to gather the seeds. A couple of years later I saw the same spot but in place of the strong pink flowers there were only dirty lavender and muddy white flowers with one or two on the pink tone; these new plants were from seed of the glorious pink penstemons.

Gardeners save themselves from chance inferior flowers by dividing established clumps of plants of known quality. This is done later in the year, phlox, Esther Read daisies, and a lot of others, and we shall speak of it at the proper season. *

Having decided to grow your own perennials, what is the preparation for the seed-bed? First of all get a handy place to work; a table or bench about waist high will suit most people. Kneeling on the ground to do this work is inconvenient and even painful. If you are lucky enough to have a small greenhouse or lath house, materials will be greatly simplified, but this is not essential, for you can move things off the tool

*(See also "Other Fall Duties" — October: second week.)

bench by the window in the garage, or even work on the porch.

SOIL

What kind of soil is best to start perennial seeds in? Loose soil is best and you can mix it yourself. All you need is to sift the soil when it's dry or slightly moist through a screen mesh five-eighths or one-half inch, because you want the soil particles thoroughly loosened. To make the soil loose and friable add to it equal parts of leaf mold and sand. Mix no manure nor peat with this preparation for you are preparing only a seed-bed not a foraging ground for driving roots.

HOW TO SEED

How do you sow perennials seed? It is easy but don't wait for a windy day. Just fill the flat or pot with the mixture you have prepared, firm the soil with a brick or wooden tool designed for the purpose. Pressing down the soil will lower the level from one-half to three-quarters of an inch below the rim of the box. This is about right. If the soil mixture had not been thoroughly watered when it was prepared, then after placing it in the flat and pressing to firm it there, sprinkle the soil until it is saturated. Do this before you scatter the seed;the presence of water is important in the seed-bed. This procedure is not like that of springtime sowing because summer is a difficult time to plant perennial seeds due to the California heat. In spring you squeeze a handful of the prepared soil; if it stays compact there is enough moisture; if it falls apart the soil is too dry. But the method just described I've seen done by "the world's greatest gardener," as he calls himself. His secret is soaking the flat thoroughly, even sterilizing it with boiling water poured over the flat and then cooling it before sowing the seed.

After scattering the seeds over the prepared soil in the flat cover lightly with dry soil. The coarseness or fineness of this covering will be determined by the size of the seeds. Seeds in general should be covered to a depth equal to two or three times their diameter. Run into the kitchen and borrow the "bowl strainer," it's handy to sift the soil evenly over the seed. For the coarser seeds the depth may vary considerably without doing any harm. With the finer seeds it is often fatal to more than barely cover them;many times very fine seeds are merely pressed in and not covered at all. But in summer I would advise amateurs to cover the seeds to contact more closely the moist soil below creating a perfect bed for the seeds to germinate in. The next step is to cover the seed flat especially if warm weather prevails. Use a sack, covering the flat completely. This differs in an important respect from springtime planting in flats because now you have the weather against you. In winter or early spring you would use a piece of glass and several thicknesses of newspaper but now being summertime with a high daily temperature you may achieve good results without glass. Then you take your flat of seeds to a dark place in the basement or in the garage, but watch it like a cat watching a gopher hole.

CARE As soon as you see the seedlings have actually pushed through the ground the sack covering should be removed. From then on after the seeds have begun to sprout it is no longer darkness but light they want. Bring the flat out of the basement or garage. But the delicate seedlings are not ready for full strength sunlight, we must protect them a little; what they need then is subdued light for the next few days because some perennials are very slow in getting started and need protection from direct sunlight. You cover the flat a second time with cheesecloth or muslin or lath frames especially prepared with the laths close — no more than a half inch apart, just enough to let the sunlight in slowly; otherwise the seedlings might burn up.

TRANSPLANT When seedlings have developed their second pair of leaves you may transplant them. A good trick is to loosen carefully the soil they are growing in so that it falls away from the roots. This permits you to pick up the individual seedlings. A new flat is prepared with loose mixed soil, firmed as already described. With a blunt-pointed stick called a "dibble" punch small holes a half inch wide and an inch and a half deep. Place in the hole the seedling and with a pressing motion close the soil around the roots. These holes are best put two inches or four inches apart according to the respective size of the plant. After your seedlings are planted water them well; give them shade from the sun for several days while they become established in their new home. In a few weeks they will be ready to plant out in the garden.

What about weeds that come up in the flat? If you sterilized the soil with boiling water there'll be no weeds. However, when weeds do appear the best time to pull them is when you bring the flat from the basement or garage. The weeds definitely come first so that you can pull them with assurance at this time before their roots get anchored.

WATER

What about watering the perennials after they have passed the seed stage? Watering is perhaps the most vital of all activites in connection with the growing of seedlings. Can I give you a rule? No rule can be laid down for this except to counsel that never after the seed is first moistened should it be allowed to dry out. A seed germinates once if it is given the desert treatment then it is good night! Apply the water gently with a fine sprinkling can so as not to wash the seeds or the soil covering them.

Now there are some other problems to seed germination; let us take the primrose for an example. Primrose seeds are slow to germinate unless you save your own and sow them as soon as they ripen; even then some of the seed will not come up until the following spring and from others there will be never a peep. Some perennial seeds take a whole year before they germinate; for example, the Japanese primrose and the tooth-leaved primrose.

Then there is the rule in good gardening which tells you never sow different types of seeds in the one flat. All kinds of troubles come from disobeying that one.

BROADCAST SEED

So much for sowing seeds in flats, but professional gardeners have a trick of starting seedlings without flats. I called on Arthur Taylor who I met years ago; he's head gardener of an estate on the Peninsula, and he has right along given us many fine suggestions for good gardening. He said, "Come over here I want to show you something." We reached a shady walk and under the trees Arthur pointed to a little green patch. "Look, what do you see there," he said with a broad smile. I got down for a good look and saw hundreds of little primrose plants. "How did you get them; what did you do; what happened?" I asked. "Those are Primula malacoides, the 'Baby Primrose'; and over there are some foxgloves; and all I did was to shake out the seed pods last spring just where the plants were growing; and Nature does the rest," Mr. Taylor said. He went on, "Scatter the seeds where they've been growing; you selected the spot in the first place because you either knew or thought it would be suitable; you noticed perhaps the spot was shady and that there seemed to be enough moisture in the soil at all times; your plants had a successful show; so you shake the seeds there and they'll grow of their own. That's what I do all the time," he said. And all over his garden Mr. Taylor showed me little clumps of volunteer plants. There were cup and saucer campanulas, hollyhocks, Siberian Wall Flowers, forget-me-nots, and columbines. "As a matter of fact I'm too busy with my other duties in summer and by merely shaking the seeds onto the rough soil where the plants grew it saves me work and time; besides the plants come around in season when they're supposed to." He said further, "Now it is a hard time to prick the plants off but like those forget-me-nots that naturalize themselves all over I'll leave them until fall when I'll shift them for the first time; then they will be big enough. I'm preparing places for these seedlings right now. Come over to the lath house and I'll show you something else," he said.

PROTECT SEED

Over by the lath house in a sunny spot a plot ten feet long by five feet wide was all spaded up nicely graded with a little lath frame over it. "What I did here," said Mr. Taylor, "was to mix into the soil, sand, leaf mold, and a little cow manure. I spaded it deeply, pulverized everything, watered it down and now at this time of year the sun prepares it for those seedlings I'm going to move in the fall. They will be spaced about six inches apart; and by and by they'll have strong fibrous roots, really a clump of strong fibrous roots, that'll be in perfect shape to put in the perennial border in spring. By doing it this way my plants actually reach flowering stage quicker and surer because they grew sturdily and vigorously with a good root system."

SELECT

What guides your selection of perennials to be grown from seeds for your garden? Those that reproduce well, such as the golden flax. Stick by those that are hardy, as the coreopsis; that are vigorous, as the day lily; free from pests and diseases, as the perennial asters; plants that are good for cutting, as the chrysanthemums; and that give a succession of bloom, as the blue scabiosas. Plants that do not require constant staking, spraying, dusting, or even cultivating belong in the perennial border because there the gardener looks for a glorious display over a long period. Here, for example, belong the columbine of surpassing grace with beautiful streamline flowers. And while we are on the columbines it might be well for me to caution that you purchase regularly new seeds or new plants to mix with your own because many times your own seedlings do not possess the long spurs; and even then you can expect the unexpected with columbine seedlings. We can't overlook the fact that Nature's pull is inclined toward quantity; it's man who goes in for making what he calls improvements.

Then your choice of perennials may also be guided by the character of the plants. Penstemons are native from Alaska to Central America with one hundred and fifty species; some dwarfs ideal for the rock garden, some growing to four and a half feet tall. All of the penstemons are prolific seed bearers. The seeds are fine; plant them now and later transplant the seedling easily. Penstemons planted at the right time, even seeds from a mixed packet, will give you interesting results with the odds all in your favor; they are easy perennials and good to handle.

There are many other perennials to be recommended for seed propagation. Salvia officinalis, the common sage that has been growing in European gardens since 1597, its home is around the Mediterranean. Then there is the red sage, native to Texas and Mexico; the forty-niners brought it to California. But perhaps you want to study the catalogue and make your own selection.

SEEDS OF BULBS Before we leave the subject though a word about bulbous plants produced from seed. The question is why grow bulbs from seed? Commercial growers offer standard types, but from seed you may get new kinds; many interesting and beautiful species are seldom offered in bulb form. Seed is more often available and if the hobbyist wants the unusual he may have to resort to growing seeds to attain his wishes. For example, Liliums and Gladiola species; several rare types make fine perennial subjects; unusual bulb iris and the very desirable crown Imperial fritillaria. I just happened to mention the name of this imperial fritillaria to a gardener and right away he said, "Where can you get seed of it?"

But now's the time to plant seeds of bulbous plants; put them in the soil, they'll germinate by spring; next fall you will plant them out, mulch them, mark where they grow, and after a while they will bloom. Blue and white agapanthus, amaryllis, cottage tulip, gray hyacinths, including the miniature and the strange iris that looks like a dwarf cornstalk with dropping leaves, Iris bucharica.

The Opportune Task: While your soil in the open ground is sun dried get it ready for sowing seeds and planting seedlings. First with a heavy screen clear out the sticks, rocks, broken pieces of glass and the like. Next screen the soil again through a five-eighths or half-inch wire mesh. Then wet the pile down to encourage weed germination. Your soil then will be ready for mixing with sand and humus materials for general garden use. Repair your flats, make sure no holes remain in the bottom pieces of wood, and that these pieces of wood are not set too far apart, one-eighth inch apart is enough. Also hammer down loose nails that can tear holes in fingers and clothes.

Other biennials to be grown from seed:

Bellis perennis
Campanula medium
Echium wildpretii
Glaucium flavum
Myosotis alpestris
Oenothera hookeri (Evening Primrose)
Papaver nudicaule
Trachelium caeruleum

Other perennials to be grown from seed:

Anchusa azurea
Anemone japonica
Armeria vulgaris
Campanula isophylla
Cerastium tomentosum
Dianthus caryophyllus
Erigeron mucronatus
Francoa ramosa
Gaillardia aristata
Gerbera jamesonii (Transvaal Daisy)
Geum "Mrs. Bradshaw"
Heuchera sanguinea (Coral Bells)
Hunnemannia fumariaefolia (Mexican Tulip Poppy)
Scabiosa columbaria
Statice reticulatum
Stokesia laevis
Viola odorata

STEPHANOTIS FLORIBUNDA

STEPHANOTIS FLORIBUNDA the Madagascar jasmine, a vine native also in Malaya, possessing shiny leaves and waxy white fragrant flowers 1 - 2 inches long deserves special attention. In summer from May till August take plant out into warm lath house. WATER carefully, not too much in the summer; keep the plant on the dry side; in fact this vine likes to dry out once in awhile. However, while your plant is in the lath house spray it overhead, the water keeps down insect infestation. Ants, scale, and mealy bugs love this twining vine. Proper use of Diazinone, Summer oils, and Nicotine discourages these pests. In late August return specimen to the home. There do not place underneath a pan as you would with other plants because you do not want too much water standing. In spring you may add new soil, some plant food, and start plant off with plenty of water. Keep the roots confined in pot, don't over pot by placing plant in large container. Tight-rooted, Stephanotis grows best.

CHAPTER 35

HOW TO MAKE CUTTINGS OF PELARGONIUM; MARGUERITES

(August: Third Week)

We have questions on pelargoniums and iris; these are timely, because now is the time with pelargoniums to make cuttings and with iris to shift them if you are going to shift them this year. With both, you have to catch the bus!

Our first question asks: "When do you make cuttings of geraniums and how is this done?"

Geranium cuttings should be made now, so that they will make roots and be established by November and December; then your new plant will give you flowers next spring. Now is the time to begin. But first of all, let us understand the principal kinds of pelargoniums we are dealing with. To the beginner the name geranium means pelargonium hortorum, pelargonium domesticum, and pelargonium peltatum. Pelargonium is the generic name. The gardener calls the hortorum, the common or garden form, by the name geranium. He calls the Lady Washington, which is the fancy or show form, by the name pelargonium, and he calls the trailing form the ivy geranium

KINDS First, the common or garden geranium, because all summer these have been blooming. They are about at their best now, and in coastal gardens will bloom right through the winter. If not of too sappy a growth, they are hardy to mild frost attack. These flowers usually arranged in a ball are easily seen because they stand up on tall stems high above the leaves. Older blooms now have exchanged their colorful round petals for pointed long crane bills, the seed carriers. The common garden geranium has been called Zonal, because its leaves are often prettily zoned in light and olive shades of green. They have been called horseshoe because the zone markings are in the shape of a horsehoe; and fish because of the unmistakable odor of fish in the foliage of some early varieties hybridized a hundred years ago; and bedding because they have been much used out in the garden.

Some grow up as high as a house, others that are pygmies live in a pot, and some are scented geraniums in a class of their own. They have oil in their leaves, and their flowers are usually of a soft lavender rose and are usually small.

Now for the second kind, pelargonium domesticum or Lady Washington. These are not hardy against the frost, and in most gardens require winter protection. The main stem holding up the flowers is short, letting the flower head sit on top of the leaves, instead of standing high above them as in the garden geranium. These Lady Washington flowers are individually larger than those of the common geranium and have loose petals which carry large blotches and contrasting dark lines which give bright value to them. They stand up not like a ball, as in the garden geranium, but appear as a loose bouquet above the leaves.

The third kind is the ivy or trailing geranium, pelargonium peltatum. It is planted to cover sloping banks, to cascade from window boxes, or to hang from pots. In general, then, these are the differences between the common or garden geranium, the Pelargonium or Lady Washington geranium, and the trailing or ivy geranium. They grow somewhat the same, and the procedure of making cuttings is identical.

Now let us go out into the garden and step over to a common geranium. Right out there in the open sun, against a fence where the wind doesn't get it, notice the strong green stems. In my plant they stand up two and a half feet tall. Then there are others less green, more brown and yellow. These I am going to pass by because I am now searching for green firm growth. Take hold of a green branch at the very tip, notice how soft, how willingly it bends, but as you go down the stem you will notice the stem becomes firm and does not bend so readily. That is the growth you want to CUTTING

SELECT take for cuttings. Firm, active, green wood. In my plant, the section five or six inches below the tip is just right. On some of the side branches the tip four-inch growth is just right. Also, notice that many of the side branches as well as most of the tip growths are fat, and short-jointed. That is the best material for cuttings because out of it will grow shapely vigorous new plants.

Now, how do you make the cut? Should the knife cut above a joint, through a joint or below a joint? A joint, by the way, is the swelling in the stem just where a leaf stalk breaks off. It is also called a node.

HOW CUT Since tip cuttings are the best I select the top four or six inches, and with the sharpest knife I make my cut straight across just below the joint. I make a clean cut.

Suppose now you do this, then turn the cut surface up, look at it carefully, and you will see a ring surrounding a large center part, and surrounded outside by a narrow band of firm stem. That ring is known as the cambium layer. After a while all along the cambium layer, if you have made a neat cut, will develop a callous, a "warty growth" as some gardeners call it. This callous must develop first because the roots come only from that layer.

But this is getting ahead of the work. When you have made the cutting, take off the lower leaves, at least at two joints if the cutting is four inches long. When you have removed the leaves you will see remaining at the joint two little stipules, appendages that sit on the stem. They always accompany the leaves, and in young growth they are green, later they turn brown and are brittle, breaking up easily to the touch. Take off these appendages because they often hold moisture which will rot the cutting. Leave the upper tip leaves on your cutting, do not take them off because later they will help it to a good start. Make several cuttings of the common geranium, then place them in the air for an hour to permit the raw cut to seal over. Now go out to your Lady Washington. Notice how many branches are tall and leggy, trying to grow up to the top of the fence like their cousins the common geranium. But notice also that you see the same kind of tip growth, green and vigorous — that is, if you have given your plant plenty of water all summer. Now take the cutting. Select firm young growth; beware of sappy slender growth, keep to the firm young growth. Make the cutting identical with the one you made on the common geranium.

Now step over to your ivy geranium. Lift up a long branch. Notice the new branches that shoot out all along the sides. You can select the firm short ones, about four to six inches long, for they make the best cuttings. You proceed the same way. Be sure and let the raw cut surface seal over. After you have made your cuttings they are ready to go into the sand.

Any coarse sand is good. Most gardeners prefer fresh river sand, like Marysville No. 2; some even select sand with a good deal of gravel in it. Don't DON'T take it from the beach, or the sandy dust that makes dunes. Dip the cuttings into hormone dust then gently push all your cuttings down in the sand at least one and one-half inches deep; this will be two joints under. Make that sand sit firmly around each cutting.

I happened to be visiting Mr. Matthews one day. He was setting his cuttings. He used a tow-inch wooden block which he pushed up close to the row of cuttings. He grabbed a hammer, of all things. What would he do to the delicate cuttings with that? He pounded the wooden block and he said to me, "This is my secret of getting every cutting to make roots. This pounding makes the sand snuggle closely. No cutting waltzes around, and with each one firmly set in the sand, you have your only assurance of every cutting making a callous and then making roots."

I also went around to Mr. William Schmidt. He had no hammer; he had the garden hose and was compacting the sand with a good soaking.

After you have placed all your cuttings, then give them a thorough soaking. Thereafter, be sure the sand never dries out. The idea is to keep the sand moist, not sopping wet. Your cuttings should have light, neither a dark cellar nor the hot sun. In about four weeks or so, your cuttings will be rooted. How can you tell? Just pull gently; if the roots have becomes established your cuttings will not come out. Dig your finger down, and when you lift up the cutting, you will see a knobby fat callous covered with a beard of white fibrous roots. Your new cutting is ready to be potted. A mixture made up of one part loam, one part leaf mold or peat and one part sand is good. Do not use manure.

POT SOIL

"Is this the only months in which to make cuttings of geranium?"

August and September are definitely best to start the Lady Washingtons, because if you wait another month they'll be retarded in blooming next spring until the hot weather is almost upon them, and that means their best time for blooming will be gone. With the common geranium it doesn't make so much difference because it blooms all summer. If you plan for a big show of geraniums, especially in pots and particularly if you grow them on a roof garden, in a porch or window box, cuttings can be made in May and June, and they will give you flowers in the winter time. Now is a good time to make cuttings of the ivy geranium too.

Occasionally you get hold of a sprig of common geranium or Lady Washington which you like. In that case, a single cutting can be rooted in a glass of water, like oleanders and other plants. The main thing then is to seal the cut surface in the air for a while, before putting the stem in water. Select a light window but not a sunny one. Hide the glass behind black paper.

PRUNE

"When should the Lady Washington pelargoniums be pruned?"

Now is a good time to start to prune the Lady Washington. If your plant has grown big and bushy, if it has a crown of heavy branches, you should give the plant a heavy pruning. Do this by cutting out inner crowding branches, by cutting off broken outer ones, by cutting back wild ones that shoot up beyond the rest of the plant. You prune now so as to enable your Lady Washington pelargonium to send out new fresh growth while climate and growing conditions still prevail because on this new growth will appear the flowers next year. For example, if you do not prune now, then your plant will have so much old unproductive growth that it will be unable later to give you a show of good flowers. Another benefit of pruning the Lady Washington pelargonium is that you enable your plant to grow compact instead of sprawling and loose. What is meant by old wood? Wood or stems that have already given you a crop of flowers, stems that have now turned from green to brown, from soft to hard growth.

"My Lady Washington pelargonium has grown up leggy. There is more old brown growth than new green. How shall I prune it?"

In this case you must reshape your plant. That is, you can prune all of the branches back, prune them down to the last good green healthy leaf, making the cut just a fourth of an inch above the joint. There the leaf bud, which is dormant at the base of the old leaf, will grow and a new shoot will develop. Usually if you prune back an old stem below the green leaves, leaving it leafless, that stem dies out.

There is another side to this question. If your plant is in good growth, has a compact shape now, then all that is necessary will be to thin out here and there branches that have already bloomed, and keep watching the plant until December at which time all pruning should have been completed. Thus you will oftentimes be able to enjoy a few flowers in fall from your established plant.

Remember you may use the pruned branches to make cuttings. Remember too, if you discover insect enemies, now is a good time to clean them up. Spray your plants thoroughly, use a summer oil if you find mealy bugs; look for ant nests if your plant is in a pot or box. *ENEMIES*

And the second part of this question: "When should the common geranium be pruned?"

In the spring after the frost has gone is the best time to prune the common geranium. Vigorous plants in the garden can be given a severe cutting back, all old and dead branches can be cut out, and spindly weak ones too. Potted plants, however, require a pruning in proportion to their size, but prune to permit the light to reach in and encourage the new basal shoots.

And now another question: When do you make cuttings of the marguerites?"

Right now. This goes for both the white and the yellow forms. All you have to do is proceed as you do for your geraniums. Select the tip growth, the upper four inches of active green. Make clean cuts, strip off the lower leaves, and put the stems right away into the sand. Pack the sand down tight, water, and your cuttings are on their way. Like the geraniums, first they make a callous, then they make roots. They will do both quickly if you go ahead now.

In warm summer it's war on crabgrass! In hot weather it grows furiously, seeds germinate everywhere, plants come out in all bare spots in the lawn, they pop up in the perennial border, they hug sunny shoulders around shrubs. Once the seed germinates under the warm sunlight of June-August nothing stops growth; in a few weeks it literally crowds out the regular lawn! Control: Water soluble chemicals are used; follow directions on the container. One application is not enough to completely destroy crabgrass. Two treatments at intervals of seven to ten days apart is usually required. Plan to work on Saturday. On Wednesday give the lawn its usual drink, for the roots of the desirable permanent grasses should not be thirsty during crabgrass treatment. On Saturday when the sun shines hot right on lawn, mow. Then spread the crabgrass herbicide. Follow instructions on container. After application leave lawn untouched for at least two days, do not water. In that period the herbicide will have begun its work with crabgrass turning brown. Water the lawn on the third day, it will need it, but the crabgrass won't since it is dying. Kill crabgrass in hot weather, do it early, then no seeds will be formed. Learn the difference: crabgrass is an annual; Bermuda grass is perennial with deep roots and a tough wiry shoot. Nothing kills it, thus gardeners learn to live with it and make it serve.

CHAPTER 36

WATER

(August: Fourth Week)

All hearty, thriving, living things, plants and animals, are mostly water. If the proportion is reduced, even a little, they suffer. If it is reduced further, they die. That is why one of the big divisions of gardening is water.

But wild plants of California get along without help. How do they do it? First, only those are left which can do it. The others which can't do it have long since thrown themselves out. But those that remained — how did they manage? They either plunged their roots down into the crevices of the bed rock which make little odd-shaped wells of water. Such are the junipers of the mountains, and the morning glory of the valleys. Or, they go dormant during the dry weather and wake up again when the rains come — the buckeye and the little goldback fern and the native beardless iris. Or, they store water in special reservoirs protected from evaporation by thick leathery walls, such as the succulents, including the barrel cactus.

But a garden is a different enterprise. We are not content to have our plants go dormant, for summer is the very time we want them to explode into foliage and flowers. We are not content either to limit ourselves to the deep rooters or to the fat water storing succulents. What we want is plants from climates all over the world, many from humid climates, even from the rain forests (the tree fern for example). And very many with shallow roots. In other words, our gardens are oases — they are spots of special artificial climate established here in the half-arid California. Every plant we bring in involves a problem of watering.

What is watering? We, in imitation of rain, pour or sprinkle the water onto the ground. Where does it go? How much of it do our plants get? That depends on where you are in the garden. Under the birch and willow tree your pansy would go thirsty even in a downpour, for the marauding roots of these trees suck it all up. It depends also on the cross section of the soil. Let us suppose that it is sandy six feet deep resting on sloping bed rock. Your water will pour down through almost as fast as though there were no sand there, and will then coast away on the bed rock. Fifty barrels of water, measured precisely through your hose. Or, instead, at the top you have two feet of spongy ground — ground that holds water. This can be for example a loam; that is, a certain mixture of sand, clay and humus.* Or it might be sand and peat such as we have in the bogs of the delta. Or it might be a black mixture of adobe and humus. This two-foot thickness of spongy soil, whatever its composition, rests, let us say, on seven feet of clay which in turn rests on deep gravel. Now what becomes of your water?

It first saturates the sponge, and thereafter the excess leaks down to the clay surface. The clay acts as a bed rock and if it has a slope it drains the excess off; if it is level or pockety, the excess water rises, even to the surface, and you have for yourself an artificial swamp and, besides, a problem of drainage.

STUDY SOIL

If the excess does drain away, your two-foot porous soil layer holds tight to its water and constitutes an ideal growing medium for the roots of your water-loving plant whose forebears lived on the edge of a pond! You can see that in watering you want to know where you are in the garden and what kind of material you are pouring your water into. This is so important that you will do well to put holes down, plenty of them, to see what you've got. The surface may look like any surface. But what's out of sight is far from important and individual.

Let us assume that you have in your garden a thick layer of good spongy soil. You put a young stock plant in it. How does it drink in its water? It has a little

*For a more complete discussion, read the chapter on "Soils" September: Fourth Week.

tap root, two inches long and radiating little threads which near the end break out into a brush of tiny white hairs so close together that they look like feathers. The threads instantly with intense eagerness start squirming around through the grains of soil, hugging them tight, and drinking through the hairs as they go, and they plunge into the flakes of humus. But if the water disappears, they stop short; if the ground goes dry the hairs die back to the threads, the threads die back to the tap, and eventually the tap dies and the whole plant goes out. But even if you turn the water on when only the hairs have died back, the plant has suffered a shock and you'll have to work like mad to bring it back.

Or suppose you have good sponge, but poor drainage below. Or that you left the hose running all night. Whichever it is, you have your own private swamp and your little plant is being drowned. But does a plant breathe air like an animal then? Not exactly. But there must be air circulation in the soil, as well as water. One reason is that plants and decaying matter exhale gases which become poisons unless they get away. Another reason is that if air is excluded certain bacteria multiply against which the roots are helpless, and so they rot.

Every winter, nervous voices assail me through the phone and on the sidewalk: What in the world is wrong with my stock? First, all the leaves turned yellow; then the tip growth lost its fresh greenness, quit growing, and stood absolutely still, just moping. I dug it up; half the roots were rotted off.

I answer these nervous voices by asking: How did the soil look when you pulled up the plant? "It was sopping wet!" Well, that was the trouble every time. With many annuals this happens if the cold rains come before their roots get well anchored. And it happens with many established plants if contrary to all their wishes their roots have to stand in a swamp. The Cedrus deodara, for example, used as a Christmas tree and then set out in a low pocket in the garden, where every time water comes from anywhere it gathers there — this tree, in the succeeding summer, yellows and drops its needles by the thousands, until it is only a bare skeleton of branches with little bunches of tip green growth holding on for dear life. But it is too late. The roots are rotted and the tree is doomed.

But the biggest problem in watering in California is not too much but too little. This is what the 200,000 new gardeners must learn. For we have six totally dry months per year when if you don't water intelligently to suit each kind of plant, you have a suffering garden, thirsty and diseased. In April you have prepared your fluffy, porous soil layer and the late rains and the early spring watering have conditioned that soil with a full quota of moisture. But as the ground warms up, the sun blazes down, and furnace winds blow, and our dry summer gets fully under way, that moisture is pulled out faster and faster. The roots down below are working overtime, every stem is pumping away all day long and the precious water is being pulled out from the leaves by the dry air. This is happening all over the state, that is why the Los Angeles Aqueduct, the Hetch Hetchy Dam and the Shasta Dam were constructed. We just have to have water to put back into that porous layer. And we have to put it back in the right amount. How do you tell what is the right amount? If you have too much, moss will grow, especially in shade, and black-slime. And as I have said, the plants stand still or positively begin to die off.

KNOW HOW WHEN

If too little with annuals such as zinnias, petunias and ageratum, the leaves start to curl in two or three days; then turn papery brown and brittle, and blow away. In the course of time the flowers get smaller and eventually all you have is sun-scalded green stems with a tuft of green immature leaves at the tips. In the shrubs such as the snowball and the strawberry bush, the leaves lose their color, mostly because red spider and thrip come running when the plant goes hot and dry. And harvest time comes; you step over to your nectarine and when you pull one down you notice its tight skin, you bite into it and find it hard and juiceless. Or you grab a peach, bite into it and find the flesh rolls like rubber;or you gather some oranges and when you peel them every one is like cork instead of fat and squirting juice everywhere. In summer with all kinds of food plants as almonds, walnuts and grapes, the harvest tells at once if enough water had been given the plant during the growing season; where it was withheld the crop is below par, lacking in size, in meat or juice, and in all-round quality. This means that next year you are going to be more careful, you are going to be more watchful. A good way is about June the first to take your shovel and dig down into the soil, dig down two feet; take a look down there and see what is going on. If the soil is dry a foot or eighteen inches below the surface in June just think what the condition will be a month or so later. Some plants go dry awfully fast, the roots, especially the little tip roots we mentioned earlier, have a lot to tend to; in moist soil they can do all their work, in dry soil they stop; and if it is a fruit tree the swelling and ripening of the crop is impaired; and sometimes the tree throws the crop down to the ground, so alarmed does it become with its thirsty condition. If the plant is in the flowering stage, especially with the oranges and lemons, it drops most of the flowers and the remaining ones it permits to grow only small and stunted fruit. Water is the only answer. Get it there at the right time. In California during the three summer months and often into early fall we must keep the water down below, we must pour it on so that the roots can drink it in, the stems can pump it up to the leaves where it can be used for the ripening of the crop, and for new growth so important for years to come.

TEST

But what is the right time, and how much water should be applied will evidently vary with the plant. We can illustrate by putting plants in seven groups, according to their water needs. At one extreme is the cactus; the next the drought-resistant geranium whose ancestors lived in South Africa where they have six rainless months, just as we do here. Next the bulbs, such as the tulips, which can sleep in the hot sun, and come wide awake with leaves and flowers during the rains. Next alfalfas and conifers which plunge their roots deep and keep on growing when the surface is bone-dry. Next the oranges which must have both bright sun and water. Next the hydrangeas and fuchsias and begonias which must have constant water not only for blooming but for survival. And last, at the other extreme, the aquatics, the water lilies and water hyacinths — true water plants.

Let us remember that all plants whether from swamp or desert need special watering when they are young. For example, a young fruit tree which you have just brought into your garden from the nursery will require much more attention during the first season when it is getting its roots established than it will during subsequent seasons. Even your seedling cactus while it is just taking hold will have to have water.

California gardens have all these groups: we have taken a palm from the sunny Canary Islands, the wisteria from cool Japan, a cactus from the Colorado desert, and fuchsia from the moist cool Americas. Each plant has its own water requirements; we must recognize them.

Unfortunately, these plants are often so huddled together that if one is properly watered, another alongside is dying of thirst, and still another is being drowned. Golden Gate Park of course handles the problem of variety in a professional manner. They perhaps have 50,000 different kinds of plants growing there; all under artificial conditions; in the Tea Garden some come from the lofty Himalayas, some from the cold wet forests of Japan; over at the cactus garden all come from the thirsty desert, and in the Arboretum they have made subdivisions of plants from Australia, Africa, and Mexico. In the Mexican section they turn on the sprinklers every night, so that those plants can get their daily supply of water in imitation of their daily showers at home. In the Park, the overhead sprinklings which would wet the visitors in the daytime are postponed till night, but the plants get their daily supply.

Now let us consider how some of these ideas take

form in the actual watering that goes on in the garden at the present time. At the last meeting of the Garden Club, the question up for discussion was "How Should the Summer Garden be Watered." "Soak it," said a voice in the back of the room. "Just a minute," interrupted another from the side. "That all depends," he went on. "Now take a plot out in the blazing sun, and take a scorchingly hot day; you have to be careful. Annuals and the perennial border have to be treated differently from the established fruit trees. When the temperature is normal, 65 to 75 degrees, even up to 80, you can give your annuals and perennials out in the sunshine water from an overhead sprinkler. But when the temperature runs above 80, then you have to use a special technique, particularly on the morning that starts out hot, when, for example, by 6:30 it is already 70 degrees. Then the gardener must get all his top sprinkling done before nine o'clock. He sprays the water over the tops of all his flowering perennials and annuals by that time. This will permit them to dry off before the sun gets too hot. We always have to bear in mind," he went on, "that, with overhead watering, the hot sun blazing on them will cook the flowers and leaves, and will set the plants back for weeks." Someone asked him about overhead watering when the temperature is normal. His reply to this was, "There is no danger then in overhead watering directly in the sun. The idea is to get enough water down to the roots."

"Is it safe to let the watering go till five o'clock in the evening on these blistering hot days?" was the next question. "That depends somewhat upon the amount of moisture already in the ground. If the ground is dry, better irrigate; otherwise you can wait till evening. Then sprinkle overhead and the foliage will have a chance to dry off before night comes." "And how about irrigation for trees, shrubs and vines when the day turns out hot?" queried one of the younger men. "Certainly; you can soak the roots with a good stream of water and you'll help your plant; I've seen hydrangeas for example, with their large leaves, hold up pretty well on scorching days when the roots were given a big drink by irrigation. In fact, for the perennials and annuals you can irrigate on hot days and keep these plants in good condition," was the answer from the most experienced gardener in the group.

One of the other men rose from his chair and said, "What about irrigation versus overhead sprinkling in general?" Right away a champion for overhead sprinkling took the floor. He said, "I feel your plant gets a better watering; that is, it gets in more water from a fanned overhead sprinkling than from irrigation because the water is taken up not only by the roots but also through the leaves, especially when the spray reaches the undersurface as well as the upper surface." "Yes, it cleans the foliage too, by washing off accumulated dust," said the man sitting next to the speaker. "It saves time," said a gardener long at the trade as evidenced by his weathered face and strong hands. "While the sprinkler is spraying the water in one place I can pull weeds, set stakes, and tie fallen branches or twigs and get the next plot ready for the sprinkler; my hands aren't locked to a hose; I can do other chores while the sprinkler sprays the water. And too," he went on, "I can work in the sunny plot and spray in the shady plot, and move around, spraying the water where it will do the most good."

DON'T

"However you apply water, don't overlook drainage," said the president. We'll discuss this subject in another chapter.

And one other phase of this subject — what about water and the winter garden? The newcomer to California must realize that fall is a critical period in his garden, and he must begin to take into account the water that is in the air; and he must also take into account the lengthening shadows. Humid hot air combined with the lengthening shadows brings mildew to his plants, to his dahlias, zinnias, and lilacs. These plants then must not be watered overhead in fall, in fact the first hint of mildew must be the signal to cut out all overhead watering, and for a stepdown in amount. Again, he must concern himself with the moisture in the soil itself. Too much in the fall will

WINTER WATER

mean trouble if not death to many of his plants in winter. For example, if he keeps pouring the water on the roots now, he will stimulate sappy growth which at the first frost followed by bright sunlight will wreck that tender growth by bursting the cells and tearing down thin walls within the leaves, the twigs, and even in the stems of the plant, so that within a few hours all that will be left of a prosperous, too sappy growth is a drooping mass of black twisted leaves and tip growth in the plant. What he must do is to watch his soil in fall; if he finds it dry he should water it, but not enough to make it cold and sopping wet. If he finds it moist he should withhold additional moisture, especially in places where he has tender plants growing. He must watch at all times that water does not stand; we have mentioned this already, but it won't hurt to remind you that a whole lot of water standing in one place will make the soil muddy, will make it so fine and so tight that it will shut off the air from the roots so that in the course of time they and the plant will die.

Plants associated with pools; some are happiest submerged as Myriophyllum, parrots feather; others with roots in pots or boxes sitting on the bottom or near the margins of the pool, as Japanese iris, nymphaea lotus, and lilies; and still others placed around the pool in the landscape design:

Acer palmatum, and varieties
Agapanthus
Azaleas
Bamboo
Begonias
Berberis thunbergii var. atropurpurea
Billbergia
Chamaecyparis obtusa nana
Chamaecyparis Wisselii
Cotoneaster salicifolia
Cistus purpureus
Cupressus nidifera
Cyperus alternifolius
Cordyline angustifolia (Dracaena)
Elaeagnus pungens maculata
Euonymus radicans var. argentea variegata
Erigeron mucronatum
Ferns in variety
Cytisus racemosus
Hebe (Veronica) cupressoides
Iris, Japanese
Juniperus chinensis procumbens
Lobelia
Moraea sp.

Nandina domestica
Pinus mugo
Pinus tabulaeformis
Podocarpus gracilior
Pittosporum philly-
raeoides
Prunus, weeping cherry
Sciadopitys verticillata
Saxifraga, sp.
Sarcococca ruscifolia
Willow, weeping

The Pool.

CHAPTER 37

INSECTS IN THE SUMMER GARDEN

(August: Fifth Week)

We devote an entire chapter to insects in the summer garden. Let us look about. First, how many kinds of insects do we find there? Two, those with sucking mouthparts and those with chewing mouthparts.

But the chewers are in greatest number. Many have been there since early spring but now in the late summer their destruction is apparent. We'll discuss them first. The chewers are in greatest numbers because they love warm weather, they specialize now on foliage and bright flowers, they move into the vegetable garden, they get into the berry patch, they fly up into the fruit trees, and some are busy in the roots.

How can we identify these chewing insects? The Good Book says, "By their fruits ye shall know them"; but we shall say, by their works ye shall know them. There are the beetles such as the western striped cucumber beetles, with yellow bodies and black stripes. They go for the tops of beans, beets, corn and sunflower plants. In the larva stage they go for the roots and eat linear holes in the stems of the young cucumbers, melons, corn, and pumpkins. And there is the western twelve spotted cucumber beetle found now in almost every garden section of the state. These are commonly called the "Green Lady Bug". Both of these beetles are known as diabrotica, the scientific name being generally understood because the insects have become so bothersome. Have you wondered what insect chewed into the flowers of the zinnias; have you wondered what devastated the petals of the dahlias, the asters; and how many times have you looked for the insect that carved out chunks in the leaves of your chrysanthemums? Diabroticas certainly move around the garden. They are controlled by sprays or dusts

12 SPOTTED BEETLE

made up of Rotenone, Pyrethrum, Malathion, or Diazinon. In using dusts be sure to apply when there is no wind and most important of all do the job early in the morning when the dew is still on the foliage so it will stick; and the insect is present because he loves a bed in a flower. The dry dust and the moist dew is as good as a wet spray. How do you do it? Blow the dust on both sides of the foliage; keep to the windward, and

DON'T don't blow it on yourself for some of them irritate the skin and will continue to do so even after you have washed them off. Stand away from the plant when dusting otherwise you will not cover both surface of the leaves. Apply dust for diabrotica control every five or seven days; they hate the stuff and soon get out; they hate dusts even more than they hate sprays, so when they are around keep all growth of the plants covered and you will have an effective repellant. Let me caution though, don't bury the plant with dust, but cover completely. A little is more effective than too much. Remember too to read directions on the commercial dusts because some of them should not be used on vegetable and food plants that we eat since they contain poison.

Right here I want to remind you that we have not been speaking of the friendly little red lady bug, it is not a diabrotica but is one of the most active and beneficial insects friendly to the gardener. She eats the aphids as well as one of the mealy bugs.

The elm leaf beetle will turn a beautiful elm into a skeleton by mid-summer;because new broods can keep it that way for the rest of the year. Power sprayers are needed for proper control and most communities attend to this along the streets through their public service departments. However, commercial experts may be called in where a garden elm has been attacked, because small sprayers or dusters are entirely impractical for home use on large trees.

Insects have different tastes. First you noticed only the flowers and occasionally the tender tips of the plants were ruined, but now as you look around you notice damage is confined only to the leaves. Insects are fussy that way, for diabroticas specialize on the flowers and here another beetle called the black vine weevil takes for his tidbit only the leaves. Have you found leaves with clean-cut crescent shaped chunks bitten off the margin? Especially on the pyracantha, camellias, olive, lemon, orange, pittosporum, they do beautiful work on the lilacs, they just scallop the edges; they'll take the privet hedges, and even the rugged honeysuckle vines. The cut is always the same, each bite looks like the next one all along the outside margins. This mutilation makes your plant unsightly. Right now everybody is talking about the brachyrhinus, the scientific name for this black vine weevil. The scientific name has become commonplace by the insistent diabolical activities of the bad actor himself and indeed of the many cousins in the "tribe" of brachyrhinus. LOOK

And another thing, these black-brown thorny beetles do their work at night; that's why you seldom see them. How do you get the best of them? Just spray with Diazinon (see page 494) in the evening. And you can get sprays made up of oil and one or more insecticides which thoroughly applied will discourage this beetle. "Use good commercial insecticides; they get them" said one of the gardeners at one of the meetings. And Mr. L. R. Cody said be sure these poisons thrown on the ground to control brachyrhinus do not contain metaldehyde because that material chases them away and they won't eat any of the poison put out to catch them.

Caterpillars go through the garden like voracious monsters. Hanging up in the laboratory at the university I remember a picture of a vigorous man making an ugly face and holding between his big fingers a furry worm, as he said, "So it's you who's eating my plants alive." Well, the other day looking over my potted plants I found a busy caterpillar chewing away on the leaf of the golden mirror plant. I picked him off just in time for he was making off with many leaves. Hand picking is one way to get rid of caterpillars but where numbers have invaded, pyrethrum dust or an insecticide spray can do a more satisfactory job. Sevin controls caterpillars too. The same is true of the smooth worms, light green and about one-half inch long found on the oak trees. They come in successive broods all through the summer, and some years they've been terrible, leaving the oaks looking brushy and thin. There will be more in November and still another crop in December, especially on the trees that are not sprayed. Heavy infestation demands the help of an expert. If you find these "worms" on smaller shrubs, with the strongest sprayer you have cover the plants with a summer oil, or other insecticide. Both the fuzzy caterpillar and the smooth green worms prepare for winter by going into the chrysalis stage from which they will emerge as moths next spring, ready to do it all over again. In this group too there are the measuring worms that trouble geraniums at night. In the day time they crawl in between and pull the leaves together saving themselves from the heat. Keep an eye out for them too. Some as pupa hang in the trees, others drop into the ground and pass the winter there.

Slugs and snails feed on many plants. We discussed their control last spring when they began marching out into the flower beds;* and snails also go up into the orange tree and into the genista bush. Just keep an eagle eye out for them and give them one of the prepared poisons.

The earwigs, authorities tell us, are becoming a serious pest in the Bay region and in other sections of California. They hide away in nice cool, moist places during the day but come out at night eating holes in leaves, nipping off seedlings as soon as they pop out of the ground. Right now the second brood are starting to feed on tomatoes, snapdragons, young veronicas, and pyracanthas, though they like also decaying vegetable materials. What do earwigs look like? They have a shiny black-brown body, long rather than round and flat, and they are equipped at the tail-end with a pair of forceps that are easily recognized. To control earwigs a special bait has been prepared which is

*See Garden Enemies (February: Second Week.)

liberally put around in little piles where they are known to be. After three or four days dead bodies of the insects will be discovered. Another trick in catching earwigs is to stuff moistened paper or excelsior into a five-inch pot and turn it upside down. Every morning plunge the pot into hot water and you will find you have killed scores.

We now come to the second class of insect, those with sucking mouthparts. In this group always in summer and fall, the etchers are found attacking plants that have been neglected and allowed to get dry. They etch the leaves, then pierce the cell and take out the plant juices. They include the mites and the red spiders. Both work in the summer and often several broods appear in a season. Go out and look at your almond tree, the foliage will look very grey, the green luster of the leaf is gone. Mites are the cause of this. Pretty soon the mites will lay eggs on the twigs and stems of the almond, they winter over in little ruby red globules, the eggs; are ready for work next spring. But the red spider on the other hand, though in the same family as the mite, winters over in the adult stage, hiding in the bark, twigs, or at the base of the shrubs. Now in summer they lay eggs which hatch right along. One of the cheapest and easiest methods of control of mite and red spider is to water the plants overhead. Cold water hampers their activities. Keep your plants growing vigorously. Summer oil sprays, according to direction, will take care of them. You are quite likely to find them on the leaves of viburnum, strawberry tree, abutilon, birch trees, and a lot of others. Sulphur dusts too are helpful, especially on hot days. Look into Diazinon (see page 494).

Late summer, warm weather, and dry soil brings out the thrip. Those brown spots on the viburnum and pyracantha leaves; those spots on the fuchsia leaves, on citrus, on the woodwardia fronds, and on the dahlia buds are caused by thrip, tiny insects with rasping mouthparts. And what they can do to rhododendrons and azaleas; that dirty fly spot appearance on the leathery leaves; that's the work of the thrip all right.

"I think it is the most despicable insect there is," said Professor Isabel McCracken of Stanford at a Wednesday garden meeting, "because it ruins the plant now, goes into the ground to come back next year, to raise the same rumpus." She went on, "The symptoms are very evident; the leaves look seared because the thrip sucks all the juices from the under surface then the sun burns and sears the top of the leaf." They love flowers too, as gladiolus which become whitened, curl, and look deformed with the leaf blades yellow. Keep your plants in good growing condition. We want to remember many insects are busy in the warm summer months. Keep an eye out for them. Take a good look in the morning, another at noon, and still another in the evening. Early discovery will enable you to protect your gladiolus, zinnias, and vegetables too. See page 494.

We might review now what we said last spring about aphids and mealy bugs; they give many gardens serious trouble. We described also the scale insects that attack such plants as the citrus, lilacs, ferns, oleanders and a host of other plants. Now, late summer, the mealy bugs should be called to your attention because they particularly enjoy warm weather. Lantanas, gardenias, fremontias, and ceanothus will often be "alive" with mealy bugs. Should you find them on your plants get busy; first, water the plant down well, water it overhead, soak in the water at the roots because you want to awaken the plant to active growth. Then get an oil spray and either early in the morning or late in the evening, after the hot sun has passed the plant, spray generously. Use a summer oil spray, any of your favorites. Wait ten days and give the plant another spraying; and ten days later give a third treatment. But you know there is a partnership between the insect aphids and mealy bugs and the ants, which gather their nectar. When you have one you have the others. So let us consider next the ant, that paragon of industry.

ANT. He has something that Hitler aspired to — a total government with everybody inside contented; everybody outside miserable. He is not to be despised either for efficiency or for character. His orderliness, persistence, courage and loyalty are marvels. He is a home builder too. He divides up the work — some tend the eggs, some the larvae, some clean the house, some fight intruders; nobody loafs or even dreams of it.Some are herders — they herd the aphids and mealy bugs, putting them out to pasture on your

Ants and Aphids.

choicest plants and they regularly gather the nectar and bring it back to the nest. The colony centers in the queens, several of whom live pleasantly together. They are bigger than the others — look until you can identify one — for so long as a queen is still there the colony still has life in it. It is though the colony were all one body with several queens acting as interchangeable hearts and the workers as interchangeable legs, arms and mouths. Everything is expendable. It's hard to beat an arrangement like that. If you flood, the next instant those not drowned grab eggs, larvae and queens, and gallop off to a dry spot. They have alternative nests. Or they can set up a new housing project anywhere at the boundary between dry and moist ground — under a paving block, along the edge of the path, especially down the edge boards (header boards) close to the house underpinning, under dry leaves, under the dry skin of the humus pile. To my dismay I once found in my humus pile ten colonies each with ten thousand members at least.

The ants are admirably organized for what they want. The trouble is they pay no attention to what we want and as fast as we build up they tear down and despoil. And they are ambitious to inherit the earth — after the warm days came this summer many appeared with wings to start their nuptial flight. The young queens were migrating to form new colonies.

With the warm days, the war of the ant against man begins in earnest. They send out from the nest columns which might be thought of as tentacles, to forage. They will eat meat. If you step on a snail the scavengers will be there in no time. For this of course we should thank them, they are our best garbage collectors for dead bugs and even dead birds. (They will attack and eat young birds in the nest, just out of the eggs.) They would carry off an elephant, but if you have any dead elephants you had better dispose of them yourself. They eat other kinds of ants too, for here in California we have little left but the Argentine. The Argentine have not whipped the termite, however, though they will eat the larvae if they get a chance.

They will eat sweets. That is why they come into the house where too often we suddenly for the first time realize their existence and make piercing cries for help. The taste for sweets is the reason also for their interest in their cattle, the aphid and the mealy bug.

In the neglected gardens these foraging columns, these long flexible tentacles, go squirming along their established pathways from dawn to dark, and even through the night. They have to stay together. If the individual falls out he is lost and dazed. Half may perish but it still goes on. What does it do to the garden ? Have you ever seen a cherry tree with the leaves out at the tips curled tight ? That is black aphids attended by the ants; the column has marched up the trunk. Such trees will have a column going up and another going down.

The whole garden can thus be taken over by this cooperative monster. Well, how do we stop it ? First, we strike at the monster's heart, the nest. It's position is wonderfully advertised for invariably the column leads to it. But it may lie in a thicket where it is hard to get at. That is one of the disadvantages of thickets and one of the reasons for clearing them out. As I have said they like the boundary between moist and dry ground. They like the shelter of bricks and flat rocks. To find the nest you'll have to keep on looking, follow the column — but there is a reward — it is like fishing. The column won't stop dead at the next and plunge out of sight there. The individuals will maneuver around it in a novel dispersed formation which you can recognize. Moreover in the mating season the winged ants will be there. And at any time if you dig with a stick or screw driver you will turn up white oval eggs half as big as an ant and you will see the alarmed workers pouring out of the ground carrying them to a place of safety. Put down holes three inches apart to cover the area, shake in a little cyanide powder from the snout of the can in which it is sold — and in addition take care not to breath too much of it — and plug the hole with moist earth. Slight moisture always present in the nest releases cyanide gas which is that used in our prisons for another kind of enemy. This gas will creep through the ground and kill the heart of the colony. (It will kill children too; keep the can locked up.) Kerosene oil or many insecticide preparations, if they saturate the ground, are equally effective. Put in a stake and come back next day to see if any are left.

ANT CONTROL

The more usual attack is made, not in the nest, but on their columns. Ant sprays and dust are scattered on window sills and sinks where the ants are found in the house. Or a poison syrup is put in cans or bottles close together all around the house. The idea is that after feasting the ant, who never learns that this bottle isn't a giant ant-cow or aphis, runs back to the nest and refeeds it to the young. This method does in fact break up the column! the ant goes away after while.

Now one more item before we finish with ants. If

your potted plant becomes infected with ants set the pot in a bucket of poison, very light oils, for example, used according to the directions; leave there until the bubbles are out; then dip the foliage in the bucket. Let the pot drain and your ants are no more.

Above all, in any of these treatments keep at it regularly. You can rid the garden of ants by simple intelligent persistence. You must meet organization with organization. Once the habit becomes fixed, it will take little time. The method of attack whether on nest or column must be thoroughly applied or it will be like trying to kill a criminal by cutting his hair.

The Opportune Task: Go after the insects of the summer garden, spray wherever you find trouble. Don't forget the shady sections as well as the warmest parts of the garden. There are the pelargoniums and geraniums; look them over for mealy bugs for instance. And at this point let me remind you now is the time to make cuttings of geraniums for new plants for next year. I'll remind you too that rhododendrons and azaleas can be given food for the last time this year. Use the 6-8-6 fertilizer or the acid food fertilizers that you have been using; apply and soak in.

HYDRANGEA HYDRANGEA to keep blue, lavender, etc. Add one pound of aluminum sulphate to five gallons of water; make three to seven applications ten to fourteen days apart. Never pour this solution on dry soil, always water plants first. Thereafter to keep soil acid and flowers blue, use one ounce of aluminum sulphate and one ounce of iron sulphate to two gallons of water. Treatment also makes foliage dark green. In containers color change takes place faster than in garden grown plants. Ball bluing can be used as a second method. Put blueing balls at root crowns; or place 6 balls to one gallon of water. Must put on when new growth begins; repeat later; and by the time the buds form (when flowers open too late) result is a beautiful soft light blue. (See pages 318-321).

Chapter 38

FLOWERING TREES OF THE SUMMER GARDEN

(September: First Week)

Our talks for the next three chapters will comprise a series on summer flowering plants. In this we discuss trees, the next chapter shrubs, and the third chapter the vines. My reason for presenting these discussions is to make available information that will prove useful to you in your plans for additions and rearrangements in your garden next fall or winter.

Early this summer a lady asked me, "What's that tree lit up like a golden candelabra; you see it everywhere; in Saratoga, San Jose, and in Oakland." I asked her in reply, "Did it have nice clean leaves that look something like an elegant fern; and was it 25 or 30 feet tall?" "Yes, and the flowers were full of honey; I parked my car under one tree and after I came back I found big sticky drops all over it," she replied. "Did you look at those flowers?" I asked. "Not particularly, but they were orange-yellow," she said. "Well, if you looked harder you would have noticed the flowers were held facing up toward the sky, one-sided really, and most of them were carried in the upper branchlets of the tree. You came upon one of our most prized fast growing trees that was introduced from Australia. They call them Silk Oak, or Grevillea robusta. These trees are always neat looking except when the seed pods hang on; in that respect they are like other Australian plants as the acacias. We in California can use these trees in the open garden and as you have noticed as street trees. In the tropics they plant them to shade young coffee plants. But in the east they use silk oak as a potted plant for the conservatory. And in the New York Botanical Gardens I saw a specimen growing in the high glass house. Silk oak won't take severe frost."

Give them a sunny spot somewhere away from the sitting areas to miss the dripping honey dew. This is all we need to say about the silk oak.

Haa-ka-randa is the way I used to say it because it sounded so good but that is not the way to pronounce this name at all. Then I tried Jack-a-rrranda; but that sounds too operatic; and the managing director of the broadcast station whispered, "Albert, never roll your r's in the microphone." Now I call it Jacarandá because that is the right pronunciation of this Portuguese name (Zhäkarandã). Jacaranda is a tree native to Brazil.

In San Carlos along the main street in a lot where the theatre now stands a tree grew for years that every summer threw out a great show of blue flowers. The newspapers along the peninsula carried a story when the tree came into flower. Garden lovers came for miles to see it; nurserymen were swamped with requests for young specimens that the thrilled visitors wanted to plant in their own yards at home. And garden clubs announced under "new business" in the month of June this discovery on the local landscape. Because here indeed, only a stone's throw away, was to be seen a strange tree in full bloom. Strange because in our climate this tree wasn't supposed to grow, much less bloom, and here was one with a trunk almost too big to hug. But horribilus dictu, that is, horrible to tell in plain language, the ax got it to make way for a new building.

But don't worry — specimens had been planted all around the Bay region and many of them have succeeded in blooming. This is a compliment to our climate. In San Diego I saw a tree 60 feet tall in full flower and that was in a warm protected section of the state. Jacarandas prefer a warm exposure to a cold one, in fact, must have it or else they will freeze back. You gardeners in the warm foothills will find an ideal spot, you in the flat districts be sure to plant your tree in a protected corner. Put it near a warm wall. Two lovely trees in Palo Alto planted in just such a position being shielded from killing frost, have grown well and produce flowers every year. The idea is that, just as with many tropical vines, if the specimen can go through several winters without frost killing it, it will have made hard wood enough to take the cold.

What does the Jacaranda look like? The leaves are the most characteristic; they are fern-like, but whereas the leaves of the silk oak resemble the heavy leaf of a woodwardia fern, those of the Jacaranda suggest the delicate leaves of a maiden hair fern. The leaves of this tree are finely cut; think of the airy plume of a tropical bird and you have the picture. In mild climate these feathery leaves remain on the tree until late spring and when the flowers appear they drop. The flowers, of course, constitute a second charm. I saw Jacaranda in full bloom on a trip to Los Angeles — my first introduction to this tree. A whole street was crowned with waving lavender blue flowers that melted into the sky. The flowers in large loose panicles waved out from the ends of the twiggy branches, as most of the foliage was off. I waded through petals ankle deep. Each flower was tubular like a little curved thimble.

Jacaranda is a clean tree. It seems to have no enemies except frost. A missionary from Madagascar told me they use the wood for cabinet and finish work because of the very fine close grain, capable of an exceedingly smooth surface. Since my first acquaintance with Jacaranda I have seen in bloom small trees grown in large pots; they were handled like tender hibiscus.

In 1935, you remember, San Diego put on a little exposition. That summer after presenting a lecture in Los Angeles I jumped onto a train to go down to see it. As others have said before, there's nothing like stolen sweets and as I had to play truant to get this trip in I certainly was pleased. For that matter, the discussion of the next tree comes out of that trip. At one of the stops along the line my eye caught sight of a tall tree ablaze with red blossoms, all the more brilliant because there were no leaves and the ground underneath was covered with glowing coals. The trunk had a strange shape like a champagne bottle. "What in the world is that?" asked the man sitting next to me. And passengers crowded up to the windows to get a better look. Everybody wanted to know all about it. Although this was the first time I had ever seen the Flame Tree in bloom I spoke up and told them all. In student days I had studied pressed, old, brown, dried flowers so I knew their shape but at the station was the tree itself. You never want to study herbarium specimens when you can get a living thing like that. Each flower is like a little bell, put a handle on it, hold it with the handle downward, cluster them together, and that's the way it comes on the tree. This is the flame tree, or the Victorian Bottle tree, native of Australia. Brachychiton acerifolium is the Latin name meaning leaves like the maple.

Think what a street lined with them would be. When I got home I hastened to tell everyone about the new tree that had come into my life. But you don't have to go off to San Diego to see them; if you hurry you can see one just finishing flowering in the inner quad at Stanford University. You'll find two trees there and they seem to alternate in throwing blooms. The best one grows fifty feet away from the entrance to the chapel, on the right-hand side as you enter. In 1937 it bloomed almost as well as the one near San Diego and since then it has bloomed several times but not every year. The trees have to attain a certain age before they start to bloom.

If you try one in your garden, plant it in a protected spot, guard it from severe frost, but don't pamper it.

We have been speaking of the silk oak, orange-yellow flowering; the jacaranda, blue flowering; and the flame tree, red flowering. Now for one that produces large fragrant flowers that are like saucers of snow against the summer blue sky. "What makes flowers like this?" asked a girl at the restaurant one day showing me one of these saucers. "It's the southern magnolia," I said. "Is it a big tree?" she asked, still holding the flower that measured ten inches across. "Yes, it becomes a very large tree reaching to 80 feet tall. If you plan to grow one in your garden be sure to give it lots of room." I forgot my lunch for a moment and went on to tell her the largest magnolia I ever saw was on the old Flood estate in Menlo Park. In fact there was a pair of them. They had been planted on the lawn way out front of the residence and had all the room in the world to spread and that is just what they need. The trunk out of the ground was five feet through and the first branches to lead off were two and a half feet in diameter. They had broad crowns and did not look much like the young trees that you see so often growing in parking strips. Of course, planted in 1879 you'd expect large trees now. Be sure to plan for future growth and don't crowd your specimen when you plant it in your garden.

A gardener complained to me the other day, "Magnolias are dirty trees; they call them evergreen but I'm always raking up fallen leaves." "But say," he said, his scowl giving way to a smile, "did you ever watch a magnolia bloom open? The other day I picked a magnolia bud and took it home to lunch; it was like a great big ivory rosebud. Before I went back to work the petals opened out and rested back hiding the green shiny leaves. A thing my children learned that day was not to put their fingers on the petals — they blacken." Inside are the stamens and golden anthers surrounding a little green delicate cone. This cone grows as the flower gets older and contains the seeds. They are bean shape and turn red when ripened. They possess the same fragrance as the flower and down south are made into perfume.

Lately after a broadcast I dropped in to see Mrs. Breen at San Mateo; she has been a mother to many amateur gardeners down on the peninsula and of course she has added much to How Does Your Garden Grow. "I think," she said, "that every garden should have a scarlet flowering eucalyptus," pointing to a vase of it some friend had brought to her. "Especially gardeners up in the foothills away from the frost," she went on. Right now in gardens all around the Bay region eucalyptus trees are flowering. Some are brick red, some pink, the one Mrs. Breen had was copper, others orange, and once in a while you'll see one which strangely enough is white. The flowers have no fragrance but the bees visit them in swarms; and the ants in armies. They have no sepals or petals — the color comes from the stamens. The whole upper crown of the tree will be in full bloom at the same time. Afterward big seed pods like bowls of smoking pipes develop and in these bowls the tiny seeds are formed.

When you hear the name eucalyptus, you immediately think of El Camino Real or Sutro Forest in San Francisco where trees grow to reach up to weave around among the stars. But these giants are the common eucalyptus. The scarlet flowering kind that we've been talking about is a dwarf only 50 feet tall, and kept down to suit garden space. They suffer from frost injury and one should protect a young tree until it gets well established as we suggested for the jacaranda. I might add, besides this scarlet flowering eucalyptus there are other ornamental forms worthy of your consideration, as the golden flowered eucalyptus with brilliant red pointed caps to the flowers which themselves are fluffy golden yellow and "Southern Cross" eucalyptus with blue-grey flower buds that open into lovely primrose yellow flowers and red ironbark that produces pink flowers.

There are many more flowering trees of summer; I will list a few but give only a statement about each one. Has your son back from the Pacific told you about the Japanese Pagoda tree; it's sometimes called Chinese Scholar tree. It produces cream-colored flowers in clusters and will grow in dry soil. Then there's another tree that is the tallest of the hibiscus family; the blossoms are like little half-closed hollyhocks; it's a mallow. The tree gets 40 feet tall and every summer interested parties ask me the name of that beautiful tree in bloom on Waverley Street and Hamilton Avenue in Palo Alto. It's named for a Spanish physician and botanist of the 16th century, Andreas Laguna, and the second part of the name is for Colonel Paterson, Lieutenant-Governor of New South Wales —

thus Lagunaria patersonii — with Primrose tree a common name. The flowers are a beautiful shell pink and I have seen the ground littered with fallen flowers at this time of year. The trees will grow in full sun, but if planted where some shade falls in the afternoon the flowers will hold their rich tone longer.

The Opportune Task: Visit around today, go out and get acquainted with a half dozen new flowering trees. Visiting is one of the real delights in gardening; you pick up so much information that comes in handy later.

Here are three important items of your opportune task. First, today is your last time to feed your acid-loving plants — camellias, rhododendrons, and azaleas. It should have been done in August and already we're one day into September. Give them the same food you have been feeding before, the so-called acid food. To a plant four feet tall give a cupful, to a smaller plant, one-half cupful and then water it in right away. Second item; now is the time to make cuttings of pelargoniums and geraniums. Take plenty, select sturdy tip shoots, don't take any leggy drawn stems. What is a sturdy shoot? Young wood with a crown of good healthy green foliage; below along the short stem are at least four joints, each bearing a healthy green leaf. Select the lowest one and under the joint with your sharpest knife cut it off. Cut right under the joint, cut straight across — then you will have a perfect rooting surface. And take the leaf off too, but don't pull it off because where attached to the joint pulling will make a tear which is not the ideal condition. Then lay your cuttings exposed to the air for several hours. Cover up the foliage part, just let the ends of the stems lie exposed so that they will seal over and make ready for the callous to be formed later. All geraniums, pelargoniums, carnations, and many other plants must callous, so that they will not rot when rooting, and also that they may seal in the little moisture already present.

In the meantime get a flat, put two thicknesses of newspaper in the bottom, then fill the flat with coarse sand, pack it tight in the flat, water thoroughly so that it settles with no air pockets, and it will be in good condition for the cuttings. With an old license plate or something similar, push into the sand almost to the bottom of the flat, working back and forth to create a little valley. Then all along, insert your cuttings, two and a half inches into the sand. Pack the sand snug against each cutting. After you have filled the flat give them a good watering. Let the flat dry out a little before you place in the cold frame, greenhouse or porch.

The third item in our Opportune Task is a caution about watering from now on. Fall and cold weather are on their way. Here's the idea. Beginning today do all your watering during the warm hours. From ten to three o'clock is good. Why? Mildew is coming along and will soon be creeping in. We fight it by keeping our plants warm, by letting them dry off before night and by defending the ground against moss and cold.

And still another opportune task in the summer garden is to study the shade there. See where the shade is dark, where it is lightened by beams of filtering sunlight. Certain plants will demand full shade, others will be happier in partial shade. The following lists contain plants known to grow satisfactorily and bloom too in shady places.

Tolerant of full shade.

Columbines
Ferns of all kinds
Japanese Maples
Iris foetidissima (Gladwin Iris)
Iris japonica
Ivy of all kinds
Nandina domestica
Oxalis
Sarcococca ruscifolia
Violets
Acanthus

Shade where sun percolates through.

Astilbe
Aucuba japonica
Azaleas
Brunnera macrophylla
Bulbs in variety, narcissus, etc.
Brunsfelsia
Camellias
Cyclamen
Daphne odora
Fuchsias
Heuchera (Coral bells)
Hydrangeas
Laurel, English
Justicia
Maples, Japanese
Quince, Japanese
Jasmine, Star
Honeysuckle

Chapter 39

FLOWERING SHRUBS OF THE SUMMER GARDEN

(September: Second Week)

We'll make a tour of inspection. We have been busy, each of us, with problems of our own; so let's take a holiday and look at what the neighbors have been growing. A lady who attended one of my lectures told me recently every Sunday on her way to church for months she passed a garden that had all sorts of wonderful plants in it. And around Easter time she got enough nerve to open the gate and ring the bell and ask the owner the name of a very fragrant shrub that was then in full bloom. It was a daphne she found and the man who answered the door bell was so pleased to have a stranger interested in his garden that he invited her to see his special collection at the side of the house that was hidden from the street view. Now they are exchanging notes and ideas all the time. All I'm interested in is to get you to go around — go to at least three places; make an old-fashioned call; just look; you'll find the experience a restful change and I'll wager you'll come home thrilled with new ideas too. The reason I tell this story is I am taking up the subject of Flowering Shrubs of the Summer Garden. I can't describe all those shrubs;there are too many and that isn't the best way to do it anyway. I'm going to take you out into some gardens and see examples of these shrubs. And I want to invite you to go out on your own accord and see not only the shrubs we talk about, but many others.

In the tour which I take with you now we shan't ask how they got the plant nor concern ourselves with the question of its rareness or strangeness, but how we like the plant and where we could use it in our garden at home. And, because we wish to cover ground on this tour, I shall stick by the plants themselves and plan for the future.

We do this with our eyes open especially for the shrubs that we can put in our gardens this fall to bloom next summer — shrubs that our neighbors have but we have not. The idea is not to find a certain plant for a certain spot in your particular garden, but to note where each one in general thrives in the garden, as in full sun or partial shade.

In East Palo Alto I called at a house set back from the street behind a grove of oak trees. Planted all around the grove were dozens of hydrangeas, a won-

HYDRANGEA derful example of mass planting. "You see those beautiful hydrangeas," the owner said. "Well, I can't take any credit for them; my husband thought up that idea and he planted every one himself." These hydrangeas stood six feet tall; every stem was topped with a great big pink flower. Those pink flowers were like the crest of a sunlight wave that hid the foliage below and as we stood gazing upon the sight the thought suddenly came to me that mass planting is certainly the best way to get the most from these shrubs in the garden.

Hydrangeas are among our best summer flowering friends. Though all of the garden forms drop their leaves in the winter, they make up for it after coming into bloom by giving color far into the fall months. And in cool coastal places as San Francisco I have seen them bloom in winter. Hydrangea macrophylla the principal kind in our gardens are pink in most parts of Central and Southern California, but invariably blue in the northern districts from Eureka to British Columbia.

BLUE This blue is due to iron in the soil. You can get it here by every two years adding one-half pound of aluminum sulphate to each square yard, or for potted plant, three ounces per gallon of water. Your pink blooms won't change to blue before your eyes, the results come gradually (if the next crop), over a number of years and you will have to keep up the application at intervals.(See also page 308.)

"Hydrangeas are in their infancy for people don't know how pretty the new forms are," said Frank Morrelli, who has been specializing in raising hybrid hydrangeas. Frank used to be a jobbing gardener having learned the trade in Santa Barbara. "But I always liked hydrangeas," he said, "and I've been collecting them for a long time." I went over to his place and saw growing under his special lath house rows planted to many different colored hydrangeas. Frank told me he had sent all over the United States, England, and France to make this collection and he had forms with red, deep rose, pink, and pure white flowers. None of them had flower heads as large as the hortensis from which they had been hybridized, but they certainly had unusual color tones. As we looked over the lath house Frank said, "Some of these plants grow strong like the parent, others as dwarf in habit. This one called Strafford is a strong-growing form and it produces the largest blooms of all the hybrids. The flowers are a carmine red," he said. "And over here is Percival — one of the best of the hybrids because you can depend upon it to bloom. Some of these hybrid hydrangeas are shy bloomers, but Percival always throws a mass of flowers; it's a profuse bloomer. They are a deep rose and Percival is very popular because the flowers keep well when cut and this form is the only one with fringed margins to the sepals." Further on in the row was Merveille, the finest deep pink form Frank told me. Europa is a lovely blue. (See page 308.)

HYBRID

We moved over to the other section of his lath house and there I saw two white hybrids. One is called Moulliere, and "It's the best white form; it's the favorite of the florists," Frank told me. "But this other one named Engel's White is also a favorite because it can be grown easily in a pot and it has flowers of clear, pure white. Engel's White is a plant of dwarf habit, only becoming about eighteen inches tall but every branch or stem carries a bloom," Frank remarked. "And one more thing, be sure to tell them all of these hybrid hydrangeas can be grown in the garden; all they need is a partially shaded place, same as camellias or fuchsias. What they need most is plenty of water during the summer season. And tell them when they take the plants home from the nurseryman's

CARE

lath house to plant in the garden to give the hydrangeas a light sandy loam with a lot of peat mixed in. They don't like adobe," Frank stressed.

"Then as with all hydrangeas," he continued, "when the foliage gets yellow and sick looking, the plants need a working over. I always dig them up, shake the roots — not too rough — then I correct the bad soil condition by adding lime or gypsum and finally after adding a little well-rotted cow manure, I reset the plants and they start off new again."

CHLOROSIS Chlorosis or yellowing of new leaves takes place in other plants besides hydrangeas. Azaleas and rhododendrons suffer especially when the peat has decomposed, the soil has packed and become hard, improper environment for root growth. Besides with city water calcium piles up. Chlorosis can be prevented by the application of iron sulfate at the rate of 1 ounce to 2 gallons of water;or 1 pound per 100 square feet of soil.

On a garden tour over in Marin County I saw a whole hillside planted to hydrangeas. They were protected from the direct sunlight by the high shade of oaks and buckeyes. All hydrangeas like shade because excessive sun will curl the leaves and stunt the flowers; but in partial shade and with sufficient moisture hydrangeas will bloom so successfully that the flowers actually hide the foliage. This is especially true with macrophylla where it is not uncommon to see flower heads eighteen inches across. And these are attainable also when plants are grown in large tubs. In fact, hydrangeas are among the finest summer flowering shrubs that may be grown in tubs or boxes.

"Why do hydrangea blooms droop and wither when I pick them for the house; they don't even last through a luncheon?" is a question often put to the nurseryman. The reason is the seed bearing part of the bloom hasn't developed yet. To make this clear let us look carefully at the bloom to see how it is made up. The biggest part of it is composed of sepals, which as you know make up the container of a flower. These in the hydrangea are large, flat and of course, sterile; that is, they do not produce seeds. Almost hidden in the center is the true flower; before you pick your hydrangea find the flower. If it is closed in a ball, leave it;if it is open so that you see the stamens and anthers, it is waiting both for the bee to bring his pollen or for you to bring your shears. Now in some gardens, you can see hydrangeas with a flat head of small purple flowers in the center surrounded with a ring of sterile flowers made up entirely of the large sepals. They are like butterflies about to light upon the true flowers in the center. The climbing hydrangea belongs to this type. And Frank Morrelli tells me a good additional safeguard when picking flowers is to smash the stems and plunge them into hot water as you do for dahlias; then the flowers keep indefinitely. *HOW CUT FLOWERS*

Now the oleander. What does it look like? They are big shrubs spreading out like cornucopia baskets upside down; and all summer are lighted up with fragrant blooms like a candelabra. The single blooms are red, shell-pink, white and cream; the doubles are deep rose and apricot, or salmon and recently a new double red. *OLEANDER*

The strong branches shoot up from the base of the shrub if it is growing well. The leaves are lead-gray green and lance shaped and big clusters of blooms keep unfolding at the end all the time.

Just the other day on an estate in Atherton I drove for a mile between banks of oleanders. For full open sun they can't be beat. The gardener told me that you make sure they have plenty of water in the spring, but the shrubs do better on the dry side when they are approaching bloom period, because development of the flowering bud is encouraged instead of development of the luxuriant bush wood. And, by the way, all nurserymen when selling oleanders caution never to chew the leaves, stems or any part of the plant because all are poisonous. *DON'T*

The other week I went to see a garden in Menlo Park that was designed in 1887. Leading up to the front door on either side of the slate steps were two plants in pots. The lady told me some of these were 44 years old. These plants are woody-stemmed, three feet high and produce new shoots which carry large flowers. The flowers attain five inches in diameter, hollyhock shape, and come in the shades of copper, yellow, pink, red and white; the famous hibiscus of Hawaii. Each fall these plants are carried to the glass house for winter protection. (See page 84.)

HIBISCUS

Every summer patrons of the Community Play House at Palo Alto pass a lovely garden facing Middlefield Road in which are four high shrubs. The bushes are covered with lavender and shell-pink flowers that look like hollyhocks. Invariably some one calls me up asking the name of these shrubs and I have it all ready for them; the Rose of Sharon. This is another kind of hibiscus called shrubby althea, botanically. These high shrubs are woody plants which drop their leaves every winter and send out new ones in the late spring. They are Oriental plants grown in China and India for centuries. In old California gardens you might see great big specimens.

You will remember my old friend who made me mow her lawn — well, she has plants which die down completely each winter to spidery roots like rhubarb, and when spring comes each year throw up new shoots with large dark green leaves. Late in summer these carry huge blooms, often the size of eight-inch breakfast plates. Red, white or pink and look like a huge silky hollyhock. This is the third kind of hibiscus.

Now let's go on to still another. The other day a gardener brought me a strange plant; he wanted to know the name. He said he found it growing in a neglected garden where to his astonishment it blossomed all summer. Well, he did me a real favor when he brought me a nice big sprig — so many times I get a stingy leaf with the question. "What is it?" There is little I can do toward classifying it. This sprig possessed airy, fern-like foliage. The blooms were long and spidery with yellow petals and red stamens that stuck out beyond the rest of the flower. The flowers were in clusters and they continued to open up and reach fullness in succession. The shrub is called by the name Paradise Poinciana. It comes from the tropics and under favorable conditions develops into a small tree. Just to keep things clear I might say there is another plant called Bird of Paradise, but it's an herb from South Africa and you often see the cut flowers in florist's windows.

One summer I dropped in to see the late Mr. Pilkington who had been a nurseryman all his life. He had in five-gallon cans a row of shrubs that were ablaze with color — every plant holding up masses of royal purple flowers as high as three and one-half to four feet above the containers. I asked him what he did to get that effect. "Frost," he said. "The frost killed them down to the roots. They came back strong in the spring and you can see the results. So I tell people to always prune them away back if the frost doesn't do it for them."

PLEROMA

This bush is called Tibouchina by the Indians of tropical America, and that was the first name given the plant. Many gardeners prefer to call it Pleroma or Glory-bush. It attains a height of six to ten feet with soft velvety grey-green leaves and stems that produce large reddish-copper buds that open up into large flat purple flowers. The flowers open several in numbers at the same time — are three inches across and are truly a royal purple. I saw in Santa Cruz the other day a glory-bush that was a mass of purple bloom which were supported on straight loose branches with here and there an old leaf that had turned brilliant red, an indication its work had been done. In the foggy frostless parts of the Bay region this plant can be depended upon for fine flowers every year.

I went out to the Academy of Sciences one day to see Miss Alice Eastwood up in the Department of Botany. The late Alice Eastwood has for years been working on the plants of California so I asked her what she thought was the finest summer blooming Escallonia. Escallonias, you know, are found in gardens throughout this state. She said, "There are many fine escallonias and they bloom all year round, but the pure white one called Montevidensis with the round head of blooms is the best for summer. At Stowe Lake," continued Miss Eastwood, "there is the largest specimen to be found in the city and the men of the park call it the butterfly bush because when it is in bloom these insects come to it by the hundreds." Escallonia montevidensis grows into a large rounded shrub and every branch and shoot will produce a ball of pure white flowers. If the shrub is given an annual pruning so as to favor new wood, each summer about early August the white flowers will bring to the garden as much color and interest as do the old-fashioned lilacs in spring, because both flowers are displayed alike.

The Opportune Task: Go visit the park or call on your neighbor whom you think is a good gardener. Don't talk politics but talk gardens and How Does Your Garden Grow. There are many summer-blooming shrubs and you will want to think about them now. Ask the names of any strangers if they appeal to you — get acquainted with them so that you can add them to your garden in the fall. There's that low shrub called Jacobinia. Ask about it. It has deep rose-pink flowers and leaves the color of the copper-beech. Then there is that very fragrant plant, Cashmere Bouquet. They grow either three to four feet high and bloom, or eight to ten feet high and bloom as I've seen them up in the foothills of Saratoga. There is the Datura, Gabriel's Trumpet, Ceratostigma willmottianum, named for Miss Willmott and a hard worker in the field of gardening; and the gardenias; there are lots of summer shrubs that you ought to get acquainted with. Just look around, ask the name of the plant, and if they who grow it do not know the name then ask for a twig and a bloom and seek your nurseryman.

Certain perennials are entering their annual rest period. Acanthus, Bear's Breech is an example. Leaves now are floppy, yellow, or brown lying on the ground. The plant is resting. Cut those old leaves to the ground; cut all flower stalks too. Look for snails and slugs down at the old crown of the acanthus. Clean them up. Fall rains awaken the roots and from them grow lush, clean leaves. Your plant returns then to its resplendent classical form.

Chapter 40

FLOWERING VINES OF THE SUMMER GARDEN

(September: Third Week)

Let us take another tour and this time keep on the lookout for plants that climb and creep. All around us are vines that cover walls, that conceal unsightly spots, that run over roof tops, that blanket wide spaces, that climb on other plants in the garden. All of them produce flowers, some large and beautiful, others small and often hidden. The summer garden has many spots of bright color created by vines growing there.

Why are we talking vines at this time? So we'll be prepared for this fall; we want to get acquainted with them; we want to know them so we can use them in our gardens this fall when we make alterations there.

Have you ever taken time to really look at a vine and see how it is able to reach up into a tree, or how it is fitted to climb a wall. The bright color they give us in the upper reaches of the garden is the direct result of efficient mechanical devices for holding on.

I remember studying vines in the class of plant physiology given by the late Dr. George Peirce at Stanford. He invited the class out to the experimental gardens. "Look a moment at those plants and tell me what you *STUDY* see," he said, pointing to a little redwood tree wnich was almost hidden under a vine. We scurried around on all sides but before we found an answer, Dr. Peirce asked further, "Is the vine going to smother the tree?" Some said yes, some said no, for we knew it was only the annual growth of the common manroot vine. "Now look once again and tell me how that vine is able to climb up the tree." "It has tendrils," we all yelled. "Yes, and what is a tendril? You see a tendril has no leaves," he went on. "A great many vines have tendrils. They are one of the most useful gadgets in the plant kingdom because they not only enable the vine to climb up a tree, but they can stretch like spiral springs and no matter which way the wind blows can yield and still hold on."

All the students scratched down that useful fact and when we looked up from our notebooks the professor invited us to move to a little shed over at the side of the experimental gardens. There Dr. Peirce pointed to another kind of vine and told us to look hard. "What do you see there? Is it like the last one?" he asked. We saw leaves as big as a valentine card standing out six to eight inches from the side of the building; they were rustling in a little breeze. "How does that vine get where it wants to?" he asked. We looked again and like a flash one of the bright boys yelled, "It has little holders like the darts the kids throw in the games." "Those are suction pads," said the professor, "and have you ever tried to pull one off a pane of glass?" I didn't say it, but I knew the answer all right, because I've washed many a window on my journey through a college education. When you try to pull those pads off the glass the stem comes away and leaves them stuck fast. And the only way to get them loose is to use a razor blade. Dr. Peirce said, "This vine is the Boston Ivy. Its original home is Japan. It will cover great expanses of walls and for that reason is often planted in landscape work. Roble Hall for instance, our largest girls' dormitory is completely covered with Boston Ivy; in a way the plant can become a detriment as it can muffle a building, obliterating the texture, and even weakening the architectural lines."

Dr. Peirce's field trip makes me still conscious of vines.

As you know, Santa Clara is one of our fine garden towns. I was there the other day. On a west wall of a Spanish house in the full afternoon sun my eye caught a great splash of red. I stopped the car immediately to find what it was. To my astonishment all that color which extended up above the second story and across the whole side came from one vine. I rang the bell and asked the lady about it. She smiled heartily when she heard my question. "Where did you get that vine; and how old is it? *KINDS*

"You know," she began, "we used to live in Santa Barbara and we saw this vine everywhere; on the old houses, and planted on the new lovely mansions. It's a wide-spreading vine, as you see, and those vines down there seemed always to be in bloom. When we came up here to live eight years ago and built our home we thought we couldn't have this vine, but when we saw a marvelous specimen of it in Carmel our hopes were raised so here it is in our garden. It sort of swept along the ground for awhile, but about the second year it started up the wall." I looked at the vine closely and saw that it had suction pads like those of the Boston Ivy — little disks that stick to the wall. Its name is the Evergreen Trumpet Creeper and its home is Mexico. While the Boston Ivy has inconspicuous flowers and showy blue berries, this vine has large red trumpets in clusters of four and eight.

Now back to Palo Alto. "I want to cover up that wall," said Mr. Hooper to the nurseryman after he had come to Palo Alto from San Francisco and had bought a large estate completely surrounded by a brick wall. "I don't like that bristling broken glass the former owners cemented along the top to keep the boys from climbing over. What can you suggest?" "I know of nothing better than the cat's-claw vine, that likes to spread and climb high. In fact I've seen it cover whole roofs and the entire side of houses," responded the nurseryman. "What does it look like?" asked Mr. Hooper. "The vine is evergreen and can stand a lot of frost. The leaves are shiny but its greatest charm lies in the canary yellow flowers." As a rule it takes a few years before the blooms come because a young plant has first to get established before the claws will take hold. After that the vine grows like wild fire and will cover a wall completely; next the blossoms start to appear and they come in such numbers that the upper part of the plant is a golden draping blanket. "But how do you plant this vine?" asked Mr. Hooper. "That all depends, sir, upon two factors. This vine is going to be included in a landscape scheme, therefore it's going to be with a lot of other plants. In other words there is going to be root competition. So be sure your gardener prepares for this by deep fertilization of the soil before the vine is planted," he said. "And what is the second?" pressed Mr. Hooper. "I'm coming to that but let me finish about soil preparation," continued the nurseryman. "You see vines grow big and cover astonishingly large areas of wall space; they attain age; they produce a lot of wood, twigs, and foliage besides quantities of bloom; we must prepare for this or else our vines will fail to come up to expectation and do only a halfway job," said the nurseryman who felt this was the time to drive the point home for thorough preparation of the soil at planting time. He went on, "Now the second important consideration with vines is that all of them need moisture. Have you ever seen a vine covering a wall with the upper part dead — 'burned back' as the professionals say. Boston Ivy is seen often in that pitiful plight. It just didn't get enough water and to save itself started economizing by dying back in the upper parts. This is going to be planted against a wall that is a difficult spot because, as under the eaves of the house, it will get a little water, unless you make a special point and prepare for it. Dry soil is no good for vines or any other plant for that matter; even cactus like a little moisture. Well, excuse me, I didn't mean to give you a lecture but I know you want a good vine and that's the way to get it." That's how the cat's-claw vine went on Mr. Hooper's wall, and today you can see it doing all the things the nurseryman promised because it was well cared for.

Now our tour takes us to Menlo Park. Last June

the professional gardeners met at a member's home and at the corner of the house was a vine called the Star Jasmine. It was in full bloom — little pure white flowers that perfumed the whole yard. "I see you have trained that vine on copper wire; doesn't that burn the vine?" asked one of the club members. "Well, you're right, any wire can injure a vine on a hot day but in this case you see the vine is really growing under the shady protection of that big oak tree. For twining vines like that star jasmine I use strong manila hemp cord and if I can get any old electric cord with insulated cover I use it," said one of the other gardeners. "Yes, and you can unfasten and pull them down when you want to paint the house too, " was another contribution to the discussion. "It's one of the best evergreen vines I know of," said the president of the club. "Well, for that matter you can prune it, keep it cut back and grow it like a low shrub, " said one of the boys who gardens up in the foothills of Los Altos. "In fact, where I work we trained this twining star jasmine so that it grows alongside a brick walk. The ground slopes away from the walk on the east side and that bank is covered with this vine grown shrub fashion and it's a knockout." "That ought to make a wonderful tumbling carpet of foliage and attractive, especially with those fragrant flowers," said one of the boys. "After the blooms are gone, about August up in the hills, some places a little earlier, and others maybe as late as September, then prune, but the way to do it is to get to the main branches. They are low down in there;then prune where the old shoot first breaks from the main branch. The secret is to keep the new shoots coming from the body of the plant. These shoots carry the bloom. You have to be careful. It's not a whack job — it's really a special job which must be done right. Whacking results only in a lot of dead leaves and the plant looks burned."

STAR JASMINE

Now before we leave the twining vines let me remind you to look for that very fragrant white flowered vine from Argentine called Chilean Jasmine. They are in bloom right now. We must not forget either the

Chinese Wisteria that keeps on blooming throughout the summer. It and the Japanese Wisteria with the long pendulent flowers are also vines that twine.

So far we have discussed vines with tendrils that included our own common manroot, and to which belong others as the passion vine, and that favorite of many the cup and saucer vine from Mexico; and the grapes that are soon to be harvested. Then we discussed the tendril vines that have holdfasts or little disks, as the Boston Ivy and the evergreen trumpet creeper; and the third tendrils with a claw, as the cat's claw trumpet vine. Then we moved over to the twining or twisting vine, the star jasmine; wisteria, the morning glory and hops are other good examples but there are still other kinds.

In 1940-41, I presented a series of lectures in Marin County and one day the group met at the Walker residence in San Rafael. There for the first time I saw in bloom the Burmese Honeysuckle. I took a colored picture of it. The plant grows as a scandent shrub; that is, it scrambles up anyway it can, resting and pushing against a wall.

The gardener had tied the specimen up against the wall and like a great blanket it draped over the upstairs porch. The flowers were six to eight inches long, they were slender, tube-like with the open end two-lipped; and the stamen and anthers resting on the lower lip. Up on the porch the flowers were a clear yellow; a few older ones had some orange-red, and those that had dropped to the ground were dull ochre. The plant I saw that day was indeed a blanket of golden-yellow, laid on shiny large green leaves, and the fragrance permeated every section of the garden. Mrs. Walker told me she gave it the warmest and most protected section of her garden. Later on I saw one in San Francisco with fewer blooms, but it proved to me this tropical vine will grow in a somewhat cool climate.

Now of course honeysuckles are natives not only in the tropics but also throughout the temperate regions. We have four climbing natives in California. Several of the kinds, including Burmese, are strongly scandent, that is to say, they scramble up any way they can resting and pushing against a wall or fence or they reach up through strong stems.

I remember along the railroad tracks coming up from Richmond, Va., to Washington, D. C., seeing the trumpet vine, the common trumpet creeper now grown in many California gardens. And in Williamsburg, Va., where John D. Rockefeller, Jr., has brought back an entire early American town, I saw this same plant grown as a hedge. This is possible because this vine grows into stiff woody stems; these may be pruned back to strong buds each year and the new wood brings out fresh foliage and clear trumpet-shaped flowers every summer. These which are orange-scarlet come in great clusters. "Yes, that may be so," said one of the gardeners in discussing this vine at the club not so long ago, but the trumpet vine is a nuisance when it starts to sucker all over the garden. It will come up in the lawn, in the walk, and in the shrub borders; I have to keep whacking away at it all the time," he said. Well, this gardener speaks the truth all right — the vine does sucker but many amateurs plant it anyway because they like the orange-trumpet flowers. And all over California you can see arbors, gateways, and fences planted to the trumpet vine. But look for the one called Grandiflora.

In this group of strong, stiff-stemmed vines there are the Bougainvillea which when well established shoots up ten to fifteen feet in the air. Then the side branches come and upon them the flowers are produced. So be sure never to cut those spear-like shoots DON'T that break out from the roots; tie them back or train them where you want them to grow and be sure to look out for the sharp-pointed hooks. I saw a bougainvillea at the University of Santa Clara that covered a wall one-half block long. It was growing in a court and faced the full afternoon sun. It was in full bloom and that was something.

About chrysanthemum time you can see on garden tours, especially in Santa Barbara and San Diego, the famous Cup of Gold. It's a strong-growing vine with shiny stiff leaves and flowers that open in a large cup. And in spring you see also the woody bush jasmine with single yellow fragrant flowers; the commonest jasmine of all. Both of these vines belong to this group of scandent shrubs.

Another group of vines common in our gardens include those with aerial rootlets. Two are well-known forms — the English Ivy and the creeping fig. I can only mention them in our discussion today because they have insignificant flowers, especially the creeping fig and we are interested in those with showy blooms in the summer.

The last group of vines includes those using leaf stalks to reach up — they are known as clasping petioles; they grow loosely; the garden clematis belong to this group. Everyone knows the clematis, the small flowered forms as Virgins-bower, that has either white or rose-pink flowers;and the large flowered type such as the ever-popular purple form, Jackmanii. There are quite a number of these large flowered hybrids from the Orient and what they want most is a rich, moist and well-drained soil. All the climbers like lime or gypsum mixed in the soil.

Another member of the loose-growing (clasping petiole) vines is Maurandia. I have the blue form in my garden and it is covered with flowers all summer long. It's a dainty vine also from Mexico and has proved hardy in many places in California.

A word about the trailers is in order and among the best is the trailing lavender lantana. It loves a sunny spot and blooms all summer. Trailers don't travel far, but they are useful to cover ground and hide scars in embankments.

The Opportune Task: Do today for vines the same thing I told you a week ago for the summer flowering shrubs. That is, go out and see these things yourself and more besides. Once you start you'll find them everywhere.

Chapter 41

IRIS

(September: Third Week)

Now is the time to work over your iris. That is if they require shifting. Last June and July you could have performed this office but if you did not do so then, you can do so now in this fall month. You'll know if you have to shift your plants when you remember how well your iris bloomed last year, and when you look at the plants themselves today. We know iris are divided into two main groups, the bulbous and those with fleshy food rich rhizomes. A rhizome is a stem of root-like appearance, horizontal or oblique in

position, lying on the ground or subterranean, bearing scales instead of leaves, and usually producing annual roots from its lower surface which move into the soil to perform their important duty of food and moisture gathering. The bulbous iris you cannot see now for the bulbs are hidden below ground and there is no foliage showing at this time of year. But those iris in the rhizome group are very much in evidence. Let's go out to the iris plot now and take a look. I mean of course to the bearded iris, the Iris germanica, which have been much hybridized. Are the clumps crowded?

Do you see among the green leaf blades dead straw colored ones? Are the rhizomes sticking far out of the ground? Do you see vigorous weeds that have intruded and now are growing wild among your iris? Recall how your iris bloomed last season. If you recall small blooms on short stunted stalks, then you'll agree with me now is the time to shift this clump of iris. Now step over to that second clump of iris which also has rhizomes. Notice how strong it grows. See how well the leaf blades stand up, clean of any marks right to the tip point of the blade. You may notice a few straw-dry leaves still attached on the outer parts of the rhizome. These you may grab firmly at the bottom and pull, they peel away readily. If some of the green leaves are beginning to shrivel you may cut them back, but that is all that will be necessary for this clump of iris is in vigorous growth and promises tall stems of fine blooms next spring.

CARE

But for that first clump you'll have some work to do, and here are steps to guide you to start your iris on their way to giving you quality bloom. You must realize iris can multiply quickly. They can fill up a plot in a few seasons. Then when they get crowded the roots are not able to support the rhizomes which in turn are powerless to send up strong growth to give fine blooms. The time comes every three years, certainly by the fifth year when most iris must be shifted in the garden,

For the benefit of your notes I might state again you can move your iris in June or July or in September. Iris are very drought resistent. They can go through our long hot dry summers. In fall when our rains usually begin they may be moved easily. Growth always begins at that time. So September is a good time to move iris and here are the eight steps: One: with your spade lift the clump. You notice it has a central large rhizome off of which on either side like the outstretched wings of a bird are two other branching rhizomes. In fact you may find more, then the simile of the bird doesn't work so well because he couldn't fly, at least not gracefully with three or four

MOVE

wings pointed in different directions. Two: slice through this clump where each of the branching rhizomes are attached to the mother. Three: then pull the rhizomes apart; that is cut off all the dead parts of each rhizome, especially the old mother one. It may in fact be pretty much gone and can be disposed of. Or you may observe the older part of the rhizome has shriveled up, and remains still attached to a vigorous growing section at the opposite end. You'll cut away the old dead part. But the younger rhizomes that I likened to the wings of a bird you'll notice how firm and vigorous they are. More than that you'll observe how young shoots are starting out all along these younger rhizomes showing a promise of strong growth to come. Fourth: now cut back all the foliage. Cut each shoot back to three inches. You may do this now because you are starting off your clump as a new individual and you are anxious to get strong root growth this coming year; the season after next you'll get your quality blooms. Let me make clear an important point here: if your clump was in vigorous growth, that is the leaves stand up clean and firm, you wouldn't in all probability need to lift and shift your clump of iris, and you certainly would not put your pruning shears anywhere near one of those green leaf blades. Iris should not be cut back every September because you see the neighbor is cutting his back. Such indiscriminate pruning simply robs the rhizomes of their blooms. But in this case since we are beginning over again we do a thorough job, and that is why I say cut back all the foliage to three inches above the rhizome. And before you get through with the rhizome look at the roots on the underside. All the dead dried up roots you may pull off, the broken ones cut, but the new firm ones, those just starting out from the rhizome, they are ivory white and are just ready to plunge into the soil, these you leave along. It's because these roots are just barely getting under way and are unable to support a lush growth of leaves that you have to cut the leaves back to three inches. If you left them long they would merely wilt on you and look flabby.

Now you can place them all in a pile and cover them with a wet sack while you proceed with step number Five. This is to prepare the ground for the new planting. With your fork or your spade thoroughly loosen up the soil, scatter some bone meal, a pound to every 12 plants when spaced a foot apart. Thrash that bone meal well into the soil. This is step Six. And if you discover your soil is stiff or you have a heavy soil that does not break up easily, then scatter some wood ashes or soil sulphur in the plot. Rake the area over, get it level and you're ready to set out your plants. Seven: after you have placed your rhizomes in the soil remembering to leave them at least a foot apart (this is so that they will have room in the next two years to fill into clumps) — remembering also in placing these rhizomes in the earth that you leave the upper part out of the ground — after you have placed all your rhizomes in the soil, then turn on the sprinkler and soak them well.

Give them a good soaking once a week for two weeks after resetting them, this so as to make sure the roots will begin at once to grow and perform their all important duties. But you'll be interested to note that the rhizome doesn't always get into growing condition. For some time it is slow about sending out new roots. In that case too much water can bring rot in the rhizome. You'll have to keep track of your newly set iris. And Eight is really a caution rather than a step. Iris do best, that is grow strong and bloom profusely, in full sunlight. When the rhizomes are buried in deep shade the leaves grow limp and the plants seldom throw a flower. Give them as much sun as is possible. Of course iris belong in the perennial border and they grow well on sloping well drained ground too.

I might call your attention to one of the fungus enemies, you recognize it as dark brown or black spots on the rhizome. Take a sharp knife and cut these out, and if you see them on the leaves cut them off too. Then drop the plant in a bucket of water in which a nursery-recommended fungicide has been dissolved.

Let the rhizomes soak for a half hour, then spread out in the sun to dry. And when you reset your iris, select a brand new place. All of this is health insurance.

And before we leave the subject of planting and care let me add a few more pointers. For one thing be careful with the use of lime. Gardeners have found too much has a tendency to cause the rhizomes to rot. The bone meal you worked into the soil is enough. Fertilizer: you can sprinkle a little each year, a light feeding of some well balanced fertilizer. Superphosphate is good; or a dusting with well-rotted barnyard manure including sheep manure if applied lightly is helpful. And see that your plants get a good soaking either from the rains or from your sprinkler every two or three weeks from early fall till late spring. California winters and dry springs are a great disadvantage to the iris. You can prevent the ground from baking by carefully cultivating the soil around your plants, thus encouraging fibrous root growth. But again as I have already told you your iris can be dried out in hot sunny soil all summer and do well season after season. They dislike shade and they dislike standing water.

FEED

Here is information to classify iris. As I have already told you the common garden iris, the botanical Iris germanica, is also called bearded. I'll explain why the upright petals are "standards" — those that bend down are falls. I suppose after the fashion of Niagara Falls! Now these falls are sometimes like the chin of an aspiring young boy who looks yearningly at his father's electric razor, but so far has no possible excuse for using it. Other falls however are so endowed as to meet the young boy's fondest dream with a kind of soft whiskers. It even exceeds the dream because it can be golden, ruddy, or wonderful to relate, multicolored, and it is indeed an adornment. But there are several kinds of bearded iris, and popular among them are tall ones and dwarf forms. As an example of one of our tall flowering stemmed iris is a fairly new one first seen in 1933-34, and now listed as Happy Days. It was hybridized here in California by

Sydney B. Mitchell, who developed gardening as a hobby into something which rates very high professionally for he turned out to have an intuitive skill. And by the way Mr. Mitchell wrote the chapter "THE IRIS IN CALIFORNIA" which you can read in Bailey's Cyclopedia of Horticulture. And by the way again I'm just now trying to figure out whether there can be any logical relation between this iris and the name, which full of anticipation I gave to my house as soon as the roof was on -- the name Happy Hours. When Mr. Mitchell's iris is in bloom you see as many as seven to eight immense flowers as crowns perched at the tips of branches 40 inches above the ground. These flowers appear every season and each single bloom will measure as much as seven and one-quarter inches from top to bottom, and three and one-quarter inches across. The standards as I told you have petals that stand upright, are a clear yellow, and the falls are a rich orange yellow.

KINDS

A tall bearded blue iris is Santa Barbara, blue petals with a golden yellow beard on the fall petals;and a long time favorite in pink tones is Frieda Mohr. Here the fall petals have a slight tinge of lavender. Of course new forms are being hybridized each year. This work is going on at a great rate in Oregon, back East, down South, and in several districts of California. I would suggest that you study the catalogues. And feeling a certain sympathy for the growers I will not suggest that you do what I found one of my friends doing, that is, collecting these catalogues to furnish not his garden but his library with these astonishingly beautiful pictures!

And still in the tall stemmed bearded iris are a number of bearded forms that flower again in the autumn, types that send out surprisingly fine flowers from September till November. This out of season flower production is inspired by the fall rains. In Iowa, Minnesota, Illinois, Oregon and California hybridizers have selected from these forms and have created new types giving them such lovely names as Autumn Frost, a blue, Golden Cataract, a bright yel-

AZALIA MACRANTHA

Grown in container

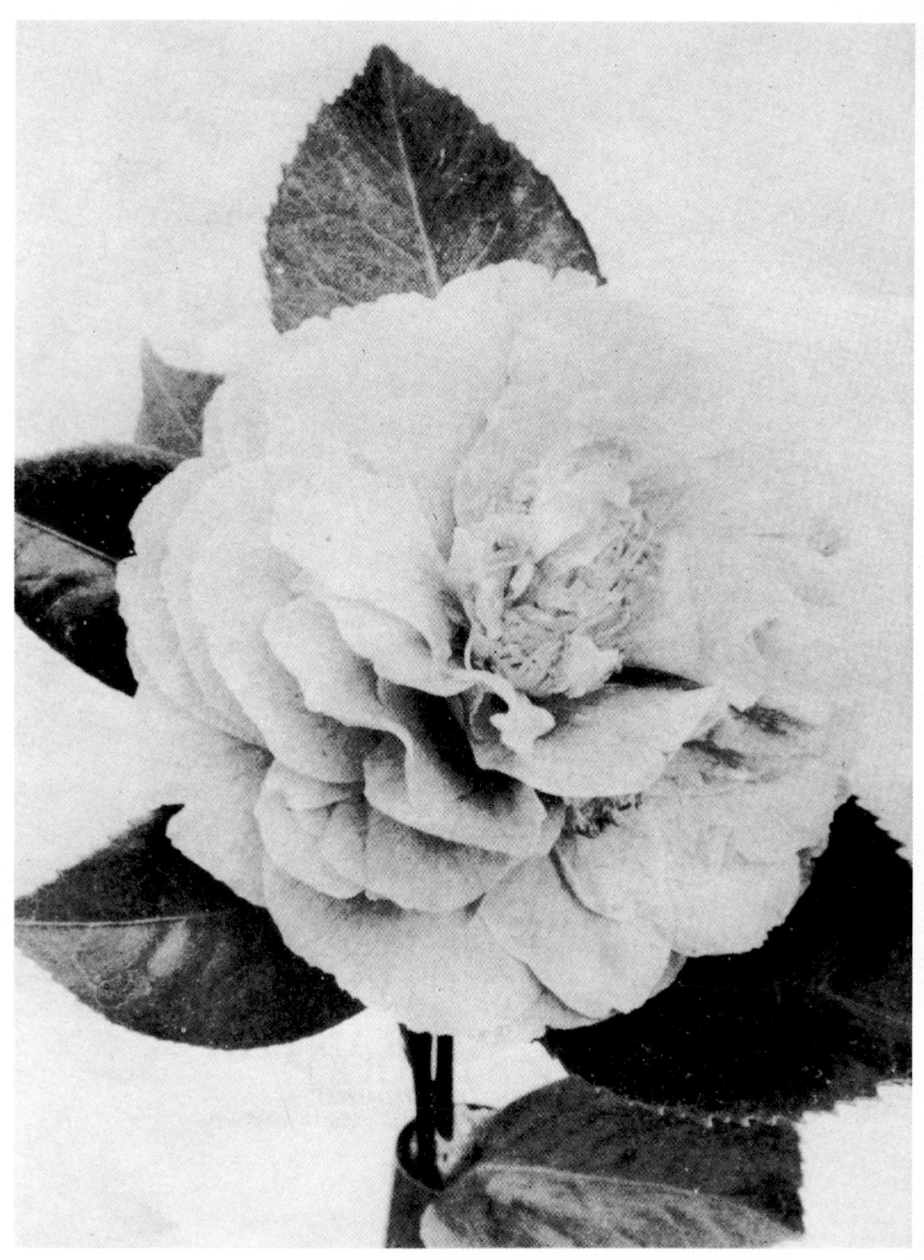

CAMELLIA

"Gov. Earl Warren"

Introduced by J. E. EDWARDS

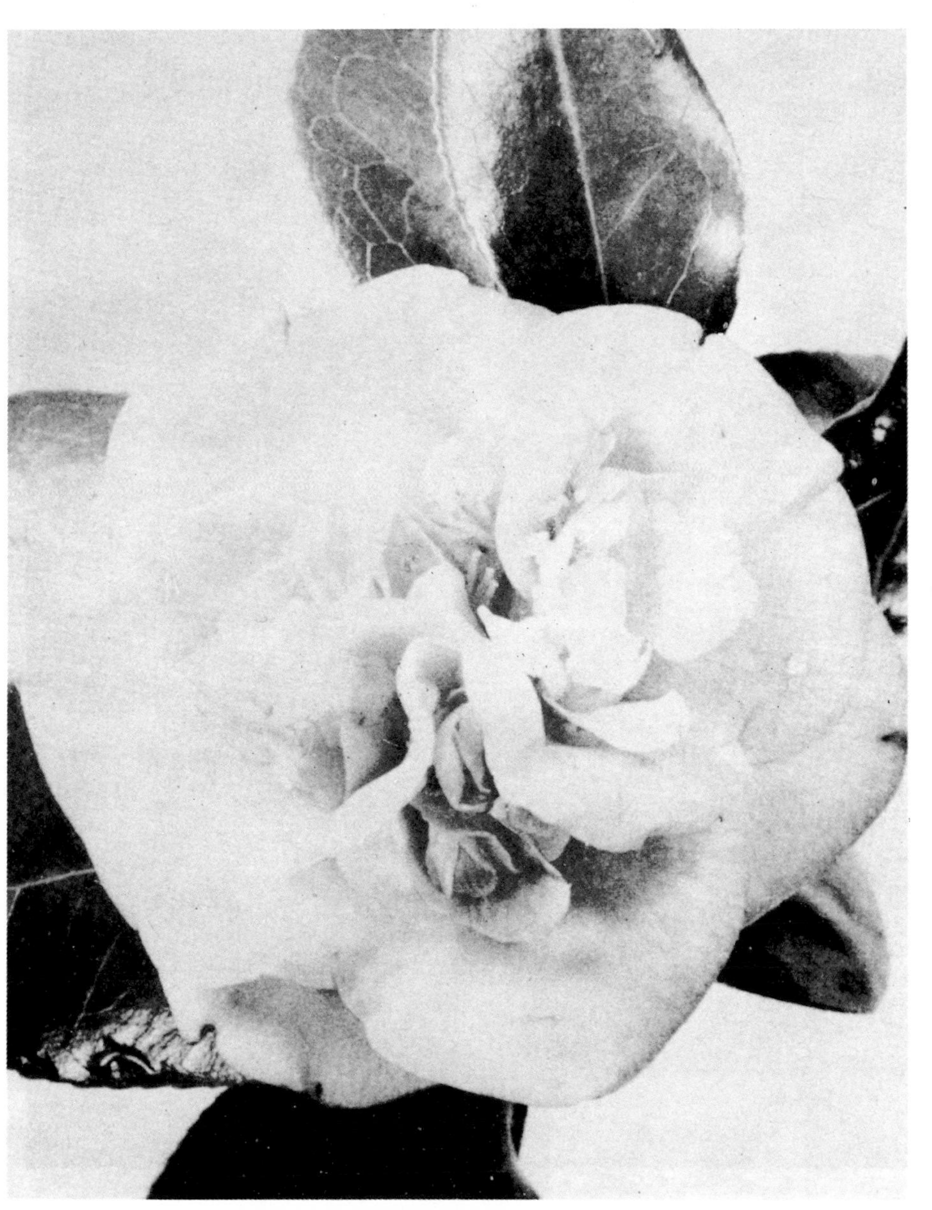

CAMELLIA

"Emperor of Russia"

FLORAL PERFECTION IN RHODODENDRON

RHODODENDRON
Growing in Golden Gate Park

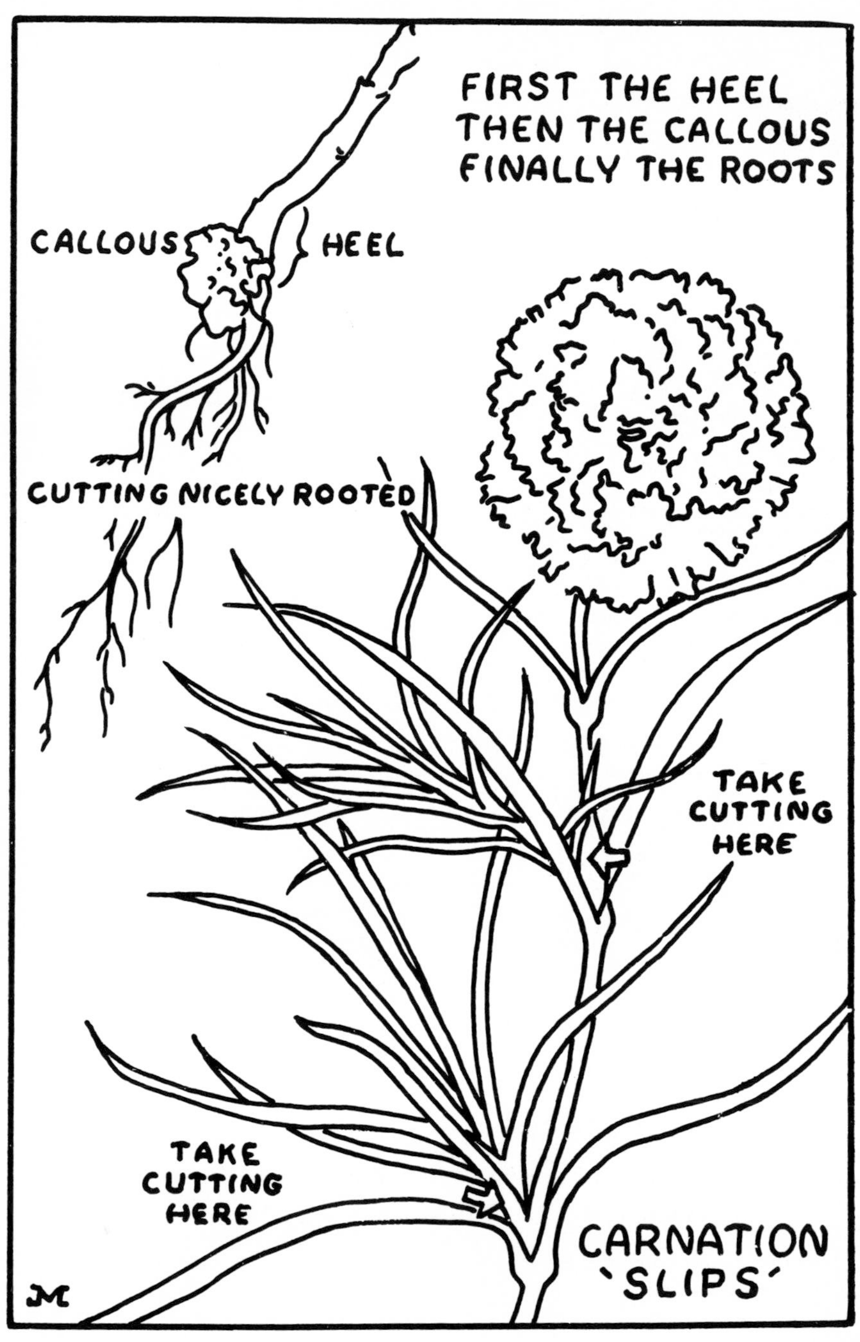
FIRST THE HEEL
THEN THE CALLOUS
FINALLY THE ROOTS
CALLOUS
HEEL
CUTTING NICELY ROOTED
TAKE
CUTTING
HERE
TAKE
CUTTING
HERE
CARNATION
`SLIPS´
JM

HOW TO PLANT PEONIES

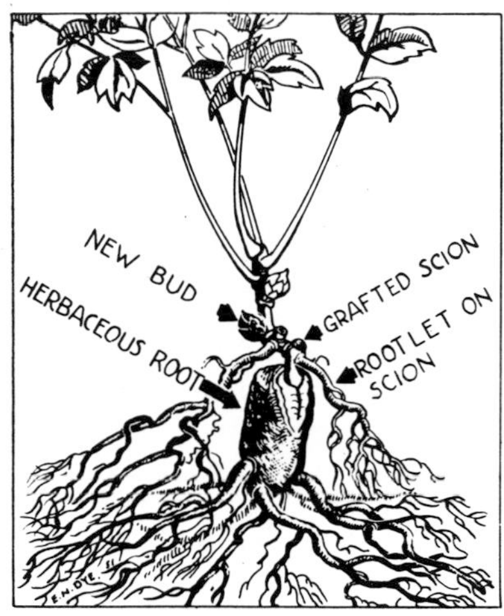

This is a grafted plant on herbaceous peony root. Note new roots developing from the Tree Peony stock. This is 3-year graft.

Same grafted plant pruned and set in planting hole. Soil must be friable for good root growth. Note planting depth.

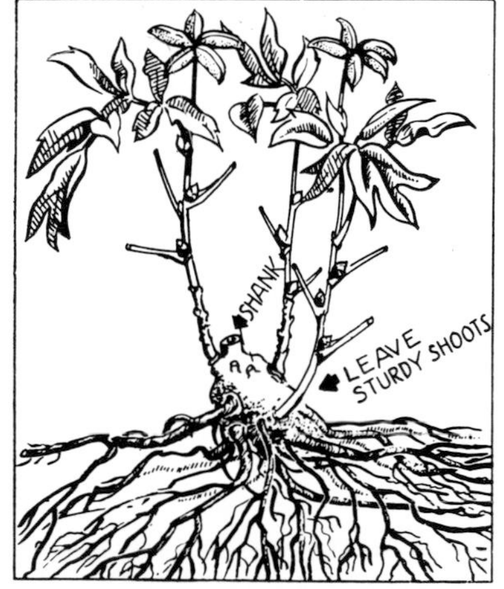

This seedling plant is about seven years old, as dug from the field.

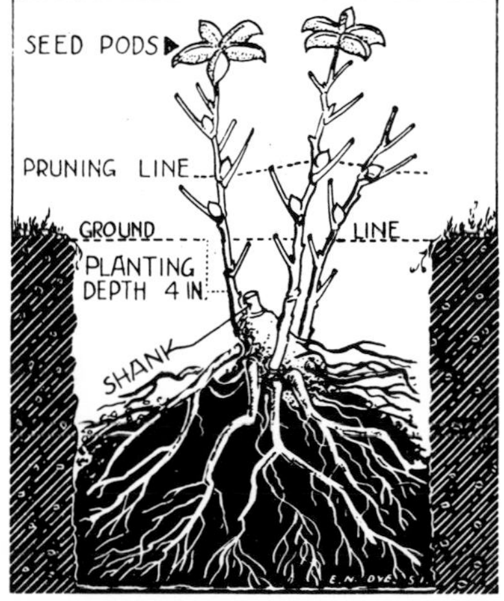

Same seedling set in hole. Note planting depth and pruning line.

FOOD PLANTS

Annual and Perennial Vegetables

low, October Blaze, large red-purple and Equinox with rather small flowers of several shades of violet-blue. I think these names have been inspired by the beauty of what they have to see and can imagine. One hybridizer being in a state of mind in which he says "I won't sell it, I'll just keep it."

In all the iris there is a wonderful range of color, as another enthusiast said, "They're a lot easier to get than orchids, and that's why we go and forget them. We think orchids are wonderful, and we just take these flowers which are no less wonderful for granted." You can select from blues of every hue, violets, purple, mauve, and mauve blends, light pink, brilliant coppers, reds evenly blended, yellows, creams and bicolors. And for the tall bearded iris and among these autumn flowering here are some more names Setting Sun, Indian Night, Shining Waters. (I can imagine some one erecting a tablet in his garden bearing all the beautiful names he could find.)

Twice blooming iris grow and increase so fast that they make a year's growth in five or six months, and that's the reason they are ready to bloom again in the fall. To encourage this second blooming, plant the rhizomes in loosely prepared soil, in full sunlight; water them frequently and cultivate lightly to prevent them from going to sleep for the year at the outset of summer. Two year old clumps have a better chance to mature the side shoots necessary for second blooms, CARE as they have become established, but have not become too crowded. And of course after the third or fourth year, each clump should be taken up, divided and reset. This work is best done in July.

And now I want to turn your attention away from these tall bearded iris to those which grow in the direct opposite, that is those that hold up superbly gorgeous blooms on short stems. They are known as dwarf iris or miniature bearded iris. This group is the result of crossing two distinct species, one of which is pumila, a stemless iris found in the old Austria-Hungary, South Russia, and the Caucasus; the other is chamaeiris, a native of Southern France and

Northern Italy, which produces flowers on stems six to ten inches in height. By crossing these our modern dwarf or miniature iris have been produced with all of the charm and beauty of both species, on the flowering stems of chamaeiris, and with all of the ruggedness of the latter rugged variety. The results of these crosses have been flowers of startling beauty and they bloom generously. Some of them blooming in both spring and in fall. One named variety is Boquet, white and heliotrope. Another is called Black Bird, flower stem only six inches, midnight violet. Tan Toy is a true tan-brown. All of these and many more grow well and do exceptionally well in rock gardens or on hillslopes.

Now a word about our Winter Blooming iris, Iris unguicularis, popularly known as I. stylosa. It grows in great clumps or tufts on the dry hills of Algeria, Greece, Asia Minor, and Syria. It brightens those dry rocky hills, and it brightens our gardens here too from November till April with sweetly scented well formed flowers that are of a very deep purple with large falls and standards; or a lavender with delicate small falls and standards but with a stronger fragrance than the purple form; or with white flowers possessing a slight yellow tinted streak, and more fragrance than the other two forms. Iris stylosa unlike Iris germanica has no stem to the flower; what you find as a stem though a foot long is simply the elongated style. You find the seed pod way down at the base of the tufts of leaves.

When the tufty clump finishes blooming then anytime from April to July is a good season to move the plants. In California around July is a good time to do this work which may be done once in four years. However in my own garden my clump has grown in the same place for over six years and is still doing well. But when you do move your clump the idea is to take up the old tufts, break them apart and set them out afresh. You'll discover as you dig up your plants that the old roots have dried up into brown wires, long brown wires that start off from the mattlike tuft, and new ones will be pushing. The native haunt of this winter blooming iris gives us a hint of the kind of soil they want; they get into trouble in rich soil, in it they prefer to send up leaves, hundreds of them, a yard long, and not one bloom. So set out your clump in a sunny place, near a wall, at the base of an apricot tree in my garden or near some busy rooter as a perennial aster whose roots give any neighbor the keenest competition and your Winter Iris will bloom away. Of course as you reset your plants you'll give them some water, don't let them go bone dry. As to fertilizer at planting time a little bone meal thrown in is good, but nothing more, no rich soil remember. It has been found sandy loamy soil is better for them than rich adobe.

So far, as you know, we have been speaking only of the bearded iris, but there are many other kinds. For that matter botanists have listed over 100 species of iris, with innumerable garden varieties. I do not intend to discuss all of these but there are some others besides the bearded iris which you should know about. Put down beardless iris next. Every spring commuters from the Peninsula glancing at the hills of South San Francisco can see thousands of iris rippling in the wind with their delicate lavender white blooms. There are beardless iris, and belong to Iris longipetala. Native iris grow in many sections of California and when they are dotting the hillside with beautiful pink, white, lavender, purple and buff flowers, the gardener finds it a difficult task to keep from digging up the clump and taking it home. It will not move when in the flowering stage; a better way is to collect seeds later; or arrange to transplant in the early fall when the rains begin and the plants themselves begin a new cycle of growth. Our native California beardless iris stand up about a foot high, but in Louisiana, another form grows up to two to four feet tall, and carries flowers that are maroon shaded and of unusual colors.

Another group of iris popular in the California garden is the Siberian, and some enthusiasts consider them the most elegant of all irises. They are easy to grow and are prodigious workers. They love to show their flowers. From one clump as many as 50 flowers appear. They grow on long thin tubular stems, have ornamental grass-like foliage, and their flowers of many shades, blue, soft pinkish-lilac, wine red and sparkling waxy-white make excellent cut flowers. Here in California as at home in Europe and Eastern Siberia they love moisture. You may place them near a brook or place them in the pool where the clump of roots at water line can sip to their hearts content. They like humus too and do well in the sunny places. But what they and the Japanese iris also, in contrast to other forms, do not like is lime in any form whatsoever. Once I threw a handful of lime down to the roots of my Siberian and Japanese iris. They started to turn yellow the very next day, and the clumps looked worse and worse, finally I lost them all. And mentioning Japanese Iris let me remind you of the fine planting of them in San Francisco's Golden Gate Park. They grow near a little stream which escapes from the pools of the tea garden. Every year you can see these big summer blooming iris, they sit up there like huge saucers, and you can admire their wide variety of colors. Each flower crowns a long stem and each petal spreads out flat. The Japanese Iris, which is one of the lovely groups, we won't be able to discuss fully this time. I might mention the parks in Seattle have a prize collection of Japanese iris which bloom best in late June or early July.

All of these iris may be shifted in the garden at this time. Just as new growth is about to begin. Bear in mind thorough preparation of the soil, and work with the idea this job will not come up for some time to come. Do a good job in other words. The iris I've been talking about all grow from rhizomes or in clumps, but finally there are those which grow from true bulbs. The Spanish, Dutch, and English iris, that don't come from England but Portugal. You place their bulbs in the ground in October, put them down at least three inches below the surface of the soil. And select a permanent spot, because you don't have to disturb them unless they become diseased.

Iris is a great study, a big one, and there is far more to it than I have hinted in this discussion. Bailey gives 20 pages to them in his cyclopedia. Maybe you'll want to go to the public library and study up on them.

And one last thing to remember about the iris; the whole subject is entwined and bound together by a haunting perfume.

And now for the Opportune Tasks. Of course working over your iris is the big task this time but we have another opportune task of a very different kind — that of paying attention for a moment to the American Association for the Advancement of Science. As the clocks were striking 12 noon on September 20, 1848, the rules of a society, the one which I have mentioned, were read and adopted. That society had a membership of 46. This year it is celebrating with great satisfaction and even excitement its hundredth anniversary with a membership of 40,000. How does this concern us gardeners? Well a suggestion of how it concerns us is given by the fact that on the cover of the magazine Science which has an anniversary number this month, September, 1948, is a portrait of the wonderful Liberty Hyde Bailey,* 90 years old. He you know is the editor of Bailey's "Standard Cyclopedia of Horticulture" to which all gardeners make tracks when they need information. (I must say it is written in a pleasing lively style). Mr. Bailey was once president of the American Association and that association actually is a clearing house for the sciences. They tend to fly apart like electrified particles, each group working by itself and forgetting all the others. It's the Rotary Club of Science. It's what you might call a conference of all the scientific faiths where the horticulturist looks to the geologist, the geologist to the chemist, and the chemist to the physicist. What do you suppose our gardens would be if it were not for the active and intensified efforts of chemists, microbiologists, plant explorers, geographers and geologists? Actually all learning is one, but learning is so prodigious in quantity that we can hardly help dividing it into little pieces, and yet the nature of things require

*Deceased: December 1954.

we keep bringing them together. It's something like the strife between naturalist and the utter need we feel at this moment that the nations of the world cooperate in all those matters which incur the risk of war. So let us rejoice that this American Association for the Advancement of Science is in a powerful way promoting cooperation between scientists and that this cooperation is actually at all times transcending national boundaries. Scientists all over the world have a yearning to work together and that is one of the finest hopes of all.

COMPOST PILE

July-September are good months to work over your compost pile. Plan and work it right and you get excellent material from your compost in six months! What you do is turn the pile over and over, wetting it down generously each time you turn it. Always select a sunny spot, not a dark shady one, and build the compost there. Wheelbarrow onto this pile, old leaves, pest free clean green vegetable matter, grass cuttings which have first been permitted to wither, wood shavings, even coffee grounds can be used. Pine needles, redwood, cypress green, bay, walnut leaves belong in a separate pile since they break down slower. Build the pile up one foot, then on it add a one or two inch layer of fresh manure to promote bacterial action (heating). On top of this add one inch of garden soil to "sweeten." By layer build pile to height of five feet. As each layer is built sprinkle water to moisten without making things soggy wet. After pile has stood five feet high for three weeks, turn it. Build a new pile along side the old. Make sure outside materials of the original pile goes to the inside of the new one. Use no chemicals on compost pile; fertilizer may be used when material goes into the garden.

MULCHES FROM BARK

Get acquainted with the various available processed forest bark mulches. These are ideal as mulch, soil conditioners they can be combined with soil as growing medium. All are excellent too as top dress for container plants maintaining moisture and proper temperature at the root zone.

Chapter 42

(A) SOIL

(September: Fourth Week)

What is soil? Mineral matter; that is, ground and decayed rock plus decayed organic matter. More specifically, gravel, sand, clay and humus. Humus is the decayed organic matter. It is the residue left after the bacteria and moulds with which every soil is swarming have made off with the part that yields easily. It is what is left of the animals and plants and it is somewhat resistant to decomposition. It is dark brown to black, and it has the great advantage of locking up for a while the plant food elements carbon, nitrogen, phosphorus and potassium, and letting them out to dissolve in the water for the plants to use. Remember that plants devour only liquid food and that therefore the effect of humus as a feeder is quite different from that of chemical fertilizers, because it is slower than the chemical fertilizers which dissolve instantly. (Not bone meal and basic slag sold commercially.) The humus always carries the bacteria and moulds as essential constituents. Actually, if we had no bacteria and moulds we would have no soil, and no plants. Some of these however are far from benevolent; they are deadly, and it was long a mystery how the soil escaped becoming a poison bed where everything would die. The discovery in the soil of the benevolent moulds such as penicillin and streptomycin, at least in part resolves this mystery. The bacteria and moulds then are under some kind of natural control so that they work for us rather than against us. For example, if you pull up a clover plant you will see little clusters of bumpy nodules which house bacteria which have the marvelous office of seizing nitrogen and oxygen from the air and converting them into nitrates, one of the principal plant foods. Ammonium,

HUMUS

you know, is one of these nitrogen products. Your orange tree needs such products, but the tree could stand forever in the bath of nitrogen and oxygen which we call air without getting a scrap of it. It has to be put together first either by the bacteria or in some other way.

TEST The mineral matter, gravel, sand, and clay, you all know. But you're not likely to know what their proportions are in your soil. Take two handfuls, shake it up in a quart mason jar of water and let it settle. The gravel will be at the bottom; next the sand increasing in fineness upward; next the clay; next the dark brown or black humus; and floating on top undecomposed straw and sticks. You may have for example a fourth of an inch of gravel, half an inch of sand, half an inch of clay, and an inch of humus. This corresponds to a sandy loam. There are of course all mixtures. If you dig a hole down to bed rock or to solid clay and take samples you are likely to find the humus mainly in the topmost foot. But it isn't composition only that is important to you. The soil, as we have said, must contain air and water if anything is to grow in it. It must have a loose texture — it must break up into grains — not into chunks — and when wet, the grains must still keep their identity and not squash together into mud. Clay, you understand, is anything but granular. The only openings in it are what are called capillaries, that is hair-size openings, and they carry so little water that we can use clay to puddle irrigation canals and so stop them from leaking. Clay holds little water and little air, and in clay the good bacteria are smothered, and those bacteria racketeers which can live without air, begin to thrive and take over. Instead of feeding the roots, they rot them. The clay is made granular by the addition of sand and humus. Thorough cultivation of this mixture and exposure to the air and sunlight flakes up the clayey soil and speeds the change. What we want is a fluffy spongy soil layer to hold water and provide a medium in which roots can thrive. A soil with good texture crumbles in your hand even when it has some moisture. It must not become plastic when wet. It must not make deep wide drying cracks when dried, nor must it turn to dust and blow away.

All soils are made up of these constituents. But the combination varies with the topography, and climate. In this part of California the lowland around the bay has much loamy soil with the accent on the clay constituent. Some of the richest and deepest soils are found here. Near the creeks where plants have thrived for hundreds of years, the loam becomes thick and rich. When I got my land on the creek in Menlo Park my basement, seven feet deep, was still floored in loam. The hillsides are often clothed with adobe or reddish clay or can even be rocky. The soil has been washed off, or eroded, to use a term which has unpleasant suggestions. But wooded hillslopes hold their soil and are often good.

In San Francisco, the yellow sand of the dunes has been enriched by past labor and trainloads of humus until it has become transformed from desert to garden which supports the most finicky plants. Then too, Telegraph Hill has its natural rocky soils, and the Mission its loams.

Now, although all plants like food, one thrives best in one kind of soil and another in another. The kind of soil in your garden therefore dictates what will grow there and what you, if you know your business, will plant there. Unless of course you are ready to change the soil over by digging out clay here and adding sand there and dumping in the humus. This means you have to know your soil — in other words, get the facts.

That garden is going to be yours for a long time. Know every inch of your soil. Whether you are a beginner or not, a good practice is to make a soil map; locate your areas that are mostly sand or gravel and therefore light; those which are mostly clay and are therefore heavy, and those that are in between. Here is where you take those samples. Perhaps you'll find a spot that is always soggy — or maybe in former days a stream ran across your land and left a streak of coarse gravel with a poor soil begging for nourishment. After you have made your survey, you'll be ready for the question, "what can be done now for the garden soil?" That will depend upon the type you have in your garden. If your soil is loamy, you have the best kind. Loam is an admixture of clay with enough coarse materials to secure permeability to air and water, ease in cultivation, deep root penetration, and free drainage of surplus. You have loam if your sample shows a quarter humus material and when wet or dry is still crumbly. You can keep it a good loam by the addition of organic materials taken from your compost pile, and scattered over the garden every time you place a plant there. (A compost pile you know is where you artificially prepare humus by putting together weeds, cuttings, fertilizer, lime and some soil so that they decay in a hurry.)

ADOBE But if your soil was full of cracks and was hard and dry all summer you have adobe; but don't moan about it because adobe is one of the richest soils in our State. Adobe cracks because the clay particles are so small. They are smaller than the dust particles that float in the air; they pack together and each particle carried moisture so firmly attached that it won't drain down through. The roots are unable to creep freely in it as they do in a loam. Turnips and bulbs which have to push the soil bodily out of the way, grow dwarfed and all out of shape as though they had been tortured. And after this ground is watered, the crowded clay particles, with minute spaces between them begin to act as a wick as soon as the sun comes out, and the surplus water promptly draws back up to the surface and evaporates. And you must know that adobe often holds more organic matter than better looking soil. Locate it and mark it down on your soil map.

But all adobe needs is to have its disposition improved. How can this be done? You can improve the workability of adobe, first by getting all the strawy manures, compost and peat you can lay hands on. These materials thoroughly mixed in and spaded under are decomposed during the winter, and next spring your adobe will have that disposition improved and will work up easier. I know a man who, through persistent use of peat over a six-year period completely reformed his adobe. He was constantly mixing it in, a little at a time. Take your wheelbarrow, fill it with any humus material, dump it and spread the load over an area six by nine feet. Then dig down deeply with a fork; take only small chunks of earth, the fork carries them better than big chunks, which are sure to fall all over and make nothing but a sloppy job. Turn the soil, the humus which you spread on top will now be down underneath. There it will do good.

SAND

If as you make your map you find your soil is sandy, then what should you do? Sand lets the water sink through freely. If the ground is too sandy to the depth of several feet, it may let the water get away, and the amount that sticks to the sand grains won't be enough for the plants. The sand needs humus too, both to supply food, and to make a water-holding sponge. That will change it into a kind of sandy loam; and that is why we tell you, especially in the sandy soils of San Francisco, Carmel, Fresno and Eureka, to always plant with a shovelful of humus; it makes the sand more retentive of moisture as well as more productive. A woman who lives in this city said to me, "For eighteen years I have put all my vegetable parings, cabbage and lettuce leaves in my sandy lot here. It has helped to improve my yellow sand-dune soil. Now it is dark, showing the presence of humus material, and my flowers grow better and better."

In order that your map will be complete in its charted information, you should in fact sample your soil, not only for its proportion of sand, clay and humus, but also for its ability to hold water like a sponge. Punch holes in the bottom of a gallon can. Fill it with your soil and pour water measured in a milk bottle, until it begins to run out the bottom. A good spongy soil will hold astonishingly more water than a poor one. To carry the test further, try another can with four handfuls of peat mixed in, and if your soil is deficient you will see clearly what peat can do for you.

An excellent practice is to take enough samples all over the garden so that you know what the texture is, that is, where the mellow crumbly ground lies, and where the streaks of gravel, sand or clay; what the proportions are in the top soil between humus, clay and sand; how thick the top soil is; how thick the poorer soil underneath; and how deep the soil to the hard pan, blue clay, or rock on which the soil rests.

Some of you, alas, will find nothing but harsh gravel or clay with scarcely a trace of humus; for the contractors in building your house have brought in an unintelligent power grader which turned your ground upside down and buried your top soil six feet deep. If that's it, you have to start all over again to make up in a couple of years for the loss of the product of a couple of centuries. It can be done; you can bring in soil stripped from some other place or you can enrich your sand and clay with manure and other humus.

On your map you'll mark down where the clay is in your soil, and you who have clay soils, that yellow stuff, very poor in humus often found in hilly San Francisco, must especially pile on the compost, work it deep, and the winter rains will do the rest.

Everyone at this time of year may work for soil build-up and soil correction. Do it before the rains become to heavy. How? Dig deep, use a pick, a shovel, or fork or spade, and like miners dig away in the packed ground. Turn it over, level it up, rake it down. Digging soil up and leaving it rough in the garden is identical to the farmer's plowing his field. You dig it when it is reasonably dry of course, keep out of it when it is squashy, don't forget to go down deep, break it up and the air with its nitrogen and oxygen will get down there too. Making over your own garden soil is better than bringing in new. The idea in the garden now is to get the soil loose, to improve the drainage where it has been found to be faulty.

About this time last fall I called on Herbert Double, head gardener of an Atherton estate. He was busy in his glass house, but as I approached him my eye caught sight of several piles arranged in a semi-circle in his enclosed yard. There was a mountain of old oak leaves, and garden rubbish that recently had been gathered. Next to it was another pile, which had been thrown through what Herbert called his "rough screen" of coarse chicken wire. A few feet away from this pile of rough screened leaf mold was one that had been worked through a finer screen. Then in this work yard were several bales of peat, one of which had been broken into and lay scattered loose on the ground. I saw other piles; here was white river sand, there was a scuttle full of wood ashes, and near it a sack of gypsum, and over there some old cow manure.

I wanted him to tell me in his own words what he was going to do with all this stuff, so I asked "What's going on here?" His face broke into a smile as he replied, "Did you ever see the makings of a cake laid out on the kitchen table? Well, these are the makings of my garden soil. Now come into this shed here and I'll answer that question, 'what's happening here'," he said as he led me to a shelter where the rain never reaches. Inside was a last grand pile. "Run your fingers through that," he said, "and tell me what you think of it." With no effort at all I shoved my hands wrist deep and pulled out the softest, spongiest, lightiest soil that was slightly moist, that I had seen for some time. I could distinguish particles of leaf mold, peat, sand and loam too. It poured through my fingers like foam in a wash pan, "How did you get this wonderful mixture?" I asked. "From those piles out there, as of course you already know, but some of the stuff that went to make up this soil is as much as three years old, from all of those outside I mixed up this one pile of soil, and this is what I use for my plants. I share this generously with everything I put in the garden. When I plant fruit trees, pines, oranges, daphne, roses and geraniums, and when I set out the seedlings like delphiniums, sweet williams, and snapdragons, I use this soil. Just take a look around this place and results will speak for themselves," he said pridefully, as he pointed across the lawn in a bed ablaze with gold chrysanthemums. "They are beautiful," I remarked, but my mind was thinking of that pile of soil. "What about fertilizer, do you use any?" I asked. "That depends on what I'm going to use the soil for. You see, some plants will want fertilizer in their mixture — roses, or delphiniums; others will want none, as heather, so I mix in the fertilizer proportionately as I dig into the prepared ground," he responded. "And that goes for the gypsum also. I don't use it for all the plants. My whole idea of mixing this soil is to have a vigorous, light, airy medium to set new plants into, or to spread around established ones I wish to encourage. An application of a mixture like this gives a new life to my plants."

KEEP CLEAN

And finally, let me caution you to keep your soil clean. Very soon now you will be pulling out annuals and perennials that have finished their show for this year. Examine the roots for aphis, mealy bugs, or for root galls. Or you may be taking out a diseased shrub; for example, a Fremontia, a beautiful plant when it is grown well, a miserable mess when it is unhappy and ailing. Oftentimes that sickness starts from the soil, where at the roots mealy bugs have taken possession. Go out and destroy these diseased, insect-infested plants, but do not stop with just pulling up and burning old brush; keep at it and clean up the soil too. Dig it up, turn it over, lightly spray the alarmed insects with an oil spray, later wash the soil with a flood of fresh water and work intensively to get rid of those root insects. Get the sun onto the soil, leave it turned up rough for six weeks or so, and stick with the job till you get rid of these enemies so willing to take up residence in your soil.

PEAT

We must not overlook bog soils and marsh soils which include peat and muck. They are poorly drained soils or developed from accumulation of plant remains. Peat is plant remains better preserved than humus because it has been immersed. You know how much longer timber lasts when it is wholly under water than when it is kept moist in the presence of air. Peat and muck cover a total area in the United States estimated at 79,000,000 acres. They exist under a wide range of climate and vegetation, but most extensive areas are in the Southeast, the Great Lakes states, and the Pacific Coast region. In the Everglades of Florida there is an extensive area; in Virginia and in Maine there are peat and muck areas; up in Wisconsin and Minnesota. In the Klamath area of Oregon and Northern California and again in the delta region where the Sacramento and the San Joaquin meet there are peat and muck areas. Of course it is found in Europe also and on a big scale. In Ireland for example it has been one of the principle fuels.

KIND OF PEAT

There are two kinds of peat: woody and fibrous. The woody peat is found in the swamp forests of spruce, tamarack, and arborvitae in the north, and various conifers, maple, elm, and ash farther south; and that of the Everglades in which often there is found buried whole logs and stumps in woody peat and muck areas. But reed and sedge marshes, sphagnum moss and heath bogs, underground stems, canes, rushes and grasses build up fibrous peat. Some of the fibrous peat is developed from a mixed open growth of canes, bay shrubs, myrtle, and gallberry.

And one of the best known areas of muck is that found in Florida bordering the southern shore of Lake Okeechobee. The muck here is developed from black organic sediments from aquatic vegetation. It contains some silt and clay, is dense and sticky when wet but shrinks and becomes quite hard when dry, develops surface cracks with angular fracture and crumbles into a granular mass. Underneath the muck is a brown fibrous sedge peat resting on limestone rock. The climate of this region is subtropical and humid.

And our own peat areas are built up mostly on tule, reeds, sedges, rushes and water plants. At Klamath in Northern California and Southern Oregon, the tule peat is characterized by brown fibrous porous and poorly decomposed plant remains. And the peat of the Delta region in Central California is likewise built up on tule reeds, and water plants. *

In spite of the fact that often true black mucky soils peddled to put on your lawn are often poor, some of the

*See December: Third Week: Questions and Answers "What is peat?"

cultivated muck soils are extremely rich. It depends of course on the amount and the condition of the organic content. Muck soils have proven very rich in Florida at Lake Okeechobee; good crops of sugar cane, onions, cabbage, beans, tomatoes, and peppers have been produced on it. Sometimes it has been found by students of agriculture that in spite of a 12 foot depth of this muck soil built up by centuries of rotting vegetation, lettuce and such vegetables grown upon them spring into leaf in a few days, swiftly reach luxuriant maturity but lack taste. Beans for example mature in 6 weeks flat on muck soils in Florida. Furthermore it is to be observed on the peaty soils of the Everglades where the water has been drained off that this soil is overly rich in nitrogen, and though the weather provides a longer growing season yet the peaty soils are pestered with mosaic disease, and root rot. Let us not forget that winter vegetables grown under glass often have the same trouble, even their colors may be pale and vapid.

In the Klamath area the peat soils have supported crops of rye, clover, barley and tame grasses — that is — European and American grasses all mixed together — but as time has gone on good crops have given way to poor ones as the water table dropped and bad salts accumulated at the surface.

In the Delta region of Central California as soon as they diked off the land it blew up in an explosion of productivity, and soon away from there were being hauled boat after boat, train load after train load, and now fleet after fleet of trucks bearing away the precious fuel for life. A man on Mars watching this Delta country would have seen it within a few years change from an expanse of water dotted with dark islands, which if he had a big enough telescope, five times as big as our two hundred inch, he would have seen to be covered with tule. And then suddenly the water disappeared from over them, the tule too, and all the great area became black, then clouds of dust rolled up like smoke on a battle field, and through spots of clearing he would see plows at work by the score. And then as the season advanced he would see it all turn green, and little clusters of buildings appear here and everywhere.

At this time, halfway through the twentieth century this soupy land is being kept in order by huge pumping engines working like giant slaves all up and down the place. It is more fruitful than ever producing huge crops of potatoes, corn, sugar beets, onions and celery. For certain crops such as asparagus whose roots go racing through that light fibrous soil, there's no place in the world like it.

But there is an enemy standing outside waiting; the whole Pacific Ocean wants to get in there, and sometimes he sends in his advance agent in the form of a death dealing saltness. This is one of the reasons for the Shasta Dam and is one of the arguments for the vision of a dam lower down across the Sacramento River which would keep the Pacific out where it belongs.

So far I have been discussing kinds of soil. Now I shall speak of the means by which huge quantities of soil are transported and deposited in such a way that they now carry some of our richest agricultural areas. I'm now thinking of Delta areas. The river comes out of the mountains carrying ground up rock and organic matter. It suddenly finds itself free of its containing walls and fans out widely to right and left. There it drops its load of sediment. *MOVEMENT*

I remember seeing in the wall on the Panamint side of Death Valley a sharp narow defile coming down the wall. It looked no wider than a pencil. Suddenly at the base it opened up wide and from it like wheat running out of a pipe had erupted all the rocks brought down in 5000 years. They spread out a mile to each side and far toward the middle of the valley. Some years ago we had a terrific rain storm that kept up for a week, after the sun came out I went up on Telegraph Hill and to my astonishment I saw a reddish brown muddy river flowing swiftly through the bay toward the Golden Gate. I'll never forget it, and I began to figure what would become of that mud. And then I thought it must have happened thousands of times before; and I went down the hill straight to the office of the U. S. Gov. Naval Department and on a hydrographic map of the Golden Gate saw a beautiful fan, showing the bottom out there in curved lines arching beautifully around the entrance to the Bay in the shape of a fan. As you know except for the channel the water out there is shallow over a big area.

Then as you may not know the gold dredges up near Folsom, Oroville, etc., are working in fans made up precisely with this same mechanics. The coarse gold stayed back up in the mountains but the very fine gold as it was released by the rock pounding and grinding against each other was suspended in the swiftly running water and carried out to the flat country and there dumped with deep gravels in big alluvial fans. The ordinary miner couldn't handle it at all because it was mixed up with too much gravel, in fact there was only a few cents of gold stuff. About 1900 some one built a boat with a steam digging machine something like a floating steam shovel, and the amount of ground they have turned over by now is one of the eight wonders of the world.

This is merely leading up to the use of soils in agriculture. The earliest great agriculture projects of which we have record, that of Egypt and Mesopotamia (Mesopotamis means middle of the rivers) were both on alluvial fans which mechanically are identical with the ones I have described. In these two places the silt of the fans includes organic matter, the climate is warm, and the proximity of the rivers make irrigation reasonably possible. Here the land was often refreshed by floods from the rivers and perhaps a foot of new soil laid over the crop impoverished old soil. An old friend who once lived on the Ohio River in the Mississippi valley tells me that when the land there was flooded in this way the farmers waiting for the water to recede would bet among themselves on whose land the new soil would be dumped, and who therefore would have the bumper crop that year.

The Mississippi Delta is one of the great ones in the world. Delta you know is a fancy Greek name used because their letter D is the same shape as a fan. This fan indeed is a huge one. You remember in Huckleberry Finn a place was mentioned 40 miles below New Orleans. If the Mississippi hadn't brought that silt there, that would have been out in the deep water.

Coming back in California again we have here a great deposit made by the Colorado where it comes out of its canyon. This as you know spreads and spreads until it reaches far into the Gulf of California. The fact is the gulf at one time reached a long distance farther into California and Arizona, and finally the Delta dammed off a part of it. The water inside dried up and shrunk until all we have left is the Salton Sea well below the level of the ocean. The Imperial Valley is made on this Delta. You know what a garden it has become within the last 30 years. A wonderful combination of sun, soil, and water.

TASKS

Red spider mites thrive during hot summer months. To keep them off the laurel, viburnum, rhododendron, azalea, lemon, orange, Choisya, and privet plants, be your garden in San Rafael, San Diego, Stockton, or Palo Alto, give plants water. Spray plants overhead, let water fall like a torential rain. "Red spiders are poor swimmers." In rainless July-September occasionally water shrubs overhead, especially broad-leaf evergreens. New chemical control: Diazinon; see page 494.

From July-September you can find sooty mold on leaves of your bay tree, oleander, laurel, cotoneaster, gold dust plant or privet hedge. Look at every permanent plant; with sooty mold notice how the brushy outer branches keep sunlight from the leaves of inner ones. Prune crowding branches even if it requires drastic cuts. Let the sunlight in; sooty mold can't take sunlight full strength. Trees casting dark shadows encourage sooty mold; could that overhanging branch be pruned; will more sunlight reach the understory growth if you thin the tree? Soapy summer oil sprays discourages sooty mold; nicotine sulphate discourages aphids too, often the companions of sooty mold.

Chapter 43

(B) FERTILIZER

(September: Fourth Week)

Let us discuss fertilizer. What is fertilizer? How long has it been used, how has its use been developed and what is the supply?

Fertilizer, either organic or inorganic, is food which is added purposely to the soil; it enables it to be fertile and to grow fruitful plants.

HISTORY Fertilizing the ground was certainly known to the earliest primitive gardener. By observing the effects of the droppings of their animals in open pastures, the first farmers learned very early the value of animal manures for growing plants. And the use of all kinds of animal manures is an ancient practice in agriculture. Four thousand years ago in the Nile Valley farmers used a stone sickle, and three thousand years ago farmers fastened together two sticks and made the first hoe. 1500 B. C. farmers took one year in seven to rest the land and let volunteer weeds and herbs take it over and thus give it a chance to renew its strength. When Rome was at its best, much was written about agriculture, as for example Cato, who classified soil, Varro who stressed green manuring for rendering soils more fruitful, Virgil who wrote in his poems "vetch planted one year gave full heads to the grain the following year," Columella who stressed soil improvement through drainage and the growing of good crops through the use of dung and green manure, the name they gave to turned-under vetch, and Pliny also recommended green manuring in ground where turnips were to be grown first and grain later.

Cato the Elder wrote practical books to help farmers of his day. He taught crop rotation, recommended the use of leguminous plants for soil improvement, the importance of livestock in farming and preservation of manure. "What is the principle of good agriculture?" he asked. "To plow well. What is the second? To plow again. And the third is to manure."

China, a nation which has never known a dark age, a nation where learning has never been pushed totally aside, produced the plow as early as 2600 B.C., and originated silk culture. It has had to produce much of the world's food supply and has learned the value of all kinds of fertilizers to raise more crops on few acres.

And reviewing further the use of primitive fertilizers, we know the North American Indians used fish for fertilizing their corn, and those of South America use guano, the excrement of sea birds. Wood ashes, compost, and waste wool have also long been counted among the early fertilizers.

And back in Europe again, during the Middle Ages agriculture was characterized by a three-field system of rotating crops: grain, root crops and bare fallow. And as governments with central powers became more established, as land became fixed on more secure bases of ownership, agriculture began its long climb. Printing came to enable ideas and new methods to be broadcast, and then the new science of agriculture was wonderfully sharpened by chemistry. As a matter of fact, a whole chain of events now took place. In the early 1600's the fallow system was abolished and in its stead the growing of clover and other legumes in rotation was practiced. In 1660 Boyles, the pioneer British chemist, published his book, then in 1731, the idea of inter-tillage and cultivation was introduced. In 1770 Arthur Young the Englishman who exchanged ideas with George Washington wrote, "Who knows but there may in the walk of agriculture be compound manures powerful enough to give fertility to the earth vastly greater than anything we at present know of." Then in 1832 Liebig the great German chemist turned to animal and plant physiology, seeking to discover the laws of natural growth and development. He investigated and exploded old superstitions and put agriculture on a scientific basis. His book stimulated fervent inquiry into agricultural problems. Liebig illustrated to the world there could be no exhaustion of carbon and ammonia, as the supplies in the air were constantly renewed by fermentation, whereas the supplies of mineral elements in the soils were limited. He taught that the function of fertilization materials was to restore to soils the ash constituents, or mineral elements, removed by crops.

Liebig's thesis suggested to him the application of the so-called "law of diminishing returns" and the "law of the minimum" to plant nutrition. He said: "The crops on a field diminish or increase in exact proportion to the diminution or increase of the mineral substances conveyed to it in manure. By the deficiency or absence of one necessary constituent, all the others being present, the soil is rendered barren for all those crops to the life of which that one constituent is indispensable." Liebig experimented endlessly and one of his greatest contributions to knowledge was his clear forceful statement that plants absorb simple substances like water, carbon dioxide, ammonia and minerals, and convert them into complex organic compounds.

All this time there were other encouraging discoveries. In 1656 Glauber, a German medical student of early forms of chemistry, while studying in Holland found certain salts, which we now know are nitrates, stimulated plant growth. And a hundred years later, Home of Scotland made a similar discovery regarding potash salts. From early steps in scientific analysis of plants Wallerius of Sweden concluded that "humus" was the nutrient of plants. Also in Sweden Scheele in 1772 isolated nitrogen, which he called "foul air" because it wouldn't support a flame; and in the same year Priestly in America isolated oxygen, which is the part of the air which does support a flame. And two years later he discovered a combination of oxygen, nitrogen, and hydrogen made ammonia, which he called "alkaline air". Already in the same year that oxygen and nitrogen were discovered in England (1772), Leicester discovered that crushed bones gave him a wonderful crop. And because that was the time when people were insisting upon what it was that made the difference, chemical work went ahead. The Earl of Dundonald in 1795 showed the secret was the alkaline phosphates contained in the above.

In Switzerland in 1804 DeSaussure observed that ammonium salts stimulated plant growth. All of this led to the discovery of chemical fertilizer. Lawes of England in 1843 proved ammonium salts in chemical manures resulted in strong wheat plants. This was a great step because in 1798 Thomas R. Malthus of England had advanced the terrifying theory that the population was bound to increase at a faster rate than the food supply, and always war and pestilence would be killing off the surplus. Once it was known that nitrogen was a major element in fertilizers, industry instantly set to work to provide it. Ammonium you remember contains nitrogen, and the traders saw a chance to do their part in supplying this element for huge natural deposits of nitrates were known in the rainless regions of northern Chile. Natural nitrate of soda is one of the oldest nitrogen fertilizers used by farmers; it was first shipped to the United States in 1830, and to England in 1835. Today it is also manufactured as a fixed nitrogen product.

The Germans were able to carry on the First World War only because they had found they could make nitrates out of the air, and thus became independent of the nitrates mined in Chile which would have come by ship. The United States also built plants in this country and we can now produce an enormous amount of nitrates synthetically. As I said a moment ago, the traders brought to England from Chile raw nitrate products in 1835, but soon thereafter the same traders began to bring guano from the neighboring islands of Peru and Ecuador. Davy had already analyzed guano (1805) and found it consisted of one-third ammonium salts.

And let us be reminded of what happened on one of these islands. A sailor, Alexander Selkirk, shipped out of London in 1703, and he and Captain Stradling, being quarrelsome people, snarled at each other all the way across the equator, and down the East Coast of South America, around the Horn and up the West Coast. And finally Alexander, spying an island and yearning for the quiet which seemed to envelop it, screamed for all the world to hear that he would rather spend the rest of his life over there than sail another day on this *!*?!* ship.

"All right," said the Captain in a deep bass voice. "Lower the boat! Over you go!"

Selkirk stayed on the island four years and four months, and once back in London, having had no one to talk to for so long, he filled the air with words, just as some of us do today more than two hundred years later; it seems to be a persistent urge. Anyway, he told his story to all and sundry and finally to the great narrator Daniel Defoe, who went home in a hurry, sat down at his desk and wrote the history of Robinson Crusoe.

The point of all this is that the place where Alexander spent his time resolving he'd never quarrel with a sea captain again, especially if his name was Stradling, was the island of Juan Fernandez off the coast of Chile — one of the very islands where the early traders found one of the thickest and the most exquisite blankets of guano that it ever was the good fortune for the discoverer to see. We wonder if Alexander appreciated it when he got there or ever had the slightest suggestion of an idea that it would sometime be transformed into lush gardens thousands of miles away.

Guano is taken off the coast of Peru from about forty different places along the mainland and from the Chincha Islands which have the largest and richest deposits. Seventy or eighty years ago the Peruvian government supported itself richly on guano. At that time the guano, which had been accumulating for centuries, was two hundred feet deep. The nitrogen content was from 12 to 16 per cent. Sea birds as the pelican with its cavernous beak and the booby (so called because of its stupidity) along with the guanay who settle the island feed on fish which come out of the Antarctic via the cold Humboldt Current and these fish are saturated with proteins rich in nitrogen. The birds roost along the coast and on these and other islands and since rains seem never to fall there, the guano stays put. For years Indians from the mainland harvest the guano. They do this once every two and one-half years; the birds obligingly move away for four months and the men go to work.

The second major component of fertilizer is phosphorous or phosphoric acid, which was recognized in the startling progressive experiments of Lawes in 1839. He just had to improve his fields in order to get better sheep, and so he experimented. One day he went out to the farm, poured sulphuric acid over a bucketful of bones, and he produced a superphosphate. He was so pleased with the results that he applied the same acid treatment to rock phosphate (apatite) with equally good results. He realized immediately he had found what he was hunting for — a fertilizer element which he could spread over the ground to grow better field grasses for his sheep. That was over a hundred years ago, and in the following year, 1843, he organized the Rothamsted Experimental Station and his factory for making chemical fertilizer. Materials used today in the manufacture of phosphates include ammonium phosphate, ground phosphate rock and basic slag. High grade rock phosphate which can be ground up and put on the land has been produced for many years in the Southeastern states of this country.

Much of the material is used in the very states in which it is found. And in our Northwest have lately been developed huge tonnages of lower phosphate rock laid down in ocean bottoms and then elevated into mountains. It is one of our great natural resources and will keep our fields green for hundreds of years.

And finally potassium, the third major element in fertilizer. You will remember in 1756, a Scot discovered potash, like nitrogen, stimulated healthy plant growth. For years the principal sources of potash were wood ashes, ashes of seaweeds and common salt. The Stassfurt potash deposits in Germany were discovered in 1857, and came to be worked in 1860, but little was made of these potash salts by farmers until after 1890. And after that time they became one of the great exports from Central Europe; fleets of ships carried them to many parts of the world. Then the sea has been found to hold an enormous reservoir of potassium salts. Before the Stassfurt mines in Germany were worked, France used to have "salt gardens" along the coast where the supply was drawn upon.

In the World War, we here were forced to hunt around for potash. In California, in Mono County at Searles Lake (which is not a lake at all, but rather a frozen bed of salt crystals through which holes are pushed and the brine pumped up) we found our source of potash.

It is good to realize what stands behind our immense food-producing agriculture, and also behind our home gardens. And what about the change since the days of horses and automobiles? That old joke of the farmer hunting for a tractor that will do everything for the farm that the horse used to do — he certainly has to watch out for all the machinery working on his farm; the land may become impoverished.

And still other fertilizers have come into common use. The produce of sewage treatment plants is an excellent high grade fertilizer, containing 5 per cent nitrogen and 3.5 per cent phosphoric acid. Two cities, Milwaukee and Pasadena, have established regular plants using sewage sludge for the production of fertilizer. The extension of this practice throughout the country will eventually save for us a huge quantity of organic matter which is now wasted to the rivers and oceans.

Tankage is a refuse from the slaughterhouses and from other places. This fertilizer contains ten per cent of nitrogen. And some of the not commonly known sources of fertilizer materials include the waste stemmy parts of tobacco which contains as much as ten per cent potash as well as a little nitrogen. The water hyacinth, a fresh-water, stream-flowering plant which was introduced from South America and has now become a terrible pest, has been dried and found to contain four per cent potassium. It has been widely used in vegetable gardens for cabbages, potatoes and sweet potatoes. Much experimental work has been accomplished in India with the water hyacinth and there they have found it has very promising possibilities for fertilizing material. We have already mentioned seaweed known poetically as "the poor man's manure."

This slight sketch suggests to you the hundreds of years of trial and error experiment which have gone into compiling our present searching knowledge of fertilizer. Now what can you and I do to determine if our plants are hungering for food? First, we must consider the signs. For example, did your apricot tree fail to put on growth last year; did you notice there were no new strong shoots sent out? Or were your corn stalks weak with the leaves yellow instead of rich green? Or did your zinnias languish and put out only small sickly leaves and stingy blooms? Were your potatoes tardy in sending out new tip growth and green leaves? These are signs in plants as clear as the signs of malnutrition in starving people. In particular they mean nitrogen hunger. These are signs of nitrogen hunger which prevents the plant from putting on good growth. On the other hand, maybe your corn grew like Jack's beanstalk and never gave you an ear, or your apricot put on wild growth and never set a bloom or fruit — this means too much unbalanced nitrogen in the soil.

LACK SIGNS

As a second example, did you notice all the leaves of your apricot tree the same size but all of them yellow? Did you place in your garden a rose, but the roots never moved in the soil and no new shoots develop and there it "stands still" as the nurserymen say. Or have you noticed some of your plants take longer than is necessary to throw blooms; the flower production is retarded? This is phosphorus hunger. When plants get all the phosphate they require, they produce full heads of grain, full rounded peaches, and kernels in the walnut. And beautiful blossoms on your lilies.

A third problem: do you notice your apricots lack

sugar or even lack the characteristic apricot flavor? Or you seem never to get any good seeds from the pods of your lilies? Or you have observed your delphiniums have been attacked by fungus diseases? Or did you find whole sections of the tomato leaf turn brownish yellow and break down? These mean potash hunger. Potash is a governor, it balances the other two, the nitrogen and phosphorus.

In order to use fertilizers correctly, the gardener must first study his soil conditions. He must find out what is lacking in the soil and determine what his plants are hungering for, and then he must provide it. Some prefer to mix their own formulas. Others use special preparations already made up to include the necessary ingredients. Whatever the method, a garden with a variety of plants should have a "larder" with some of the following on hand:

KINDS Bone meal. A safe slow fertilizer. A favorite for roses, bulbs, citrus and general garden use. "Steamed," which has had the fatty substance removed, is quicker acting than "raw" and is alkaline in soil reaction. One gardener I know always dumps a can or so of it in a bucket and then pours water on it, leaving the mixture to stand overnight before putting it in the hole at planting time. He feels the soaking in water gets the bone meal sooner on its way for root use.

Blood meal. A protein fertilizer rich in nitrogen. Effective for lawns, water lilies and many house plants.

Cottonseed meal. A dependable food to stimulate growth in azaleas, heathers, rhododendrons, camellias, and deep-rooting Transvaal daisies. Also good for roses; some people use it once a month; two level tablespoonfuls to a plant when new growth is out about two inches (April through September).

Aluminum sulphate. This is a chemical agent used to acidify the soil for rhododendrons, azaleas, heathers, laurels, and other acid-loving plants. There is also ammonia solutions, sulphate of ammonia, and ammonium nitrate which are good foods available for hungry plants.

Ammonium phosphate. Miscalled the "universal fertilizer" by some people, because it includes two of the three principal ingredients, that is nitrogen and phosphorus. It is a quick stimulant and is good for rundown lawns, hungry trees, shrubs both evergreen and deciduous. It is also good for citrus trees, berries, vines, vegetables, and many flowers. But remember this nor anything else is a panacea. Before you can supply the dietary needs of your precious plants, you have to find out what the needs are. In other words, what the plants are hungry for. This takes more than the blanket assumption that some particular fertilizer is total, including potash.

Chilean nitrate. This is relatively pure salt, the nitrate of soda we have already spoken of. It contains almost 16 per cent nitrogen. It is used principally as a direct application to the soil as side or top dressing. It is mixed in with commercial or home preparations and is mixed specially for greenhouse use. There is also cyanamide and seed meal available for plant foods.

Leaf mold. It contains all kinds of food for hungry plants. In fact, every plant in the garden will appreciate leaf mold in the soil into which it is trying to plunge its roots. Oak leaf mold is most commonly thought of, but other good kinds which may be included in any mixture include the leaves of madrone, maple, and the needles of pine trees. Acid-loving plants in particular hunger for leaf mold.

Calcium sulphate, or agricultural gypsum should not be overlooked. Though not considered a plant food in the strict sense, nevertheless its work, especially on heavy soils such as adobe or tightly packed ones as clay, is to prepare them for the proper use of the true plant foods which growing roots are always searching for in any soil. Lime (Calcium carbonate) also belongs here.

I've listed, the nitrates and so forth, but you want to watch your step in using the chemicals or you will

USE burn your plants to a cinder. People have to know what they are doing when they apply chemical fertilizer. If you are a real amateur and you want to play safe, get some of the ready mixed chemical preparations sold under a respected trade mark and then study the directions and follow them precisely.

There is still another source of fertilizer: fish meal, the scrap from non-edible fish and waste from fish canneries. After the fish have been cooked with steam and the oil pressed out, the residue is dried and ground and sold for fertilizer. Also from the fish is a liquid form of this fertilizer. Fish meal contains on an average about eight per cent nitrogen and six per cent phosphoric aicd. And there is another feature to fish meal. Once a ton of fish meal stood on the docks along the coast. It was during late summer when warm sunny days had chased away foggy ones. Desperately the dealers sought to have those sacks of fish meal removed. At last a barge was sent and the stuff hauled away. So grateful were the dealers that they gave the captain ten extra bags.

"It's good for the garden," they said.

The captain gave them to his mother. This was back in 1936, and the captain's mother attended regularly my garden classes. She offered me three sacks which I threw into my car and drove home. This was early October and my chrysanthemums were coming into bloom. I decided to feed them fish meal.

I engaged a helper. He said he knew all about fish meal, and he proceeded to feed my chrysanthemums. My garden isn't a very big one and I didn't have too many chrysanthemums, but when I returned I found he had spread over the ground two and a half sacks. Well, that would never do! I jumped into my old clothes and the two of us swept and scraped up fish meal, but were able to fill only part of a sack. For six weeks I knew, the neighbors knew, the postman knew, and the dogs and cats down the street who ran in to dig and scratch knew, and the big buzzflies knew that Mr. Wilson used fish meal in his garden.

But there was one innocent man in the block who

understood nothing about agriculture and gardens. One morning he looked over my fence and said: "Albert, where does it come from? First it seems to come this way, and then it seems to come that way, and this morning it seems to come from here."

So I gave him a little lesson in the realities, explaining to him carefully a great mistake had been made, for the stuff had not been put under the soil right. All that he could reply was, "WELL! What a lot of technique there is to gardening!"

GINGER

Opportune task: GINGER: In September look at your ginger; it is going to bloom? Is your plant in the sun; does it get enough water; do you see bloom buds forming? The ginger in California wants warmth. Your clump throws up more sturdy canes; the leaves grow broader, and the flowers unfurl better if the plant has been given a warm place and one which offers partial shade. Place the ginger against a warm wall, near a fence, or near a hedge for it can meet the competition even with privet roots, near a pool or grow it in a tub. ROOTS: come from fleshy rhizomes; you shift them only when they are fully dormant, January-April. Once in three years is often enough. Plants have gone dormant when leaves turn brown and the stalk fall off the rhizome. Then a pinkish bud, an eye (several) sitting on the horizontal rhizome will show. Dig up the rhizome, cut into lengths of about one foot, each with an eye. The active roots will show on the undersurface of the rhizome. SOIL: including adobe prepare the new spot well; loosen, enrich with manure or commercial plant food. Make clump planting. Space rhizomes 18 inches apart. Eye should be flush with grown level. Settle roots with water. During growing season May-September water ginger. In winter keep soil on the dry side. ENEMIES: In spring snails especially chew the tender shoots as they unfold. Snails chew so that rivet-like holes appear in the leaves when they fully unfold. Control: poison baits. Zingiber officinale: cream, yellowish-green flowers. Hedychium: forms of this ginger-lily grow successfully in California. H. gardnerianum, yellow flowers.

CHAPTER 44

SWEET PEAS

(October: First Week)

Mr. Ernest Matthews is our authority on the subject of sweet peas. You know we have had many questions about them, and today, though this isn't our regular question answering program, nevertheless I am going to use this opportunity to get them answered.

Matthews: Let me say that there are many ways of growing sweet peas. Gardeners everywhere, getting at it in their own special ways, have good results; I do not wish to say that my method is the only one or the best. It is one I have worked out over the years. It has given excellent returns, and I am quite willing to pass it on to your readers.

HISTORY Wilson: Suppose, Mr. Matthews, I start off with a little historical background of the sweet pea. The latin name of this annual is Lathyrus odoratus. It has a climbing habit of growth; the leaves are tendril-bearing. The flowers are in shades of blue, red or white, and in many combinations, and as the name indicates, it is fragrant, and each flower produces a seed pod one to one and a half inches long, filled with brown or black seeds. And there are four main varieties of Lathyrus odoratus. The original sweet pea, discovered in Sicily in 1688, was a small flowered form limited to purple and maroon and it became the parent of all others. From it was developed the Grandiflora, which means large flower. The flowers of the Grandifloras are all upright and hooded-standard type, and possess the closed keels. They are much grown in the United States, particularly for color ef-*KINDS* fects. The second type is known as Early-Flowering sweet peas, developed from the Extra Early Blanche Ferry, selected in New York in 1895 after five years of hybridization. They have been popular with the greenhouse men, who grow them under glass for the florists' trade. The third type is the Cupid sweet pea; it spreads on the ground like verbena, sometimes being from 18 to 24 inches in diameter and rarely growing more than six to eight inches tall when in full bloom. It has however very large blooms on short stems; and from these Cupid sweet peas come the white Cupid variety called so because the seeds are white. And fourth, the Spencer sweet pea; these have bold upright wavy standards and open keels. They were introduced in 1901 by Silas Cole, a hybridizer, who first came across these wavy-petaled forms in the garden of the Countess Spencer. They produce more flowers and for over a longer period; have longer stems, larger blossoms, and are more beautiful than the old Grandiflora variety. And out of the Spencers have come recently the Cuthbertson sweet peas that are particularly adaptable to California growing conditions. And not sweet at all, because it has no fragrance, is the Everlasting pea;it has large and rose-pink or white flowers, but no fragrance;it is a perennial which comes up year after year from the root; it produces, it blooms, long after the Spencers are finished, and the flowers come clustered on one stem. And finally, the Seaside pea or Beach pea with purple flowers. Mr. Matthews, how do you go about planting sweet peas? What do you look for first when you are getting ready to set out your sweet peas?

Matthews: First I choose the location which catches the sun all day in winter and spring. Also I look for new ground, where sweet peas have never been sown before. Sweet peas grown in shade are bound to send up weak and spindly growth, and weak, spindly growth means a stingy flower crop and oftentimes no flowers. *WHERE PLANT*

Wilson: I noticed last year when I called on you, your sweet peas were growing out in the middle of an open plot, but, Mr. Matthews, what about these city people; can they grow them against a board fence or against the wall of their house?

Matthews: Certainly, sweet peas can be grown against a fence or the wall of the house; but here the idea would be new soil.

Wilson: And now, Mr. Matthews, perhaps our most significant question today: what about soil preparation? What do you do, and what do you recommend for the amateur to do in preparing the soil where he is going to grow sweet peas?

SOIL Matthews: I have grown them in sandy soil; such as you find in San Francisco; I've grown them in adobe which you find in Oakland and many other districts of California; and I've grown them in clayey soils such as you find in the foothills. But in every instance I've pitched in and prepared those soils for the particular crop of sweet peas I was planning on. In other words, when you grow sweet peas, spare no care in the preparation of the soil. As a matter of fact, a good sunny position is of prime importance, but thorough preparation of the soil is essential to strong growth, long stems, large blooms, better color and most desirable of all, a longer blooming period.

Wilson: Then you would say that any ordinary soil is good for sweet peas provided you do something about it; and tell us what you mean by thorough preparation of the soil.

Matthews: Sweet peas are deep rooters, so I dig a deep trench eighteen inches wide, twenty-four inches deep. By digging a deep trench, I enable the roots to go in every direction and to gather up both moisture and nourishment. The fleshy root action of sweet peas will not penetrate unworked soil; many times I've traced roots of sweet peas down four feet deep.

Wilson: Just what do you do at the bottom of the trench?

Matthews: I turn it over too; when I get down the twenty-four inches, then I take a pick if it's hard, or take my spading fork if it is not packed, and I turn over that floor of the trench. I loosen the bottom well, throw in a good layer of cow manure and dust this manure and the pile of soil waiting to be returned to the trench with bone meal.

Wilson: How much bone meal do you use?

Matthews: If my trench is twelve feet long, I

scatter one-half pound in the bottom; and another half pound on the pile of soil. But remember, sweet pea roots love a deeply mulched soil. That is, light and loose down there; the idea is to have a rich store of food awaiting the roots when they reach down after the plants get going.

BONE MEAL

Wilson: Mr. Matthews, you said a moment ago that you always select a new place for your sweet peas.

Matthews: Yes I do, but I know this isn't possible everywhere. When the same spot is used season after season a little more planning is required. A few weeks prior to sowing, you prepare the trench, working over the soil thoroughly as I have just explained. But in the bottom, dust in some slacked lime, then stir it in thoroughly. We all know that soils that have been cultivated for some time often get acid, so that legumes such as clover and sweet peas will not grow or at least they languish. Lime corrects acidity and furthermore it unlocks plant food that would not otherwise be available in soils which are not acid. I always use lime for example in clay soils; it makes them porous.

Wilson: But you don't scatter it around every year.

Matthews: No; that isn't necessary; and further crop change will correct the acidity naturally.

SUPPORT

Wilson: Before we go on, tell us how you prepared the support for your sweet peas. Last year I saw you had a support higher than my head.

Matthews: Just as soon as I finish the soil preparation,. I go ahead and build the frame. I design it to fit tightly right over the trench three inches above soil level. Sweet peas have twining tendrils; and tendrils want to climb. I like to use two-inch chicken wire; some gardeners use string, others buy prepared nets, but I build my frame of chicken wire, drawing it good and tight. Then, no matter how high up my sweet peas grow, they have a strong unyielding support. The result is upright growth without weak flopping curved stems.

Wilson: And now what is your method of sowing the seeds; do you just tumbel them in the trench or ...

SEED

Matthews: Not quite. You know back in England we used to say, "Well sown is half grown." Give every seed the best possible starting condition. For example, you never want to scatter seeds of any kind on wet ground. What I mean here is don't sow seeds when the ground is too wet to work; the soil must not stick to the shoe or to the tools. The soil in the trench must be firmed well before sowing, then you must rake the top loosely and you can cover the seeds easily and effectively. What I usually do for my sweet pea seeds is to sow them one inch apart and about two inches deep, and cover each one firmly with screened soil. I mean soil that I have shaken through a quarter-inch mesh screen. This provides a lightness which enables the seedling to move up easily.

DON'T

Wilson: I'm interested in what you say about screening, Mr. Matthews. Do you want to tell us why you have developed this method of using only screened soil around the seeds?

Matthews: Of course, straight sand around each seed is all right. But I have used the screened soil because it assures the new root just breaking through the seed coat a ready food supply. You see, it is essential for each seed to be in close contact with the soil particles so that the root may attach itself to them as soon as it leaves the seed; the food supply in the seed is quickly exhausted once growth commences; the seed must be surrounded with moist soil particles for the moisture taken from them softens the outer coat, and enters the seed carrying with it oxygen which sets the machinery of germination in motion. Furthermore, the soft and fragile young shoot cannot be expected to push its way through hard lumps; it won't try to.

Wilson: And you would agree the depth of seed planting must be a compromise between limitations of the seed and the need for keeping it moist throughout the critical germinating period. Most seeds germinate quicker and better with only just a bare covering of soil.

Matthews: Indeed, and once germination has begun it must proceed unhindered or the seedling dies. A seedling must fend for itself with its new roots and new leaves before all stored food has been taken.

Small seeds you must cover lightly; large seeds you cover deeper, and sweet pea seeds are best covered two inches under. But let me take a little more time and explain just what I do in making this trench; you see, after I prepare the soil I build up my trench to about six inches of the top. Then I sow the seeds an inch or two apart in furrows two inches deep. The object of sowing the seed a little below the ground level is to protect the delicate seedlings because there is a degree of tenderness after germination and that little depression in the soil provides protection. When the sweet peas are planted at soil level, especially in the winter, they are exposed to the winds and suffer from cold.

YOU COVER SEED

Wilson: Is it your practice to soak the seeds first before sowing?

Matthews: I never do; they might rot. But it is my practice to protect my seeds from the birds. When the job of sowing is completed, I put over the trench a tight-fitting wire screen. I make sure it covers every possible place where those little fellows will look, hunting for a gate so that they can go in and grab up those seeds. And, Mr. Wilson, before you go on with your next question, I might say to you that I have found it a good practice to scatter a little sulphur, agricultural sulphur in the trench just a moment before I put down the seeds, because sometimes lurking in the soil is a disease known as the wilts that is just as ready to attack those seeds as the birds are.

KEEP BIRDS OFF

Wilson: What do you do when your seedlings have gotten up to three inches?

Matthews: Then I usually draw a little soil to them, and give them a light top dress of peat. This peat is important to sweet peas in the winter time because a light dressing of peat moss tends to keep the soil warm, keeps the ground from packing and it cuts frost which will never penetrate the peat; and another thing of importance to me anyway is that peat looks neat.

PEAT PROTECTS

Wilson: Do you believe it is a proper thing to pinch back the seedling after it has reached up to the frame?

PINCH

Matthews: I certainly do; the leader usually becomes blind; that is, it runs out and there's no leader at all. So I pinch back when the growth has reached five inches high; what I do is nip off the top two inches with my finger nails or a sharp knife, and usually a bottom growth of four or five eyes has already started. But here again keep only two or three of these eyes for that is enough to carry on and to grow up and make strong healthy vines.

Wilson: Sweet peas put in the ground now will grow during the winter but with the rains that pack the ground, don't you advise cultivation?

Matthews: Yes, I get busy with my cultivator every time I see the ground pack; I never let the soil bake either, but keep it loose; it's possible to cultivate safely within six inches of the vine; and when the vines are doing well, I give them a top dress of manure.

Wilson: Sometimes as for example in February the rains stop for a while. How do you water sweet peas then?

Matthews: I like to irrigate, that is let a stream of water flow into the trench; I don't like to sprinkle sweet peas because overhead watering encourages mildew. It's important that sweet peas have moisture at all times; never let them get dry or thirsty.

Wilson: You said a moment ago when you see your vines are doing well you give them a top dress of manure. Do you want to tell us your other ways of fertilizing sweet peas?

FEED Matthews: Yes. I always give them additional fertilizer when I see the vines beginning to throw their flowers. Just as soon as I see a little color in the swelling flower buds I give them a little chemical fertilizer; I sprinkle one of these at the roots and then I water well in. I usually repeat it every two or three weeks and this I have found helps to keep up good color in the blooms; and it also keeps my vines interested and encourages them to keep going longer.

Wilson: Perhaps the next question won't seem necessary to our hearers because they all think they know how to pick flowers; but what method do you use in picking sweet peas and how often do you go after the crop?

Matthews: There's no particular rule, but cut the flowers when they're ready; don't ever let them remain on the vines too long; I have found when flowers are left on the vines the next crop comes on short stems; seed formation is hastened; and the plant soon gives up, feeling its work is done. DON'T

Wilson: I have found few flowers in the garden that are entirely free of enemies and troubles; what do you feel is the main cause of the dropping of flower buds?

Matthews: I believe one reason for sweet pea buds dropping rests with soil preparation. The soil was thoroughly prepared in the trench but wasn't firmed before the seeds were sown, or the trench and soil were firmed, but that the top inch or two wasn't loosened just before sowing of the seed. Second, too much water will make the buds drop, especially water remaining up at the seed level. In heavy soils this often happens; one method of overcoming this is to scatter sand over the seeds when they are sown; then cultivation enables the excess to get away. A third reason for bud drop in sweet peas is too much food; it is better to leave them a little hungry than to stuff them. This applies to all garden plants; it is far better to apply two light feedings than one heavy one; and finally; sudden cold nights will upset growing conditions and flower buds drop as a result. BUD DROP

Wilson: And what have you found to be the worst insect enemy of the growing sweet pea vine?

Matthews: I think the aphids are the worst enemy; I go after them with a spray of nicotine sulphate; I never use an oil spray on my sweet peas because the oil discolors the blooms, and even weakens the vines.

Wilson: And how do you clear up the fungus disease — I mean Fusarium wilt.

Matthews: Yes, we occasionally find our vines wilting down; first the leaves turn yellow, the plant gets sick and starts to wilt. It is a soil-borne disease, we don't know much about it; but two things are helpful. Pull out diseased plants the minute you discover them, and burn them. And second, find another place in the garden to grow your sweet peas in.

STREAK Wilson: I have heard two gardeners at the club talk about the Streak Disease of sweet peas. What can you tell us about this?

Matthews: It's very simple; streaks of yellow appear in the foliage, in the stems and in the flowers themselves. The whole plant turns yellow, gets limp and ultimately gives up altogether. Just yank them out when you discover these sick plants; burn them and go over the trench with a light dusting of sulphur; cultivate it in but like the Fusarium wilt there is no known cure, though I believe every experiment station in this country and at home in England is working on this problem.

Wilson: What are your favorite sweet peas?

USE Matthews: My favorites are among the Early Spencers: Daphne, a beautiful soft pink; Shirley Temple, a rose pink; Early Mariner, a blue; Vulcan, a crimson; Harmony, which is white.

Wilson: What is the most interesting use of sweet peas you have ever seen?

Matthews: I have seen marvelous effects in boxes and tubs where the vines are trained up on supports to look like delicate and lustrously colored screens. And then in England a single vine is grown to produce a single flower; the idea is to see how long a stem and gorgeously big a bloom can be made to result. I think they must have to set a guard during the last week or two. Anyway, I remember when I was a child looking up at the delicate burst of colors fluttering like a big butterfly far above my head.

Wilson: Did you ever know anyone who thinks the sweet pea is the best flower on earth?

Matthews: Yes, Mr. Cuthbertson of San Francisco, whom I know very well. All his life he has devoted his best to sweet peas, and he has finally given us the variety now known as the Cuthbertson strain.

Wilson: Well, Mr. Matthews, I certainly want to thank you for coming up to our studio today and giving us in your clear way so much information, valuable information on the growing of these long-time favorites. I would say in all of this on sweet peas, we should never forget that well-prepared soil is the answer for good growth, good blooms and strong color. A year ago, I got a letter which I've been remembering ever since, because it expresses vividly and from a place where few of us stand, the preparation of a row of sweet peas.

It begins: "You have mentioned the blind several times in your Sunday morning 'How Does Your Garden Grow' broadcasts. I belong to this group, and though I do not find it possible to do much gardening, I now and then do a little digging and planting, but so far without good results. My Boysenberry vines never did grow more than a dozen or so berries and the two apricot trees got some kind of blight and the leaves dried up.

"Last Sunday you explained how to plant sweet peas. This interested me particularly because when I could see I always enjoyed their beauty, and I still enjoy their fragrance and imagined beauty. And so I got half a dozen packages and ten pounds of commercial fertilizer and went to work today.

"I wondered what the neighbors would think of the trench I was digging along the 15-foot side of my guide-dog pen. Well, when my twelve year old boy,. Gary, got home from school, he came out and right away asked 'What are you doing, Daddy?' I grinned a little and said, 'What does it look like?' 'A ditch. But gee, Daddy, why are you digging it so deep?' It was fifteen or eighteen inches deep and as wide as the shovel. I told Gary I want to plant sweet peas. Gary didn't believe me and this made me laugh. Then he didn't believe me for sure, but I explained what you had said, so he lost his incredulity and said he would help me.

"Gary and I spread a layer of the commercial fertilizer. Next we filled the trench half full of soil and again spread in the fertilizer from one end to the other. We covered this with soil until the trench was about an inch or two of being up even with the ground. Then the boy planted the seeds an inch apart and about an inch deep all along the bottom of the six-foot chicken wire fence. As a finishing touch, I had him sprinkle the rest of the fertilizer on top of the sweet pea trench bed. And so we used ten pounds of commercial fertilizer altogether.

"I will let you know how this venture comes along. The soil here is quite sandy. I may have used too much fertilizer, but I doubt it. The sweet peas will have a soft deep bed for their roots, a good fence to climb up, and plenty of sunshine.

"While I was digging the trench I enjoyed the smell of the fresh damp earth. I reminded myself of the way potatoes smell when you wash them under the faucet before baking them. I chopped out and broke away roots here and there. I cleaned the loose dirt out of the trench by turning the shovel upside down and pulling it toward me. This piled up the dirt and made the trench smooth and clean."

He signs his letter Verne L. Nelson.

The Opportune Task: In this first week of October let us take note when rains come early we must spray early to beat the fungus diseases which are encouraged by them. Remember that though next year's leaves on your peach are safely wrapped tight in the buds, their fungus enemies are already generating on the branches so as to pounce on them the instant they open, and to your horror make the leaves curl helplessly next spring. Get out and save them with your squirt gun. And what else do you spray for besides curly leaf? You spray for the shot hole disease of the apricot, of the almond, cherries, prune and plum; then on the pears you spray now for the "blister or bud mite."

PESTS TO THINK OF NOW

These trees may be sprayed right now with bordeaux which you can buy ready-made on the market; follow directions on the label and add A. Wilson's direction to turn your nozzle like an acrobat, first upward from underneath, then horizontally from the sides and then downward from above like a good summer shower. The idea is to saturate every twig and branch all the way round, and now's the time. (For the blister or bud mite on the pear, instead of bordeaux you use lime sulphur.)

LIME SULPHUR

CHAPTER 45

OTHER FALL DUTIES

(October: Second Week)

Fall is the season that belongs to the perennials. We work for them now so that they will work for us next spring and summer or next fall. Our work is to move the plants, to feed them, to water them and to protect them from their enemies. How do we do this; where do we move the perennials to; why do we move some perennials now, and some later, and what are the tricks involved?

We move perennials now because they are at their lowest ebb; they lie exhausted from their summer's work; they have not begun next year's work. Many of us have found our perennials, including the iris, have grown too crowded; there is too much growth for the soil. The water we pour on these perennials is doing no good; it can't get down to the roots because the soil around them is packed hard like cement. It needs to be loosened. We move perennials because we have discovered the need of a better adjustment. Our violets, for example, have failed to grow or produce a flower because the ground is dry. Growing conditions still prevail to encourage lively root action among the new plants we put back into the garden; the soil is still warm, and the climate is favorable too.

CLASSIFY What kind of perennials are we working with? The beginner and near beginner must first classify his perennials; he must classify them according to type of root action because what he does now depends upon the type of root he is placing in the soil. For example, some perennials spread through roots which move underground as a submarine, and spread everywhere as perennial asters, salvias, oriental poppies, and snow-in-the mountain. Other perennials increase by bunching up the crowns as cowslip primroses, coreopsis, and Transvaal daisies. And still others increase by producing new bulbs or rhizomes at the base of the plant as lily of the Nile, belladonna amaryllis, daffodils and iris. Spreading perennials as the asters and salvias must be pulled apart and only the young new shoots returned to the soil. Bunching perennials as cowslip primroses and Transvaal daisies can be broken apart;the new eyes or rooted new shoots can be selected and replaced in the garden. Bulbous perennials should be separated with the young bulbs reset at a depth which your wise neighbor or nurseryman will advise you about. How is all this work managed?

You realize that with all types of perennials a common principle governs this work; that is, old and spent *CARE* roots are destroyed, new shoots and young roots are saved and replanted. The professional gardener plans his work a few days ahead. He sprinkles down the spot. Otherwise the roots of the old clumps would be so tightly woven and the whole soil so opposed to spading that he would almost have to bring in a pile-driver. He waters thoroughly both the old plot and the new one where he is going to set the plants later. Another thing he does is to have a wet sack alongside so that he can throw it over the clumps while he is working over the area. This helps to keep them from suffering too much from the direct sunlight. If the plot is watered a few days before more soil remains attached to the roots, they don't dry out so easily — the young plants get established quicker in their new home.

We move perennials every few years as we move the iris. Then we take everything up. We are selective. We throw out all dead roots, we remove all dried-up leaves, and we examine all parts of the plant for weakness and insect attack. We save only the full and plump rooted new shoots; they are ruddy green as in the perennial aster; or clean straw colored as in the coreopsis, or purple-green as in the salvia. The roots that go with them are firm and plump ending with white feathery rootlets. As with iris we limit the day's work to what we know we can finish by night. All young perennial plants suffer lying out in the air and sun.

After all the plants are out get a load of loose, partly rotted, pulverized cow manure, not too old nor green lumpy horse manure. One method is to spread the manure over the ground and then spade it in; a second method is to spade the ground first, then put the manure on and with a hoe chop it in; a third method is to spread the manure over the ground after the plants have been set in, but before the final watering takes place. Experience will use each one of these in accordance with how deep the fertilizer is needed. The beginner will do well to use the second method, that is, spread the manure on the ground and with a hoe chop it in. The ground should be deeply spaded, all old matted roots, stubble stalks, and broken off, watery, sappy stems and foliage should be thrown out. Just the other day I passed by a yard where a gardener was turning the soil. "Look at those robbers," he said, pointing to a pile of wiry, stringy roots. "Those intruders come from that privet hedge and that tree at the margin. They sneak into this plot every chance they get. My only way to keep them in check is to spade this plot a full spade deep and that is why you see this pile of old roots," he said.

When the plot has been spaded it should look like a dinner table covered with a clean cloth and ready to set. Best results come if the gardener uses loose rough manure; beware of lumpy stuff because it will be sure to upset plant growth later. Spread it two and one-half inches deep; too much causes leaves to curl and turn yellow, to lumpy, causes wild growth in some plants, and stunted growth in others. The ideal for all perennial roots is loose manure, preferably on the dry side when spread and worked in evenly and deeply.

The next step after the plot has been enriched with manure and leveled off is the spacing of the new shoots. How is this accomplished? The old clumps have been dug up out of the ground, those no longer useful thrown away, only the young shoots remain. These are examined closely, broken roots are cut back, injured shoots are rejected, and only young shoots limited to a clump that will fit on the scoop of a trowel are finally selected for planting. Just as with the iris they are arranged in triangles each clump one foot from its neighbor if it is a bunching perennial or bulb and 18 inches if it is a spreader. Work them in — do not jam them in. The roots of such spreading perennials as asters and salvias are fanned well out. The roots of the bulbous plants as the lily of the Nile, agapanthus, rest in the soil, but are not pounded down into a hard tight place. Looseness is the very essence of planting new perennials in a plot being started for the seasons to come. Of course, resetting your perennials in the garden is finished off with copious watering. And the best way to do this is with a fine spray from the sprinkler. The object now is to get the soil to settle snugly around the little clump of roots, and a misty fall of water, drifting down gently upon the loose soil excels irrigation. The object is to establish even moderate moisture around the plants when they have just been moved. The roots are temporarily idling and until they get moving, too much water will bring on rot.

PERENNIAL KINDS TO WORK NOW

What kinds of perennials do we work with in October? What kinds do we work with later after the ground has been soaked with heavy rains? And what kinds do we leave until spring? The ones we put in now — their roots apart going as soon as the rains start falling. They move right along with the rain and once the roots are running full swing the shoots will start to keep up with them. But of course the beginner can't go wrong if he moves at this time only perennials which will go safely through any weather including downpour of rain, frost and cold winds. These are called hardy, such as ajuga, coral bells, coreopsis, columbines, campanulas, gaillardias, geums, phlox, baloon flower, delphinium, doronicum, and perennial asters.

THE HARDYS

After the ground gets well soaked in December and January we shall move those hardy perennials which now have not finished their work but are still hard at it, as Esther Read and Marconi daisies and the hybrid penstemon.

Then the perennials that we leave until spring are either tender or have the weakness of rotting in winter if disturbed now. Among them are Transvaal daisies, verbenas, geraniums, dahlias, chrysanthemums, fibrous begonias, and scabiosa. When moved in the spring they go right ahead and there is less trouble.

The whole subject of moving perennials in the fall depends upon the location. Among the Oakland hills, for example, some perennials were ready for shifting a long time ago,others like false dragon, dragonhead and penstemon are still in bloom and mustn't be disturbed yet.

SEEDLINGS

We have been speaking so far of perennials that have to be separated. Let us give attention now to the new seedling perennials which are ready to be planted out in the garden. You raised from seed three months ago, or you can get from the nurseryman, delphiniums, foxgloves, columbines, sweet williams, primroses, violas, wall flowers and pansies; if they are strong, healthy seedlings they can be placed in the garden now. Where do they belong?

These young seedlings go in soil prepared in the same way as for their bigger brothers the young rooted new shoots. In addition make certain that they fit the sun and shade. Foxgloves and columbines like partial shade; they give better results if they get half a day's direct sunshine. Primroses also like partial shade for they hold their color better there; but sweet williams, violas and pansies will do their best in sunny spots.

I was talking the other day to a specialist in violas, Mr. F. W. Davis of San Francisco. He said, "When it comes to setting out my young seedlings I give more attention to soil preparations and spacing than when I am resetting old clumps. I prepare the plot thoroughly working into the ground a liberal amount of well-rotted cow manure and as much leaf mold as I can get because seedling violas like a light soil that holds on to the moisture. Leaf mold and humus creates just that condition. Violas plunge their roots deep, they want to be cool, so I plant the seedlings so that the crown will be a half inch below the ground level. Violas like also protection from the mid-day sun but they suffer when put in too much shade, so I always select a spot offering a balanced exposure. Another thing about violas especially, though it can go for pansies too, is that they should not be crowded together in the plot. Plants can be spaced six to eight inches apart — any closer gives their enemies a good chance to abide and destroy. Amateurs in their desire to develop a mass effect often crowd the violas and pansies and this frequently results in trouble. The moisture content of the soil where violas are growing must be watched very carefully. One day it rains and there is plenty of moisture and the next day strong winds blow up and the soil dries out. Again the gardener will soak the soil too much while watering and too much water always brings on rotting. Perhaps no other type of plant placed in the fall garden requires a more rigid timing in application of water than the viola." What Mr. Davis does is make certain that the ground never gets either soggy or dry. He works his fingers down into the root zone and with his experience can tell in an instant what it needs. All of us can learn to do the same.

VIOLAS

The Opportune Task: Learn which of your perennials need to be worked over now and go to it.

There are other items of the opportune task. For one thing, put away some dry soil for potting plants later on. I saw a poor gardener once trying to dry out rain-soaked soil on a garage floor. If he had stored his soil before the heavy rains came his troubles would have been solved. Now is a good time to shovel up soil from the garden, screen it to get rid of rock and other undesirables, and then store it in a dry place.

PROTECTIVE WINTER MULCH

Another job for this time is to prepare the oranges, lemons and grapefruit trees for the winter. Put a heavy mulch four or five inches thick of rough leaf mold, compost materials, or straw on the ground all around the trunk of these trees. This mulch helps wonderfully as a protector against cold. But under no condition give any more water to the citrus trees planted in the garden. It is better for citrus trees in the garden to go into the winter thirsty; in that condition they take the frost. Give them no water. Those in tubs and pots are in a different category of course.

TREE PRUNING

Another useful job especially for the beginner and near beginner is to start pruning the fruit trees. Early last summer you remember my telling you of Mr. Ernest Matthews' recommendation to prune back wild, sloppy branches. Well, now you can take another crack at it; before all the leaves on these fruit trees have dropped off. Now it is easy to see the difference between live bud wood and dead useless stuff. Make clean cuts and all large ones paint over with tree seal. Last month I saw a prune tree where a large branch was ripped off by the wind. I told the gardener to take his saw and finish the job. He made it neat — he evened up the edges — he chiseled back the wood to a smooth surface and then he sealed over the scar.

THE BEGONIA

Still another item; think of the safety of your prize tuberous begonias now outdoors. Review "Begonias" (May: Second Week); see also "Planting in Winter" (December: Second Week); see also "Questions on Tuberous Begonias" (December: Third Week).

PEONY

It's the peony that gets most of your attention this week. Are you planning to move your peony to another location? Have you discovered your peony refuses to bloom because you planted it in too much shade? Has your peony remained a scrubby, dinky plant which has never given you a bloom in five years? Then it's a good plan to move it to some other place. Last April,

Mr. Toichi Domoto, our guest speaker, told us all about peonies, and his parting words were "October is the best month to transplant peonies." I promised then to remind you and repeat his information. First, the herbaceous peonies. He said for the herbaceous peony that you need at least six hours of sunlight — twenty-four would be better. Dig up the soil, dig deep, "I recommend a hole twenty-four inches in diameter and eighteen inches deep" were his very words. Right now your herbaceous peony has bronzy leaves, many of them have fallen to the ground. The plant is just going to sleep and now's the time to move it: Push your spade deep down so that you get under the roots; pry up carefully just as you do with the trowel under the tuberous begonia. And how does a root look? It is fleshy, suggests long sweet potatoes joined together at one end. That is the important end. You will notice many of those rose-colored eyes, which are the dormant shoots, are wrapped around with the stems of the old leaves. Mr. Domoto said, "That eye must be covered just so when you place it back in the soil. Not so shallow that the sun's rays will blind it; not so deep that the moles will run into it; but just two inches below the level of the soil." This is important because too many amateurs push their peonies too deep or leave them standing out of the soil too far. Two inches is what Mr. Domoto recommends as the proper depth for herbaceous peonies. Now before you put the roots back into the ground after you have dug a good hole, you may scatter bone meal, and churn it in; but do not give any other fertilizer, as Mr. Domoto said last spring. It is not necessary. You carefully throw the soil over the roots; build a basin and wash the soil down by filling that basin several times with water. So now is the time to plant peonies and if your nurseryman has been holding your order till fall get it and plant right away so that the roots will be well established by next spring when new growth begins.

Another task for your herbaceous peonies, those not to be moved, is to prune all the old leaves off now, this for the sake of health. You want to get rid of enemies; for "clean culture" as Domoto called it. Cut the herbaceous peony stems clean to the ground;gather up the old leaves.

If you have found it necessary to move your tree peony, or a friend wants to give you a clump from his old plant, now is the best time to handle the job. Select full sun; don't jam a tree peony into a shrub border, or hide it under a spreading tree; give it room, give it lots of room. The roots will go down as far as you prepared the soil for them, and later on they will travel four or five feet away; so do an especially good job. Tree peonies are long lives; I know of one growing in the same place for 45 years and still blooming and doing its best every year. Use only bone meal; place the plant deep enough so that the stems will spring up from the roots at the ground level; make your basin, fill it with a mulch, compost, straw and leaf mold is good too; and water in so the soil snuggles down to the roots and your plant is off to a good start. If your established tree peony is tall and has a weak stem than nail a metal hoop to a stake, drive it down the hole so that the hoop puts its arms around the plant and keeps the stems from slopping over. And here also, if your nurseryman is holding your order, call for it now and get your new peony into the ground. Again, for tree peonies that are not to be transplanted it's a good thing to practice clean culture. Examine the stems, look for scale, look on the underside of the leaves for thrip. Gather up all the fallen leaves, spray the plant overhead with an oil spray, even bordeaux in the winter will help to control die-back, a fungus disease fond of tree peonies. Look around to see if it has come upon your plant. Another thing, prune out dead twigs from your tree peony.

DON'T

HOW TO PLANT

Opportune Tasks:

Those seedling delphiniums -- have you got them out in the garden yet? They should have gone into the ground in September, but you can still put them out if the weather hasn't been too wet. Set them out; give those that you put out in September a top dress now. Right in the crown you can put the mulch, and in between the rows you can later put a shovelful of manure.

Chrysanthemums — look at the colors and get the names of the varieties you like, so that you'll be ready with them for next year.

Frost: Now is a good time to give thought to frost. Do you have a hibiscus, gardenia, bougainvillea, choice fuchsia, young citrus, ginger, lantana, Lady Washington pelargonium, or choice geranium established in your garden? Prepare all of these and any other plant that you suspect is susceptible to frost injury. One way is to crown the roots with a mound of leaf mold, compost, peat, and even sand piled around them will help to keep roots from frost damage. Gardeners often permit their tender trees, shrubs, and vines to go without water before the cold weather is due, this to check young tender growth and also to get roots and their crowns on the dry side before frost. You must mulch also your potted plants such as the clivia, heliotrope, cinerarias, marguerites, jacobinia, geraniums, begonias, etc. (See index frost, further reference.)

Opportune task: Before rains come clean up under trees. Rake up dry leaves, twigs, seed pods, needles now while ground is dry. Wet leaves do not rake easily, they are heavy to pile and wheelbarrow off to the dump. Nor do wet leaves burn readily. Now clean up under pines, acacias, eucalyptus, cedars while ground is still dry.

October till December are right months to set out wall flowers. Use them in places where sun lingers in the winter garden. Spade soil loosely; work in manure, it suits wall flowers. Space plants 12 to 15 inches apart, they grow busy. Always pinch back wallflower seedlings. Complete the whole planting, make a neat bed. Water in the seedlings making sure the soil settles around the roots. Protect wall flowers from aphids and snail, too.

Protect plants now. Top dress roots with humus mulch, peat. Mulch shields surface roots from hot winds, sun, and cold.

CHAPTER 46

CARNATIONS

(October: Third Week)

See Illustration Page 506

Our subject is carnations. We speak of them now because there is work to be done this fall if you want these plants for next year. But before we come to that, let us consider where this plant comes from. Carnation and dianthus is a perennial given its name by Theophrastus, who lived 300 B. C. Dianthus means *HISTORY*

divine flower because, as a group, most of them possess fragrance. Carnations have been favorites among all peoples; in England they call them gilly-flower, and by the 16th century had appeared many red and white tones originating from the flesh-colored flower, The gardeners of Italy, France, Germany and Holland with their ideals of what this flower ought to be added so many hybrid varieties that in 1578 Gerard wrote that "to describe each new one would be like numbering the sands."

In Europe for years these carnations were kept in cold frames or coolhouses during the winter, and as spring approached the plants were brought outdoors to bloom. No flower was expected to appear until the month of July when there was a great profusion of blossoms, but for a short season. This limitation and others too inspired hybridizers to develop the perpetual-flowering carnations, kinds which we discuss today.

In this country by 1858, the carnation established itself as one of the leading flowers for commercial growing, standing second to the rose in favor and importance. There was a hybridizer named Frederick Dorner, for 22 years he worked hard and unlike Burbank he kept detailed records and out of thousands of crosses he left superior carnations. One thing he succeeded in was the development of a strain of carnations distinguished for its easy-growing habit, its freedom and steadiness in producing flowers, a diversity of colors and adaptability to commercial growing. Today the quality has been improved until the highest developed varieties produce blooms measuring four and one-half inches in diameter and are carried on rigid stems three feet long.

FLORISTS CARNATION

But what kind of carnations am I talking about? What kinds can you grow in your garden? You may remember in your mother's yard the garden-pink, and sometimes it was called pheasant's-eye pink. This is a low growing tufty plant of neat persistent foliage with medium-sized white and rose-colored flowers of powerful fragrance that appear in spring and summer. We do not mean this type of flower. Nor in this great group are we speaking of the sweet williams, Dianthus barbatus. Nor are we talking about the annual carnations started from seeds in January and blooming the same year. What we are talking about is the large flower the florists call carnation; how far this has come on its way to us may be seen by comparison with its ancestor, the humble spicy clove pink, native to the Mediterranean. Where do you get these carnations? You may buy them from your nurseryman or you may propagate them. You may get slips from your friend's garden but be sure you know the variety and color. The old-fashioned methods of layering plants out in the garden where they are growing is best done in July. We are discussing carnations now because the season for starting new plants is from August through October, though greenhouse carnations are usually taken in spring and new plants set in August. You may take cuttings from healthy plants now and by spring can have strong plants to set out in the garden. Just how are cuttings made? When you pick carnation flowers along the lower section of the stem are two or three little shoots. These may be taken off the stem carefully — always take the shoots from near the base of the stems — but here's the all-important trick. In taking off a little shoot do not pull off or tear the skin of the cutting; if accidentally you tear the cutting, then with a sharp knife make a new cut. All cutting shoots should be placed in gritty sand; get them into the sand as fast as possible. Dip them in rootone or hormone dust first and your chances of success are greatly increased. If you have only a few cuttings to root they may be placed under a mason jar and a partially shaded spot is helpful. Those of you who plan to root many new shoots may proceed as follows: get two flats, knock the bottom out of one, put it over the other and nail them together. Fill this double flat with gritty sand which you may get under the various names — Olympia or Marysville River Sand No. 2. Fill the box full up then thoroughly soak; water the sand just once, flood it until the water runs out of the bottom as it will from a colander. This treatment packs the sand firmly throughout the flat and that is just what carnation cuttings want. With a narrow dibble the thickness of a lead pencil push holes into the sand, into these holes set the cuttings making sure they go well down in the sand. Pack the sand firmly around each cutting. A sheet of newspaper should shield them from the direct sun for a few days. Set your flat of cuttings up on bricks or blocks of wood so that excessive moisture will get away easily and drainage will be good. Carnation cuttings make a callous, a little wart first, then in about 21 days the new roots break out. Be sure and watch the moisture content of the sand; keep it moist but never soaked because the cutting does not take up moisture until the roots have been formed and start to

CUTTINGS

DON'T

function. And remember what we told you before — water only in the morning hours so that excess will drain away before nightfall.

CARE How do you care for your new carnations during the winter? When your plants are rooted they may be placed and left in pots all winter and kept in a sunny porch or under glass until spring when you will plant them out in the garden.

LAYER Another method of increasing plants is to layer them in the soil where they are growing. This old-fashioned method is usually done in July but may be done now. A low shoot is selected, a slit four or five inches back of the tip is made halfway through the firm stem — a few of the leaves at that section of the stem are stripped off where the slit is made. The slit is made in the following manner; either from the top or from the bottom the stem is cut halfway through; the cut is made preferably at the joint — that is where it swells a little. Then this section of stem which is only partly cut through is layed on the loose soil and covered with sand. Sand is piled over the slit cutting to hasten root formation and also to help in transplanting later in spring. The promising shoot must be kept firm and fairly upright in the soil by means of a wire peg or hairpin placed over the stem near the slit. If the soil is kept moist during dry weather there will be few failures.

Most of you prefer to grow your carnations in the garden and you'll wait until spring before putting out your new plants. It is possible to grow carnations in pots — some of you may wish to do so. It is to these folks then that I continue our discussion this morning.

POT In a month then these new cuttings will have formed good roots. When rooted, pot them in two-inch pots. When the top has grown to five or five and a half inches cut it back and re-pot into two and a half- or three-inch pots. This sets the plants back but it causes the plant to branch out and become short and blocky. As your plants grow you will shift them into larger pots, from three-inch to four-inch, five-inch, six-inch, seven-inch, up to eight-inch; the best size in which to grow potted carnations. The amateur must remember to sift his plants into pots consecutively larger and not skip around because there is always a balance between soil, roots, and pot; a pot too large upsets the balance; it can be fatal. Good potting soil is two parts loam, one part sand, and no manure. Use bone meal, it brings no diseases. Now more on soil. Even those who are going to plant their carnations in the garden next spring will get something from Mr. Ernest Matthews' reply the other day to my question, "What kind of soil is best for carnations?" "Loamy soil inclined to sandiness; as a matter of fact," he continued, "any garden soil is good if it is deeply dug and made light by introduction of sand. But never put leaf mold around carnations because leaf mold tends towards the acid and these plants do not like acid soils. The most important answer to your question, really," he went on, "is to make sure drainage is good. If you have adobe soil to work with break it up with gypsum or lime. Carnations like soil loose and friable. Let the roots go deep so that in summer they will be cool and light cultivation will not disturb them."

SOIL

DON'T

Now for watering carnations. Let them dry out occasionally, don't keep pouring on the water because the roots will surely rot and get into trouble; let the soil dry out once in a while; it's good for carnations, but watch them every day. When the top soil becomes powdery, apply water and at the slightest sign of wilting give them water. Overhead watering both in pot culture and in the garden keeps down their insect enemies.

WATER

But since carnations must be grown well to be satisfactory and to give good results, professionals make a practice of setting out in the garden new plants every second year. They may however remain three or four years undisturbed. In planting out in the garden the new plants should be set about three-fourths of an inch above the soil level so as to make sure of drainage. A good trick is to set the plants out in rows, alternate the clumps so that the ones in the front row can spread out to the open spaces between plants in the rear row. A little trough can be established; even a wooden trough with holes bored on the sides is good; the roots of the plants will go down into the trough and watering by irrigation can follow. As a matter of fact, if the roots are kept cool down below, heavy watering will not be needed.

FEED What about fertilizer? Professional growers of carnations feel the plants do not need fertilizer, either manure or chemical. In carnations especially rank, soft growth will produce only weak blooms. But if the gardener feels his plants are being taxed by a heavy production of bloom he may apply to advantage a handful of Milorganite to each plant. "It inspires the plants to keep up production without softening up the new growth," said Mr. Matthews. Again the gardener may apply safely manure in liquid form. Application should be only when the plants are in bloom or bloom stems and buds have already appeared.

DISEASES Before we go onto their enemies we might mention carnations have one bad trouble and that is the cracking of the calyx that holds the petals together. This cracking, splitting, or bursting of the calyx may usually be traced to either irregular temperatures, fluctuating days of light and darkness or to overdoses of feeding. Some varieties tend toward this fault more than others. Stemrot disease attacks carnations, especially those grown under glass. This disease develops in the soil and when discovered that soil must be turned out and fresh brought in. Diseased plants must be taken out also. Rust attacks carnations and is identified by brown-red powdery spores which burst out from swollent spots in the foliage. Spray plants with zineb, work sulphur into the soil and keep foliage dry to check rust.

ENEMIES Among the insect enemies aphid and green fly attack the bud and tip growth; but red spider and thrip especially are the worst. These enemies attack the bloom and discolor them. A liquid preparation made up of Diazinon, applied according to direction, will take care of these enemies. Under glass such preparations as insecticide gas bombs help in the control of insect enemies. For these pay strict attention to instructions on the containers and above all never use on carnations sprays with an oil base; even a harsh spray of water alone thrown upon the carnation foliage is bad because it washes off the bloom, the bluish colored dust which naturally covers the foliage. The loss of this bloom from the foliage weakens the plant.

Does the carnation fit the garden design? It does fit the garden design only in very carefully selected places. To begin with, the first garden hybrids were loose growing, were inclined to flop on the ground. Later in France a rigid-stemmed variety called "tree carnation" was developed. This pleased the florists and the variety became a favorite. But even today many carnations have weak stems and for that reason these plants, unlike the hybrid petunia, can never be considered a beautiful garden type. Unlike the petunia the carnation should not be given a prominent spot in the garden; it must always be given a spot in the background where it may be supported by neighboring plants. Or better yet a special place should be reserved for it in the garden. Professional gardeners find carnations important enough for a separate study.

USE

Because the flowering stems are weak, they must be provided support. Frames made of wood or bamboo or of galvanized wire with transverse cotton strings, creating a supporting network are what the growers use. Or individual stems may be tied to a bamboo stake. Carnations are no good without support. The idea is to support the flowering stems so that they will keep the flowers off the ground where they would become spoiled through mud splashes and where pill bugs and slugs would ruin the bloom petals themselves.

What sub-climate do carnations demand in the garden? In coastal sections carnations must have sun and afternoon sun is best because petals are likely to burn when early morning sun falls upon the dew-covered flowers.

After the plants have been set in the garden the idea then is to develop a stocky growth rather than a spindly plant. A good plan is to give the young plant a pinching back — that is, pinch back the tip growth;

PINCHING

usually one pinching is enough for the results is a bunching up brought about by many new basal shoots being started. However here I must report that a specialist at the Fiesta said for glass house culture he feels in order to get a strong stocky plant it must be pinched back three times. Pinching is nothing more than a nipping back done with your fingernail; the tip of the uppermost part of the growth nipped right through the heart of the little stem. The result he said is from each shoot three new branches develop below. If this trick is followed you will have instead of one spindly plant, dozens of shoots loaded with flower stems.

In the hot valley and in the desert region, partial shade is recommended. You must remember this, put it down in your notebook, and I'll tell you in spring about it again. As a rule carnations grow and flower better in the sunny garden, but strong sunlight fades the blooms. And you'll remember next spring two weeks before you plant your carnations, you will spade the ground, spread steamed bone meal, and well-rotted cow manure too. After you spade the plot deeply you will leave it dug up for two weeks and then conditions will be right for planting.

GET READY

GROW GREEN HOUSE

I asked a banker down the peninsula about growing carnations in the glasshouse; they are his hobby and have been for years. He said, "There's nothing to it. I always make it a point first to whitewash the inside of the bed with hot lime where I'm going to grow the carnations. I let it dry and this starts us off nice and clean. Another thing I do is to prepare the soil weeks ahead out in the sun. I mix in the bone meal, some cow manure, sand, and loam; it's all kneaded together thoroughly and it is slightly moist when I put it in the bed. The rest of the growing is easy except that I hang inside the glass house cheesecloth on the glass frame to keep the sun from burning the blooms. I disbud when the blooms start developing because I like large flowers as you see in this boutonniere. It came from my glasshouse this very morning," he said.

Now for the Opportune Task: If you want large-size blooms for the rest of this month, disbud your garden carnation; that is, take off all but one good bud to each stem. If you want nice carnations for Thanksgiving or Christmas pinch back or nip back each stem; this will throw all the energy into new succulent growth that will carry the flowers for the holidays. And look again to drainage; it is important for carnations. Here's another item. I went to Saratoga the other day. Along both sides of the highway I saw orchardists irrigating their pear and prune trees. I asked one farmer why he was watering them now. He said, "The crop has been harvested; it's been warm lately and I felt the roots needed a drink so that the buds of next year on the young branches would not suffer. I want to make sure my blossoms will come," he said. You might dig around your home orchard trees going several inches deep; see how dry the soil is there; around the peaches, nectarines, apricots, and plums; all the deciduous fruit trees maybe need water.

Another thing, water the hedges now. If they get water now after the long hot summer, when the rains come the roots will spring right to it. And while you are playing the water around sprinkle down the plot where you plan to grow your bulbs. Sprinkle the spot, later spade it, because before the month is out you and I are going to discuss bulb planting.

Still another item; if your zinnias and French or African marigolds have finished their show, rip them out. Turn the soil over, leave it rough, let the plot lie under this hot fall sun, and it will mellow the soil and will prepare it for the annuals to be planted in the winter garden.

ROSE CUTTINGS

Fall is a good time to make cuttings of roses. The steps are quite simple. Water plants thoroughly the night before you make the cuttings. Select firm green wood. Cut stems about eight inches long. Choose a partially shaded place for your cuttings. Place cuttings one-half their length in soil. Never let the soil dry out. Rose cuttings made in the fall are often well rooted by spring at which time they may be transplanted to a permanent place in the garden.

CHAPTER 47

ANNUALS IN THE WINTER GARDEN

(October: Fourth Week)

This morning let's you and I take the wheelbarrow out into the garden. We work now so as to have flowers in late winter and in early spring. You folks in the mild climate along the coast of Eureka, San Francisco, Long Beach, and Carmel will have many flowers in December and January. We away from the coast with our cold and short days will have only a few. So we'll load the wheelbarrow with all the tools, the rake, the spade, the fork, the pick, the hose, and in our pocket let's carry a sharp knife.

In Europe you know, they have done this for hundreds of years but there they have to plant their annuals in the glasshouse. Here in the mild California climate we can grow in winter the same annuals outdoors where the weather doesn't freeze for more than a few nights in succession. You may wonder, why plant annuals out in the garden now when summer is gone and the rains soon will pour down? The answer: if we plant now when the ground is still warm the little plants will reach down, gather strength, and get a terrific head start for next spring. We will remember vividly what calendulas, forget-me-nots, snapdragons, violas, pansies, stock, cinerarias, and primroses do in the garden — how they enliven the scene — how they dress it for season to season among the more permanent fixtures, the perennials — and how, therefore, in our design we must make room for them among our perennials. They fill out the borders and we remember to find out when perennials and annuals will be in bloom and make certain that their colors will harmonize when they overlap.

In the foreground we put in low bedding annuals as violas and pansies; in the background the tall uprights such as larkspur. We remember to protect the sensitives such as cinerarias, from frost and cold winds. And we give all kinds as much as possible of the pale winter sun. Above all, the charm of annuals lies in masses of brightness and we therefore take special pains now as always. Even in the frost belts, if we get them in now so that they get in some good licks of growth, our garden will begin to show this brightness in the warm days at the very crack of spring. That is the privilege of California.

WINTER LIST

And what are winter annuals? They are the annuals that are hardy here — that will stand weather, heavy soaking rains, cold winds that bring frost. Here is a list which you may have, a list of hardy winter annuals that may be set out now as little plants; calendulas, fearless against weather; forget-me-nots, blue-eyed, low growing or tall; cinerarias, best when protected from the worst weather; nemesia, showy in scarlet, blue, orange, and white; pansies, favorite of all that will bloom right on until early summer; Primula malacoides, feathery dainty, tender lavender, to rich salmon rose, dark velvety wine red, soft lilac, and pure white; stock, fragrant and bright; snapdragons, crowns of positive colors; violas used as annuals; and sweet peas, a test to the amateur.

So we are out in the garden with wheelbarrow and tools. Maybe we haven't yet yanked out those old dried-up summer flowers. We'll pull them then — African and French marigolds, the ragged petunias, the ageratum — all that have finished flowering. We'll throw them into the empty wheelbarrow or sack and carry them back and dump on the compost pile. Now we've cleared out the trash, what will we do with the soil?

SOIL

The only difference from standard soil preparation is that we take special pains with drainage. We pick our best spade or shovel depending upon which tool each one likes best. We must dig deep, especially heavy soils, and the subsoil area must be loosened also. An expert tells me, "At this time of year I go at my soil with a sharp pick. First, I throw up to one side the good top soil, then I spade down as deep as my spade. As a rule I throw out the spaded soil too, then down there I pick away as deep as I can hammer in the pick. I do this purposely to break up the hard packed soil; it isn't what you call hardpan, it is just heavy, hard and solid and I'm after the best drainage I can get for the winter garden and this is a sure way to get it." He went on, "In England you know, when I learned this trade they didn't let us dig deep like that unless we threw into the trench compost material. It is such a job to prepare the ground in this way that we want to keep it so the job wouldn't have to be done over again too soon. Alongside of me as I worked my wheelbarrow is piled with compost and as soon as I pick a little trench I throw in a layer of it and then fill in with the top soil I saved to one side. Drainage counts in the winter especially in the rainy season. Nothing like loose soil in winter," he said, as he pinched my arm by way of emphasis. Of course this is old stuff to many of you. But to you beginners let it sink in like a bee sting! The expert continued, "I have found both in San Francisco and in the Santa Clara valley that the farther down you go with the spade and pick the better the root action and the higher up the stems of the flowers will go."

DRAINAGE AND LOOSE SOIL

The beginner and near beginner can learn from this lesson. He can spade his ground as deeply as possible, he can trench it, and throw into the bottom of the trench compost material. He can fill in the rest with top soil; if the plot is too puffed up, with a little water he can wet down the plot and it will settle. The humus below will become humus soil, plant roots will race through it, following the little trails of water as they trickle down through.

HOW

With soil thus prepared the annuals can take any weather that may come. Heavy rains will pass right through the soil, drainage will be sure. If the rains can move through the soil easily the top ground can keep on the dry side during the wet season and then when one ounce of sunshine comes the plants will reach up for the light with strong stems and healthy foliage and they will have energy to throw good blooms later.

For winter annuals the soils as those in San Francisco have no trouble with drainage; as a matter of fact, they must be worked so as to check too rapid runoff of moisture, to check the development of little rivulets. How is this done? The soil is made heavier and more absorbent with humus. At the Fiesta I spoke to Mr. Julius Gerard, Superintendent of Golden Gate Park. He said, "You will notice that in the 'valley' near the Conservatory, we maintain many displays of bedding plants and in the winter we especially aim to keep them as high and dry as possible. The beds are raised approximately eight inches above the surrounding area. By raising the beds, we are assured that the roots of these plants have perfect drainage; they never suffer wet feet; further there is no chance of the soil souring from lack of proper drainage. As a result we provide a show of colorful plants throughout the year."

Should manure be used in the plot where winter annuals are to be grown? That all depends. In the first place you may remember in the opportune task of two weeks ago I told you to spade the ground rough, spread manure over it and chop it in. Maybe some of you spaded the manure in deep; if you did that, so much the better. For that manure is breaking down and is becoming an integral part of the garden soil. It is all right to plant winter annuals in that soil. The burning power of the manure will have been spent by the time the roots reach it. But those of you who have not done this and want to plant immediately, it is better to proceed without manure of any kind. Because it is better first to permit the roots of your winter annuals to get established, to attain a good anchorage, and a good spread through the soil. Manure freshly spread with no time before young plant roots get to it is not good at this season of year for it usually rushes the plant into rank unhealthy growth which suffers at the first fluctuation of the weather. Besides such manure can burn the roots, as the professionals say. You may

MANURE

use safely compost material. Loose, humus rich soil will permit a slow steady growth of stem and foliage. Later after the plants have grown strong and are ready to throw blooms food may be provided as a top dress.

STOCK Annual stock is something of an exception and is one plant that keeps gardeners guessing. Let me quote from a letter from Mrs. Stuart of Carmel who, you remember, wrote about pelargoniums. "I have tried for years to grow plain garden variety stock. I broke every rule in the book this time when I planted stock and you should see my vigorous plants blooming full time. To begin with, I planted the small plants directly into freshly manured ground. The manure sticking up like a sore thumb. I hadn't even had time to dig it in." This result is less astonishing than it sounds for some nurserymen pile bone meal and almost fresh manure, both chicken and cow, and get wonderful results from their stock. But remember that the professional can use devices that the amateur cannot. The amateur had better stick by the rule of well-rotted manure or none at this time. Otherwise he get will sickly yellow leaves crowded with aphids and stunted, lopsided flowers.

How should winter annuals be planted? "Separate them to manage them. Above all in the winter avoid over-crowding; it's dangerous where it wouldn't be in summer. Refrain from filling in. Lay them off far enough apart so you can cultivate easily, to let the air pass around each plant, to let the winter sun fall all over the foliage," said the late Charles Gamblin when we discussed this subject. "I like winter annuals to be far apart so that none of the foliage touches another plant, excess water and rain drip falls to the ground and not upon the leaves of its neighbor. With full sun all around the plant there is less trouble and less disease," he said. In the small garden that most of us have every bit of space should count. When the weather is ugly we usually stay out of the garden but this neglect will not penalize if the winter flowers are not jammed in too tight a bunch.

It is a good thing to plant winter annuals small,

when they are strong and growing actively. Stock plants for instance move best when they are taken out of the flat and planted in the garden when they are not over two and a half to three inches high. The roots suffer less from disturbance; there is no stop in the growth of the plant. Stock in particular must develop strong roots before the cold weather comes or else they stand still as the nurserymen tell you. The roots rot and this rotting continues all winter and the stunted plants finally die.

At this point may I go back to Mrs. Stuart's letter that just happened to arrive at this favorable moment. "With fear in my heart I cut the center stem out of every plant. You should see those plants now! The side branches that have never matured on my stock before are a foot long now and blooming furiously. The adventures of gardening is ever fascinating." Yes indeed, many nurserymen recommend pinching back stock when they have reached five to eight inches tall; then cut back the tip two inches and the result is as Mrs. Stuart describes so vividly.

CARE

How do you care for hardy annuals in the winter garden? One thing of course is to keep down weeds; they also are hardy winter annuals. Pull them and cultivate around the plants. Make it a practice to cultivate in the winter, especially after a pounding rain, don't let the top soil become packed tight, keep the top soil loose. Periodically examine the soil; moss creeping in means poor drainage, or too much water.

PESTS

Remember too in the rainy weather snails and slugs start moving;during the warm summer months they lay low, they don't like dry ground but it is surprising how far they will travel over moist ground. Put poisons around for snails and slugs.

So far we have been speaking of the hardy annuals that you started several weeks ago from seed in flats, or you are buying them now from your nurseryman. Each seedling is going to be lifted out of the flat with the long hairy roots holding onto a little soil. You will carefully drop the little plant into a little hole in the prepared garden spot. With your trowel you will work the roots into the ground and after all from the flat have been planted you will settle them in with a little stream of water from your hose. Let the stream be the same as you would pour water from a tea kettle. A "water wand" is good for settling soil around freshly planted annuals. The soil falls in with the water right around the roots.

But what about broadcasting seed just where they are to grow? This is a fine method for many winter annuals and some gardeners sow stock that way too. Seeds to broadcast include Shirley poppy of lovely colors; godetia, with delicate cup; Bachelor button, Virginian stock, and sweet alyssum; larkspur, clarkia, and linaria with all the colors of the rainbow. If you have good clean soil, soil that has lain open to the sun between plantings, then broadcasting seeds will be little trouble. But there is a trick to this, and let me read what we said about this last winter.

KINDS

We can't afford to throw these about in the wind and let them fend for themselves as Nature does. We must help them. For most of them we must find a place where the sunshine, later on, will blaze down and warm the ground. And that place must not be so big as to exceed our powers for we are amateurs you know. Then we prepare the ground. It must be aerated and nitrified. It must be loosened up. It is not yet conditioned. If the roots use their energy fighting their way through the soil, which is still compact, they will throw up nothing but bitter disappointment. Use your square-edged spade or four-pronged fork to ruffle up the soil and break all the clods a foot deep. The soil now is fairly dry but if your soil happens to be moist, grab up a handful, squeeze it, if it coheres like a ball of putty, leave it alone. Wait until it drains. Do not tread on it and do not work it until some day you find it beginning to crumble in your hand. The next step is to introduce fertilizer, bone meal, manure, or compost. You may throw on the fertilizer and work it in with a cultivator, or if you choose, chop it in with a cultivator, or if you choose, chop it in with a hoe just so you get it well mixed. Use a fine manure, not great

HOW

chunky wet stuff. Then you grade the area. Do not wet it down, just grade it by raking the soil level and getting it fairly smooth. Next you scatter your seeds. A good trick is to mix with the seeds still in the packet a little dry sand and shake well. In this way being separated the seeds will distribute evenly and your garden will flower everywhere instead of giving deserts here and forests of crowded pygmies there. After sowing, draw an iron rake back and forth. Do not work the seed too deep. They merely have to be covered and mixed with the top soil not pushed down to China. A light top dressing of screened leaf mold is good. The last step is to water down with a fine spray from the garden hose or water can. Don't irrigate. Think of a misty rain. This being the cold season there will be little chance for the bed to dry out. You still have to think of those engaging marauders, the hungry birds, who can pick up seeds and pluck away tender shoots with wonderful thoroughness. Colored strings, dangling bright discs, old lace curtains, or surplus camouflage nets will all help to warn them off. Nor is the earnest cat to be despised as an ally. At this point those who love both garden and birds are bound to shudder with the miseries of conflicting loyalties.

DON'T

PROTECT

And now for the Opportune Task: Figure out today what you are going to do about winter annuals. Remember your garden will be gloomy in the dark months unless you take action now.

Opportune task: Daisies (Esther Read, Marcony, Shasta, etc.) soon will bloom no more. Now clean out each clump; get rid of slugs, snails, pill bugs, mealy bugs too. These tight clumps make good hiding and wintering places for such pests. Crown plants with sharp river sand, to discourage pests, and to encourage new root formation. Add light dress of compost and leaf mold; leave for winter. In spring when daisies are ready to be divided and moved all of the little side plants will be rich with new roots. Do this same task for chrysanthemums.

Chapter 48

COLOR IN THE AUTUMN MONTHS

(November: First Week)

We discuss autumn color because this is the season to enjoy and to study our deciduous plants, trees, shrubs, vines and some of our perennials whose leaves also have a habit of turning color when their season ends. This is the time when our mountains are covered with a Paisley shawl, dotted with rich purples, dark reds, flaming crimsons, brilliant yellows, deep golds, and soft oranges. And a season when in gardens all about us our plants burst into flashes of brightness before going into their long winter rest. I want to give you the names and the descriptions of kinds of trees, kinds of shrubs, and kinds of vines which you will want first to see in your neighbor's garden, and then in the nursery, or which you may have already discovered growing in your district, but whose name you still seek; with this information you can proceed to plan to place them in your own garden. Now is the last time this year we can discuss the subject.

In spring it is growth we look for, in autumn it is fruit and color. Farmers call it "the harvest", and to gardeners it is a harvest of a different kind. But what is this fall color, why does it happen, why does it end, and in what plants do you expect to find it? The botanists tell us it is a matter of the ending of photosynthesis. What is photosynthesis, that wonderful change going on in the cells of a leaf during the hours of sunlight, a change going on quietly, and doing the work which is the very basis of life itself? No one yet has learned exactly how photosynthesis goes on, but we know what it does. Any plant all summer long has green leaves, and in those green leaves photosynthesis has been going on — water was taken up by the roots

WHY

and pumped into the leaves; carbon dioxide was taken from the air and under sunlight in the leaf cells, first starch and then sugar was manufactured. In fall this work comes to a stop, and the green fades out. But each leaf under the green has had concealed the vivid coloration which now delights us. It was there all the time.

In this country it is in the New England forest, from the shore to the highest mountain of New Hampshire that we get the greatest display of color in our deciduous trees. This year I took my vacation late, expressly in order to visit this region, and what a brilliant display they put on! First there was the red maples, the leaves turning a fiery red, and then the sugar maples whose golden leaves light up the hills or brightened the roadways with their cheerful tones; they are the most popular of all. The sweet gums (liquidambars) come next, they are natives from Southern Connecticut down to the Mississippi Valley. This tree which in midsummer has warm sweet juices runs the maples a close second in the gala autumn show. Then there was the tupelo; in New England fifteen days ago in the forest I tramped ankle deep on crumply fallen leaves and came upon tall tupelo trees cropping up in the hills and valleys and I saw in these trees rainbow colors with a rich crimson predominating. And when I pinched off a twig and chewed a leaf it tasted sweet. And scattered here and there in the woods I found the Sassafras, which too had a sweetish and an old familiar flavor;the leaves of the Sassafras are individual; never can you find two alike on the same twig; but they turn a fine color in orange, dull red and copper. Nor should we overlook the oaks,traditional source of tannin, their leaves too turn the deepest red and the deepest purple in the autumn hills. In general if the sap is sweet the autumn leaves will tend toward gold and crimson; and if the sap is pungent and full of the taste of tannin the leaves show the deepest red and even purple.

WHERE

Why does it happen? The quiet scented summer suddenly draws to a close, autumn begins with a gentle wind stealing up from the Southwest;in the orchard you see everywhere a rain of golden leaves with sunlight playing upon them; like snowflakes they fall or fly from the bough, lose themselves in the soil to take part in its activities. The season was named from the behavior of the leaves and continues until the last leaf is down. Its duration depends upon your district. Fall seems never to come to our warm seashore cities of Southern California; there the leaves hardly turn color at all, and many refuse to drop forcing the fresh leaves of spring to push the old leaves off when the new season begins. Fall arrives tardily for us here in the Bay region, where our cool fogs modify our weather so regularly. It long has passed for the Upper Sierran region where for example the aspens with snow all around are stripped bare of their golden coat. And it is just coming to the foothill district and in our fruit growing valleys. How has autumn come to your garden? Take a look and see if you have had an early fall show, if you are now enjoying a midfall show, or if you have still the promise of a late show to come. Here is a list:

Trees that give an early fall show.

TREES

American elm, Ulmus americanus, leaves turn a butter yellow
Red maple, Acer rubrum, always a favorite
Sugar maple, Acer saccharum, always golden
Sassafras, a new tree for the California garden
Japanese persimmon turns early in the fall with orange and copper leaves

Midautumn trees.

Big-leaf maple, Acer macrophyllum, grows native from California on up to Alaska
Box elder, Acer negundo, its leaves turn yellow
Tulip tree, Liriodendron tulipifera, the large leaves turn first yellow and then bronze, and all through the tree you see the mixture of green, yellow and bronze, so that you witness there the progress of autumn itself

Sweet gum, Liquidambar styraciflua, colors from purple to red, pinkish, buff, and yellow. You get the best effects with sweet gums if you place them in groups.

Trees for late autumn color.

Birch, which turn a beautiful yellow with flecks of light

Ginkgo biloba, the Maidenhair tree from Ancient China, I found ours here turn a richer gold than do those in the East

Linden, Tilia americana, a soft lovely yellow

Chinese willow, with its golden drooping branches

Horse chestnut, with sail-like large bronze yellow leaves

Kellog oak, bronze with flecks of red, wild in the mountains of California and of which you often see cut boughs in florists' windows

Black locust, its leaves turn yellow

Swamp cypress, a member of the pine family; the leaves turn from grass green to copper bronze before they drop. In Golden Gate Park they have a beautiful specimen. Every autumn worried amateurs anxiously inquire about "that dying tree", but it's just the way that the tree chooses every year to pass the fall season.

So far, we have limited our discussion to the larger trees which offer autumn color in their foliage. But in California we have a number of smaller trees, those that reach only 25 feet or so. So our next list will be:

Small trees for autumn color.

Japanese maple is the best of these; the leaves turn red, yellow and crimson

Scholar tree, Sophora, from China; the leaves turn golden

English hawthorn; gold leaves and red berries

Washington Thorn, Crataegus phaenopyrum, whose glossy leaves turn deep red with cluster of lustrous red berries lighting up the tree every fall

Crataegus lavallei, named for a noted French botanist; its leaves turn copper, red and yellow, supported by huge red berries

Chinese pistache, Pistacia chinensis, whose leaves take on the most brilliant fiery red and crimson color just before they drop. Up in Chico in the Government Plant Importation Station, there is a famous row of them;people come a long way every fall to see them.

These are but a few; there are many more.

In this discussion of fall color in the autumn garden, we would be omitting a great section of the subject if we failed to discuss the shrubs, the lower-story plants. We in California are fortunate in having a wide selection of evergreen shrubs to choose from, but there is a galaxy of deciduous shrubs which in spring burst into fresh flowers;in fall shine out in rich autumn colors. They celebrate the seasons in the shrub border. So our next list will be:

Shrubs for autumn color

SHRUBS

Pomegranate; leaves golden in fall when they drop, but a delicate, shiny copper in spring when they unfold

Barberry, Berberis thunbergii; leaves turn red, and the berries set the bush on fire

Deciduous azaleas make up a great group whose leaves turn soft colors, mostly bronzes; they bring in a bright note in the shady spots; this is also true of ferns and even for large-leaved hydrangeas

Spirea and forsythia, with yellow bronzy leaves

Snowball bush, properly known as the European Highbush Cranberry, has beautiful colors

Oregon grape, classified an evergreen, in a hot spot in the garden will turn the most astonishing color of red in the autumn months.

Vines for autumn color

VINES

Wisteria, with its golden leaves, climbing on a pergola

Boston Ivy, with red and crimson leaves in fall

Virginia Creeper, with five-parted leaves which always turn a fiery color
Grape, of course, its variety of color making it always popular.

In California, it is agreed we do not have the ideal conditions for autumn color effects. But there are certain tricks you can do to heighten the effect in your garden. First, of course, select only the types of trees you want;consider the range of color in the plant. Next, give thought to the position in the garden you place your plant. The more sun you can give the greater the effect. Give thought to the manner in which you place the roots in the garden; give them a chance, spread them out, don't shove them into a poorly prepared hole. And, most important of all is the matter of water. For instance, in order to get a good color effect in fall, it is wise to withhold the water in late summer. A good plan is to give the roots a long drink in mid-July, let that suffice for the balance of the year, and then your shrub or tree or vine will reward you with a brilliant display. When you place an apricot, a peach, a hawthorn or a spirea in a moist, well-watered lawn, for example, you'll find the autumn coloring fails to stand out because growth has been kept too active right up to the last minute.

STUDY

PERENNIAL

And among our flowering perennials there are a few noteworthy ones offering autumn colors in their foliage. The herbaceous peony with purplish tones; the creeping plumbago (Cerastostigma willmottianum) is very effective under the pomegranate; being low, it makes a wonderful ground cover either for bank or in parking strip; the leaves turn a deep, rich wine-red color. In San Francisco, the running wild strawberry is used to bind the sand; in it we have an especially attractive display of red colors in the foliage. You all have seen the geranium, where an occasional stray leaf shows up in an attractive red. And the so-called ground orchid, Bletilla, whose leaves turn a beautiful yellow. Nor should we forget among the succulents you find those which turn orange, yellow and red, as "Baby Toes" for instance.

And now for the Opportune Task. Take a tour around your home district, examine the trees in the parking strip, visit the parks in your area, look particularly at the Japanese cherries, the flowering crab apples, and at some of the plums; they are among the finest colorful fall plants. Visit your friends' gardens. Get the names of, the character of, all the flowering shrubs. Consider the old-fashioned snowball, or the tree peony, and with your list visit your nurserymen, select your favorite or give him an advance order to be delivered this winter — a list of plants you have seen and like and that you have thoroughly considered as suitable to fit into the design of your garden. Let that plant, tree, shrub or vine bring its fall color so that you'll have a harmonious picture throughout. Now, remember, is the time, before all the leaves have dropped, while all glory is yet with us, to make your selection.

During the war, many enlisted men from California were sent to Jefferson Barracks. In 1942 I was one of those men, and on a late October day, five hundred of us arrived for duty. Jefferson Barracks is situated on a high bluff facing the mighty Mississippi River, ten miles south of the city of St. Louis. What a place this turned out to be for a botanist — a vast forest, a last stand of the noble American deciduous forest trees. This by the way was a part of the great hardwood forest known throughout the plant world to be only on the North American continent; this was a part of the forest our forefathers cut their way through from the Atlantic Ocean to the western borders of the Mississippi Valley. A forest that Linnaeus, "father of modern botany", wanted desperately, though in vain, to see and study. Anyway, the Army sent me to this glorious place. Here I saw for the first time our native American persimmon, the kind possums fatten up on for winter. I saw sturdy red oaks, and ancient pin oak trees; hackberries, shaggy bark hickories whose leaves turn a brilliant yellow; and the flaming sumac I saw time and time again in the hills and valleys all through the Ozarks as we journeyed to our place of duty. All these kinds and many others growing wild, painting autumn colors everywhere. The floor of the forest was carpeted with purple and lavender asters, and goldenrod and many other Eastern perennials.

One bright day, shortly after our group of five hundred tenderfeet had arrived, and while the place was still new and full of interest to us, we were marching and going through maneuvers out on the drill field. It was "right dress, left dress, right face, left face, forward march, left oblique march, right oblique march and to the rear march." All of a sudden we heard the sergeant yell, "Company halt, one, two." We came to rest, and then he roared: "There's a galoot back in the ranks looking up in the sky all of the time," and as he approached he screamed in a most unfriendly voice, "Private Wilson, what's the matter with you? What are you looking up in the sky for?" "I'm looking at those trees," I replied, somewhat embarrassed. "Trees!! What trees?" yelled the sergeant with an incredulous, unappreciative expression on his face. "Those beautiful trees," I explained, and by this time the men in the formation showed signs of nervousness as they cast their eyes first to the sergeant and then to Private Wilson. But it was too much for the sergeant. He ordered: "Glue your eyes on the neck of the man in front of you — that's where all you men better keep looking. Forward march!" The next day on the announcement board I found my name pinned up for special duty. I was promoted off the drill field and right into Kitchen Police!

GRAPEFRUIT

Note. It was in Jefferson Barracks that Wilson ate his first pink grapefruit! A grapefruit is the result of a mutation from the shaddock. The rough skinned shaddock produced what is called by gardeners a sport because it springs from a genetic change, can reproduce after its own kind. Unlike other citrus fruit, grapefruit grow in clusters!

Chapter 49

CAPE BULBS FROM SOUTH AFRICA AND NATIVE BULBS OF CALIFORNIA

(November: First Week)

Planting bulbs in fall is our subject. You must learn which bulbs have to be planted now, and which can wait till another day.

What is a bulb, and what do you know about bulbs? Today we know exactly what a bulb is because our information is definite. Botany students are trained to be accurate in the use of such terms as bulbs, rhizomes

and corms. In my student days I studied with Professor Douglas Houghton Campbell of Stanford University. I was one of the fortunate students to be in his last class. You'll be surprised what he said about bulbs. Here are some notes from his lectures:

BULB FUNCTION

"With few exceptions the body of a plant always shows a clear separation into root and shoot; and the latter normally consists of the stem and leaves. The stem is the axis of the shoot which serves primarily to support the leaves and raise them to the light. It is also the medium of communication between the roots and the leaves — the stem is a highly specialized conductive tissue — but while the stem is primarily a structure for support and conduction of food, it may be buried in the earth, and replace the roots to some extent, as in the plant called Coral-Root that grows wild in our mountains; but more commonly the subterranean stems, i.e. the bulb, mainly serve as reservoirs of food for future use. From them green shoots grow and live for only a short time, only long enough to ripen the seeds and prepare the starch and other substances which are stored up in the underground stem for next season's growth; good examples are shown in the dog-tooth violet and the tulip. Such underground stems are especially common in the plants of cold or dry regions where growth is interrupted by drought as in many California and South African bulbous plants." Bulbs in these countries have only a short season of growth. Among the true bulbs as the botanist classifies them are: The dog-tooth violet, the wild Tiger lilies, the beautiful Mariposa lilies (Calochortus) these are among our native bulbous plants. Narcissus, and hyacinth of the garden, and the onion in the vegetable yard are also bulbs. Some, as the hyacinth, tulip and narcissus have thickened fleshy layers wrapped all around them, while others as the Tiger lily, madonna lily, have overlapping scales. What is called a true bulb may live indefinitely as a single unit or may increase by splitting.

A wonderful thing about the true bulb for flower production is the fact that in well-matured bulbs, the flower buds are actually encased within the bulb at the time you plant, and are there surrounded with stored-up food materials. The flower is inside the bulb, all folded up. That is why hyacinths, and narcissus will bloom if the temperature is favorable without even soil or water. The bud within a dormant bulb was created while the foliage was maturing the season before. Therefore it is important to remember that, in all true bulbs, next year's flowers were being produced while this year's foliage was maturing. No less care should be given to bulbs after they flower than before.

TUBEROUS BULBS

Why do I say true bulbs? Because there are also tuberous bulbs, and cormous bulbs. What is a tuberous bulb? We all know the Irish potato — Solanum tuberosum — which by the way is not Irish at all, but American Indian. It's a modified underground stem and like Argus himself, has eyes all over it. And there is the Dahlia and the Sweetpotato; which sprout from buds on the stem end or "neck". There is also the tuberous anemone, and the ranunculus with small tuberous roots. The main duty of the tuber is to serve as a reservoir of food so the little shoots can feed until their new root system is able to gather in food of its own. And what is a cormous bulb or corm? The corm like the tuber, and the rhizome commonly called a bulb is botanically different. Calla is a rhizome. But the freesia is a corm. When you pick up a corm it feels hard, it is all one piece, and is not made up of scales. It contains no flower bud. A corm can be rough, long,

CORM flat or plump it can be two and a half inches in diameter as in a gladiola, or four inches long as in a Jack in the pulpit. A corm is merely a collection of food in a shell. Have you ever dug up a gladiola and found a hard, clean-looking corm clustered around with little ones and all of them riding on a big shrivelled one? The mature corm has withered and died after a growth, and has been replaced by the new corm. Both in the gladiola and our own native Mission Bells (Fritillaria) when you see little offsets do not remove them unless they come away easily because the larger bulb is mothering the little one yet. The cyclamen that grow so well in the cool greenhouse or in the shady garden the Autumn Crocus (Colchium autumnale), and the baby gladiolus are other examples of corms. Some of the corms like some of the true bulbs will bloom without soil or water. Haven't you seen Autumn Crocus in dry dishes on the mantle throwing out cheerful flowers with never a drop of water or a speck of earth? Well there is a corm for you, it's a fibrous coated corm from which these flowers grow.

We leave out the tuberous bulbs, and concentrate on the corms and a few of the bulbs, all of which need immediate attention. Most in this group ought to be in the ground not later than the first of November. Some of the true bulbs and tubers — the daffodils, hyacinth, tulip and ranunculus can wait a little.

The ones we plant now are either natives or brought from South Africa, the so-called Cape bulbs. We must do certain things for them now in order to get the flowers we want next spring and summer. The time of planting is related to the new cycle of growth which is identical in California and South Africa, for in both places it starts with the rains. Take as an example the freesia, the corm throws up leafy blades in

the cool moist season, and is already to throw out the flowers before the hot weather comes. How many times have freesias received as Christmas gifts failed altogether to bloom. We planted too late, these corms couldn't get established in time to do anything before the hot weather. They will have to wait another year. Of course there are plots where freesias come up year after year, even if planted too late they will get established in time. NO BLOOM

Following are lists first of corms from South Africa and then of California bulbs. After the lists I'll tell you how to plant. First there is Gladiolus tristis, the only fragrant gladiolus which we have. Prof. Campbell introduced me to it in his garden; it possesses cream-white flowers, on slender stems, it sends out a rich fragrance from sunset till dawn, and never in the heat of the day. Once you plant it you always have it. And it has the virtue of not getting thrip for it leaves out too early. Another South African is CORM LIST the Watsonia that give its flowers on tall spear-like stems in late spring and summer. The finest Watsonias I've ever seen were growing in the sandy loam of Santa Cruz, California. They stood above my head as I walked along the rows. And the flowers are of all colors from white, through rose, pink, and lavender to brick red.

Then there is the Star of Bethlehem, Ornithogalum, which send up its papery white flowers unfolding in a ball cluster on long stems. And there is a lovely gold one too.

Every spring people bring me for identification a little flat petaled flower with all the color tones of a Cashmere shawl. It is a Harlequin-Flower, or Sparaxis. I know a garden near the old town of Santa Clara that has a plot of sparaxis which hasn't been touched in 30 years. Every year they light up that section of the garden rivalling anything in the whole valley. And of course there is its cousin, Ixia, which is taller and produces each spring striking funnel shaped flowers.

Babianas get their name from the baboon that eats their bulbs. Keep after your nurseryman till he finds some for you. They grow about a foot tall, throw red or purplish blue or white flowers in spike-like clusters. Another good one is Cape Cowslip (Lachenalia). It is a small bulb, and the flower is tubular; you may get them in shades of red, yellow and sometimes white. Finally there's the Calla, both the white, which we saw at Treasure Island on stems 6 feet tall, and the one often grown in pots, the little golden calla with rich glowing yellow flowers supported by leaves that are mottled or spotted with white. And last of all the Amaryllis.

Of the natives, most of which are bulbs — is the Mariposa lily Calachortus. It grows wild from British Columbia down through California into Old Mexico. Mariposa, the Spanish word for butterfly is used because of the markings on the flower. You can find one from among the rocks of the High Sierras, another in the sagebrush regions, as far east as the Great Basin, and still another in the Mohave Desert. All have flowers of beautiful shades, and many have been given beautiful names including Amabilis, the lovable. Then we have in California the great tribe of Brodiaeas. A cardinal red one tipped with a flame of clear yellow which they call Firecracker Flower Brodiaea ida-maia, another of clear violet blue is the California hyacinth; still another is the Harvest brodiaea Brodiaea elegans, because in the fields after the grain has been cut these plants shrewdly shoot up and bloom, safe from the sharp blade of the harvester. The whole field awakens to a stand of glossy, purple flowers waving on tall stems. Another brodiae has white flowers; another golden; and still another a deep rose. Brodiaeas are hardy, easy to grow; they are among the loveliest of cut flowers, lasting even as much as two weeks. They fit the garden design best in little colonies either in sun or light shade of deciduous trees, and also in niches in the rock garden.

Another native bulb is the dog-tooth violet, Erythroniums. It is an enchanting woodland plant — hardy in the coldest parts of the United States. I saw acres of them one June in Glacier National Park, pushing up their golden flowers with snow all around. The leaves themselves are richly mottled. In the garden the dog-tooth violet should be planted in groups. The flowers are in delicate tints of white, pink cream, lavender, bright yellow and deep rose.

Besides these brodiaeas, mariposa lilies, and dog-tooth violets, there are two other California natives with bulbous rootstocks that ought to go into the ground right now. You perhaps have heard of Mission Bells, or Chocolate lilies; botanically they are Fritillaria. These fine plants are divided into 3 groups, based on the character of the bulb, the kind of soil, and the condition of light and shade. The first group are woodland plants, in partial shade the stems are stout, stands one and a half to three feet tall. The roots are low conical all in one piece, their sides thickly covered with small round white rice-like off-sets. The finest form is called Scarlet fritillaria, F. recurva, it has bell shaped red flowers, the throat flecked with yellow.

In the second group are found those which love best the full sun and grow well in loam or clay soils. One of the finest in this group Miss Eastwood of the California Academy of Sciences called F. purdyii, after the late Carl Purdy who discovered it 36 years ago. On stems only four to nine inches tall one to seven large waxy white bells, flecked with purple develop each spring.

In the third group is found only one form that does not require as much shade as others of its group, it delights in full sun and perfect drainage, but will grow in sandy or gritty soil. Fritillaria are odd plants, they have two different sorts of leaves. If they do not flower they have single, very large leaf; if they do flower they do not have this leaf at all, but circles of leaves around the flower stem. They are steady bloomers but are apt to rest the year after flowering. Now, what of planting.

I have lumped these South African and California bulbs and corms together because planting methods are identical. All demand perfect drainage; all must have moisture during the growing season, .and when the bulbs or roots are ripening for next year; and during the summer must be left perfectly dry. They have the same habits of rest, the same of growth.

CARE

For all do one good job, and then as Mr. Purdy always recommended, "leave them alone". If there are active roots, get the bulb or corm back into the ground just as soon as you can for the air and light will rob them of weeks of growth. Select the right spot in the garden for the right bulb;most of them love the full sun, as the Star of Bethelehem, the brodiaeas, and sparaxis; some prefer partial sunlight as the Mission Bells; still others love to grow in the cool pockets of the rocks as do the dog-tooth violet. Here are notes on planting:

HOW PLANT

Brodiaeas: Plant bulbs two inches apart, cover two and one-half inches in soil. Will grow in adobe if drainage is perfect; friable loam clay or sand is good. No manure whatever. Protect plants from gophers. Autumn Crocus, Crocus speciosus: plant corms not later than November; space three inches apart and three inches deep, in ordinary garden loam. A plant similar to Autumn crocus is the attractive Colchicum autumnale. The botanical difference in the crocus is an Iris with three stamens whereas the colchicum is a lily with six stamens.

Calla: tuberous root stock for white form, and flat corm for gold form; plant both three inches deep; grow best in loamy soil which may be enriched with manure; full or partial sun. The small white calla, and the yellow one may be grown in pots.

Cape Cowslip (Lachenalia): do best in enriched soil, sandy loam; should be kept moist once growth begins; open sunny spot. Plant two and one-half inches apart, space two inches apart, about one and one-half inches under surface. They grow very well in boxes and pots.

Cyclamen: the hardy miniature cyclamen: tubers just resting in the earth, do not cover crown, soil rich DON'T in humus best.

Dog-tooth Violets: (Erythroniums) set bulbs upright when planting; with two or three inches of soil covering tip, two inches apart gives room enough. Any loam or gritty soil, loose, but rich in very old leaf mold. Partial shade best.

Freesias: sunny spot, prepare soil well, plant corms two inches apart, one inch deep; fine for boxes and pots. Mission Bells (Fritillaria) both forms that like partial shade and that like full sun must be given well-drained soil fairly rich in leaf mold; two and three inches deep, three inches apart.

Ixias: sun lovers, two and one-half inches apart, two and one-half inches deep.

Gladiolus: three and four inches deep depending upon size of corm.

Sun best, will grow in partial shade; but the gladiolus are different in that they are more summer growing; you may hold these out of the ground for a while; around January to March is a good time to plant.

Mariposa Tulips, Calochortus: plant bulbs two inches apart, cover two and one-half inches soil. Will grow in adobe if drainage is perfect; friable loam, clay or sand is good. No manure whatever.

Star of Bethlehem, ornithogalum: full sun, three and four inches deep in good soil; any soil.

Sparaxis: sun lovers, two and one-half inches apart, two and one-half inches deep. Remember to favor these with a place in the garden that won't be disturbed even under a birch tree, or flowering cherry is all right, if the sun can reach into the spot.

Watsonia: four inches apart, five inches deep, full sun best.

And now for the Opportune Task: Find the spots in your garden where you'd like to have some of these delightful South African bulbs and California natives. Scour around and find them, and then make one grand job of planting. They'll be lots of fun and long lasting.

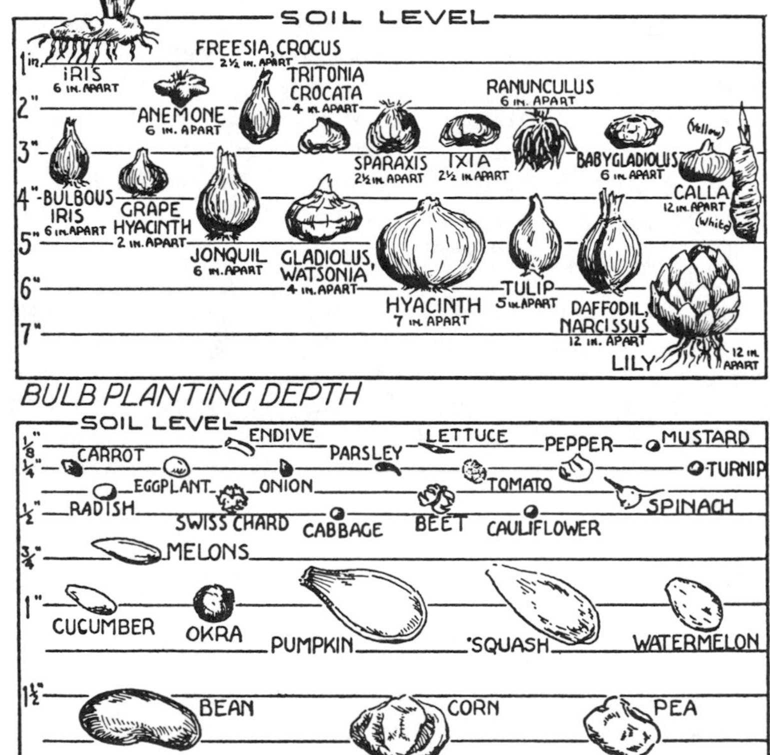

BULB PLANTING DEPTH

VEGETABLE SEED PLANTING DEPTH

CHAPTER 50

PLANTING IN FALL THE DAFFODILS—NARCISSUS BULBS

(November: Second Week)

I told you of true bulbs as the onion, daffodil, hyacinth, and tulip were characterized by having a thickened fleshy layer wrapped all around them. I said what is called a true bulb may live indefinitely as a single unit or may increase by splitting. A wonderful thing about the true bulb for flower production is the fact that in well-matured bulbs the flower buds are actually encased within the bulb at the time you plant

and are there surrounded with stored-up food materials. The flower is inside the bulb all folded up. This knowledge permits us certain privileges in planting these subjects in the design but it requires also certain duties for their welfare. For one thing from now on the earlier you plant them the earlier they bloom, the later you plant them the later they bloom; that is why Christmas present daffodils and tulips give excellent flowers long after the others are gone. And the all important duty required of us if we wish to succeed in keeping these bulbs year after year in the garden is to care for them after they have produced flowers as well as before they flower. That is, to care for them while their leaves are still green and before they have gone into the long summer sleep.

WHERE

But whenever we plant we must do certain things in order that these bulbs will be able to throw up the blooms that the catalogues promised. First, position in the garden. This is very important especially with bulbs that are to remain in the same spot year after year. Moreover, they must be planted so that they are conspicuous when in leaf and in flower so that they are hidden and forgotten when warm weather comes and the bulbs are resting. Therefore instead of taking over the prominent border they are better planted towards the background associated with more lasting perennials or massed in groups throughout the design.

Certainly these spring flowering bulbs as daffodils and tulips should not be permitted to dominate the garden when their foliage is nothing but straw colored blades of drying leaves going down as the bulb below ground is building back its strength. Their beauty is passed and they must yield the limelight to other flowers. These permanent bulbs should be woven into the picture where they may be permitted gracefully to make the show when they are blooming furiously in spring and where gracefully they may bow out of the picture when their season is over. How is this accomplished? One way is to group daffodils, for instance, in with the shrub borders to mass them in stands under the birch tree, near the flowering peach, almond, or Japanese quince. And in little swales of the hillside garden or in among the rocks. Naturalize them. I know a garden where daffodils have been planted for 33 years. They have been multiplying and developing in that spot undisturbed so that now there is a stand that looks indeed like the work of nature itself. The epitome of good gardening is to make the garden look as though it always was there.

For this discussion there is enough to tell about daffodils alone to engage our full time. I'm going to keep the talk on tulips and hyacinths until later.

Daffodils are mighty fine bulbs for the garden. You select with the help of your nurseryman fairly permanent bulbs that throw up good strong stems, that hold up under beating rains and wild winds. And forms with flowers that hold up too. You don't want flowers bowing in the mud. You can select those too, that multiply nicely in the garden; once established they do well by themselves. In your selection go for the types you really enjoy, the good ones as you judge them. Let them be the foundation of your collection.

Do you know what a daffodil is, do you know what a narcissus is, and do you know there are eleven groups of narcissus? Well, a daffodil is simply the English name of the Latin Narcissus. Any narcissus is a daffodil; narcissus is the name the botanists use when they get together; daffodil is the name we use in the garden. If you are going to plant daffodils you must learn the differences. Let us look into these groups.

KINDS

Group One —

Yellow trumpet daffodil: trumpet is long, or longer than the segments. The best example is King Alfred. This bulb has been growing in gardens all over the world for 50 years. King Alfred starts the season; blooms come out in February through March. There is a sub-group here with white and yellow tones. It is known as a bicolor daffodil, the best example is Mrs. Krelage. It's very sturdy.

Group Two —

Incomparabilis; that is, in English, the incomparable. Here instead of a trumpet there is a cup only but the cup is large. (The cup measures from one third to nearly length of the segments.) A good example is Fortune with long cup with red-orange frills and brilliant yellow perianth — that is, the petals all one piece. Another good example is Havelock.

Group Three —

Barrii, named for some Mr. Barry, cup measuring less than one-third the length of the segments. This form of daffodil is better in the cooler regions for the cup burns in Central California gardens. Diana Kasner is an example with pure white perianth, large fluted yellow cup, deeply frilled.

Group Four —

Leedsii; after a man named Leeds; cup white, cream or pale yellow, perianth white. Leedsii narcissus are often called the Chalice Cup daffodil and one of the famous forms in this group is Lord Kitchener with pure white petals, frilled cup of lemon-yellow. And Tunis, which has a cup edged apricot color, is a form used extensively by daffodil breeders in California.

Group Five —

Includes Jonquils, named from the Latin word for reed; these are narcissus that are classed by themselves because their leaves are like reeds, they are round instead of flat. Jonquils have delightful colors and scent the garden with a sweet fragrance of spring. Good ones are Buttercup and Golden Sceptre. Jonquils will throw up from each bulb three to six flower stalks and some of them have clusters of two to three flowers to a stalk.

Group Six —

Named for the poets and is known as Poeticus varieties. A good one of the poeticus narcissus is Snow King with glistening white petals that are exceptionally broad and flat with cup with a broad red edge. And the ever-popular Pheasant's eye is another. Included here too is Actaea that just loves California. It throws up strong flowers of broad petals.

Group Seven —

Includes the Poetaz narcissus, a derivative of Poeticus. They include groups of flowers on long stems, each bloom small with short cups and white petals. Gardeners select from this group for concentrated color effects and one of the finest is Klondike with golden cup and yellow perianth. Also Laurens Koster and Medusa are good examples.

Group Eight —

Polyanthus or bunch narcissus; these are the reliable standbys for winter bloom in the house. Here is included the Chinese Sacred Lily that are grown in bowls, the flowers appear in clusters, with white perianth and golden-yellow cup and of course very fragrant. Similar to the Chinese Sacred Lily is Soleil d'Or with large clusters of dark yellow flowers bright orange cup flowers. And they bloom early.

Group Nine —

Includes those narcissus with drooping flowers, they are called triandrus.

Group Ten —

Includes the cyclamineus whose flower petals curve back and which plants love partial shade though for many gardeners they are sulky performers.

Group Eleven —

Includes miniature narcissus, the little "crowns of jewels" of the rock garden.

For a long time the experts have divided daffodils into eleven groups and they have insisted that if you are going to plant daffodils you must learn the differences. But now happily for us with their tremendous breeding and cross breeding those experts can hardly tell them apart themselves. In the fall of 1948 the late Mr. Sydney Mitchell at the California Horticultural Society meeting in San Francisco told us that they have regrouped the daffodils into trumpets, cups, saucers and miscellaneous.

TRUMPETS

And within some of these groups there are certain variations as between bunched and single flowers. The trumpets: a good example is the large trumpet King Alfred. The trumpet is long or longer than the sepals, and this bulb has been popular in gardens for more than a generation. For us it starts the season. It's a golden daffodil with a bold uniform giant trumpet. Another example is Aerolite. It has a long trumpet, chrome colored, with a soft primrose perianth (that is the ring of sepals standing up). There is also Tres-serve. It has been popular since 1923. It has a deep canary yellow giant trumpet two inches across cut deeply into lobes, with a paler perianth. Among the trumpets of medium size is Mrs. Backhouse, the famous "Pink Trumpet Daffodil" named in honor of a hard worker. Its apricot pink turns to a deeper pink at the fringed edge of the trumpet. This belongs to the old class of Leedsi daffodils. And a good example of the white trumpet is Beersheba, a magnificent flower with large, pointed perfectly flat perianth, standing at right angles to the trumpet, which is beautifully formed, slightly funnel shaped, and nicely flanged at the mouth. The whole flower is a clear white of good substance, and with this vigorous grower goes a free bloomer.

CUPS Examples of cup flowers to include among the old classification of Incomparabilis is Carlton, one of the largest of this group. It has a very large broad flat perianth of rich lemon yellow and a nicely proportioned frilled crown of the same shade. It is a vigorous grower. Lucineus is a rich bright yellow blossom of large size. The perianth is flat and at right angles to the cup. Fortune has a flat overlapping yellow perianth and a coppery red orange cup. In the old Leedsi group, still in the cups, there is Netty O'Melveny. It has a small cup of clear lemon yellow and a white perianth. And among the old classification, the Barrii, and still in the cups, is Diana Kasner. It has a white perianth and a large fluted yellow cup with blood red frills. And as a final example among the cups is Firetail. It has a broad petaled creamy white perianth and a crinkled orange cup.

SAUCERS Examples of the saucers. Here in the old class poeticus belongs the Actaea, a prized one that has readily adopted California. It has a broad saucer-like snow white perianth with a cup broadly margined in dark red. Snow King is another with glistening white saucer perianth with exceptionally broad petals and a cup with a broad red edge. And finally, Pheasant Eye, a clear white, perianth somewhat reflexed, and small yellow cup edged in deep scarlet. The flower possesses a rich spicy odor.

There is the group called bunch flowered daffodils and here is included the ever popular Soleil d'Or which has large clusters of dark yellow flowers. The cup is a bright orange. *BUNCH*

Monarch belongs here. Also Laurens Koster. It has large bunches of white flowers. The perianth is white. The cup is fluted and a deep orange yellow and the flowers possess a delicious fragrance.

The jonquils are a small group that have rush like rounded leaves, greener than the grey foliage of the other narcissus. They have several flowers to a stem and all are fragrant. Golden Sceptre is a good example.

The triandrus daffodils all have drooping flowers and Thalia, an all white bloom, is a good example.

And then there is the group which includes various species and hybrid daffodils. The Bulbocodiums, the Hoop Petticoat or Medusa's Trumpet daffodils come from North Africa.

Bulbocodium Monophyllus or Clusii carries a white hoop petticoat. It will grow best in the rock garden.

Bulbocodium Conspicuus is the yellow Hoop Petticoat with rich golden flowers of hoop-petticoat form and rush-like foliage. There are others but the important point about these Bulbocodium daffodils is that on no account should they be given manure. Then there is the Juncifolius, the miniature rush-leaved daffodil, a charming species ideal for rock garden or for pot culture. The flowers are small, rich yellow, fragrant, and their original home is in the Pyrenees.

There is much more to it than what I have outlined. If you genuinely want daffodils go to your local library and read about them in Bailey's Cyclopedia of Horticulture. Supplement what you read by asking your nurseryman for catalogues illustrating the eleven groups.

Of course in all of this the thing you'll want to do is take a catalogue and leisurely go through it studying the various groups to acquaint yourself with the daffodils.

Check off and make selections to add to your collection, label them with a good permanent label, I *LABEL* mean with a label of metal so that the name doesn't rub out in a few years, and you'll learn exactly the kinds of daffodils you have.

You know hybridizing is a fascinating art and daffodils are a great favorite because not being self pollenizing they are easy to handle. You keep them under control because you do the pollenizing yourself. It's done a great service for you. For example here in California they have hybridized a variety that fits our warm dry climate. If it were not for the hybridizers we wouldn't have daffodils adjusted to our climate. Those that flourish so well in Northern Europe would bloom at the wrong time and cook in the sun. They're still working on the problem of getting daffodils with some kind of steel reenforcement in their stems that will make them stand up bravely and brightly in the downpours of January and February for you know many of them bloom at that very time and again and again, as I have mentioned already, fall with their faces in the mud. The hybridizers have slow, plodding, persistent methods and nowadays they have an immense source of systematic knowledge available This particular task is a hard one, but they will accomplish it.

HYBRID

Here is a short list of lately hybridized quality daffodils. The hybridizers themselves include them in their own collection. You will do well to consider them in yours. Every time you place daffodils in the garden think of the complete picture. The plan is the thing you know. Think of the flowers that go in front of the daffodils and what goes in back of them. Think of the trees that flower above them. One thing to be sure is to have accent in the garden, but above all, think of the picture. For example Lavestale is a giant trumpet daffodil with ivory white perianth and a trumpet of deep cream yellow. Havelock is a smooth well proportioned flower of a good plain yellow. Peggy is as perfect a flower as you'd find. It is slow to increase, but it's a jewel with shiny-petal white flowers. Cornish Fire has strongly colored brilliant flower of a good size with yellow perianth and widely expanded cup of fiery orange scarlet. John Evelyn is one of those daffodils much sought after. It has white and yellow and lemon-yellow flowers. Charmant is a well-rounded, substantial flower carried on a stiff stem. Its perianth is purest white and crown a bright scarlet-red. Nairabi is a striking large flower with immensely thick smooth rounded white perianth of fine quality and a large expanded much frilled cup of intense solid orange-red. Of course here again you want to run through the catalogues. Many of them carry the hybridizing information, parents and date. Select your daffodils to your liking.

Of course your daffodils will go into your garden and stay many years; they are nearly pest resistent, they are distasteful even to the gopher which works such disaster to your tulips and gladiolus. He has evidently been reading the books of the chemists who have found daffodil bulbs contain strychnine, that vigorous poison. The gopher is guilty sometimes of picking up your daffodil and dropping the bulb in some place not figured in your design. But you'll remember that the main point to the daffodil which doesn't come out at all in the descriptive items I have given you is that at the first hint of spring it can leap out of the cold ground and give you one of the finest effects you can ever see in any garden. Wordsworth felt this effect keenly. He said: "I saw a crowd, a host of golden daffodils — beneath the trees, fluttering and dancing in the breeze."

But long before Wordsworth our great Shakespeare knew all about it. He said: "daffodils come before the swallow dares and takes the winds of March with beauty." And I wonder if he didn't do some gardening on the side.

But then of course we have to remember that if he did all those gorgeous things he describes in his plays he would have had to be the very busiest of all transcendent geniuses.

Now about planting daffodils. I speak here to the beginner and near beginner. You employ of course such recognized good gardening as deep digging, frequent cultivation, proper fertilization, heavy watering CARE while growing, light watering while dormant, complete maturing of foliage, careful observation for disease control. You challenge the right of every bulb to enter your garden; is it the variety you want, the variety you really enjoy? Is it clean of enemies and disease? Examine all bulbs carefully especially gifts from friends' gardens! For though the daffodils mostly enjoy good health and the nurseryman's is sure to be all right, there is a disease called "mosaics" that can be passed around in gifts. Remember that if planted correctly in permanent spots, the bulbs will multiply and in time your garden will abound with quantities of quality plants. The gophers for some reason best known to themselves, go around them. Since permanency is the ideal with these bulbs do a good job in planting. First, make sure drainage is not only good but perfect; if it isn't that already, you make it so. Go after the soil in the good old fashioned way with pick and shovel. Get down there deep, improve the soil with humus material, bone meal is good and it is possible to purchase food prepared especially for DON'T bulbs; but use no manure for manure only excites wonderful green leaves and no flowers. Sun or shade, depending upon the likes of each type of bulb planted; in one book I read, morning sun and afternoon shade's good for narcissus and since daffodils always bloom towards the sun, plant bulbs for the southern exposure if possible. Be sure to set each bulb in a pocket of sand. Push the bulb into the sand so the disc at the bottom rest in it; this helps in several ways; one is sanitation, another is sand makes for ease of moving the bulbs when that is desired and the bulbs multiply better when encased in sand. This is especially true with large bulbs but in using sand with small bulbs or corms as the South Africans we spoke of last week, it is better to mix the sand with the humus soil before planting. The sand will help to lighten the soil. Small bulbs and corms need food soon, sand offers no food but the humus soil does and it is not the best thing to encase in sand the small bulbs or the corms. The true bulb which has its food all stored up in the layers wrapped around the bulb, the sand is all right. Remember to plant daffodils deep, 4 to 6 inches underground depending upon variety. And then after all planting is completed, water well. Start them off with a good soaking and if the rains don't follow be sure and continue watering once a week because good flowers next spring depend entirely upon vigorous root growth now.

A Precaution for Bulb Planting

For all bulbs about to be planted good practice suggests dusting with an insecticide. This protects the narcissus, tulip, lily, hyacinth, etc. from soil borne pests. Drop bulbs in bag, dust generously, shake vigorously. The dust-covered bulbs then may be set out.

The Arms of This Garden Reach Out and Embrace the Distant Hills.

CHAPTER 51

TULIPS

(November: Third Week)

We devoted our last chapter to the narcissus, the daffodils. We told you there are eleven groups, some of them produce very fragrant flowers, some have large trumpets, some produce their flowers bowing toward the ground, still others produce clusters of flowers while a whole group of them like best the hidden places of the rock garden.

Now we speak of the tulip and furthermore we do something different. We report an interview with the late Peter Valinga of Burlingame, California, a native of Holland and a specialist in bulbs.

Tulips are somewhat special; for instance, we can use them in the design alone or we can bring them into the house as cut flowers. Again for tulips you have to do one thing that is not required for the narcissus; that is, protect them from gophers. Gophers will clear them out every time.

We discuss tulips today because they can bring to the garden their enchanting beauty next spring only if we plant the bulbs now and only if we do certain things for those bulbs now.

The home of the tulip is Asia Minor but few flowers have been so long cherished as the flower from this bulb. In 1554, they were growing in the gardens of Constantinople and soon afterward were brought into Western Europe. They are called Dutch tulips because in Holland since their arrival they have been cultivated and improved so that today the gardens of the world look to that country for the supply of new bulbs. At one time there was a tulip boom and fortunes were made and lost. Dumas' famous novel The Black Tulip was written concerning this time. Mr. Valinga, do you want to tell us something about the importance of the tulip in Holland, your native country? What is the place of the tulip bulb in Holland?

Valinga: Tulips have been cultivated in Holland from 1634. Flowers have played an important part in the home of all Hollanders bringing to them a cheer that lifts the bleak days of their harsh climate.

Wilson: How did they count during the current war?

Valinga: The bulb industry survived because all the fighting was done in the Eastern part of Holland whereas the bulb fields are situated behind the mile-wide row of sand dunes along the North Sea on the West coast of Holland. On account of this lucky break we have today improved varieties that were actually hybridized and propagated during the war. I can report also that the folks at home used them for food. First they cut off the roots at the disk where they break from; they peeled off the dry shell, then sliced them up like an onion after they cut the folded-up flower out and put them in whatever else they could get. The flavor is terrible; cows like them well enough but people find them bitter. For thousands they made the difference between starvation and survival.

Wilson: We know that the tulip has been hybridized for a long time and therefore the different kinds overlap. Yet, the experts choose, at least to some extent, certain kinds for certain purposes. Tell us what are the principle kinds.

Valinga: There are three main groups of tulips. The Darwins, named in honor of Charles Darwin the eminent English biologist; and these bulbs are comparatively new having been hybridized within the last 40 years. Darwins have large square cup flowers. The second group called Breeder with flowers shaped like an egg with an outside sheen of a plum and the third group, the Cottage tulip with the pointed petals of a lily.

Wilson: I'm going to ask you, Mr. Valinga, which kind you would use for planting in the outside border.

Valinga: I can't answer your question as directly as you have put it because all of the tulips have been cross-bred over so long a period that their characters are quite similar and the three divisions have little meaning. The best way to select from the Darwins, the Breeders, and the Cottage is by color. I wish all your hearers could spend a day with me next year at the California Spring Garden Show in Oakland; that is the very place to learn how to choose tulips; how to place them in the garden. Every year at the show you can hear person after person telling how they select their tulips entirely by color so that they will blend with the drapes at the window so that the color of the garden will reach into the house and vice versa. And in all these tulips more than in the other spring bulbs you can select all colors varying even into the blue. It is possible to get almost anything you want. And a simple rule is to put dark colors in the sunny spots; light colors in the shady spots.

Wilson: Using color as a basis, describe some varieties that you would select.

Valinga: Beginning with the square-cupped ones they call Darwin, I'd take Rev. Ewbank, it is a soft heliotrope lilac; then there is Clara Butt, it's a light pink and always a favorite. A dependable fiery cardinal-red with flowers as large as a coffee cup is the City of Haarlem and the darkest tulip yet raised is the Queen of the Night.

Wilson: How would you plant these kinds in the garden, I mean in the design?

Valinga: Any one of these grouped in a plot in the garden will give a cheerful display coming along right up to the last of the spring season. It's a good rule always to plant tulips in groups never plant them in straight rows. Tulips make a striking picture when they are grouped in front of a dark hedge, when they are grouped with a background of shiny foliage; they can never make a picture when strung along in a straight row.

Wilson: Will you tell us how to use tulips with perennials. USE

Valinga: Tulips go well with perennials, but they must never be jammed in tight among them;it is better to group them here and there among the perennial flowers; mass them in spots by themselves. In that way the stems of the tulips are not hidden; they will stand up, and will hold their flower cups high so that their full beauty may be seen. And here again you can pull heavy on color to play its part in the picture. For instance, along the perennial border a pure white, like Zwanenburg, a strong Darwin type will stand out like glistening snow flakes above a sea of green foliage; or a soft lemon-yellow like Golden Harvest, one of the most prized of the cottage tulips will brighten the perennial border and compliment any other early spring flowers that might be out at the same time, as for instance the blue or scarlet long-spurred columbines. There are lots of ways of using tulips in the perennial border especially if the group idea predominates.

Wilson: What do you care to say about tulips and pansies or violas?

Valinga: There you have one of the grandest combinations possible. We can't all have formal gardens like those we saw in Treasure Island but everyone of us can have little beds of jewels made up of violas or pansies and tulips. The violas or pansies will bloom throughout winter and then in spring the tulips push up and bloom above.

Wilson: Then according to your rule of choice through color you can select tulips from all three — Darwin, Breeder, and Cottage for use with pansies and violas.

Valinga: Yes, all three types can be used but watch the color combination carefully; you can do wonderful things there. For example, with yellow viola use the one called "The Bishop", an almost pure lavender can be used. With pansies where the cool blues, lavenders and maroon tones predominate a tulip like Captain Fryat, one with dark ruby-red petals can be selected. And when white violas are massed with them a tulip like the maroon black Queen of the Night can be used in rich contrast.

Wilson: Your mention again of the maroon color reminds me of the striped tulips; you had such lovely ones at the spring show last March. Do you want to tell us a little about them?

Valinga: Indeed I do remember those striped tulips at the show. The visitors just couldn't keep their hands off them. Children, adults, and gardeners alike kept pulling them out of the vases, kept rubbing the petals, even smelling them to convince themselves they were not made of wax. They are a group known to the experts as The Rembrandt tulip; they sort of break away from the large square cup Darwin which they resemble somewhat.

Wilson: Where in the garden could they be used?

Valinga: Always put these striped tulips grouped together by themselves. Some of them are striped dark with the various shades of slate, some purplish with crooked stripes like marble cake. A good one is named Cordell Hull. It's a deep red, blotched with white and was developed during the war. And another very good one is Pierrette, a white with a purple flame. But these highly decorative tulips stand out best when planted in groups by themselves.

Wilson: I remember having in my garden once a tulip called the Parrot. That was an odd flower. It had petals that were deeply cut and were in sharp color shades of red and pink with a strong green stripe running through it. But it died out or disappeared.

Valinga: It died out perhaps because you planted it in too much shade. The Parrot tulip is one that must have absolute full sun. Or it might have been eaten out by a gopher. But, you know, Mr. Wilson, there is also a blue Parrot, a tulip which resembles an orchid.

Wilson: What tulip can be used in the rock garden? I'm thinking of course of the rock garden in the small place.

Vallinga: I was wondering if we were going to get those in. There is a whole group that is ideal for the rock garden. They are known as the botanical tulip. They are the wild forms. They grow wild over there in Asia Minor on the dry rocky slopes of the Taurus mountains in Turkey, facing the Mediterranean Sea. We could go for a walk over the dry hills of Damascus or in the plains of Smyrna and there we could pick them by the bushels. They are at home in that climate which is just like our own in California; six months, no rain, six months, torrential rains.

Wilson: Do you care to recommend one or two botanical tulips for planting here?

Valinga: Yes, there's a good one that has flowers colored white and red like a peppermint stick, it is called Tulipa clusiana. It sends out its flowers early on stems 18 inches tall. Another wild one is Tulipa kaufmanniana with flowers shaped like a water lily of creamy white with a sulphur-tinged center. SUGGEST

Wilson: Reaching this phase of our discussion, suppose we consider planting methods. How do you go about planting tulips; not only the wild forms but also the hybrids.

HOW TO PLANT

Valinga: First, I would make a sound rule. Plant no tulip in California before the last week of October, but they may be planted as late as January first. The main reason for delaying the planting date of the tulip in California is to plant the bulb in cool ground rather than in warm. The colder the soil, the better the root action. Furthermore, if the top growth develops suddenly before proper root growth below ground, which will surely take place in soil that is still warm from the summer sun, then the whole plant is weak and the flower thrown out is very poor indeed.

Wilson: The soil then must have been reduced to a certain temperature before growth develops properly.

A warm soil retards root growth.

Valinga: Yes, and another important feature of planting tulip bulbs is to provide good drainage. Drainage is even more important than manure.

Wilson: Tulips will grow in any soil then?

SOIL Valinga: Yes, light soils are best; if the soil is stiff you can make it light with peat or humus materials.

Wilson: What about manure?

MANURE Valinga: Manure for tulips as well as for all flowers tones up the plant and gives a finer color. It is all right but under one consideration, that it be worked well down into the soil a month or so before the bulbs are planted. Or if you have had no time beforehand to work the manure into the soil, then spade up the plot at least 18 inches deep, plant the bulbs and after the heavy rains come then top dress the plot with manure and let the rains carry it down to the bulbs.

SAND Wilson: Do you recommend sand with tulips at planting time?

Valinga: Yes I do. There is a very beneficial effect from sand on the root development of tulip bulbs. Sand gives a moderate moisture never excessive down at the root disc and this enables the roots to get off to a good start. Encase the bulbs in sand, and besides, it does all those things you said for it last week when you described planting daffodils.

Wilson: We have already spoken of planting tulips and pansies or violas together. But how far apart and how deep should tulips be planted when used this way and when planted in groups by themselves?

DISTANCE Valinga: Plant tulips always five to six inches below the surface of the soil. If planted in groups, space the individual bulbs within the group five or six inches apart, but if planted in the same plot with violas or pansies, then space the bulbs farther apart, for example, a foot from one another.

Wilson: At the florists' every spring, tulips are sold in pots. Can the amateur grow them that way at home?

POT Valinga: Yes they can and here is the simple trick. Select a five-inch pot, one that they call a pan. Provide drainage by placing in the bottom broken crockery.

Then the soil should be composed of equal parts of peat moss, loam and sand. The bulb should be placed near the top of the pot so that the upper half is exposed. The top soil should then be covered with one-quarter inch layer of sand. A cool spot in the garden should then be chosen and the pot plunged into the soil so that the top of the pot is five inches below the surface. The soil should then be firmed between the pots and kept moist. In California it should be watered once a week until the rains start. After twelve or fourteen weeks the plants should be four or five inches high. They can then be brought into a weak light. As soon as the shoots turn a normal green they are ready to be brought indoors.

WATER

Wilson: I see our time is about finished, Mr. Valinga, but before we leave the tulips will you tell us how to protect them from the gophers.

Valinga: Make baskets of one-half inch wire netting big enough to contain a dozen bulbs. For that matter, you can make a basket small enough for one bulb, or large enough to protect 18 bulbs. Put it in the ground just deep enough so that an inch rim projects above soil level. And then you know many gardeners plant tulip bulbs in cans or in pots and plunge them, with little drainage hole punched in, all down into the ground. That keeps gophers away all right.

KEEP GOPHER OFF

Wilson: Thank you, Mr. Valinga, for your discussion of the tulip. *

The Opportune Task: Camellia buds are nice and fat now; you want to keep them so and a sure way is to make sure that they have plenty of moisture at their roots now. This prolonged dry spell when we ought to have rain may cause some of us to overlook the camellias at this time. Those buds will not be so fine next spring if they don't get the water this fall, so investigate and if they need water provide it at once. And while you are about it, take a look also at your rhododendrons. If, for instance, the rhododendrons showed attack by red spider, the brown spotty condition, then it is a pretty good hint you have been pretty stingy with the water where they are concerned. Investigate them too and see if some water is needed.

*See also (December: Second Week: Planting in Winter.)

One of the causes for beautiful camellia buds to drop off before they open in spring is often traced directly to dry roots in fall.

Potted Tulips and Hyacinths.

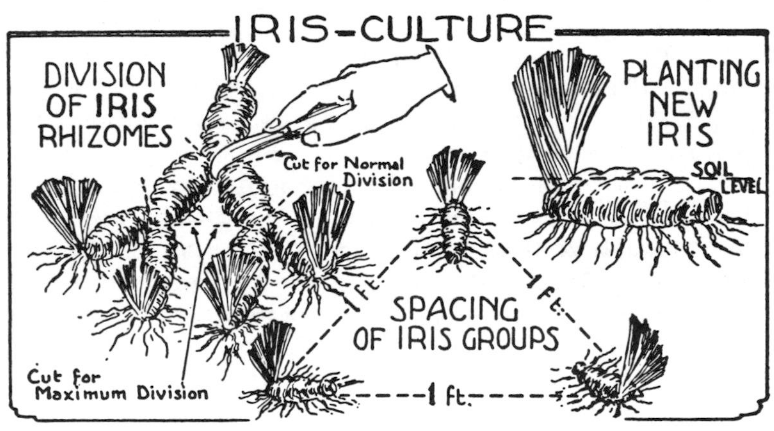

Also see "Iris", Chapter 41, pages 333-344.

Chapter 52

PLANTING HYACINTHS, RANUNCULUS, ANEMONES, AND DUTCH IRIS

(November: Fourth Week)

We promised to complete this series of talks on bulb planting. It is evident to all of us that in our California gardens we can grow beautiful flowers from bulbous rootstock collected from all over the world. It is also evident that one broadcast cannot take care of these many kinds and therefore, we have broken up the discussion first into the South Africans, then the daffodils, after them the tulips and now today, the hyacinths,

ranunculus, anemones and Dutch iris. Even this does not complete the list for there are the lilies which we discussed last winter and will have to leave out this time because we must get on to other things. These also have to be planted this fall and if you want to know about the kinds ask your nurseryman.

EARLY TULIP

But before we go on to the bulbs I should like to go back a step and answer one question sent in about tulips. "Why do my tulips start to bloom the very minute they come out of the ground? They send up a few leaves and then immediately, right down in the soil, the bloom appears; there is no stem; why is this?"

I turned that question over to Mr. Valinga the specialist on Dutch bulbs who was our studio guest. His reply, "In Holland they have developed a certain class known as 'Early Tulip' propagated so that it can be forced into bloom. It is supposed to be grown under glasshouse conditions. These special tulips are for the florist trade – are suited for pot culture only." EARLY TULIPS LIKE COLD CLIMATE. The Earlies grow best in cold hard winter climate. Warm California does not suit in the least! Here the flower of the Early throws up the bloom before a stem has had time to develop. Out in the garden they turn out failures. When the nurseryman tell you Keizerskroon (scarlet, yellow edged) is an Early tulip he means this kind is good for growing indoors; Murillo, white tinged with pink is an example of Double Early; and Tea Rose is a yellow fragrant one. Never select them for outdoor culture. Note also the catalogues place after the name H-12, H-10, H-30: H meaning the height of stem.

What Mr. Valinga told us last week about planting tulips goes also for planting hyacinths. It will take only a minute to run over the details. Tulips and hyacinths may be planted in the border, they are best grown in groups or hyacinths may be massed on a slope. The bulbs of both tulips and hyacinths should be planted five or six inches under the ground and individually in a group each bulb should be spaced five to six inches away from its neighbor. Tulips planted with violas and pansies should be spaced twelve inches apart; this for a better effect. Many of us remember the glorious display of hyacinths wherein thousands of these fragrant bulbous flowers were planted around the Lake of the Nations on Treasure Island. Those bulbs were spaced eight to ten inches apart.

HOW TO PLANT

Another useful rule about tulip and hyacinth planting is to place them in staggered rows; planting in this manner the full beauty of each bulb stands out and no bulb loses its identity. Both tulips and hyacinths do best in partial sunlight; morning sun and afternoon shade, the blooms last longer, the colors also do not

WHERE

suffer as they might under strong sunlight. They will, however, grow in full sun; the flowers may yield just a little of their precious color in strong light.

On the way home from the broadcast last Sunday, Mr. Valinga was telling me how much pleasure he got from watching the children at the flower show get down on their knees so as to smell the hyacinths better. And he added, the rich fragrance of hyacinths gives them a powerful attraction for your garden. And right now is the best time to plant the bulbs; this afternoon, that is what I'm going to do myself when I get home today.

Color combinations are simple with hyacinths. I believe it was because of this fact and the rich fragrance that the Treasure Island display was so impressive. Only three colors were used; the best white called Innocence; Perle Brilliant, a light blue, and Lady Derby, a light pink; though of course, there are other colors these three set one another off effectively in the garden.

Let us also review pot culture because you grow hyacinths in pots just as you grow tulips. I shall repeat the details for you given in last chapter. Select a five-inch pot, one that they call a pan. Provide drainage by placing in the bottom broken crockery. Then the soil should be composed of equal parts of peat moss, loam, and sand. The bulb should be placed near the top of the pot so that the upper half is exposed. The top soil should then be covered with one-quarter inch layer of sand. I might explain here the reason for this sand: it is to help you later on when you lift off the garden soil that you threw over the pot when you proceed with the next step. So after covering with sand, you select a cool spot in the garden and plunge pot and all into the soil so that the top of the pot is five inches below the surface. That, you see, is where you cover over the layer of sand with garden soil so that the bulb is actually five to six inches below the ground level. The soil should be firmed between the pots and kept moist. In California it should be watered once a week until the rains start. After 12 to 14 weeks the plants should be four to five inches high but still wholly

POT

SOIL

CARE

buried under the mound of ground. They can then be unburied and carried to a place where they are exposed to only a weak light. As soon as the shoots, which are first sickly yellow like bleached celery, turn a normal green they are ready to be brought indoors.

KINDS But there are other hyacinths: for instance, there are the Grape hyacinths called Muscari. One called Heavenly Blue and another called Alba because it is white, are often planted in California gardens. Muscari armeniacum too is a good true blue. Grape hyacinths unlike the Dutch hyacinths are not eaten by gophers; they leave them alone. And if you and I leave the bulbs alone after planting them they do wonderfully well growing in either sun or shade; they will multiply into colonies.

Then there is the Wood hyacinth known as Scilla. They come from the Old World and you will remember the familiar Greek saying, "If I had two drachmas I would spend one for bread; with the other I'd buy hyacinths." One a deep blue is often seen in the garden; the other pure white is likewise. And there is a wonderful thing about the Wood hyacinths; they do just as their name hints, they grow in more shade and darkness than any other kind of bulb. This is good to remember where those difficult spots are found in the garden.

So much for tulips and hyacinths. Do you know there are bulbs that will give you flowers that will keep coming for six to eight weeks, and do you know that these same bulbs send up a tender growth that quail and the White-crowned sparrow would dive for in the midst of a convention of cats? Well, these are the ranunculus and anemones and if you defend them from birds they of all the spring bulbs bloom the longest.

TRICKS Now there are important tricks in growing ranunculus and anemones; the bulbs should be soaked in water for two hours just before you plant them. Remember it is only two hours they sit in water; longer than that is dangerous and if they are forgotten for 24 hours it's good night — they usually rot. Some gardeners merely soak paper and between the layers place the bulbs for two days. The bulbs swell, the tip eyes begin to sprout and then the bulbs are ready to be planted. An advantage of first swelling the roots is to know the good bulbs from dead ones so that later when planted there'll be no "gaposis" in your garden.

The next trick about planting ranunculus and anemones is to place the bulbs with the prongs facing into the soil. Ranunculus bulbs are like babies' little fingers all grouped together and where the palm of the hand is, that's where all the prongs of the bulb are attached. As you plant, of course, the prongs then will be down and the sprouts at the opposite end will be upward. This was about ranunculus, now about anemones. Anemone bulbs look like a miniature top that your boy spins with a string. The point end goes down into the ground, the top or flat end is covered with a little fuzz. Both of these bulbs, the ranunculus and the anemone, are placed under the soil only two inches. A good many amateurs wait until the first good winter rains come then plant these bulbs; here to be wholly safe they should be covered with a basket made of wire screening.

But many professional gardeners prefer to start these bulbs in flats in moist sand. Then after the new growth has reached four to five inches and is sturdy, the bulbs are lifted out and planted in the garden. In this way the gardeners are sure to have their plants safe from bird attack. Mr. Valinga says be sure to plant them out in the open sunny borders because if you put them close to hedges the birds hide there and get SOIL
away with the tender growth before the plants have half a start. And out in the garden it is wise to prepare the soil well because these bulbs are very small. They have only a minimum of food stored up in them. Their new roots must be able soon to pick up food. Loose, light, loamy soil enriched with bone meal is good and after the plants have gotten a good growth, sprinkle a teaspoonful of commercial fertilizer around each plant and then soak the food in with water.

There is one more little pointer about these bulbs; ranunculus have all the red, orange, and yellow colors but no blues; while the anemones have pink, red, white, and blues.

We may proceed with the Dutch iris; they too go into the ground soon. Dutch iris go well mixed with daffodils, one form called Wedgewood that is a medium blue with large flower is especially fine planted near King Alfred daffodils. Dutch iris will come into bloom as early as March and will continue on until late May depending of course upon date of planting. It is possible to place these bulbs in the ground as early as October and as late as January. They should be planted five to six inches deep and should be spaced four to six inches apart. They are most effective when grouped with their blade-like leaves bunched together.

DUTCH IRIS

Many people have asked me if Lily of the Valley can be grown in California. The answer is yes. I know of several successful plantings in gardens around the Bay region. In one garden at Los Altos under an old bunya bunya tree I saw a sea of white pearls standing mid a rich green foliage and upon closer examination they turned out to be Lily of the Valley. Then in San Mateo there is a grand plot growing under a low spreading oak tree and in Redwood City there is still another fine group.

LILY OF VALLEY

In each of these gardens about this time of year, the gardeners clear away the dead foliage of last year and then top dress the entire plot with leaf mold and well-rotted cow manure. The winter rains carry down to the pips, the term given the Lily of the Valley clumps, and the new growth starts out a dark green. Later in the spring around April these established stand produce the much cherished flowers.

If you are going to set Lily of the Valley pips into the garden for the first time you will proceed in the same manner as for planting other bulbs. Namely, deep loose preparation of the soil. Then set the pips with the stringy roots facing downward and cover the pointed crowns about two inches under the surface. If you have large clumps, the central part is usually composed of stiff roots; these go straight down into the soil but the outer ones may be fanned out much as you fan strawberry roots. After planting apply water to settle. The fat pips usually produce flowers the following spring after planting; the slender ones must grow for a season before they can produce the flowers. But remember when buying Lily of the Valley pips to ask for those suited to growing in the garden; do not plant outside old pips that were forced in the glass house.* DON'T

The Opportune Task: Harvest Loquat. Eriobotrya japonica. Native to China, cultivated from antiquity in Japan, and long ago introduced to California gardens the evergreen ornamental loquat grows in gardens from San Diego to Eureka. This tree grows best in regions of coastal cool climate, it tolerates hot valley climate.

In the garden the loquat may be planted as background tree. Several can be grown in a row to become a tree wall, providing a solid screen. The tree serves as a climate maker since its blocky habit will deflect wind.

The loquat is a blocky tree not more than 30 feet carrying many branches mostly hidden by the large leaves. The leaves are deeply veined, noble looking and are from six to ten inches long. They are deep green above and wooly below.

Loquats produce their flowers in winter from mid-October till January the clusters of white flowers

---

*See also (December: Second Week: Planting in Winter.)

appearing on the wooly panicles at the very terminal. Every branch on the tree carries the delightfully fragrant flowers which appear with and stand slightly above the leaf clusters.

The fruit on the loquat ripens as early as March continuing till June.

Loquats grow in loamy, gravelly, adobe or sandy soils, and fertilizer is not necessary.

Sufficient water throughout the year is advised. When grown on soil too dry the foliage becomes small and dusty, the tree dwarfed, and many leaves drop to create mess and work.

The loquat needs pruning. A tree can be pruned severely and it will break out all along the trunk and side branches into new growth. Big cuts should be covered with tree seal, or a mixture of plumbers' paint and linseed oil. New growth will break below the old cut and in a few months a new crown of full-leaved branches will cover the tree. Some gardeners permit their tree to keep lower branches. These trees grow then like huge leafy balls. Other gardeners take away the lower branches creating the stemmed tree which has a rusty colored bark, decorative and interesting especially should the tree possess a double or triple trunk.

The loquat tree suffers from the attack of pear blight. Diseased branches must be pruned off.

Aphids, scale and codling moths attack the loquat tree. Aphid is discouraged with nicotine sprays, scale with summer oils, and codling moths with Diazinon. See page 494.

Propagation: Seeds which volunteer readily. Choice types are usually budded or grafted onto seedling root stock. Budding or grafting best in October and November; young smooth firm budwood, without the soft down is used. The budwood at least one and one half inches long is inserted in a T-incision, out on the seedling rootstock, tied securely, but removed when the bud has taken.

Advance: Developed by C. A. Taft. Fruit large pear-shaped , deep yellow skin, white flesh, juicy; Crop: from March to June.

Champagne: A Japanese type. Fruit large, yellow-skinned, white-fleshed, juicy, excellent for jelly.
Thales: A Chinese type. Fruits very large, skin and flesh orange, considered sweeter than white-fleshed types; Crop: May to June; best in coastal gardens.
Gold Nugget: Fruit glossy, deep orange, juicy; Crop: from May to June; best in the coastal garden.

The Pool.

Chapter 53

CLEANING THE FLOOR OF THE GARDEN

(December: First Week)*

Gardening to all of us is a new experience because every day we meet new problems; we have new plants or new soils and we have old plants for new climate. In some sections of the State, we garden under arid conditions; in others, we are favored with abundant moisture — here, we have a garden in a windy spot; there, hidden between hills in a hot valley, we have another. Now, all those gardens to succeed under California conditions, demand an intimate knowledge of plant behavior.

The purpose of these talks is to provide factual information to the gardening public — to send over these radio waves the HOW, the WHEN, and the WHERE of California gardening — to interest the novice in better techniques — to aid the professional with new tricks and to create a wider and livelier interest in the plants at hand. We want you to achieve results with your seeds and your cuttings; to succeed in the transplanting and growing of your plants in the garden. We hope that from these discussions, you will be challenged by new ideas and authoritative methods, and that your garden will run abreast of the known facts.

A feature of these programs, the "Opportune Task" will stress JUST WHAT IS NECESSARY TO BE DONE IN YOUR GARDEN AT THIS MOMENT. Watch for today's Opportune Task later.

Now is cleanup time in your garden. During this wet weather period, the gardener must stay off the soil, but he doesn't have to stay out of the garden. There are many important jobs he can do. Most obvious is the removal of dead leaves — raking them

*Wilson's Introductory Radio Talk December 2, 1945

up and placing them on the compost pile. These dead leaves, no longer useful to the living plant, now are valuable as soil builders. They must never be burned. Therefore, in your cleanup schedule collect them, pile them, rot them down and later, when they have been reduced to leaf soil, return them to the earth. This is best done as a top dressing, a mulch around the plants in the garden and a mulch for the potted plant. But now we collect them. Mulch by the way is broken plant materials which maintain a tilth-like looseness of the surface soil around plants.

Also, at this season of the year, the oak trees have dropped their acorns. A heavy falling of acorns on the lawn for instance is bad for the grass. Both they and the leaves can ruin a new lawn and damage an old established one. Definitely, in the cleanup, get rid of them especially before continued wet weather pounds them into the root crowns of the grass. Of course, these acorns and oak leaves go on the compost pile, but keep them by themselves because, unlike most garden leaves, they take a long time to break down and become leaf soil. Give them a sunny place, turn them frequently, wet them down, spray them if you wish as I shall tell you in a moment and thus speed nature's way in getting a rich leaf mold. Those of you who have fig trees, persimmon, loquat or magnolia trees must be especially diligent in raking up these somewhat leathery leaves which also take a long time to break down besides making dandy places for snails, slugs and pill bugs to hide under during the winter months.

Some of you have been slow in removing the annuals of last summer. Perhaps you see a few more buds on your zinnias, lobelias, petunias or French marigolds. Forget them, pick one last bouquet and clear out the batch so that you can plant other things for the season to come. If your soil is not too wet and drainage is good and, if you are adept and thorough in spading, you may cut your annuals down and turn them under the soil where they have been growing; but an easier way is to put them on the compost pile. Leave the ground rough; allow the rain and the sun to fall upon it.

It will do the soil good to lie unused for a while. Neglect it for a moment and, in so doing, you will give Nature a chance. Your soil will be aerating, nitrogen will work its way in — rather, nitrogen will be formed more easily through the micro-organisms in its soil — foul gases will work their way out, rain waters will travel down deep to a lower root zone and the winter sun in its kiss will sweeten the ground where other plants are to be placed. Your soil will become new through this simple, easy exercise.

When you have become satisfied that the floor of the garden has been cleaned — that you have rid it of dead and decaying leafy foliage — your next office is to top dress the soil; particularly during the wet weather when the ground holds too much moisture for spading and planting. Those of you who have maintained and built up a compost pile, may now reap the harvest and scatter this rich material in the flower bed. Be generous. Put it out three or four inches deep — put it everywhere — spread it in the way the mason spreads his plaster. The winter rains will unlock the good that is in it — the roots of the plants to come will easily find it. Remember always that humus and this material from your compost pile is nature's best fertilizer. USE IT.

WINTER FEED

Also, with the cleanup goes fertilizing. When the rubbish has been removed, top dress the entire garden with manure. At this cool season, dairy fertilizer is the best — cow manure is especially good; strawy horse manure is useful too. Use them freely. Here again top dress the ground three to four inches deep, and let the rains unloose, for the roots, the riches they hold.

Sheep, rabbit, and chicken manure likewise are natural fertilizers. These are stronger; use them carefully. We might suggest mixing them with other things; for example, to one wheelbarrow of sheep manure or rabbit manure, mix two wheelbarrows of leaf mold.

Pruning is another important exercise of the clean-up, which takes place before spraying. Because of the importance of pruning, we will devote an entire discussion to this subject. However, for the time being, wild branches and dead twigs on your plants as well as streamers on vines should be cut off. By opening the plant, by relieving the tree of useless branches, you are preparing the way for greater efficiency in the control of plant parasites and injurious insects.

After pruning comes spraying. In your working around the perennials, you might have noticed the crowns of certain plants covered with mold. These, if permitted to persist, will cause the new spring growth to develop inferior shoots and blooms. Wherever you discover these molds, these plant parasites, spray the foliage thoroughly with a bordeaux spray. In this same class falls the famous curly leaf on the peach tree, and the well-known shot-hole or peach blight. For their control, spray the trees with a bordeaux spray. Do it today, for this damp weather (December), conditions favor the development of these diseases and much of their control depends upon the fall or winter cleanup spray. There are of course many useful sprays available on the commercial market such as those to spray for control of fungus suitable for plants that have dropped their leaves for the year, and others suitable for control of insects in the winter months. But the Bordeaux mixture is probably more generally used than any other fungicide. You can find a prepared mixture of this material on the market. Use it according to the directions on the container. However should you prefer the commercial products, first spray your garden with a copper spray to control fungus diseases. Two days later, spray the same plants with a summer oil to control the insects. It is more efficient to spray these materials separately rather than mixing them together. Be sure you give meticulous attention to the directions on the container and follow them explicitly; then, you can't possibly fail in catching your trouble makers.

FUNGUS SPRAY

In using these cleanup sprays, be generous in application always in accordance with the directions, and spray the whole garden thoroughly — it is wise practice to spray the entire garden rather than select a tree and a shrub here and there for treatment — for thorough spraying reduces greatly the chances of plant parasites and insect infestation.

If any of you find your garden alive with plant diseases in insects, it might be wise to call in an expert to cover the plants thoroughly with his high pressure equipment. Later, of course, you may give the second and third spraying with your own equipment. In all instances, to achieve good results, your spraying equipment must have force enough to make the solution completely cover the plant.

Those of you who prefer to mix your own Bordeaux may do so easily. Remember the cardinal fact is that it must be freshly mixed; don't keep it over twenty-four hours because Bordeaux mixture loses its strength. Also, it is corrosive and, if permitted to stand, can ruin your equipment. The formula is: Three gallons of cold water, 5 ounces of quicklime, and 3 ounces of copper sulphate. Make the lime water by thoroughly slacking 5 ounces of lime to which add one gallon of cold water. Then, take enough hot water to dissolve the 3 ounces of copper sulphate; add to this 2 gallons of cold water. Finally add the lime water to the copper sulphate solution and stir vigorously. Always mix Bordeaux in a wooden bucket or in an earthenware pot. Remember to cover the plant entirely. Always leave spray can clean after use. When you have finished put the left over solution on the compost pile where it will do some good — not on the ground.

This solution of Bordeaux may also be used around the perennials and on the iris or other plants whose flowers you love to pick. Bordeaux does leave a little residue, a discoloration of the foliage, but this can be eliminated by an overhead spraying with the garden hose, or by a heavy dew or light rain. But in the meantime, you will have saved your plant from an ugly infestation and accomplished the main reason for spraying; the control of fungi and insects.

Then some gardeners will discover mealy bugs around the roots. Sometimes, for example, the tree dahlia will be ready to walk off the place with mealy bugs, so thick are they on the lower sections of the tall stalks; again, these bugs will be in the crowns of the Transvaal or African daisies, or on the crowns of the coral bells, around the roots of the Fremontodendron, Ceanothus, Lantana — there are a lot of plants where these fellows love to gather. In your cleanup program, you can use a good solution of summer oil sprays — use these forcefully wherever you find the mealy bug, and he soon becomes discouraged.

OIL SPRAY

FIRE-BLIGHT

"PEAR BLIGHT"

Fireblight is caused by bacteria; these enter the plant through the fully opened flowers, and occasionally through injured bark. Bees and other insects like flies carry the bacteria from the infected to a healty plant. The bacteria follow down from the flower into the pedicel and then on into the twigs and into the stem. Finally the bacteria reach the cambium cells where under the bark sunken cankers form, and that branch is dead! The foliage first turns brown, then black, but each leaf remains on the twig looking as if it had suffered a scorch of fire.

CONTROLS

Plants subject to fireblight are: loquat, pear, apple, pyracantha, hawthorn, etc. When blooms are fully opened anthers and the pistil show; then with a misty force use a diluted spray of Bordeaux; spray right into the bloom. Other materials such as streptomycin may be used. Since flowering is spread over a six week period, repeat the spraying at 5 day intervals, particularly if rainy weather persists.

A branch dead or dying from fireblight may be cut off; make sure to cut far below the diseased area. Cut into healthy wood. After each cut sterilize pruners; use a disinfectant like a good 5% commercial household disinfectant, like 1 part lysol to 9 parts water. Be sure and paint over cut areas, use the disinfectant. Water plant deeply, feed it, encourage strong new wood growth.

Chapter 54

PLANTING IN WINTER

(December: Second Week)

Our topic is Planting in Winter. Just as every day is opportune for something so is every season. Some plants have to be put in during these rainy months (September to April); now of all the year is their especial time. The bulbs because we want their flowers for spring; the wild flowers and their tame sisters, also for spring, and because we want to broadcast them, as Nature does, and let the rains help keep them alive; and the shrubs and trees, because we want to give them the advantage of wet ground, with what warmth may come to encourage a lusty start.

What we sow now governs what we shall reap next spring, and in the show of permanent beauty next summer, and summers after. First for the bulbs. The lilies, the hyacinths, narcissus, which include daffodils and jonquils, should be in already, but it's not too late. The early tulip can go in now too, but for a later spring effect, wait till Christmas. As to the lilies: though most of ours originate in China and Japan, California is rich in native forms. We must be reminded that they belong to two classes which require somewhat different planting. The Orientals, such as the REGAL, CROFT, FORMOSANUM, and GOLDBAND, are chiefly STEM rooters. That is, they get new bulbs on the stem below ground. To keep these in place the crown of the bulb has to go down at least six inches deep. Native bulbs such as the Parry, and Humboldt are base rooters, and so is the Madonna which came from southern Europe. For these the crown has to go only three to four inches deep. Both kinds are worthy of your garden, but be sure and KNOW which you are planting.

When you put the bulb in, remember that vigorous little villain called the GOPHER. He is a choosy botanist. For reasons of his own he will not touch narcissus, nor daffodils, however, if a lily has RED scales he has been known to occasionally get away with it. But he dearly loves a lily with WHITE scales and for tulips he will make a Banzai charge. Contrive to protect these in a wire netting basket.

The daffodils, tulips, and hyacinths can go into pots if you choose and when they bloom can be brought in to glorify the house. But usually they and all the others will go into the ground. Make sure they are right side up. All of us have peeled an onion and found at the bottom a flat surface. This can be found also at the base of all the bulbs, and because the roots start from here, this flat surface must go face down in the soil. And get these bulbs deep enough. They must have their crowns five to six inches down. Such deep planting permits the new roots to get a good start, to plunge into the soil where they can gather moisture and food before the green tops develop. If too shallow, the plant will suffer pitifully. POT

If the green tops develop first, the stored-up strength is taken from the bulb before the new roots have a chance to gather food, and you can count on mangy flowers. Loosen the ground. Put a little bone meal or manure at the very bottom of the hole and then push your bulb down making sure it rests on the sand. Beware of leaving an air pocket underneath. Cover and press, do not pound. The idea of all this is to look to careful bulb planting now if you would have a prosperous morning in your spring garden.

Let us now leave the bulbs happily tucked in, and turn to the shrubs we are going to set out this season. Planting in winter includes also the flowering shrubs to bring color and interest to eye level; and the trees to make a backdrop against which the garden can tell its lovely and romantic story.

Choose your shrubs with a lively idea of what they will look like two years hence, and how they will at that time fit into the total plan. They must have a purpose, in season of blooming, in color, and in design. Do not be so careless as to set them in the wrong place, and then go digging and hacking the precious roots so you can try them somewhere else. Some love sun; some love shade. Prostrate ones line the border; low ones go in the foreground, tall ones to the rear. Vines cover walls and trellises, Trees dominate the limiting background or border the paths. But, incidentally take care not to put them where fruit will come raining down on the path and pool.

Here's a list of shrubs, vines, and trees suitable for planting in winter. Time denies me the privilege of describing each one, but you can ask your nurseryman. The deciduous flowering shrubs three to four feet, high, bushy, excellent eye-level plants, start as spring begins and keep on blooming one after another, or two or three in unison, lifting the garden in a play of color. They do not punish you with work; they require only moderate attention. Select from:

SHRUB LIST

weigela, with rose pink flowers
bridal wreath, banks of snowy white
Forsythia, strung out on loose branches
quince, of cherry red blooms
lilacs, fragrant, of the old gardens, and
mock orange, perfumed white cups of June.

The evergreen flowering shrubs — old standbys in every garden throughout the state; sturdy four to eight feet high — prosper under neglect, but will thank you politely for a little water during the summer, and a shovelful of cow manure once a year. You may consider the oleander, of many colors

summer lilac, the fragrant haunt of butterflies
Spanish broom, sweet-scents the whole community
veronica, also of many colors, named for the weeping saint
camellia, the new darling of the garden; rose colored, pink and white

Of the vines: the veils of the garden, you may select from: *VINES*

wisteria, belonging to spring
honeysuckle, sometimes called the Woodbine
Boston ivy, playing in the wind
clematis, open-petalled and honest
sweet jasmine.

The trees enter every phase of the garden; they frame the picture, channel attention on the distant view; they create vistas, and develop either the formal or informal effect. Selections are made for scale and proportion, sun or dappled shade, as among: the birch, delicate, graceful, weeping like a willow; everybody loves a birch. *TREES*

pine, whispering, protective
thorny locust, fragrant with pendulant masses of rose-pink, shell or white flowers.
maple, all-purpose, shady moving with the seasons, as do the birches too
sycamore, anticipates fall by throwing leaves down all through summer
flowering crab apple, the happy nosegay and summer source of jelly
hawthorn, flower of May.

Now a word about planting. Set your plant deep enough to keep the roots from lacing the surface, and shallow enough to keep from choking the stem. Choose a happy medium. You have heard the admonition: "NEVER HAMMER A PLANT INTO THE GROUND." To the uninitiated this means dig a great hole. Dig the hole about twice as big as the container or the ball of soil. Dig deep too, and loosen the soil in the bottom.

Use a fork, spade or shovel to chop up and break it loose and friable, for the roots need to be welcomed there. Where drainage is poor, plants may sicken and die — not from pneumonia, but from drowning. Cautious people prefer to provide gravel where drainage is known to be poor.

When you dig the hole, save the top soil in a separate pile and then throw it on the bottom or on the gravel. This soil on which the summer sun has shone directly will favor the roots of your new plant. In it

Ground Level
Dig the hole larger than the plant.
HOLE SIDE VIEW
Place loose top soil in bottom.
E.N.DYE.46.

Out of container.

are the all-important life giving micro-organisms. You can add manure, too, for good measure. Your roots will thus get off to a good start. It is the early movement of the new roots pushing their way easily through nourishing soil that gives your plant vigorous growth.

If your plant comes bare root, that is, with all of the soil washed off as is the practice with most orchard trees, roses, etc., simply spread them out to their full length, shake the top soil over them as you fill in the hole, pack the soil snugly. Experienced gardeners have learned to face the scar union toward the east or

SCAR UNION

north away from the scorching afternoon sun, this to permit the scar to heal over completely and not be injured by sun burn.

If the plant comes in burlap, set it down in the hole, cut the strings, roll the covering back from the crown, working it very carefully halfway down the sides and leave it there. Fibrous roots have a way of pushing into the mesh and clinging — rough handling will break them off and cripple the plant. Finally, fill in with soil.

Out of burlap.

Should your plant come in a can, simply cut the opposite sides and pull them apart. You can lift out the plant with its cake of soil. Should it come in a tub or wooden box, set in the hole and carefully pry off and remove the staves or side boards. Always have the container close to the prepared place because, do what you will, the ball of dirt may break. If this happens, move the plant into the hole at once and proceed with restoring the soil around the roots. Set a plant one and one-half to two inches deeper than it was in the container.

HOW TO PLANT

The planting operation should close with a basin at ground level into which compost material may be piled, and water may be poured. Fill the basin three times with water. Let it seep down past the compost material each time; then fill it once again for me, and your plant will go singing on its way.

I remember long ago putting a big magnolia in the new garden of a retired judge. He said to me: "I'm not as young as you are, and I want a big tree." We got him a big tree. What a tree! It took a truck and six burly men. We didn't have the equipment that they used to improvise those glorious gardens at Treasure

Water settles soil snuggly around roots.

Island. The men pulled and tussled, pushed and grunted. The judge was there, so were his wife and son and, of course, so was I. Finally, the tree slid into place, and while we were all catching our breaths, the judge said: "Now, Mr. Wilson, will you lead us in a word of prayer." So, you see, putting roots into the soil is a serious matter, which gains success in proportion as it obeys the rules of Nature, under whose authority all gardens work.

The Opportune Task: Today (two weeks before Christmas) plant your daffodils. Select quality bulbs, set them six to seven inches deep, measuring from top of the bulb. They may also be planted in large pots. Set the bottom disc firmly into the soil. If possible select a special spot in the garden given over to the daffodils alone, this favors good practice in culture, and assures long life and encourages multiplication in the bulbs. Deep digging is best, bone meal down at the bottom of the hole is good. Daffodils need water, and heavy watering is recommended for them. After new growth has developed above ground, cultivate.

Setting out a young tree.

And now for a question that fits well our weekly schedule: How do you go about storing tuberous begonias for winter? These have been flowering all summer; by this time they have finished; some grew right out in the open garden; some in pots. If the former, go and stir your hand among them; if the stem sheds easily your bulb is ready to be dug up and stored. Remember you do not put any pressure on the stem when you feel it, you do not pull on it or jerk it, it must fall on its own account. If it does not drop down readily, the bulb is not yet ready.

STORE TUBEROUS BEGONIAS

After you have lifted the bulb out of the garden, carefully wash off the soil hanging loosely then let it get rid of all outside moisture. One way is to set it out in the sun and roll it over once in awhile so that the sun reaches all sides. But if rain should be falling then do not wash them, just set them in a flat, separated from its neighbor so that air may pass through freely. After several days of exposure to the sun and air and when one feels dry to you, then they are ready to be stored. You must make dead sure the bulb is dry be-

Note scar of bud union faces east or north away from the hot afternoon sun.

fore you place it in storage. If moisture persists, bulbs usually rot before winter is over. Now a rule in handling tuberous begonias is never to rub them at the time either of storage or of planting in the spring. I was talking recently to Mr. Wayne Sherwood, a specialist in tuberous begonias, and he said, "Once I experimented. In one group I rubbed off all the soil and scoured off the old roots, sun-dried them and stored them. In the second group I shook off the soil hanging loosely, sun-dried and then stored. In the spring the second group started off immediately after planting; new roots broke out where the old ones had dropped off naturally; but the first group which had been scoured so clean were painfully slow in getting a start and some gave up entirely. The point is, those little pin-head gnarls or swellings where the roots are attached should never be injured in the handling."

For the winter storage; place the bulbs in open flats and set these in an airy, well-ventilated, cool place. The garage is ideal; the heated basement is not so good, especially a basement where the temperature with heaters or hot water tanks can build up. The bulbs must have air circulation throughout the time they remain in storage and then, if they were properly dried off to begin with, they won't get mouldy. Bruises and cuts in the bulbs can be defended from further damage by powdered charcoal.

If your begonias have been growing in pots, place them on their sides for a few days in the sun to dry; then store them, pot, soil, and all, still lying on their sides in a cool dry place.

OAK ROOT FUNGUS

Oak root fungus is a disease in the soil and a problem in California. Many fruit trees and ornamentals succumb to it every year. The telltale is a cluster of mushrooms seen most often in the rainy season down at the trunk or stem of the victim plant. The fungus will work from the surface and follow down the roots to as much as nine feet. It works best in the root and with little moisture remains there. It works its way up to the crown and usually when the fungus reaches this vital spot the tree dies.

It is always wise to remove the dead tree, remove the stump, and dig out the roots too. The fungus does not live in the fine, fibrous roots. It is deadly in those roots of 2 inches and more in diameter.

When you inspect for oak root fungus you discover a characteristic musty odor is strongly evident. You see also the mycelium (a fancy name for the "roots" of the fungus) under the bark, growing on the wood as white hairs spread in a fan-like spread. The wood has taken on a reddish brown color in the host plant. In advanced cases the mycelium will have invaded the wood itself. Also outside the bark, the rootlike strands are black and can be seen. These are called rhizomorphs and they indeed help to spread the Armillaria fungus.

CONTROL

Though many chemicals have been applied in a desperate effort to control this disease, as of today there is no known control. The idea is to prevent the disease from getting in. For example native oaks like Quercus agrifolia, Coast Live Oak, and Q. lobata, Valley Oak, of California in summer prefer the ground above their roots on the dry side. Their roots like the warm summer soil; they don't want one drop of water from May till late September. Never establish a grass lawn, nor set out masses of water-thirsty rhododendrons, azaleas, fuchsias or hydrangeas anywhere near the roots of the native oak.

STORY

Albert Wilson bought a lot because of two magnificent oak trees growing there. They were the evergreen oak, Quercus agrifolia. Immediately he began their demise by chopping into their roots to establish a basement, and then by building a new house right over the root spread.

When the house was completed he established a glorious green lawn over the remaining injured roots. Finally in landscaping the new residence he set out dozens of water loving plants under the spread of the branches which hung low from the trees. All began in the spring of 1929, and by the end of the summer of 1958 the magnificent trees were dead and oak root fungus was running throughout the lawn!

SUBSTITUTE

That lawn area now has been given over to a mass planting of annuals, bulbs, and seasonal perennials. In other words the whole character of the garden has been changed. Even now mushroom outcrops of the Oak Root Fungus appear in that area where the oak trees used to stand. Though a few volunteer oak trees have grown (the same Quercus agrifolia) most of the shade loving plants, like the Japanese maple, rhododendron and azalea have died.

PLANT LIST

A list of plants both fruit and ornamental, known as moderately resistant to the Oak Root Fungus has been prepared. See your local dealer when making selections.

Chapter 55

QUESTIONS THE MAIL HAS BROUGHT US

Tuberous Begonias, Peat, Humus, Christmas Trees, Heather

(December: Third Week)

We answer questions. "In your discussion last week you made no mention about the practice of leaving tuberous begonias in the winter out in the garden right where they have been growing. Is this possible in the Bay region?"

To begin with, tuberous begonias are killed by freezing so ask yourself the question "Does my ground freeze to the depth of three inches?" Have you, for instance, ever found a frozen hydrant or a split faucet? In such a garden certainly tuberous begonia bulbs would freeze and rot to mush. This is what Mr. Wayne Sherwood has to say; "One early winter the rains came too fast. I had completed digging out only half of my bulbs. After the warm rain the air cleared, the ground froze up, my bulbs outside turned black, became slimy, and rot finished them off."

This makes it clear that where the ground can freeze you are taking a chance leaving tuberous begonias out during the winter. But listen to an account of the experience of Mrs. Breen of San Mateo. You remember the three-day snow spell in 1936. Mrs. Breen says, "We were caught with too much work and our tuberous begonias were left out in the frames. After the snow storm and cold spell my husband and I thought our bulbs were cooked and gone. Then in spring one day he came into the house all smiles and he said, 'You can't guess what I've learned this morning; our supposition about those tuberous begonia bulbs being killed last winter was wrong. The ground couldn't have frozen to any depth at all for every bulb is as firm and as hard as a board'." Later Mrs. Breen reports those bulbs sent up strong growth, put out wonderfully active roots, and there was no trouble at all, "Since that time," she says, "I have told others about our discovery and they have had similar success. But," she continued, "I top dress them after the fleshy growth has gone with rough oak leaves, the leathery ones that haven't yet rotted down; just crown each bulb lightly, never pile a lot of the rotted leaf mold over them because I have noticed ants love to nest in it." The question really is who can leave the bulbs out and who can't? Don't assume off hand you can or can't leave them out;know your garden and the weather is variable enough so there is a gamble involved.

Then it is possible, except in the very cold places, to leave tuberous begonia bulbs in the same place through the winter. But let us pursue the answer to our question further. Rains pack the soil and two winters can leave the soil firmly bound around bulbs. Begonia bulbs have to breathe and I believe no tuberous begonia should remain in the same spot more than one year; after that the ground needs to be worked over. When the gardener decides to move his bulbs, early winter is the ideal time to proceed. Permit the foliage to drop naturally and then lift the bulbs as we described last week.

SOIL And in the plot where the begonias had been grown, first scatter over the ground bone meal, make the soil look white, then spread out some fresh, green, cow manure, use plenty of it, spade it under, leave the ground rough all winter. Finish off the job with a dusting of soil sulphur to make the enemies gallop away! When in spring you spade up the soil you will find the green manure has disintegrated and in the spading will break up like peat.

PEAT Another question from Menlo Park is: "What good is peat in the garden; is it humus; is it fertilizer; what is the difference?" Peat is humus, it is not fertilizer. Humus is a conditioner enabling the soil to hold moisture and still have drainage; it permits free movement of air in the soil atmosphere; it also supplies plant food slowly with the aid of the micro-organisms. Fertilizer, on the other hand, supplies plant food immediately; manure, especially strawy cow manure, acts as both. Peat is a special kind of humus usually low in some of the essential elements. But the question now is, "What is peat?" Peat is organic matter which has accumulated and decomposed under water. It grows much thicker than ordinary humus because it is in basins and can't wash away. And in some parts of the world is one of the principal fuels and we want to remember coal is old peat that was buried and hardened.

What kinds are there? There are two on the market here. Our California peat from the Delta region near Stockton made of marsh vegetation including tule. It *KINDS* is fibrous and they put it through a shredding machine. And then there is the imported sold as Canadian and the European peats such as Holland, German, Danish and Swedish. What is the use of peat? Peat makes a nice medium for the roots of your plants to grow in. *USE* Mixed into the upper few inches of the soil or to the level of the feeding roots of shrubbery and herbaceous plants, peat makes a soil conditioner that works for your garden 24 hours of the day.

Why do we use peat instead of ordinary humus? You use it where you want to get or maintain an acid condition. For example, all summer you give your garden water from the tap. It tends to make your ground alkaline. On your acid lovers such as azaleas, rhododendrons, and camellias, you have to use a peat. Ordinary humus won't do it. And too, peat does a better and a more uniform job than ordinary humus in maintaining the right moisture condition, especially up at the surface where it is needed in the summer.

Where do you use the native? Native peat has something of an advantage to chop into the garden plot because it will stay in place. The imported is better for lawns as a top dress and when a new lawn is being planted. Both kinds are good for piling around the fibrous roots of the acid lovers, the begonia beds and so forth.

Always in the use of peat you do well to realize it serves as a governor in the soil. That is, in winter it will not permit the soil to become too wet, in summer it will not permit it to dry out. Peat moss after a rain storm, after you have given the garden a soaking with the sprinkler, will dry out; it does not remain soggy especially if proper drainage has been prepared in the beginning. Plant roots want a little warmth in winter — peat moss is warm. Nurserymen have learned this from bitter experience. To save costs they have covered potted plants with wood shavings. Later seeing their plants turn yellow and dying out when they investigated and picked up from the wood shavings the buried pot they found the pot was ice cold; many times the soil was soggy wet. But later, changing to peat moss the pots felt warm when they were lifted.

And then you remember Mr. Matthews' explanation why he used peat with his winter sweet peas. And still another point; such garden enemies as slugs and snails don't like peat because it sticks to their bodies and peat in the soil aids in their eradication. The nurseryman uses peat in still another way, for example in preparing a seed bed and mixing soil to be used for potting. *

CULTIVATE Now our third question, it is more of a statement than a question and I want to say that when I read it I found myself much interested. "I am still confused when in your talk you said to break up the soil at least 12 inches deep to let it aerate. On another radio program I heard 'be careful not to dig up the earth too much as you will destroy surface roots that your plants *DEEP* need and depend upon so heavily for their life'." Both of these statements have their place; the reader must be aware of the whole context in which each idea is given. For instance, deep spading and turning of the soil is the only procedure where deep-rooted perennials are to be placed in the ground — roses, for instance, or fruit trees. In such places only by the *LIGHT* preparation of the soil to at least the depth of 12 inches, though 18 to 24 inches is better, can those plants get off to a good start. But in the opposite case

*See Soils (A): September: Fourth Week.

we are dealing with established surface roots whose duty is to spread out and gather food from the local area. Such plants as fuchsias, azaleas, rhododendrons, and citrus trees all of which have delicate roots near the surface would suffer disastrously if a spade were roughly churned in among them. What the professionals do is to take an iron rake and give the area a heavy lugging. This breaks up the surface crust and permits the air a free passage. The raking is done carefully not too close to the trunks. You want to find out where the roots are for each of your plants; a good gardener always does this. It is clear then in one case we are preparing a seed bed for new roots to come; in the other case we are working over a plot where roots have already become established with feeders near the surface and which we must not injure with rough spading.

In this same letter is the following statement: "I have the gardener's bible, the Garden Encyclopedia, and it is worth its weight in military invasion money. And I have a lot of other books and government bulletins on gardens and I have attended Professor Butterfield's talks along with visits to the garden shows. But they still get me down when one says, 'bury all garden debris to create humus and keep the earth moist'; and his twin brother adds, 'rake up all garden debris and burn it to prevent it being hiding places for insects and whatnots to breed and multiply'." Here again both ideas have their place. Certainly you do not want an insect incubator, as we mentioned last week so when DON'T you rake up leaves and garden vermin, then burn them; do not pile these infested leaves in the compost. But clean, there is no better place for them than the compost pile, in a few months with proper attention they will turn into rich leaf mold. And in sandy soils the practice of putting vegetable parings and fleshy dead leaves under the ground is valuable, except potatoes which are known in some cases to carry eel-worm infection.

"And, oh yes," continues this letter, "when I bought this property seven years ago I began digging to plant my purchases and hit pieces of buried tin cans, iron, broken bottles, wire and rocks that had been buried in backyards since Pompeii fell because householders preceding me were too stingy to have them hauled off in the garbage. So I threw up my hands and my wife (oh, he couldn't have meant that) and I got out the old pick and shovel and a good Japanese friend built me a screen and we went around the yard — 3 feet deep and 4 feet wide along the fences and spaded it all up and screened out all the debris and had it hauled off. That left me with a sandy soil that would have settled down into the clay solidly had I not had 4 loads of horse manure and 200 pounds of peat moss hauled in and in addition brought in chemical fertilizers (commercial) and mixed them in and began burying garden debris for compost. Now the famous park superintendent, Mr. Miller, was called in; he ran his hands through my earth and leaned back with a glow in his eyes and said, 'What beautiful soil, what beautiful soil.' First time I ever heard soil called beautiful but he ought to know. So now things grow so fast I have enough for me and plenty for the pests, too. Gardening — ah, what fun!" he wrote. I should say our correspondent acted with admirable intelligence, energy and cheerfulness. He has the spirit of gardening. If he had been back in the time of King Arthur, Guinevere would have taken after him for you remember she said, "The man I love must have a touch of the earth." And now our next question.

CHRISTMAS TREE

"I wish you could tell us about Christmas trees." In answering this question let's go back to what I said a year ago. Many of us will want a living tree this Christmas. What kind of tree is best to pick out? How should it be cared for in the house? The tree must serve not only for Christmas week but for a lifetime afterward. It may look beautiful in your house but that's not all. It must look beautiful in your garden too — it must become part of the design there.

BAD

Some trees grow too big or too tall. The Indian cedar, for example, makes a very pretty sapling; in a small garden such as most of us have, it can become with its floor sweeping branches a monster swallowing up a great circle of your delicate path, borders, and flower beds. I saw one once that tried to push away the house! Another one, the Norway spruce, shoots up so fast that it may out balance everything else, ruining scale and proportion. And even the Douglas fir, the fragrant, deep green, aromatic Christmas tree, mounts into the sky and makes so much shadow that the only cure oftentimes, is the axe at the root. On the other hand, the silver-coated Atlas cedar, also a pretty sapling loses its branches breaking out irregularly so you may have to wait a decade before it becomes a garden ornament.

What had we better use then? The Sierra form of Sequoia is right for both house and garden. Its branches move up well above the ground; it is more compact than the coast form and it won't get to be a giant. And some other trees which have been little used for the purpose are right also: the Spanish fir, Nordmann's fir, Indian spruce, and the white fir of our own California mountains. These and the Sequoia have a natural pyramidal habit, spiring upward like picture-book trees. *GOOD*

Having selected our living tree, how shall we care for it while it is in the house? The easiest thing in the world is to kill a pet with kindness. The nurserymen who sell these trees have been so nagged with complaints the following spring that the beautiful tree is no good, that they have begun to issue directions, the import of which, though not the precise language, is as follows:

Remember that his poor young tree has never been in a house before, has never worn strings of hot electric lights, has never stood three feet from an open fire that throws sparks, and has never had its roots bound up and pushed down in sawdust or peat moss getting drier every hour in the draft of arid furnace air. And none of its ancestors have ever experienced even one of these things. Have a heart! First: plant the tree in the garden the very day you get it, if you can only let your love of a young plant get the best of you. But if you can't, no great harm will be done if *CARE*

DON'T you: Second: do not tie up the ball of roots in colored paper and forget it but set it in a big saucepan and keep it moist all the time. If you haven't persistence enough to attend to it yourself describe to young William the horrible stunted fate of saplings that have gone dry and give him a rich reward to keep it wet enough so it feels moist morning, noon and night on the outside. You don't want those delicate fibrous roots to curl and break off. You don't want that tree to stand still for a whole season and put out only a feeble tentative sprig of new growth. Third: Turn off the lights every little while — let the tree cool lest you cook its tender new shoots. Fourth: Keep it from a draft which will act on it like a desert wind, and Fifth: Above all, keep it away from the open fire and from what is no less dangerous, the cigarettes and cigars; get fire-proof ornaments if you can for even live leaves will burn. In short, while you are about it, do not go and kill off your living Christmas tree or burn up your house. Sixth: Plant it the next day after Christmas. If you are taking very good care, keep it indoors a week if you want to but that's enough for you and the tree both.

The Opportune Task: Give peat to your acid-loving plants; also young pine trees, the firs and spruces, redwoods, sequoias and cypress trees. Coniferous trees, those that produce cones, love peat; now mix half peat and half manure. And you with the roof gardens and potted plants, for those little cedars and Japanese cypress, give them a top dressing too. An easy way to handle peat from the bale or sack is to wet it down lightly a day or so before you use it. This takes the dust away. Heathers hate manure, but dearly love peat, your choice holly tree with peat will do better.

Get acquainted with alfalfa leaf meal; feed stores handle it. Gardeners dust it around the hole and work it in the soil when setting out new bare root roses, fruit trees, citrus trees, peonies, and ornamentals of all kinds. Alfalfa leaf meal coming from a legume is rich in nitrogen, the presence of which stimulates good plant growth.

Chapter 56

NEW GROUPINGS FOR THE OLD GARDENS

(December: Fourth Week)

You may be starting, not with a clean piece of ground, but with an old garden which you intend to make over. First, before you do anything, let me counsel you to take a long, thoughtful look at it. What do you see there? and what do you want it to become? Perhaps you are not used to replanning; most of us are not. You will need all the more time and caution then. Get a professional to help you, if you have to; but remember — nothing will take the place of your own individual interest and attention. If you don't know what you want, you will not get what you like.

Supposing that your old garden, as old gardens usually are, is something of a riot. The house is staggering under vines which run in waves over roof and chimney, but leave the corners bare. The lawn is more leaves and mud than grass because a stalwart old native oak reinforced by three sycamores have kept it in deep gloom. Moreover, these trees are merely the advance guard of an encroaching forest; from outside the lawn, the shrubs, trees and weeds, long unattended, have grown into a jungle.

STUDY A PLAN

The first impulse is to clean everything up, but a far better impulse is to carve out a pre-view as far into the future as possible of what the garden can be made to look like, and what you want it to look like.

Looking a long way ahead, then, what can you see? Let me answer in imagination for you. Let me suppose, for example, that you visualize your garden as an extension of the house — that one belongs to the other — one is to be viewed from the other — and one, in a sense, balances the other. You may then propose to bind the two together by means of a strong shrub border which encloses both. Enlivened and anchored here and there by a tree, this would move around the place like the shore line of a lake, not in straight lines, let us say — though that is not impossible — but swinging gracefully in and out. The bays could be given over to flowers for color, and the lawn inside could be like a mirror on which the shadows play.

But how can the house with its sharp angles and vertical walls be imagined to fit harmoniously into such curved spaces? You can imagine its mechanical lines subdued by planting — its corners by tall shrubs or trees; its foundation by low shrubs. What you need is judicious camouflage. This is not out of the question; an army expert promises to hide my house so I can hardly find it myslef. Of course, all that is wanted is enough to make the house merge into the garden rather than stand up harshly in the midst of it.

Having come this far with the idea of what you want, you can begin to figure which of the old plants you wish to clear away and which to retain. First take out the weed and rubbish. You can now see more clearly what you have and can look ahead with more assurance. But certain features, standing out, will plead for your interest and attention. Long since some one "with a robin's nest in her hair" has romantically trained a Lady Banks climbing rose up the oak tree, or a green English Ivy. These climbers, beautiful in themselves, are as appropriate here as a silver slipper on a fireman. They belong to the category of exotic foliage, loud blooms, and striking fruits foisted on a plant whose charm is its deep fissured bark, its massive head and its quiet strength. Besides they injure the tree. Their use is nothing less than an insult to Nature. Hack them away.

It appears, moreover, that the romantic planter has been at work in other places too. For here, there and everywhere we can see what is called spot gardening — one weigela by itself, one or two honeysuckles, one lilac. We can reconstruct just what happened: the dear lady of the robin's nest — if it wasn't the dear man — found these plants at the nursery and was suddenly without warning or preparation, inspired to buy and plant. If such garden impulses have landed these plants where they will prosper, it is indeed a miracle, and you can be certain they will do nothing for the garden as a design except to stand in the way of more significant planting. The features of a garden, like the pictures on the wall of your living room, must be big enough and good enough to see. Nature, a gardener with one hundred million years of successful experience, rarely works with single specimens. She groups her plants: a little grove here, a winding tree-choked gully there, a broken margin — we can't improve on that, try as we may, and we don't even want to. Let us aspire to seven lilacs, three weigelas. This goes especially for the flowers — three dozen delphiniums in a group, or a mass of petunias sweeping the carpet, will tell a finer story. And we might go so far, if we have the room, as to plan for five pines standing off in a clump all by themselves. A key or sentiment plant, if it has meaning, will not of course be forbidden, nor will a corner for specialties and blooms. But the plan's the thing, and the spotty erratics cannot, by any chance, be expected to fit into it. Destroy them or move them. PLAN

Now you can see still better, for there immediately before the house, is quite evidently a space inviting what we are pleased to call outdoor living. Shall we build a little platform of brick between house and lawn? Can we imagine ourselves established there, basking in the grateful rays of the green grass, shrub, sunlight, shadow and flowers? But what of that fine old tree there? We must decide: can the lawn go somewhere else? Or is the shade too much for the house, lawn or no lawn? Or can the tree be thinned both for house and lawn? It is a matter of reconciling attractively the several competing desires. Any successful re-planning of an old garden requires precisely that. But a fine old tree deserves a dozen trial plans before it is condemned — it deserves something equivalent to trial by jury, and if no way can be found, call in a professional. If he loves trees as he should, he may find a way where you cannot.

Let us say that you keep the tree. Now you begin to build, in your mind's eye, about the tree and the house as complementary centers of interest linked by the lawn. But you find other big old plants, too, an olive or a cedar, and some sycamores for example. If they are in the right places — as at the far edge where you can use them as a backdrop, they may be retained. But if they merely wander about unreasonably, appropriating space, blighting and possessing the very ground which you hope to enjoy, they or some of them, must go. The garden isn't a forest, you know; it needs sunlight. And it can't afford to have too many commanding features, or it won't have any.

But now, if this old garden is like most of them we shall realize that it has always had too many features — too many centers of interest, large and small. For example, blooms to cut for decorating the house indoors were provided in straight line flower beds which slash across your design. If you want such beds move them to one side or corner where they belong. You are planning, not a nursery, but a garden. If you want straight lines, which are proper enough in their place, fit everything to them — do not let them throw themselves down in the midst of something else quite different.

The centers of interest to begin with were developed at various places independently of each other and too often with reference to one aspect or one season only. Some one covered the underpinning of the house with little creeping figs, climbing roses, wisteria or Boston ivy. Now ten years have gone by and these have become not proper camouflage or softening of lines but giants more powerful than the house itself. Their shoots or tendrils fasten into crannies, hold to woodwork, stucco, and glass, and wind around pillars. This is twenty times too much and requires either drastic pruning or a new start. The climbers on the house must be under strict discipline, lest they become parasites and kill off the charm of changing shadows. And to discourage mildew, bugs, and scaly bark, the roses at least should go up a trellis, out from the house wall, where the wind and air can reach them from all sides.

There will be shrubs of course in the old garden. Some will have out-lived their prime. Some may be remarkable plants; you will keep them only if they have not grown too tall and bulging and if they lie in good relation to the borders and anchors which you wish to establish.

I have had to spend so much of this time on the idea of design and on clearing out old material, that no time is left for an equal treatment of what to plant. But that is the problem of any garden, old or new. For planning you need restraint more than anything. The old favorites of your locality are best. What thrives in San Francisco may not do at all in Menlo Park where I live, because down there we have more frost in winter and less moisture in summer. Well conducted gardens become little bits of Nature; they include the native plants which like the climate or imported ones which by experience, have been found to like it. Unless you wish to spend your time protecting them against the very weather that makes a natural garden prosper, be certain that you are putting in plants that will feel at home. L'Abbe de Litte of the eighteenth century had some good advice for us, if only we carry it out. He said don't insult Nature absurdly with expense; keep her simple charms. I especially like the good Abbe where he suggests that we can't buy our garden paradise with money alone. I know a gardener who has created the most beautiful effects in frowsy gardens, not by putting in new plants, but merely by taking out old ones.

The Opportune Task: Each day this week, view your garden.

Note: In various chapters, for the convenience of the reader I have used trade names of products rather than truly scientific identifications. No favoritism nor criticism is intended when other similar products are not mentioned. It is impossible to list all. We deal in principles.

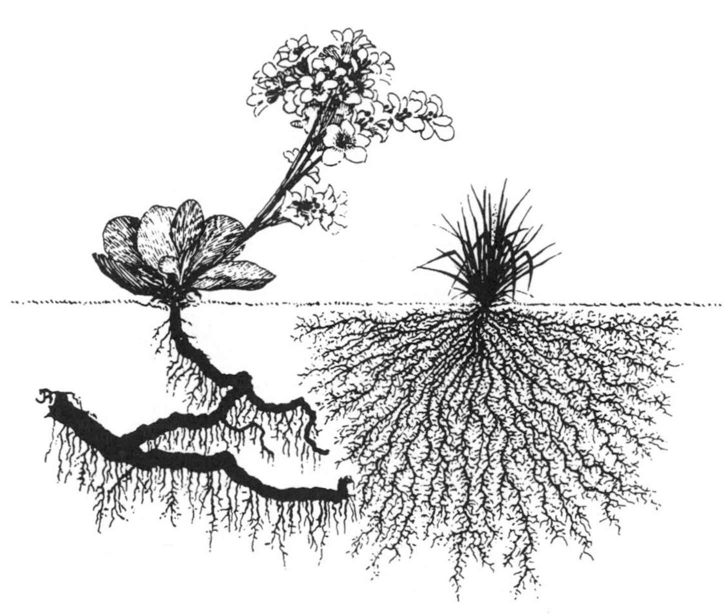

IT IS THE PERIOD BETWEEN DRINKS ROOTS LIKE BEST

Not watering daily; no! But a thorough watering with every iota of soil completely saturated. Then leave alone. As the water is taken up by the roots, and used by the plants, air will get down into the soil. Carbon dioxide will be exchanged for oxygen. A healthy plant wants air at its roots between the drinks!

GARLIC

The onion family provides vegetables that give health, and garlic registers high. Garlic grows best under full sunshine. SOIL: all soils for garlic and onions too must be rich in compost. Working soil use water soluable Diazinon turn into soil; after planting also spray lightly again to rid plot of maggots. PLANTING: small cloves of "California" white, red and yellow, etc. 2" apart; push down small clove, disc in the soil, but tip of clove barely covered. Cloves of Elephant garlic 4-5" apart, clove 3" deep, especially in gardens of cold winter areas, i.e. North Sacramento Valley. WATER: during growing period and since bulbs size up between Feb-June soil must be kept moist; no flooding, OVERHEAD watering best in which the leaves catch water and spirals it down the stem right to the developing bulb. FERTILIZER: Trace elements (TMI)* should be worked into soil prior to planting; fertilizer and soil sulphur also is introduced during soil preparation. Cut blossom pod soon after it appears. STOP WATERING in June; 30 days later (July 4th) HARVEST: when tops begin to dry and bend towards the ground. Dig; remove all earth by rubbing off the first coat of skin; this leaves the Garlic white with natures protective shield, conditioned for preserving. Braid or tie; hang in shady breezeway; the bulbs get rid of natural moisture. PROPAGATION: while soil is still warm is Sept--October plant largest cloves; consult Farmers Almanac for root planting times.

* TMI Trace minerals; Trace elements bring good growth, flavor, and aid toward long-term storing. Farmers are realizing that without these trace elements they have only a marginal crop vs. one of quality.

City Garden

"This blessed spot, this earth, this realm . . ."

YOU CAN'T HAMMER THEM IN!

Dig deep, loosen the soil, add compost, mix everything thoroughly, and prepare a "bed" for the existing roots and the new feathery ones to come.

Chapter 57

ORGANIC GARDENING

(January to December)

Let's use the scientific meaning as we develop our ideas on this subject. We are not going to make a religion of organic gardening. In all this there are two sides; and we search the truth.

We can believe those who reach conclusions through scientific work—they have made experiments. It is not easy to KNOW a principle unless we work on it; we must pry into the problems; we all know things just don't happen. Actually what has been experimented in, what has come out of that experiment, provides us a foundation that is positive and not one that comes from "I think it should be; or I think it is", said with a religious fervor.

Feeding the peoples of the world has been a problem everywhere on this globe. Mexico didn't have enough corn; China, India not enough rice. Improvements have been achieved in Mexico, in Pakistan also. They have used plant food to improve the raising of crops. Now Mexico produces enough corn to feed its people and to export its surplus to India. The rice of the United States is different from the rice of Japan.

What kind of fertilizer achieved this? Inorganic. Is that going to have a bad effect? Do you suspect inorganic fertilizer is ruining the soil? Watch your step as you try to answer that question. Go slow, and we might find out something to help us all.

I do not have the aim of prejudicing you against inorganics in this chapter. One thing we know: everything we've got is organic. Is organic gardening hostile to science? Let us get to the known facts; let's challenge everything. Let us take note that the Chinese who have for centuries been recycling their organic wastes instead of throwing them into the sea, still continue to feed their people.

Under the satiny sand on the dunes of San Francisco our family worked all the potato peelings, cabbage leaves, carrot scrapings; in fact everything from the kitchen. Only tins, wire and bottles were taken away. As our garden prospered the sand turned from gold to dark brown, and supported plants of many varieties including vegetables and flowers.

ORGANIC GARDENING

Down the street from us lived on old lady who often passed our house with a scuttle and shovel. She gathered the droppings from the passing horses. And of course all went into her garden also on the dunes.

Years later in another district of our city I met a woman who lived on a hill. She had established her garden on rock, solid rock. Street sweepers by invitation poured their gathering from their horse drawn wagons over that rock. Certainly when I visited this woman she had a wonderful garden. The roots began in the organic material, and reached the rock which provided excellent anchorage.

When I became a student at Stanford, in the wonderful Santa Clara Valley, my professor, James McMurphy, maintained what he called the experimental garden. Early in our course he introduced the botany students to the compost pile. In fact he had three. The new or rough pile made up of freshly pruned rubbish, twigs, green grass and leaves that had fallen from both trees and shrubs. Next to this, was one he called "the working compost". "Push your hands in there", he told us students. It was warm. "You understand the bacteria are working; they are helping, and those leaves break down". Of course the compost contained old remains of plant life. However the color no longer was green but dark brown. More than that there was an odor arising which the professor called "earthy". Everything here was breaking down, and there was a little moisture evident. Our professor would have us students grab shovels and forks, and turn this working pile. We took a new place, and threw down first the top section of the pile and continued to turn till the whole had been moved. This we did several times; we discovered more and more worms, and we found each time more of the material had broken down showing good decomposition. Finally the last pile was completely black, on the dry side now, and the product was called "leaf mold soil". It was ready for use, and those earthworms ready helpers.

COMPOST

This was compost. It was more black than brown, the particles were tiny, not stringy, nor packed, nor ill-smelling either. We wheelbarrowed it around the experimental garden; spread it under trees on which our professor had budded several types of fruit. We scattered the compost under the fruit-bearing shrubs like the guava and the raspberry. Also we used lots of our compost for strawberries, vegetables and certain flowers which we always set out to study the various virus diseases.

What Professor McMurphy did for his students, nature has been doing over the ages. In every forest, under every tree, evergreens such as the California redwood, deciduous such as the Eastern oaks, and under shrubs and vines of every description leaves to the depth of several inches are found. More than that when spring bulbs complete the cycle their leaves lie down, dry up and yield to the earth the basic elements they used when growing.

If we tramp the forest floor, our feet crush the dried leaves. The floor is spongy to our step. If we take time, scuff and brush away the fallen leaves we find the soil crumbly. That forest soil maintains itself, and the gardener will maintain his soil too if he annually works organic materials back into the ground. The idea is to hold a steady state of loose, airy unpacked soil.

Fallen leaves bring down to the earth organic matter, and all organic matter invites friendly bacteria which have the power of taking from the air oxygen and making it available to roots. Organic materials help maintain good soil structure. There always is a good soil atmosphere when the soil structure is good. Just as the forest soil is never packed because of the annual autumn fall of leaves, so the gardener's incorporating materials from his compost creates and maintains a proper home for roots.

Those fallen leaves cost the forest nothing, and so compost spread under your plant will provide a rich, inexpensive addition to the garden's well being.

WHAT COMPOST DOES

Any type of soil can be improved by compost materials. Organic matter will loosen up heavy soil

- will let the water get into the soil easily
- will decrease the tendency to form concrete-like clods
- will act like a sponge in sandy soil and allow less water to leak through and get lost
- will cause the particles of soil to hang together, and to capture and hold whatever plant food it contains.

Organic matter is colloidal holding water in itself. Clay soil is also colloidal, it is heavy, and is very much packed. Then it holds water and the water stays cold. Water heats up much slower than soil; it takes many days to warm up. And plants growing in cold, wet soil just sit there, for roots to move out, for they need a certain amount of warmth.

Organic matter in the form of manures will do much to improve cold, stiff clay soil. The manure is ideal to change the complexion of any soil. Manure is food for the soil. It changes the character and of course results in better root action. The strawy manures hold moisture and in light soils can aid in keeping the earth from blowing away.

Fish fertilizer is of course organic too. It may contain as much as 10% nitrogen, 10% phosphate, and only a trace of potash. In contrast the barnyard, strawy manures will furnish 2% nitrogen, 1% phosphate, and 2% potash. Fish fertilizer is definitely food for the plant. We give it to growing azaleas, fuchsias, pelargoniums, roses and all the perennials. It is best applied in liquid form.

COMPOST AND PLANT IN THE CONTAINER

We have been stressing use of organic matter out in the garden but what about its use for the container plant. Fill the top area of the container with compost—even two or three inches deep can be recommended. The presence of the organic matter enables the roots in the container to breathe better, and to take up available moisture readily. This arrangement continues throughout the year when a blanket of compost has been provided. Compost creates and maintains a proper soil fertility.

A container plant rich in organic matter is too moist to make a good home for pests like ants. They never establish nests in such a container. Nor do grubs of certain pests. In other words moisture at the root zone is good for roots' life, but not for insect life.

ASHES FOR THE GARDEN

If a forest fire runs over the ground the humus burns up. All that remains is the ash, and we call it the inorganic or mineral matter. Ashes from hard wood like oak, or eucalyptus, and hard cherry wood are good for the soil. Ashes from newspapers and pine trees are not so good. The good ashes contain charcoal (a soil sweetener) and a percentage of potash in a useful form. Since in dry California the soil is rich in potash, the use of ashes in the garden is not urgent. In rainy districts, however, potash is less abundant, and wood ashes can be used to advantage.

We all know San Francisco's Golden Gate Park; it was started in 1870. The gardeners there piled on, and worked into the sand, all the street sweepings, strawy horse manure, they could get. In those days that was all they had to improve those dunes. If however today they were to establish a new park, I imagine they would use a whole lot of chemistry.

And looking to the future: for us in this country, as in Japan, China, Germany, Holland and England, intensive agriculture will be a necessity. The farmers can control their output, that is they can put in certain things and get certain results. If they went in for all organic, then they would have a big job excluding various pests such as bad fungus.

HYDROPONICS

Hydroponics is a method of extreme control in the growing of crop plants. More and more new answers are being reached. The time will come when the results will be a harvest twice as great as it is today. This, of course, is no reason for any of us to throw away organic materials now. They have value, great value. Remember we are coming to the period of recycling everything. In organic gardening we must recall what Mrs. Emerson of New England said when her husband gave up the ministry and began his writing career: "Use it up, wear it out, make it do."

ORGANIC COMPOST AND GOOD GARDENING

SUMMARY

As gardeners we work in the authority of Nature, we work with her materials. We have five co-workers:

1. SOIL is the first of these. With certain adjustments we can find soil for most plants in the home garden. A deep, loamy soil permits good root development and lush green growth above ground. A shallow soil grows dwarfs. Soil is as deep as roots in it can penetrate, and properly spaded soil enables the roots to travel far. The gardener must know his soil, must know when to dig it, when to leave it alone, when and when not to weed it. If it is adobe, clay, or inclined to be heavy, he will not work it wet, for it will turn to putty, and not a root will grow. Where planting is to be done, prepare the soil thoroughly, and loosely, for plants cannot be hammered into the soil.
2. HUMUS is our second co-worker: (Rotting oak leaves, compost materials, grass cuttings, vegetative materials returning to the soil make up humus). Humus is the guardian and guarantor of soil fertility; it is the prime agent of soil production. The ideal form, decaying organic matter, contributes much to plant welfare. For example, as it breaks down, it releases and contributes its quantity of the essential elements; (there are 13+). Further, it holds moisture and provides tiny paths for water through the soil. Humus feeds the useful bacteria and creates happy homes for mould, fungi, and earthworms, all agents for healthy plant growth. A free use of humus must be made every time there is planting to be done. Generous amounts of leaf mold, compost and straw should be worked into the soil. Peat breaks up adobe, oak leaves loosen any soil. What the gardener strives for is a fluffy soil; one that literally foams through the fingers at planting time. Roots newly planted will then penetrate far and the plant becomes established in vigour. Sand is no substitute for humus. Sand, remember, makes cement, and no root grows in cement. The wise gardener will spread humus as the mason spreads his plaster. Humus is the greatest friend of good gardening.
3. WATER is our third helper. Water carries to the

root ALL of its food, it must always be available. Water must move continuously on to the soil and move away, for plants demand drainage. Gardeners must learn both to turn on the faucet and turn it off. Water reaching the deepest roots encourages vigorous growth. Gardeners build basins around their older plants and, through them, direct the water to the roots. For annuals and perennials a misty spray imitating the rain is a more kindly method of getting the water to the roots. The desert offers its plants unmerciful competition for water; be sure you do not offer your garden plants such an existence. Water must be in proportion to other essentials. Too much makes a soggy soil, soggy soil is sour and cold, and in it roots soon die. Too much will displace the air, and every root must have air. "Air is Lord," said Hippocrates, and this goes for roots as well as for lungs.

4. CULTIVATION is the fourth helper. Cultivation enables air to reach the roots, it prevents water-logging. Gases such as carbon dioxide must be liberated from the soil and oxygen must become a part of the soil atmosphere. Some of the world's greatest gardeners maintain soil fertility primarily by cultivation and the free use of organic materials. The sun's baking the year before stores food in the soil, but the use of the hoe, well and deep, brings out of the earth the stored food of last year's sunshine. Cultivation maintains a loose soil, it checks any tendency toward cement-like hardness.
5. FERTILIZER is our fifth helper. Dairy fertilizer is the best for our plants. It provides food for the soil and food for the plant roots. It brings into the soil, if in sufficient quantity, an enriched humus bulk. When applied 3 to 6 inches deep it will loosen the soil and enrich the moisture at the root zone. Chemical fertilizer is used additionally, applied during the season of vigorous growth and often in liquid form. Proper use requires thorough study. Chemical fertilizer may complement the organic manures, but they must never replace

them. But manure will never do its best without the help of either LIME or gypsum. There is an old adage, "It is a poor farmer who uses manure but no lime". Lime is the governor of the soil, and all gardeners must awake to its place in nature's scheme. It is not a fertilizer—it merely conditions the soil for the dress of manure. Generally an application spread on the dry ground once in 3 years will do the trick. Manure should follow the lime; it must never be placed on the ground with it (see index: soil, sulphur).

CAUTION

Under most California soil, there predominates a limy subsoil. Additional top dress of lime could result in too much lime. In alkaline soils and hard water areas, gypsum or bone meal is called for.

KIWI

KIWI vines both male and female grow in most gardens. SOIL: kiwi roots adjust to many soils; provide loose and pliable soil when planting the vines. Raw bone meal, compost even a coffee can of TMI (trace minerals) goes well in the bottom of a 30 inch hole. Annually in winter provide a compost TOPDRESS of strawy manure – important to the fibrous roots. Roots should be planted on a slight mound.

WATER

Water: kiwi roots love water. This vigorous vine must not be denied moisture. Water is imperative to check leaf sunburn in summer. (Overhead sprinkling for two hours in the afternoon is practiced by successful commercial growers.)

Vine TRAINING must be practiced attentatively; do this in early hours of the morning for in afternoon hours canes will snap. BLOOMS appear on the laterals; female blooms are white, male blooms cream colored. Bees accomplish pollination. Female vines carry FRUIT egg-shaped 2½–3½" long a fuzz brown, harvest best vine ripened; flesh greenish, delicious, fill with black seeds. PRUNING: these vigorous vines must be pruned each year. Prune laterals back to two buds; prune early as kiwi vines like grapes tend to bleed if pruned in late spring. ENEMIES: hot winds result in leaf burn on new growth in summer.

CHAPTER 58

PESTICIDES

To maintain a clean garden we want to know the insect who creates the damage. That is, how does he eat? Does he suck up his food, or does he chew it? (See Chapter 6: GARDEN ENEMIES, and Chapter 37: SUMMER INSECTS).

INSECTS COMPETE

From the first fly bite or bee sting every one of us has swatted to kill the enemy. And as we have grown older we have become aware that insects compete with us for the plants of our garden both among the fruits and vegetables. They also attack our flowers and leave many ragged losses in our garden beauty.

PLANT PATHOLOGY

When I was a student studying plant pathology and the life histories of insects, I learned of the simple chemicals which we called upon to control them. Included were lead, lime and sulphur, arsenic, mercury and bromides. Now these have been augmented by several complex, synthetic, organic chemical compounds. They come in a wide variety of basic chemical structures: chlorinated hydrocarbons, organic phosphorus, carbamates, and some whose chemical identity is not fully known. They are recommended for a multitude of uses, ranging from highly specific to broad spectrums. Examples: control of mosquito, the defence of forest trees against insects, and certain weed control along the railroads and highways. Some of these chemicals decompose or dissipate rapidly. Others are persistent.

The chlorinated hydrocarbons are the most widely used and persistent. Residues of dieldrin, lindane and heptachlor follow in order of use frequency. Minute quantities of DDT now are so widely distributed in the environment that it is impractical to prevent exposure of our dairy animals and ourselves to this chemical.

Pesticides do not stay put. They drift through the air, and are contained in the dust. They dissolve and become suspended in the water systems of the world. We are increasingly warned to exercise caution and to maintain control.

Thus, within the recent past we have suddenly waked up to the fact that several of our new, brilliantly effective pesticides have bad effects which cannot be tolerated. The very lasting quality of DDT which cleared out malaria from long-suffering Sardinia, has been found to poison the soil of the gardens and endanger the health of the gardener himself.

The experts are busy in many parts of the world determining what we should do now. Already they have told us not to use DDT, Arsenate of Lead, Mercury compounds and many others.

PROS AND CONS

Experience is bound to yield pros and cons for certain pesticides. The dangerous pesticides have gone through an interesting cycle: thorough testing, government approval, instructions recommending caution, memorandums calling for certain restrictive measures, final removal from the market. We suddenly hear that a highly effective insecticide is highly hazardous, and we even can't buy it any more. Scientists have shown that the carbamates, the arsenics, the chlorinated hydrocarbons used in soil to control infection one year remain, even migrate to a new crop, the following year! Research by government and university will continue and reports will be issued. I recommend that each of us remain students, search the literature, especially all current folders put out by the various government authorities. I further recommend gardeners get help from qualified nurserymen in the home area, seek advice from the Agricultural Commissioner or County Agent, and from the University of California Agricultural Extension Services in the County. Addresses can be found listed in the phone book. Finally there is the U.S. Dept. of Agriculture, Washington D.C. 20250, which publishes regular bulletins.

LETS REMAIN STUDENTS

KEEP ABREAST OF THE CURRENT INFORMATION. Changes will always come up, for experience will yield pros and cons for certain select pesticides.

DO NOT USE	USE INSTEAD
DDT, Dieldrin	Sevin
DDD, Aldrin	Diazinon
DD; 2, 4-D; 2, 4, 5-D	Methoxychlor
Arsenate of Lead	Malathion
Lindane, Systox	Oils
Chlordane	Oils and Soaps
Multi-purpose that include the above	Water Spray
	Rotenone, Pyrethrum
Mercury compounds	Lime-Sulphur
Thiodan	Nicotine sulfate
Toxaphane	Dibrom

Always follow with sharp attention the instructions on the container.

LAWN-FUNGUS	ADVISED 1972*
Brown Patch	Dyrene, Fore, PCNB†
Dollar Spot	Acti-dione-thiram, Fore, Daconil 2787, Dyrene, Ortho Lawn & Turf fungicide
Fairy Rings‡	Methyl Bromide
Mushrooms	Captan
Rust	Acti-dione-thiram Daconil 2787, Zineb
Snow Mold	First wash with force of water, then dust with sulphur
Other problems	Seek advice as mentioned

Disease can appear throughout the growing season. Pour double or triple strength concentrate of Captan into 1-inch holes punched 4 to 6 inches deep and 6 to 8 inches apart both inside and outside the affected area. Alternative method: fumigate infected area with methyl bromide; reseed or resod.

* Look for changes
† PCNB: pentachloronitrobenzene
‡ Also add: Marasmius, Psalliota campestris, Lepiota

CONTROLS FOR INSECT ENEMIES

INSECTS THAT SUCK UP FOOD	ADVISED 1972*
Aphids: many types, including pear root, tulip root, woolly apple, etc.	Malathion 50% emulsive, Diazinon
Leafhopper	Malathion, Meta-Systox Sevin 50% WP†
Mealy bugs	Petroleum Oils, Malathion 50% or 57% emulsive, Meta-Systox
Root Mealy bugs	
Mites (see Spider mites)	
Psylla, pear, and pear-leaf blister mite	Sevin 50% WP
Scale	Petroleum oils, Malathion
Spider Mites, Red Spider	Kelthane 18½ emulsive, Summer oil emulsion, or Malathion 50% emulsive
Spittle bugs	Methoxychlor 50% WP
Thrips	Diazinon, Malathion 25% WP
Whiteflies	Malathion 50% emulsive, Meta-Systox
Ants protect and move about insects with sucking mouthparts	(See below)
INSECTS THAT CHEW FOOD	
Ants	Malathion
Beetles	Diazinon, Sevin, some oil
Borers	Methoxychlor 50% WP
Brachyrhinus	Diazinon
Caterpillars	Rotenone, Pyrethrum, Sevin, Methoxychlor, Diazinon

* Look for changes
† WP: wettable powder

Codling moth: see Larvae	
Diabrotica	Diazinon, Methoxychlor
Earwigs	Sodium fluosilicate, Sevin
Grasshoppers	Diazinon, Sevin, Malathion
Grubs: chew at roots, i.e. camellia, rhododendron, lawn, etc.	Sevin, Diazinon
Husk Fly: see Maggots	
Larvae: horntail, oak moth, attacking roots, or at ground level	Sevin, Diazinon
Maggots	Sevin, Diazinon
Millipedes	Malathion, Diazinon, Sevin
Nematode-worm or Eel-worm	Soil Fumigants
Orangeworms (Orange dogs)	Sevin 5% dust
Slugs (on cherry trees)	Sevin 50% WP*
Slugs and Snails, Sowbugs, Pillbugs	Metaldehyde, Sevin, Baits
Walnut Husk Fly (the maggots of)	Malathion
Weevils	Diazinon

FUNGUS DISEASES

HOST PLANTS	CONTROL: ADVISED 1972†
Almond: brown rot, shot-hole disease	Fixed copper, Captan 50% WP
Apple: scabby fruits, powdery mildew, fire-blight (Pear blight)	Captan 50% WP, fixed copper, lime-sulfur liquid
Apricot: brown rot	Captan 50% WP, fixed copper spray
Bush-Berries: leaf and cane spot, yellow rust	Zineb 75% WP, fixed copper spray
Peach, Nectarine: peach blight, leaf curl, mildew brown rot	Ferbum 76% WP, Ziram, fixed copper spray, Orthorix

* WP: wettable powder

† Look for changes

Plum, Prune: brown rot	Captan 50% WP
Walnut: walnut blight	Fixed copper spray
Grapes: powdery mildew	Dusting sulfur
Ornamentals(roses, shrubs, flowering trees, etc: many attacked by similar disease)	Controls suited to type of disease and kind of plant
Miscellaneous diseases	For the unknown seek advice from qualified nurseryman

PRINCIPLES IN CONTROL MANAGEMENT

LIST ONE—Deciduous Fruit Trees for Fungus: Peaches (flowering forms also), nectarine, apricots. Fungus enemies such as leaf curl, shot hole fungus, brown rot, mildew	Dormant Sprays Winter Sprays
LIST TWO—Deciduous Fruit Trees for Insects: Almond, apple, cherry, pear, plum, prune, fig, quince; Insect pests	Oils
LIST THREE—Evergreen Fruit Trees and Ornamentals for Insects: Grapefruit, kumquats, lemons, limes, oranges, Mexican orange, holly, toyon, daphne, trailing ivy, lantana, pittosporum, hebe, myrtle, boxwood and evergreens such as junipers, thuyas	Oils

HOW TO SPRAY

DIRECTIONS

Spray into the tree, that is all through the tree, thoroughly wetting branches and twigs, up to the tips and down into the crotches, around the base of the tree, and even on the ground.

NOTE

Severe pruning and disposal of diseased or pest ridden branches may sometimes serve as a beginning in the clean up program.

SPECIALS:

Artichokes: plum moth	Bacillus thuringensis
Carnations: mites, thrip, stem rot	Diazinon, Malathion 25% WP, Bordeaux, Sulphur
Chrysanthemum:	
mildew, rust	Acti-dione
whiteflies, aphids	Meta-Systox
spider mites	Kelthane
chewing insects	Sevin
Citrus Family: red spider mites, mealybugs, scale, aphids, Virus psorosis	Petroleum Oils, Diazinon
Cyclamen: mites	Petroleum Oils, Diazinon
Delphinium: leafspot, crown rot, damping off, mildew	Mercury compound or Dexon, Bordeaux, Sulphur
Elm Leaf: beetle	Diazinon, Sevin, Oils
Gladiola: fusarium rot of corm, botrytis	Diazinon, Sevin, Lysol
Oleander: scale	Oils, Malathion, Sevin, Diazinon
Olive: scale	
Pyracantha: root aphids,	Meta-Systox
chunks chewed out of leaves	Diazinon
Roses: black spot, rust, aphids	Acti-dione, Bordeaux, Malathion
Seedling: damping-off disease	Mercury compound, or Dexon
Strawberry plants: rust,	Copper sulphate
weevils	Diazinon
Violets: whiteflies, red spider mites	Kelthane 18½ emulsive, Malathion 50% emulsive, Meta-Systox

Note: Never use Rotenone near a fish pond because gold fish will die.

INDEX